MISSISSIPPI
CIVIL WAR
MONUMENTS

MISSISSIPPI
CIVIL WAR
MONUMENTS

An Illustrated Field Guide

TIMOTHY S. SEDORE

Indiana University Press

This book is a publication of

Indiana University Press
Office of Scholarly Publishing
Herman B Wells Library 350
1320 East 10th Street
Bloomington, Indiana 47405 USA

iupress.indiana.edu

Manufactured in the United States of America

Library of Congress Cataloging-in-Publication Data

Names: Sedore, Timothy S. (Timothy Stephen), author.
Title: Mississippi Civil War monuments : an
    illustrated field guide / Timothy S. Sedore.
Description: Bloomington, Indiana : Indiana University Press,
    [2020] | Includes bibliographical references and index.
Identifiers: LCCN 2019020822 (print) | LCCN 2019021898 (ebook) |
    ISBN 9780253045577 (ebook) | ISBN 9780253045553 (hardback :
    alk. paper) | ISBN 9780253045560 (pbk. : alk. paper)
Subjects: LCSH: Mississippi—History—Civil War, 1861-1865—
    Monuments—Guidebooks. | Confederate States of America—
    Monuments—Guidebooks. | Monuments—Mississippi—
    Guidebooks. | Monuments—Southern States—Guidebooks. |
    Soldiers' monuments—Mississippi—Guidebooks. | Soldiers'
    monuments—Southern States—Guidebooks. | War memorials—
    Mississippi—Guidebooks. | War memorials—Southern States—
    Guidebooks. | United States—History—Civil War, 1861-1865—
    Monuments—Guidebooks. | Collective memory—Mississippi.
Classification: LCC F342 (ebook) | LCC F342 .S43
    2020 (print) | DDC 973.7/6—dc23
LC record available at https://lccn.loc.gov/2019020822

1 2 3 4 5   25 24 23 22 21 20

Dedicated to my wife and fellow traveler,
Patricia
Faith, hope, love.

Dedicated to my parents,
Michael and Annie M. Sedore,
*from the North and from the South, respectively,
who formed a union that lasted fifty-six years.*

In memory of Michael Sedore's service,
US Army Air Force, 1941–1945.

Contents

Maps

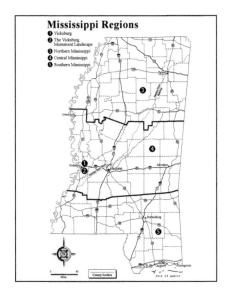

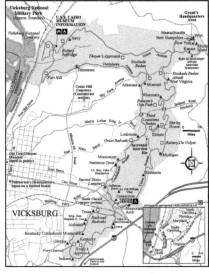

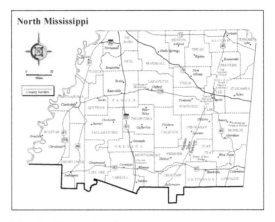

North Mississippi   202

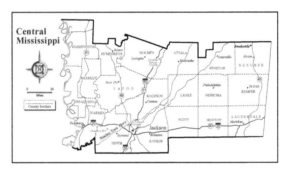

Central Mississippi   298

Southern Mississippi   356

Preface

THIS BOOK is based on a quest to come to terms with the way the American Civil War is commemorated in monument form on the Mississippi landscape. If America is a venture in exegesis, as historian Sacvan Bercovitch avers, then it seemed appropriate to test that proposition by examining the public text of Civil War monumentation in the Southern state where the decisive campaign of the war—at Vicksburg—was fought.

Over the course of four successive summers, I traveled across Mississippi in order to document some eight hundred Civil War monument inscriptions, images, and settings. We drove by car, my wife and I, often working as driver and spotter, moving from county to county for several weeks each summer. During the intervening academic years—fall, winter, and spring—the archive was shaped and edited into its present form. This task was often laid aside in favor of family responsibilities, professional obligations as a professor of English, the pursuit of a seminary degree, and preaching and ministry obligations.

It was always close at hand, however, and these "interruptions" enriched my experience with this archive. That was one of my goals for this project. It was my desire to live with the text and at least imagine something of the experience of the war that these monuments commemorate. From that experience I can testify that the words and images have a life of their own, even in the Bronx, even twelve hundred miles from Vicksburg. They form a kind of liturgy on the landscape that is worthy of extended consideration, scrutiny, and meditation.

It is on this basis that I aver that the complexity of this multimedia text has been misjudged, if for no other reason than it has never been read collectively. Other forms of media dominate public discourse today, but Civil War monuments still command public space in the way generations of Americans in the North and the South wanted the war to be remembered. The words and images emplaced in plein air on monuments across Mississippi (most of them Union) are variously cryptic, revealing, hopeful, vexing, offensive, banal, and provocative. Read collectively or holistically, it is more than this: it is a testimony to the best and worst in humanity.

Just weeks after completing the field research for Mississippi (and one day after completing the field research for Tennessee), protests erupted near the statue of Confederate general Robert E. Lee in Charlottesville, Virginia. In February 2017, the City Council of Charlottesville voted to remove the statue of Robert E. Lee. On August 10, white nationalists objected to the city's plan to remove the statue; counterdemonstrators opposed them. The demonstration descended into violence, resulting in the death of a counterdemonstrator and two state troopers. Further, it drew national attention, controversy, and opprobrium to this genre. Among other events, four Confederate statues had already been removed from public sites in New Orleans in May 2017. Four Confederate statues were removed from public sites in Baltimore in August. Also in August, administrators at Bronx Community College, CUNY, arranged the removal of busts of Robert E. Lee and Thomas J. "Stonewall" Jackson from the Hall of Fame. In December, statues of Jefferson Davis and Nathan Bedford Forrest were removed from sites in Memphis.

In the wake of this violence, polemics, and other actions, I have been led to question how to reconcile this sudden storm with a long-term movement that has no comparable history of controversy.

There are at least three ways of looking at this phenomenon, some of which I have considered in other books in this series. First, although many monuments represent causes that contemporary Americans find objectionable, immoral, or racially insensitive, numerous courthouse monuments were erected to commemorate veterans' service rather than advocate causes, in the same way that monuments were erected to commemorate the service of men and women of World War I, World War II, the Korean War, the Vietnam War, and the gulf wars. Second, many Confederate cemetery monuments are focused on mourning the dead rather than politics—again, much as many veterans' monuments of other American wars are. Not always, of course, but often enough for readers to scrutinize each monument on its own terms. Politics was one thing; monument commemoration another. A careful reading of the county, state, and cemetery monuments will show that they make only infrequent reference to particular battles. With a few exceptions, the emphasis is on collective sacrifice.

I am not Southern, nor am I a politician. I do not know what the future holds for this archive. It may not matter what the monument makers were trying to express. Every age is political, and while it may be the case that cemetery monuments on private ground are ceded sanctity, the presence of sentiment and commemoration of Confederate soldiers in public space, such as courthouse squares, may be deemed offensive and sufficient cause to remove them.

There are compelling reasons to conclude that this is because—third—monuments symbolize a continuum of conflict whose course cannot be arrested or controlled. Why this is, is beyond the scale of this book to examine, but the outlines of the phenomenon are discernable. Reflecting on this phenomenon, historian Gregory P. Downs, author of *After Appomattox: Military Occupation and the Ends of War*, writes that since the war, many of America's military conflicts have followed the same course as that of the "trajectory established at Appomattox." He continues:

> Cheers at the end of fighting are replaced by bafflement at the enduring conflict as the military struggles to fill the defeated government's role, even as the American public moves on. After defeating Spain in the Spanish-American War, the Army undertook bloody campaigns to suppress rebellions and exert control over the Philippines, Cuba and Puerto Rico. After World War II, a state of war endured into the 1950s in the occupation

of Japan and Germany. And in the recent wars in Afghanistan and Iraq, the United States military's work had barely begun when the fighting stopped—and the work continues, in the hands of American-backed locals, today.

He concludes, "We wish that wars, like sports, had carefully organized rules that would steer them to a satisfying end. But wars are often political efforts to remake international or domestic orders. They create problems of governance that battles alone cannot resolve."

This may be a reason why many Americans have evinced a reluctance to go to war at various points of crisis in history. It may be a debatable point in some quarters, and, granted, jingoism is not unknown in American history. However, Presidents Woodrow Wilson and Franklin D. Roosevelt ran for re-election—and won—in some measure on their assurances to the electorate that the United States would not be drawn into the world wars being fought on foreign soil at the time. War came anyway, but the reluctance of Americans to be drawn into these conflicts was evident. Americans can be violent, but they are not necessarily bellicose. Once embarked upon, war takes its own course. Conflict often transgresses the bounds of formal military termination. It may smolder at a level that escapes public notice or interest, but it is never quite extinguished.

The monumentation archive in Mississippi and elsewhere reflects this phenomenon. The early Civil War monuments serve the following purpose: the wartime generation and their first-generation descendants laid the war dead to rest and commemorated the service of the veterans. There is a certain necessity and decency in this act. However, the monuments they erected symbolize the continuity of conflict that Downs observes. The simple claim on a monument that these are "Our Confederate Dead" is perpetual. It places the dead in the present tense. The monuments seem staid and stable, but they represent a sustained conflict.

It is clear to this writer that the American Civil War is, at all events, an enigma that can only be understood by contextualizing it in ethical or ontological terms. For an era whose ironies never seem to end, the war's meaning and legacy was, arguably, best described ten years *before* the war, when *Moby Dick* was published in 1851. American novelist Herman Melville saw something in humanity that portended the coming of the war in his depiction of the main character, Ahab. Having lost his leg in an earlier encounter with the white whale of the title, Ahab comes to believe that Moby Dick is an incarnation of evil. Ahab engages his whaling ship—his culture, the American microcosm if you will—in a monomaniacal effort to purge an evil that he associates with the white whale. Whaling was a pragmatic if bloody industry in the nineteenth century, but the hunt becomes a deeper quest, an obsession. "He heaps me," Ahab confesses at one point—he overwhelms me. Once he persuades his crew to follow him, they, too, become intoxicated with the fervor of the hunt.

The Calvinist and Augustinian in me would reconcile this unconsummatable search for satiation by taking it to a deeper level, to a foundational restlessness that resides within the soul of humanity. Melville was no religious ideologue. "He could neither believe nor be comfortable with unbelief," is the way his friend Nathaniel Hawthorne described him. He was not a seer, an abolitionist, or a prophet, but he had the gift of an artist in sketching Ahab and his ship as a microcosm whose obsession, conscience, and madness reflected the society of Melville's time and place. The stark imperfectability of humanity apart from divine intervention compels me to be skeptical that any one creature, monument, individual, group, or cause can embody evil in such a way as to redeem the world's iniquity by its removal. In the context of the monument controversy, this leads me to think that to remove any one monument to an unjust or iniquitous cause is to leave others standing; to remove all of them would require something of the monomania that Herman Melville describes in *Moby Dick*. And this, Melville's Ahab testifies, is an insatiable quest. Ahab is a grotesque—an extreme case. But the war was grotesque—an extreme case—with millions of active participants, and its tensions continue. What troubles Ahab is the madness within, however, not without.

Death alone ends Ahab's struggle; he takes many with him to death, and only the narrator survives to tell the story (Job 1:15). In contrast, collectively speaking, the wounds inflicted by the Civil War were not fatal to the United States. The American drama is renewed when each successive generation takes up the challenge left by this legacy. In this sense, the monuments represent an incomplete sacrifice. They symbolize a perpetual disequilibrium. They commemorate a conflict whose resolution may, however, be found in President Abraham Lincoln's proclamation to the nation, North and South, in his second inaugural address: to act with compassion toward others, with the full knowledge that one may be acting in the presence of one's enemies (Psalm 23:5), and that a man's foes may well "be those of his own household" (Matt. 10:36). The lawyerly summation of this quintessential American sermon is well known: "With malice toward none, with charity for all, with firmness in the right as God gives us to see the right, let us strive on to finish the work we are in, to bind up the nation's wounds, to care for him who shall have borne the battle and for his widow and his orphan, to do all which may achieve and cherish a just and lasting peace among ourselves and with all nations."

That the reunited nation should undertake this redemptive initiative on behalf of all its citizens is what Lincoln preaches. Lincoln's counsel is respected, remembered, and revered, even venerated, but it continues to go unheeded.

Timothy S. Sedore
Pennsylvania

Acknowledgments

THE AUTHOR GRATEFULLY ACKNOWLEDGES the support, in the form of grants, of the Research Foundation of the City University of New York during the course of this project. In addition, a CUNY Chancellors Fellowship further enabled the progress of this work during the writing of the final manuscript.

I spent portions of four successive summers doing fieldwork for this project in Vicksburg, Mississippi. The staff at Vicksburg National Military Park was invariably courteous and helpful, but Pat Strange, Elizabeth Joyner, and Luke Howard were especially knowledgeable about the Vicksburg landscape and merit special mention for their expertise. D. Rose Rains offered important assistance in the closing stages.

I take additional pleasure in acknowledging the support of the following institutions: the Corinth Civil War Interpretive Center; the John Davis Williams Library of the University of Mississippi; Brice's Cross Roads National Battlefield; the Amory Museum, Amory; Holly Springs Public Library, Holly Springs; and the Mississippi's Final Stands Interpretive Center at Baldwyn. For local directions or on-site information, I thank the following persons: at West Point, Officer Toni Howard; regarding Castalian Springs, Officer Bishop; at the Yazoo City Public Library, John Ellzey; at Ripley, Mayor Chris Marsalis; at the Old Capitol Museum, Jackson, Angela Stewart.

As I noted in my book on Tennessee's Civil War monuments, I would be remiss if I did not acknowledge that many persons made this book possible by erecting, dedicating, and conserving the archive of public monuments presented here. That archive, in turn, is an acknowledgement of the service and sacrifice of the wartime generation.

As part of the research that led to this book, I visited the cities, towns, and farms where the wartime generation lived. I often found myself walking where the wartime generation walked or marched or fought. I visited their graves, and I read the correspondence and memoirs they left behind. The wartime generation had all the frailty and failings that afflict every generation. However, I also admired many of them for their strength of character, courage, sacrifice, and integrity. In the time it took to write this book, I came to know some of them as well as I do my students or even members of my family. Above all individuals or institutions, it was my spouse, Patricia Radecki, who set an example of fortitude by traveling the American landscape with me over the course of the several years and several thousand miles required to do the fieldwork for this book. Patricia was also a pivotal source of moral support during the writing. The challenge of doing this work deepened the bond between us—to her credit—and, in fact, she made this book possible.

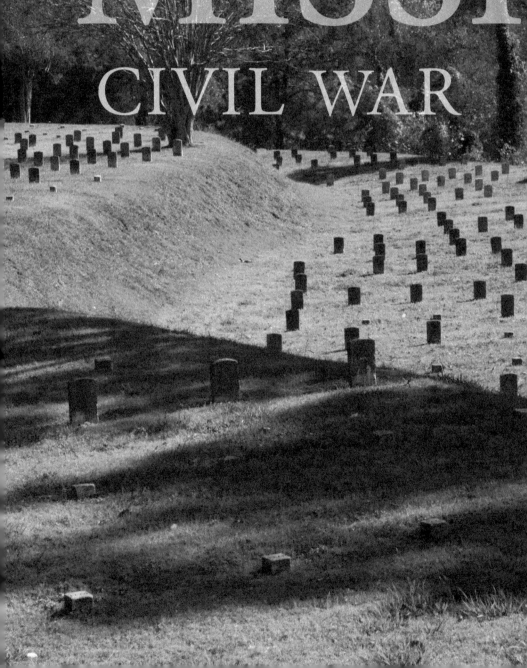

MISSI

CIVIL WAR

SSIPPI

MONUMENTS

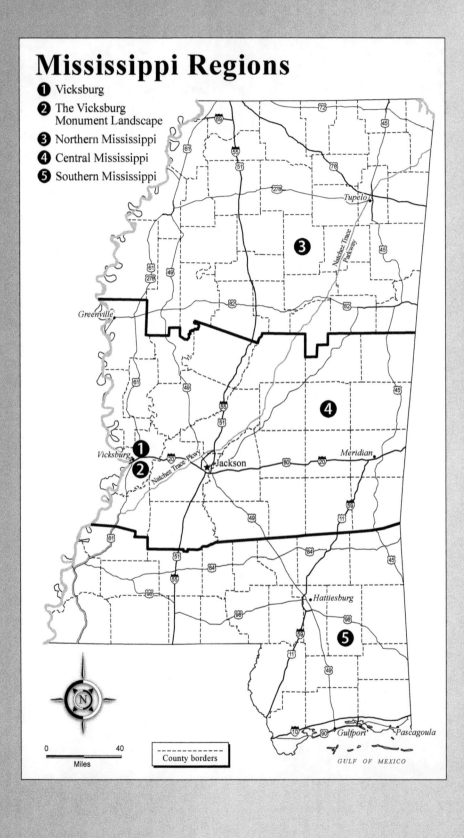

Mississippi Regions

❶ Vicksburg
❷ The Vicksburg Monument Landscape
❸ Northern Mississippi
❹ Central Mississippi
❺ Southern Mississippi

Greenville

Tupelo

Natchez Trace Parkway

Vicksburg

Jackson

Meridian

Natchez Trace Pkwy

Hattiesburg

Gulfport

Pascagoula

GULF OF MEXICO

0   40
Miles

----- County borders

INTRODUCTION

THIS IS A BOOK ABOUT MISSISSIPPI, the American Civil War, and the way the American Civil War is remembered on the Mississippi landscape. A vast panoply of bronze or granite or marble commemorations monuments stands in this state: obelisks, statues, shafts, tablets, plaques, arches, and pyramids.[1] They may be found across Mississippi, from Vicksburg to Meridian; from Beauvoir, on the Gulf Coast, to Hernando, southeast of Memphis; and from Corinth, on the Tennessee state line, to Natchez, on the Mississippi River. Today, in part because of Vicksburg's extensive monumentation, there are more Civil War monuments in Mississippi than any other state in the Union. Ironically, there are more Union monuments in Mississippi than any state in the Union apart from Pennsylvania.[2] Mississippi thus offers a unique point of contact—*Anknüpfungspunkt*—between Northern and Southern interpretations of the meaning of the defining conflict of the United States.

The monument movement in Mississippi began during the war when a marble obelisk was erected on the site of the battlefield at Vicksburg by occupying Federal troops on July 4, 1864, to commemorate the first anniversary of the Confederate surrender of this strategic city. The first county monument dates from 1866, in Liberty, Amite County.

In the Bereavement and Funereal Era, 1866–89, the need to retrieve, identify, and bury the dead occasioned memorials in a neoclassical style of mourning that nineteenth century Americans admired and emulated. Many of the monuments of the period are grim marble obelisks and shafts, mournful if dignified, affectionate but not effusive. By the turn of the twentieth century, several hundred monuments had been erected at Vicksburg, the southernmost city with a national battlefield park of the Civil War. In the Reconciliation, or Celebration, Era, 1890–1920, mourning became celebration: county seats, city centers, parks, and battlefields were chosen more often as sites than cemeteries. Monument rhetoric took a more celebratory, sentimental, or defiant tone. The movement peaked during the semicentennial of the war, 1911–15, when numerous courthouse monuments were erected—often in the form of a statue of a common soldier surmounting an inscribed shaft and base with an inscribed encomium or tribute. By 1917, Vicksburg National Military Park (NMP) had become an outdoor museum of some six hundred sculptures and commemorations, many of them in an elaborate Beaux-Arts style of the American Renaissance of the turn of the twentieth century.

Recent years have seen another wave of monumentation, as well as diverse reconsiderations of the meaning of the war. For example, the African American Monument at Vicksburg, sponsored and erected by the state of Mississippi, was dedicated in 2004. Two courthouse monuments stand adjacent to one another on the Oktibbeha County courthouse grounds at Starkville, near the campus of Mississippi State University: one monument is Confederate, erected in 2005; the other is Union, erected in 2006. The United Daughters of the Confederacy (UDC) of Texas sponsored an inscribed granite shaft at Raymond in 2002, and at Corinth and Meridian in 2010. The state of Kentucky's Confederate monument at Vicksburg was erected in 2010. The state of Mississippi's monument at the Shiloh National Military Park was dedicated on October 10, 2015, and a courthouse obelisk was erected and dedicated at Lucedale in May 2016.

The issue of what the war means and what the monumentation stands for is an ongoing, evolving, contemporary discussion with direct relevance to contemporary conceptions of the nation's core beliefs and history. Calls to drop Confederate emblems from public space were raised in the summer of 2015. Proposals have been made to honor Rev. Dr. Martin Luther King Jr. with a monument at Stone Mountain State Park, Georgia, on the site of an enormous granite bas-relief sculpture commemorating the military leaders of the Confederacy. Responding to protests, the University of Mississippi lowered the state flag that flies on the campus. The controversy was renewed in Charlottesville, Virginia, in 2017, and drew more attention and opprobrium to this genre. Contention over the state flag of Mississippi, with its emblem of the Confederate battle flag, continues at this writing.

Civil War monuments are tangible, physical reminders of a conflict that shaped America and yet still defies a full reckoning. Regardless of the future course of the history of this movement, this book will document what the first 150 years of monument commemoration have set in place and—with dispassionate consideration—analyze the import of their presence on the Mississippi landscape.

The politics of commemoration were not uppermost in my mind when I began this project. Personally, I wanted a text—that was my goal. I wanted to read the monumentation landscape as words and images in context, and I wanted to afford the reader the same opportunity to see how the Mississippi Civil War landscape unfolds as a series of interrelated testimonies, tributes, contentions, apologetics, exhortations, and sentiments that form a complex, evolving collective text.

Like other books in this series, this field guide is not a history. It is this: a detailed, one-volume overview of the central features of a salient feature of the Civil War landscape of Mississippi.

Comparison of States

The author's work in this area includes a book-length survey of Virginia's Confederate monuments, some four hundred in number. That book led, almost inevitably, to an interest in how the monument movement worked itself out in Tennessee, another scene of extensive warfare—second only to Virginia in engagements and casualties—but a theater of war in which resident loyalties were much more deeply divided. Research on the Shiloh battlefield led this author to Corinth, Mississippi—only twenty-two miles south of Shiloh National Military Park—and an interest in pursuing this thread of rhetoric to Vicksburg, Jackson, and ultimately the Gulf Coast.

One might assume that these three studies would yield fairly similar results, that the collected text would be essentially replicated from one state to the other. Not true. Civil War monuments in the three states have striking distinctions, reflecting a different experience with the war, perceptions of its meaning, and loyalties, history, ethics, and sentiments of its residents. For over a century, for example, Richmond, Virginia's symbolic importance is singular in the United States. Statues of generals Robert E. Lee, Thomas J. "Stonewall" Jackson, and J. E. B. Stuart have presided over the landscape in grand equestrian form along Monument Avenue and give the city the formality and aura of a phantasmagoric national capital. At this writing, they continue to do so.

Virginia monuments frequently define the war in terms of the defense of Virginia. The Charles City Courthouse obelisk is dedicated to "Defenders of Constitutional Liberty and the Right of Self Government." The county courthouse example in Montross calls attention to those "Who Fell in Defence of Virginia, and in the Cause of Constitutional Liberty."

The cause of the Confederate States of America (CSA) is not avoided, however. The seal of the Confederacy, with the motto "Deo Vindice"—"God will avenge"—is often superimposed. So, too, is the phrase "Sic Semper Tyrannus"—the Latin phrase on the seal of Virginia, which is translated as "Thus Ever to Tyrants."

Tennessee's unionist/secessionist divisions temper the sentiment associated with the CSA. Confederate monuments are commonly found in the towns and cities, and they vastly outnumber Union monuments there. However, on two of the major Tennessee battlefields—Shiloh and Chattanooga—the Union soldier dominates. At Shiloh National Military Park there are no fewer than 130 small unit or common soldier commemorations. At Chattanooga, Union monuments line Missionary Ridge and the heights and slopes of Lookout Mountain. All of the monumentation at Stones River is devoted to the service of Union soldiers. In fact, there are more Union monuments in Tennessee than Confederate monuments. The military victors of the war have their say.

However, distinctive sentiments are discernible in Mississippi monumentation. References to the "Grand Old Southern Cause" or to Mississippi soldiers "Marching 'Neath the Stars and Bars" at Pontotoc and Grenada courthouses, respectively, are more common than imprecations like "Deo Vindice." There is no comparison to the Warrenton, Virginia, monument's stern admonition that "God will judge the Right," for example. Imprecations against the North as the "Invaders of Virginia"—as the Emporia, Virginia, monument phrases it—are not common in Mississippi. There is not the same kind of defiance. Instead, Mississippi monumentation describes an embattled state that embarked on a destructive course of its own collective volition when it seceded and paid a full and extravagant price for doing so. Cemeteries across northern and central Mississippi, many interring the dead from the Battle of Shiloh, testify to the personal cost in terms of soldiers' lives that Mississippi bore. Corinth, Okolona, Macon, Meridian, Iuka, Booneville, Columbus, Enterprise, Canton, Oxford, Holly Springs, and Natchez are among the sites of hospitals and cemeteries where the wounded or the sick were cared for or the dead were buried, and monuments stand over the grounds. To cite historian Max Hastings in another context, their destiny was "rich in pathos, tragedy or absurdity, according to viewpoint. As so often in wars, brave men were to do fine and hard things in pursuit of a national illusion."

The Columbus courthouse grounds monument consists of a central structure in the form of a domed temple twenty-eight feet high in white marble, with sculptures of three Confederate soldiers. This is one of several Mississippi monuments that commemorate the dead not only in a local cemetery but at the county seat as well. Few county monument designs anywhere in the South venture to define the space they occupy in this fashion. In fact, temple forms of this type are uncommon in the South, but this architectural feature has a courthouse prominence at Columbus, Laurel (5.7.1), and Ellisville (5.7.2).

That legacy is, arguably, an implicit part of the legacy that Mississippi Confederate monumentation bears: Vae victis—woe to the defeated. In January 1906, when a bill was introduced in the Mississippi state legislature to erect a state monument to Mississippi soldiers at Vicksburg, it received a very mixed response. Opposition was strong for state funds going to what one legislator termed a "Yankee park." The legislation passed by one vote.

When the monument was completed in April 1912, it was the first Confederate state monument in the park. It looks impressive. Architecturally speaking, the monument has a temple form with a large stylobate or temple floor and a temple in antis—formed in part by two columns surmounted by a pediment. The central female figure is Clio, muse of history, seated above a veritable Greek temple floor, with a granite obelisk rising seventy-six feet behind her.

As large and impressive as it appears, there are, however, several features to this monument that have a more subtle symbolism. Although bronze reliefs are wrapped around three sides of the memorial depicting Mississippi soldiers in valiant, desperate combat, there is nothing on the fourth side, on the back, facing the river. It is blank. Ostensibly, funding was lacking for a bronze tableau on the blank side, although the artist, Frederick E. Triebel, proposed one. In addition, there is no inscription on this monument; there is no statement or testimony, nothing apart from the seal of the state of Mississippi and the state motto. For so large and significant a monument, it seems muted. Finally, architectural critics and Park Service officials have noted that the quality of work and materials on this monument are not as good as other monuments at Vicksburg, that it has been difficult to preserve for this reason, and that gaps and seams are apparent in the bronze work that would not be present on a work of better craftsmanship.

What is the message? In the case of the Mississippi monument it seems that the vacancy has meaning—that the space speaks, that this monument represents an unfinished and incomplete ritual. This temple space is symbolic of a valiant but doomed sacrificial defense. The Southerners at Vicksburg had nowhere to go; they had their backs to the river. After forty-seven days, the Southern army was outmaneuvered, placed under siege, assaulted repeatedly, starved out, and ultimately forced to surrender.

Perhaps the legislature did not want a monument in a "Yankee park," because they did not want a final word on the defeat. If so, then in an important sense, they got what they wanted. It is true that the war ended; it is also true that a military victory was not won. However, the conflict continues: successive waves of reconstruction, segregation, civil rights, and, on a brighter note, another Mississippi Civil War monument at Vicksburg, this one, of all things, a tribute to African Americans from Mississippi, including those who fought for the Union as well as those who served the Confederacy. They couldn't see the future any better than any one generation can, but they wanted more than a surrender site, and this the legislature won, for better or worse.

The War

Mississippi was the second state to secede from the Union, following South Carolina. The state legislature voted to secede on January 9, 1861. Over the next four years, Mississippi contributed over 96,000 men to the war effort on the Southern side, of whom nearly 22,000 became casualties, approximately

25 percent of those serving. Many Mississippians served in other theaters of the conflict, but the war came to Mississippi after the Battle of Shiloh in Tennessee, a Confederate defeat, which led to the siege of Corinth (April 29–June 10, 1862), and Confederate forces ceding the city as well. Southern efforts to retake Corinth and regain strategic initiative followed (Iuka, September 19, 1862; Corinth, October 3–4, 1862). The campaign was unavailing. The Confederate loss of New Orleans, April 19, 1862, and Natchez in May 1862 further isolated the state.

Thereafter, engagements related to the Federal Vicksburg–North Mississippi Campaign (October–December) took place at Holly Springs, December 20, 1862, and Chickasaw Bayou, December 27–29, 1862. The Union army failed. Federal attempts to bypass Vicksburg, January 1–April 30, 1863, were also thwarted, and included action at Fort Pemberton, March 11–17, 1863. But other efforts ensued: Grierson's Raid, April 17–May 3, 1863, and the battle of Snyder's Bluff, April 29–May 1. These effectively diverted Confederate forces. Meanwhile, Federal troops under the command of Maj. Gen. Ulysses S. Grant crossed the Mississippi and landed at Bruinsburg on April 29 and 30. Only a few weeks later, they converged on Vicksburg from the east, having won victories at Port Gibson, May 1; Raymond, May 12; Jackson, May 14; Champion Hill, May 16; and Big Black Bridge, May 17. They invested Vicksburg on May 18, where they besieged a Confederate army under the command of Lt. Gen. John Pemberton. They withstood the threat of an Army of Relief commanded by General Joseph E. Johnston. Vicksburg surrendered on July 4, after a forty-seven-day siege.

The loss of Vicksburg effectively divided the Confederacy in two. Control of the state of Mississippi, though still contested by Confederate forces, was increasingly subject to Federal occupation and the march of Federal troops across its territory. Union forces occupied Vicksburg for the rest of the war. Jackson came under siege July 9–16, and was ceded to Union forces. Another telling blow was the Meridian Campaign, February 3–March 5, 1864, when a force of 20,000 men led by Maj. Gen. William T. Sherman set out from Vicksburg to Meridian and returned, harassed but essentially unhindered.

Lt. Gen. Nathan B. Forrest's cavalry remained a dangerous force, but by 1864 the Confederate military in Mississippi no longer had the resources to prevent large-scale Federal movements and collateral depredations across its territory. Moreover, civil government was no longer effective, and civil disorder and crime could not be controlled. Forrest himself lamented that civilians were victims of "roving bands of deserters, stragglers, horse thieves and robbers who consume the substance and appropriate the property of the citizens."

The battle of Brice's Crossroads, June 10, 1864, was a tactical triumph, but it was not decisive and did not end predations such as the burning of Ripley in July or Oxford in August 1864. The battle of Tupelo, July 14–15, 1864, was a last stand of Confederate arms in the state.

Nevertheless, as historian Michael Ballard reports, "Mississippi was among the last of the Confederate states to be surrendered; not until May 4, 1865, did General Richard Taylor surrender his troops. Robert E. Lee had already surrendered the Army of Northern Virginia on April 9, and General Joseph E. Johnston surrendered his forces on April 26."

In many ways, however, the war has not ceased to affect the people and the landscape. Arguably, Abraham Lincoln's declaration that "we cannot escape history," in his message to Congress in 1862, proved to be more prescient than the great man could foresee. The war's legacy is still not clear. Historian John Waugh writes that the "Civil War has been a twice-fought affair—the war itself lasting four years, and the writing about the war, which is likely to never end." Thomas Beer concludes that the war "ceased physically in 1865[, yet] its political end may be reasonably expected about the year 3000." And David R. Goldsmith, in his *Still Fighting the Civil War*, ventures the judgment that the "Civil War is like a ghost that has not yet made its peace and roams the land seeking solace, retribution, or vindication."

The Common Soldier

The archetypal monument in post–Civil War America is a statue of a common soldier surmounting a base or shaft. There are approximately seventy-one statues of soldiers in Mississippi. Among the statues, forty-four are of Confederate soldiers, mostly courthouse common soldiers. There are also twenty-seven statues of Union soldiers—all of them are at Vicksburg NMP.

The soldiers can seem laconic, common, even indistinguishable from one another, in some measure because the making of monuments became an industry in the postwar era. Only four companies made statuary in the United States before the Civil War; in 1915 there were sixty-three. Confederate statues were often outfitted with a bedroll, and belts or canteens inscribed with a "CS," for example. They often wear a wide-brimmed hat, unlike their Union counterparts. Otherwise they were made in a way that was broadly similar in stance, posture, and appearance to the figure of the Union soldier. Indeed, historian Gaines M. Foster observes that many communities purchased catalogue models or types from monument companies.

To say, that "they all look basically the same" is a misconception. At the very least, the Confederate common soldier in Mississippi can be classified in four ways:

1. A funereal figure in mourning, or keeping vigil over grave sites, often looking downcast, with rifle pointed down. Examples include the cemetery figures at Holly Springs or Columbus.

2. A youthful look representing the next generation's readiness to answer the call that earlier generations answered, such as the courthouse figures at Hattiesburg, Heidelberg, or Lexington.

3. The veteran: a citizen-soldier figure who is mature, alert, in perpetual readiness, such as the statues found at Jackson's old capitol building, or the courthouse monuments at Belzoni, Corinth, Laurel, Gulfport, and Corinth.

The archetypal figure may have originated in the north. Two possibilities have been argued for: the earliest was an 1867 sculpture of an infantryman leaning on his rifle—a lifelike, relaxed figure by Martin Milmore, which still stands at Forest Hills Cemetery, Massachusetts. Another possibility is the Private Soldier Monument at Antietam National Cemetery, a granite soldier standing at parade rest. That design was adopted on September 16, 1867. Stylistically speaking, Daniel Chester French's Minute Man (1871–75) was prototypical; so too was Augustus Saint-Gaudens's Admiral Farragut Memorial in Madison Square Park, New York City (1877–81). As art historian Kirk Savage points out, the archetypal monuments represented an ideal of aesthetic perfection but are also decidedly ethnocentric, as history would have it, and thus subject to a distinct bias to Greco-white-Caucasian forms, such as the Apollo Belvedere, in evident contradistinction to other racial groups.

The figure of the courthouse or cemetery common soldier is typically posed in a classical "contrapposto" position. The figure's weight is leaned to one side; the other leg is bent at the knee. The contrapposto stance was employed by Italian sculptors who did the work for many Confederate courthouse or cemetery monument sculptures. Sources note that the stance dates back to at least the early fifth century BC when Greek sculptors employed it, but it is perhaps most famously associated with Michelangelo's David, 1501–1504. The naturalistic, idealized appearance is coincidentally consonant with an American civilian's confident nonchalance. The American citizen-soldier is depicted as a workmanlike figure. Author and World War II Marine veteran Robert Leckie described "the American fighting man" as someone with an "effortless yet wary way" about him in Helmet for My Pillow. The description seems appropriate to the statue of the common soldier prototype. He gives the appearance of being the ideal of the citizen-soldier, as a kind of reluctant but pragmatic warrior called to civic duty at a time of decision or crisis—like a common man version of Cincinnatus—but ready to return to private life when his time for service or duty is passed. He is more workmanlike than warlike, more vernacular than bellicose. He was not a martinet; he was not a machine; he was not a heel-clicker; he was not the kind to strut. He does not call attention to himself, and he is relaxed, even nonchalant or understated about his status.

As to his weaponry, he typically bears a rifle, held like a staff in his hand, in front or to the side of the body. His weapon has been called a symbol of self-sufficiency, independence, and self-defense. The rifle, the uniform, and the disposition are consistent with what historian Alexander Rose calls a "halcyon icon of every American . . . doughty individualism, rugged self-reliance, and independent spirit determined to defend hearth and home against the predations of outsiders."

These are types, but a mere listing of types is deceptive. The state of Mississippi erected a tribute to African Americans at Vicksburg, with figures of two United States Colored Troops (USCT) soldiers and one civilian laborer. Figures of another USCT soldier along with a female are at the NPS Corinth Contraband Camp, serving as counterpoints to the Confederate common soldier and the Confederate woman that are so commonly displayed on Mississippi monuments.

Finally, Vicksburg's Union monumentation is its own genre and merits separate treatment. Most of the monuments erected at Vicksburg are stylistically consonant with the American Renaissance, the period from 1876 to 1917, when neoclassical architecture was in ascendance. Many of the turn-of-the-century generation of artists and architects had a Beaux-Arts education that was grounded in the teachings of the classical period of ancient Greece. American sculptors studied at art schools such as the École des Beaux-Arts and the Académie Julian where they were imbued with an art form that expressed what one critic describes as the "concept of man's reactions to the forces of nature, to the deeds of fellow beings, and to the divine being that controlled his destiny."

The Women

Women were crucial to the monument movement's vigor and success in the South. "It is the women of the South who will preserve the legends of the war," declared Ella Clanton Thomas in 1878. The United Daughters of the Confederacy, formed in 1894, vindicated her prediction, becoming a powerful memorial movement in the early twentieth-century South. As I have noted elsewhere in this series, women's groups were fundamental to the monument movement's vigor and success. Women initiated and sustained the fund-raising for most monument projects—often for decades, until completion—and they organized the cleanup of cemeteries, set dates for decorating graves, and collected and distributed flowers. Historian William Blair concludes that women's groups—the Ladies Memorial Association and, beginning in 1894, chapters of the UDC—eventually controlled virtually all aspects of the process: conception, initiation, fund-raising, and monument design and dedication ceremonies.

Victorian ideals of women being defined by a domestic sphere were certainly articulated before, during, and after the war. The unveiling of the Raleigh, North Carolina, monument in June 1913 was an occasion taken by ex-Confederate general Daniel Harvey Hill to articulate a vision of Southern women consonant with this model. "The woman of the Confederacy was a womanly woman [who] craved no queenhood except the sovereignty of her own home," he declared. "She never thought of doubting that her sphere of action was the home, and she centered her efforts on making that home a place of refinement and comfort."

However, if this view of the role and place of a woman was ever realized on any scale, it effectively disintegrated during the war. The wartime death of men by combat or from disease by the thousands left thousands of widows and families impoverished. As Jefferson Davis, president of the Confederacy, himself observed, for the wartime generation of Southern women, "calamity was their touchstone."

Young women in mourning are depicted on the courthouse monuments at Laurel, Jones County; Heidelberg, Jasper County; and Hattiesburg, Forrest County. Statues of ordinary women—in period dress, looking careworn by their burdens—adorn monuments at Belzoni, Hinds County; and Poplarville, Pearl County. The lofty statue of a woman in the form of Clio—muse of history—presides over the state of Mississippi's monument at Vicksburg; the figure of a woman is present in the midst of a battlefield tableau in the state of Alabama's monument at Vicksburg.

Equally notable are the courthouse monuments at Greenwood in Leflore County and Raymond in Hinds County, as well as the state capitol monument to women at Jackson. Each depicts women interceding for the wounded or dying. Just how deep and pervasive was the influence of the war on the generation of women who lived through it is perhaps most vividly illustrated in the 1913 Leflore County courthouse monument at Greenwood, which depicts an officer surmounting a shaft, with two flanking common soldiers at the base of the shaft. These images are not uncommon. However, a fourth soldier, wounded, is being tended to by a woman. On the back pedestal is the standing figure of another woman, wearing a long dress and clasping her hands at shoulder height as if praying. Above the woman is the inscription "Father, Thy Will Be Done." The standing figure, clasping her hands in intercessory, even messianic prayer, intimates that the sacrifice she is called upon to make—"Father, Thy Will Be Done"—is consciously, conspicuously undertaken in the knowledge that it is the will of God (Matt. 6:10). The words are also used by Jesus in the Garden of Gethsemane on the night of his arrest and in anticipation of his trial and crucifixion ("Father, if thou be willing, remove this cup from me; nevertheless not my will, but thine, be done" [Luke 42]).

It may well be said that women were expected to fulfill domestic roles, and that this ideal was upheld, cherished, and perpetuated before, during, and after the war. However, there is more to this history. Monuments like these represent two dimensions of the role of women in the war: they mediated between life and death in tending the wounded, and they mediated between heaven and earth by intercessory prayer. No other role is presented. In both roles, the women are depicted in a kind of priestly and ministerial function: they were detached from the physical combat of war, but they were immersed in the emotional, physical, and spiritual trials of the war. The women acted; they interceded; they mediated in an intimate, vicariously priestly role. Indeed, the travail was of such a magnitude that, in a sense, the woman as priest became the sacrifice. The woman on the Greenwood monument interprets and accepts this destiny—"Thy Will Be Done."

The front was here. For Mississippi, at least, it seems to this writer that only the dead could escape the war's impact. The monument at the corner of Main and Washington streets in Yazoo City, Yazoo County, displays two statues, a Southern soldier and a Southern female civilian, surmounting a base. It looks ordinary; it may seem more sentimental than other monuments, but one can easily categorize it with "typical Confederate monuments."

Closer consideration may yield the conviction that an artistry is at work here—that a personal narrative is alluded to. Unlike the typical statue of a Confederate soldier, he does not look forward; he does not look north or south; he is not on vigil or on guard. He bears a weapon to answer the higher call placed upon him, but he looks at her, and she at him. They do not see us: they only see each other. He is in uniform, ready to depart his town and this young woman. She is in civilian dress, but she bears the battle flag. The flag notwithstanding, in some ways, this is not even a Confederate monument. It is both personal and anonymous. The figure of the man is young, as is the figure of the woman. They are not identified, but the moment between them is personal, not public, as if something unspoken is transpiring between them that is not confided to us and as if we are intruding on them. In truth, we are. Thousands of life narratives took a course that only the war could bring about. The war was personal. Its course was uncertain. Its effects were unpredictable. It broke hearts, homes, and families, as intimated here. It also freed many, lifted hearts, and established new homes and communities, as represented by the statue of the young African American female on the Contraband Camp grounds at Corinth. Some personal accounts break the bonds of intervening years. Rosa B. Tyler of Holly Springs is but one example of one woman's experience of the war, its aftermath, and its legacy. Looking back on her life she wrote, "To me then just entering upon the responsibilities of life, the war came with a shock that seemed to change my whole being. My young husband died in prison, every male member of my immediate family 'faced the foe' as a soldier; and the broad Mississippi River, traversed by gunboats, lay between me and all my kindred and early friends. People less tried smile at my enthusiasm in regard to war topics, but it will go with me to life's end."

Design and Materials

Typical postwar monuments or markers are made of bronze, marble, or granite. Iron, copper, limestone, white bronze (zinc), and aluminum as well as common fieldstone were also used. They appear in one of these forms:

· An obelisk: a tall, slender four-sided stone pillar tapering toward a peaked top.

· A slab, tablet, or pillar, sometimes called a stele: an upright stone or plaque set on a stone base—the simplest and most common form of monumentation.

· A statue: usually a common soldier, set on a stone pedestal, plinth, or base, sometimes surmounting a shaft or dado that displays an inscription.

· A plaque or tablet of bronze, marble, or granite on a wall (not included in this study).

· A relief: a carving or sculpture raised above a flat background to give a three-dimensional effect.

· A shaft or column, sometimes surmounted by the sculpture of a common soldier.

· A tablet, cast in iron, one of many posted on the Vicksburg battlefields displaying rosters, narratives, or unit positions (not included in this study).

Ceremonies

Dedication ceremonies for local monuments were momentous events in the lives of communities. Monuments were long anticipated. The fund-raising process often took decades to complete. Media, in the form of newspapers and magazines, advertised the approaching dates of dedication ceremonies, reported their occurrence, and published proceedings and speeches in the aftermath. They reported several days of festivities, successive arrivals of dignitaries, parades, dinners, and ceremonies of dedication.

A climactic moment was the dedication address. These were solemn, sentimental, sometimes politically charged moments and represent a distinctive

FACING TOP Example of an obelisk, this one a tribute to soldiers of the 8th Wisconsin at Vicksburg.

FACING BOTTOM Example of a bas-relief, a carving or sculpture raised a few inches from a flat background to give a three-dimensional effect: the 47th Ohio VI, Union Siege Line at Vicksburg NMP.

ABOVE A granite stele, in this case to the 36th Mississippi Infantry at Vicksburg: an upright stone, slab, tablet, or plaque set on a base. A less expensive, more text-oriented form of expression.

The University of Mississippi statue of a common soldier and column, dedicated May 10, 1906: marble plinth, base, dado, and column, the whole surmounted by the sculpted figure of a Confederate private soldier.

A courthouse soldier standing on US 72 outside of the Rankin County courthouse, Brandon, dedicated November 29, 1909: a private soldier, in marble, standing at parade rest surmounting a marble shaft and base.

Example of an equestrian monument, this one of a common soldier, "The Standard Bearer," the collaborative work of Henry Kitson and his wife, Theo Alice Ruggles Kitson, erected 1912, in Vicksburg.

A tablet, cast in bronze, to the 26th Iowa VI at the base of Thayer's Approach, one of many posted on the Vicksburg battlefields displaying rosters, narratives, or unit positions.

genre worthy of study that is beyond the scope of this book. None is typical. One example is the dedication address given on the occasion of the unveiling of the Oxford courthouse monument on May 10, 1906, by "Mr. Scott, the orator of the day":

> The Confederate soldier, my friends, was different in many salient characteristics from all the warriors of the world. With the exception of a few officers educated at West Point, they were entirely lacking in military training or experience. High-strung, spirited and independent, they were naturally impatient of discipline or restraint, yet they made superb soldiers. The Southern soldier, whether officer or private, fought neither for gold nor other gain. The call to arms was prompted neither by vengeance nor hatred. No unholy lust for conquest nor consuming love for martial glory summoned them from their peaceful homes to the tented fields. These men battled for a principle, in which each believed with all his heart, soul and mind. Overwhelmed at last by countless numbers and the boundless resources of a hostile world (for the South fought the whole world), the soldiers returned to their desolate homes and devastated fields; but they promptly assumed and faithfully discharged the duties of American citizens. All this was done with a Southern grace and courtesy and good humor which in time disarmed criticism and enmity, and brought peace and good will to the whole country.
>
> The war is over. Its animosities have passed away.

It is fervent, sweeping ("the South fought the whole world"), sentimental ("Southern grace and courtesy"), and hyperbolic. Ultimately, it is acquiescent: "The war is over," he concludes. "Its animosities have passed away."

Slavery

Racial servitude was a foundational element of antebellum Mississippi. Historian Ben Wynne notes that the state's "social, economic, and political institutions were hopelessly entangled in the web of slavery." It was inextricably a part of the motivation for the state's secession. It was not hidden. "During the 1850s, Mississippi established itself as the nation's top cotton producer," Wynne continues. "By the eve of the Civil War slaves represented 55 percent of the state's total population." The Ordinance of Secession of Mississippi was passed in the state capitol at Jackson on January 9, 1861, by a vote of 83–15. The ordinance was unambiguous; slavery was a central issue in secession: "Our position is thoroughly identified with the institution of slavery—the greatest material interest of the world. Its labor supplies the product which constitutes by far the largest and most important portions of commerce of the earth."

The common soldier, however, held his own credo. Wynne writes that "Mississippi's slaves outnumbered whites 437,000 to 354,000. Slavery, therefore, seemed to be an absolute necessity for the state's white citizens." However, although many white soldiers from Mississippi supported their state's position on slavery, he notes, they "fought for a variety of other reasons, too. Some joined the military to defend home and hearth, while others saw the conflict in broader sectional terms. The soldiers' motivation was generally more personal," he concludes, "than it was ideological." In an extensive survey of soldier letters and diaries, *For Cause and Comrades: Why Men Fought in the Civil War*, historian James McPherson notes that "only 20 percent of the 429 Confederate soldiers in the book's sample explicitly voiced proslavery convictions." McPherson avers that the matter was more complex, for "Civil War soldiers the group cohesion and peer pressure that were powerful factors in combat motivation were not unrelated to the complex mixture of patriotism, ideology, concept of duty, honor and manhood, and community or peer pressure that prompted them to enlist in the first place."

There is no explicit mention of slavery in Mississippi monumentation. Attention is paid to rights, including states' rights, to service, honor, justification, courage, sacrifice, sentiment, and nostalgia, but in the vast text that comprises the liturgy of Mississippi monument rhetoric, the word *slavery* never occurs. The word *servant* is used once, at Canton, on an obelisk testifying to the friendship, sentiment, and loyalty between two men of different races who served in Harvey's Scouts, a Confederate cavalry unit. The role of African Americans in the war is so vast and complex as to merit consideration about the extent to which there is an acoustic or rhetorical shadow cast over the subject in a deliberate manner or whether the essential role that blacks served in a logistical role was too obvious to mention. However pervasive and notorious was the racism in Mississippi, there are paradoxical inclusions. Historian James Hollandsworth Jr. notes that Mississippi was unique among Southern states in including African Americans in the state's pension program for Confederate veterans from its beginning in 1888. Historians John F. Marszalek and Clay Williams write that a "large but undetermined number of slaves served as body servants to white Confederate officers and soldiers, built fortifications, and did other manual labor for the Confederate Army." Hollandsworth summarizes the contribution of African American southerners in four ways:

> First, as slaves, they provided the labor that fueled the Southern cotton economy and maintained the production of foodstuffs and other commodities. Second, slaves were rented to or drafted by the Confederate government to work on specific projects related to the South's military infrastructure, such as bridges and railroads. Third, black southerners were part of the work force in the Confederacy's war-related foundries, munitions factories, and mines. In addition, they transported food and war material to the front by wagon, and provided services to wounded and sick soldiers

in Confederate hospitals. Last, a large number of black southerners went to war with the Confederate army as noncombatants, serving as personal servants, company cooks, and grooms.

They served in crucial logistical roles, but did they fight? The observations of Dr. Lewis Steiner, Chief Inspector of the US Army Sanitary Commission for the Army of the Potomac, are instructive in this regard. Steiner recorded this eyewitness description of Maj. Gen. Thomas "Stonewall" Jackson's troops departing Frederick, Maryland, on September 10, 1862, during the Antietam Campaign. It is not the western army, but it may be representative of the Confederate army's personnel:

> The most liberal calculations could not give them more than 64,000 men. Over 3,000 negroes must be included. They were clad in all kinds of uniforms, not only cast-off or captured United States uniforms, but in coats with southern buttons, state buttons, etc. These were shabby, but not shabbier or seedier than those worn by white men in the rebel ranks.
>
> Most of the negroes had arms, rifles, muskets, sabers, bowie-knives, dirks, etc. They were supplied, in many instances, with knapsacks, haversacks, canteens, etc., and were manifestly an integral part of the Southern Confederacy Army. They were riding on horses and mules, driving wagons, riding on caissons, in ambulances with the staff of Generals, and mixed up with all the rebel horde. The fact was patent, and rather interesting when considered in connection with the horror rebels express at the suggestion of black soldiers being employed for the National defense.

Notwithstanding these contributions, Marszalek and Williams observe that the "thought of a black man carrying a rifle was a horror to most white Mississippians, and the state resisted the enlistment of slaves even after the Confederate Congress authorized the policy near the end of the war in March 1865."

Who they were and what they did remains an issue. But some redress of recognition, however limited and insufficient, occurred when the state of Mississippi erected the African American monument at Vicksburg in 2004. The monument commemorates Mississippians who fought for the Union—the 1st and 3rd Mississippi / Infantry (Union)—as well as "All Mississippians of / African Descent / Who Participated in / the Vicksburg / Campaign." Mississippi thus joined Missouri and Kentucky among the states that commemorated Union as well as Confederate participants at Vicksburg. Further, a 2006 tribute to Union soldiers from Mississippi—a granite stele—stands at the Hinds County Courthouse at Clinton. More recently, the site of the Corinth Contraband Camp was commemorated by the NPS in 2009. Six life-size bronze sculptures stand on the grounds, representing the men, women, and children who inhabited the camp. As monumentation, they have an arguable place in this book. However, the figures represent an effort to address a heretofore underrepresented dimension of Mississippi's public history. They offer a significant counternarrative—or, better said, an addition—to the heritage of Confederate monuments in Mississippi.

Parameters and Method

Included in this study are outdoor courthouse and town monuments, cemetery and city monuments, and battlefield monuments or markers. Due diligence was done to document every site, but this study may have inadvertently overlooked monuments. Corrections or additions are welcome. The monumentation archive is current and accurate going into 2018. The book is intended to serve as an archive of this genre 153 years after Appomattox.

Chapter 1 focuses on 37 federal, state, or aesthetically or historically significant monuments at Vicksburg National Military Park. Chapter 2 takes a broader approach by surveying some 660 granite or bronze monuments at Vicksburg National Military Park and environs. Chapter 3, "Northern Mississippi," surveys approximately 40 monuments in northern Mississippi, including 18 courthouse monuments, numerous monuments on the Corinth, Brice's Crossroads, and Tupelo battlefields, and monuments at several hospital and cemetery sites. Chapter 4 is devoted to central Mississippi, including monuments at twelve courthouse sites, the state capitol at Jackson, and Confederate cemeteries at Jackson, Yazoo City, Kosciusko, Louisville, Philadelphia, Forest, Castalian Springs, Lauderdale, and Meridian. Chapter 5 is devoted to southern Mississippi, including eighteen courthouse sites, as well as the national cemetery in Natchez and Beauvoir, the last home of Jefferson Davis, near Biloxi.

I examined these monuments and the sites where they are placed as a collected multimedia text, albeit a widely dispersed series of distinctive texts at particular, specific locations. Assembling a comprehensive roster of texts/ monuments could only be accomplished by researching a wide range of sources, including the Smithsonian Institution Research Information System and the WPA survey of the monumentation at Vicksburg. I also visited each site in this book—every courthouse or cemetery or battlefield, including every major monument on the Vicksburg battlefield—notwithstanding the time, research, logistics, driving, and weather vagaries and hazards involved. I took these sites as they came, each having a value and interest of its own, under the premise that all of them are interesting. Each contributes to a larger understanding of this genre as well as the history of the war and its legacy. I made some deliberate exclusions, such as the excellent series of state historical highway markers or plaques, and the Civil War Trust's battlefield narratives. I excluded most but not all of the turn-of-the-century cast-iron wayside tablets and position markers erected at Vicksburg by the War Department. They number in the hundreds—750 by one count—and I judged them to be more historical than commemorative or monumental. I did not include relics or museums, such as the USS *Cairo* museum at Vicksburg or the wreckage of the *Star of the West*, which was sunk as a block ship in a channel of the Tallahatchie River by Confederate forces in 1862, but remains extant and is now under the jurisdiction of the US General Services Administration. The numbering system for the monuments used here was my own. The Works Progress Administration (WPA) surveyed and numbered the monuments in 1942, and those numbers are provided where available. In the intervening decades, however, many new monuments have been placed, monuments have changed locations, and park boundaries themselves have changed. A new survey was needed. The numbers are centered around major monuments and will, I hope, prove valuable to historians and visitors to the sites alike.

Disclaimer: I am aware that the history behind these monuments is contentious and provocative. For the record, this author has Southern roots but a Northern upbringing. I was born and raised as a Yankee; that is, I am Northern born, and I am a Union man. I work in the Bronx; I went to college and graduate school in New York. I pass Yankee Stadium on the 4 Train going to or coming from my campus; I get off the train at Burnside Avenue, named for a Union Civil War general; and my office looks out on Sedgwick Avenue, another Union Civil War general. On the other hand, I went to seminary in Virginia; my first full-time teaching job was in Virginia, and I was married in Virginia. My mother, from the South, met my father, from the North, at a USO dance during World War II and formed a union, as it were, that lasted fifty-six years. That upbringing leads me to conclude that the ties that bind the North and the South are deeper than the divisions that separated it during the war. Lewis Simpson describes a mysterious bond in the conflict between the North and South—a blood knowledge of emancipation. I would add to that meditation the words of Solomon in the Old Testament book of the Song of Songs that "love is stronger than death."

Notes

1. I will use the term "American Civil War" to describe the events of 1861–65, although the War Between the States or other descriptions may be more accurate or preferred, and the official term for the conflict is the War of the Rebellion, a description that reflects Northern interpretations. "Civil War" is rarely used on Confederate monuments, but the description reflects common contemporary usage.

I will also use the term "Confederate monuments" broadly, although some monument inscriptions deliberately avoid the use of the word. Similarly, the use of the phrase "Confederate soldiers" is one I will use broadly; however, many monuments identify their soldiers by state origin, with no reference to their status as Confederate soldiers.

Although "Union" is perhaps most commonly used to refer to the army of the United States, or the "northern" army, in the Civil War, "Federal" and "Federals" are also used to refer to the Union army and its troops, and I use both throughout.

2. Pennsylvania has an undetermined number of county courthouse and cemetery monuments. Gettysburg National Military Park also has an inventory of over seven hundred monuments, in addition to hundreds of wayside tablets.

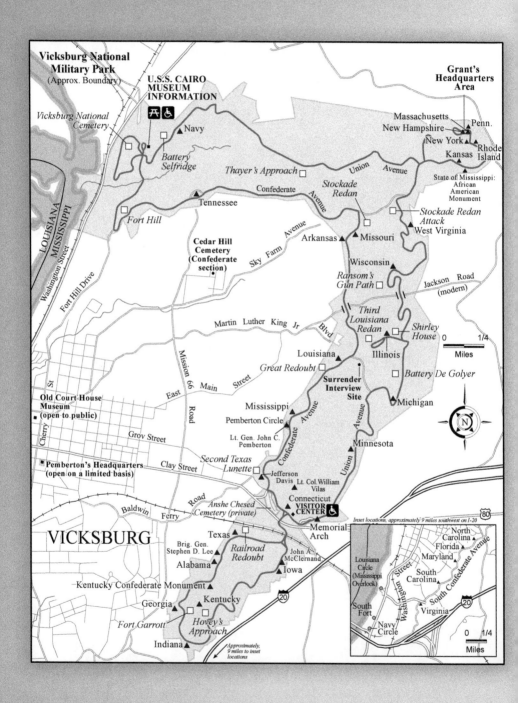

Vicksburg National Military Park (Approx. Boundary)

Grant's Headquarters Area

U.S.S. CAIRO MUSEUM INFORMATION

Vicksburg National Cemetery

Navy

Battery Selfridge

Thayer's Approach

Confederate Avenue

Tennessee

Fort Hill

Union Avenue

Stockade Redan

Massachusetts
New Hampshire
New York
Kansas
Penn.
Rhode Island

State of Mississippi: African American Monument

Stockade Redan Attack
West Virginia

Arkansas
Missouri

Wisconsin

Cedar Hill Cemetery (Confederate section)

Sky Farm Avenue

Ransom's Gun Path

Jackson Road (modern)

Third Louisiana Redan

Shirley House

Martin Luther King Jr Blvd

Louisiana

Illinois

0   1/4
Miles

Mission 66

East   Main   Street

Great Redoubt

Surrender Interview Site

Battery De Golyer

N

Old Court House Museum (open to public)

Grov Street

Mississippi

Pemberton Circle

Lt. Gen. John C. Pemberton

Michigan

Minnesota

Pemberton's Headquarters (open on a limited basis)

Clay Street

Second Texas Lunette

Jefferson Davis

Lt. Col. William Vilas

Connecticut

VISITOR CENTER

Baldwin   Ferry   Road

Anshe Chesed Cemetery (private)

Memorial Arch

Inset locations, approximately 9 miles southwest on I-20

US 80

VICKSBURG

Texas

Brig. Gen. Stephen D. Lee

Railroad Redoubt

John A. McClernand

North Carolina
Florida
Maryland

Alabama

Iowa

Louisiana Circle (Mississippi Overlook)

South Carolina

Kentucky Confederate Monument

Georgia   Kentucky

Fort Garrott

Hovey's Approach

Indiana

Approximately 9 miles to inset locations

20

South Fort

Navy Circle

Washington Street

Virginia

South Confederate Avenue

20

0   1/4
Miles

Louisiana / Mississippi

Washington Street

Fort Hill Drive

Cherry St

1

VICKSBURG
NATIONAL MILITARY PARK

ROM A MILITARY STANDPOINT, the bluffs and ravines overlooking the Mississippi River near Vicksburg formed a natural fortress governing passage on the waterway. These features led to the appointment of Confederate Major Samuel Lockett, chief engineer of the Department of Mississippi and East Louisiana, to design and oversee the construction of a defense line around the city beginning in June 1862. Prodigious work was done. Ultimately, there were nine forts, redoubts, or strong points connected by trenches or rifle pits stretching for nine miles in a semicircle around Vicksburg.

Given the strength of its fortifications and the importance of the Mississippi as a means of communication, transportation, and offensive movement by Union forces, Vicksburg came to be regarded as the Gibraltar of the Confederacy. "Vicksburg is the key!" President Abraham Lincoln famously declared, early in the war. "The war can never be brought to a close until that key is in our pocket. . . . We can take all the northern ports of the Confederacy, and they can defy us from Vicksburg."

After a prolonged campaign of maneuvers and repeated setbacks, the city came under siege by a combined force of Union troops commanded by Maj. Gen. Ulysses S. Grant and naval units—the "Brown Water Navy"—led by Admiral David Dixon Porter, some seventy-seven thousand men. Defending Vicksburg was an army of thirty-three thousand Confederate soldiers commanded by Lt. Gen. John Pemberton. An "Army of Relief," commanded by General Joseph E. Johnston, was poised near Jackson. The Southerners repulsed several direct assaults on the siege lines by Federal forces, but after a forty-seven-day stand, it became clear to Pemberton and members of his command that no relief was forthcoming and that starvation loomed for the Army of Vicksburg and the civilian populace. Pemberton surrendered the city and his army on July 4, 1863.

The Vicksburg siege was the culmination of the longest single campaign of the Civil War. It left nineteen thousand casualties on both sides. It was also the greatest defeat of Confederate forces during the war and ranks—with Gettysburg, the battle of Tenochtitlan in 1521 in Mexico, and the Battle of the Plains of Abraham in Canada in 1759—among the decisive battles in the history of North America. Historian Terrence Winschel notes that as a result of the fall of Vicksburg "the vast Trans-Mississippi (that portion of the Confederacy west of the river) was severed from the Cis-Mississippi (the heartland of the Southern nation east of the river)." He continues: "This cut major Confederate supply and communications lines that helped support Southern armies in other theaters as well as a civilian population in growing want of sustenance. Trapped in the coils of the giant anaconda, Confederate Colonel Josiah Gorgas, chief of the Ordnance Department, lamented that 'The Confederacy totters to its destruction.'"

The surrendered Confederate army was quickly disarmed and disbanded, and its soldiers and sailors were paroled. Most of the Union forces were freed to move on to other campaigns. It is notable, however, that some Federal troops remained to occupy and garrison the city and that an active Federal presence has never departed from Vicksburg. The city retains the features of an 1863 battlefield, but it is also the place where the North won and established a permanent Federal presence in a Deep South city, as historian Christopher Waldrep observes. Noting that the war "shifted the balance of power between the states and the national authority," Waldrep concludes that the "Vicksburg park memorializes many things, but it marks that shift of power too."

The transition of the battlefield to War Department site was some decades in the making. The Vicksburg National Cemetery was established by an act of Congress in 1866 and was administered by the War Department until 1933. In 1898, Vicksburg National Military Park (VNMP) became the last of five national military parks established by the Congress of the United States in the 1890s. It is the southernmost of the five national military parks. As a national park, it was laid out according to the principles of landscape architecture developed by such figures as Frederick Law Olmsted and Calvert Vaux. These principles in turn were inspired by the rural cemetery movement of the nineteenth century. Mount Auburn Cemetery in Cambridge, Massachusetts, founded in 1831, was a model for numerous landscaped cemeteries in the nineteenth century. Mount Auburn and other "rural" cemeteries of that genre also inspired a movement for public parks. In consonance with this Arcadian ideal, Vicksburg became the site of an extraordinary collection of art. Some 95 percent of the monuments erected at Vicksburg were completed prior to 1917, during the course of what came to be known as the American Renaissance. Art historian Michael Panhorst observes that most of the memorial art and architecture was built in the Beaux-Arts style popular following the "World's Columbian Exposition" in Chicago of 1893. At Vicksburg today there are more than 1,330 monuments, markers, tablets, and plaques. It may be the largest outdoor museum of sculpture and commemoration in North America.

There has been continual change at Vicksburg, in part wrought by the forces of nature and in considerable measure by dint of the currents of history, politics, and economic change. Supervision of the park and national cemetery was transferred from the War Department to the National Park Service on August 10, 1933. Under the aegis of the NPS Department of the Interior, extensive repairs and renovations were undertaken by the Civilian Conservation Corps

(CCC). Much of this was for erosion-control work on the battlefield topography and some was designed to "restore" the original battlefield features. The loess soil of the Vicksburg battlefield, which is highly erodible, was reinforced by the planting of thousands of tree seedlings that dominate much of the landscape today.

A comprehensive survey of the Vicksburg battlefield's monument and wayside tablet holdings was conducted by the federal Works Progress Administration (WPA) in 1942. Ironically, the survey was done in anticipation of scrapping tablets for their metals for military use during World War II; 145 were removed and have yet to be replaced.

Another wave of change took place in the late 1950s and 1960s, when the southern one-third of the park (154 acres) was "quitclaimed" to the City of Vicksburg in exchange for other historic property. The monuments on the land transferred to the city are still maintained by the NPS, but the changes allowed the expansion, development, and suburbanization of Vicksburg and Warren County.

Further changes occurred in the 1960s under the sponsorship of the National Park Service's Mission 66 program. A new road was constructed outside the park—Mission 66 Road—to eliminate local traffic in the park "and provide for a self-enclosed tour route to enhance visitor safety and enjoyment." The current visitor center was also constructed as part of this program, and the main avenue through the park—alternately Union and Confederate Avenue—was converted into a one-way road in 1971. The Park Service's assessment of the Mission 66 changes emphasizes the greater ease of movement across the battlefield: the efficiency that has been achieved was deliberate and intended. NPS literature observes that the tour was redesigned so as to "move people through the battlefield park in the most efficient manner possible while still giving the necessary details of the actions."

It is at all events a unique juxtaposition in North America. Vicksburg National Military Park reflects the influence of the rural cemetery movement of the mid-nineteenth century; the American Renaissance in monumentation and War Department commemoration at the turn of the twentieth century; WPA and CCC restoration in the 1930s and early 1940s; and the NPS preservation and oversight, as well as the efficiency and sense of movement inculcated with its landscape redesign in the 1960s as a legacy of the Mission 66 initiative.

The landscaped recreational opportunity it affords local residents is, arguably, unparalleled for a city of its size. At eighteen hundred acres, the park is more than twice the size of Central Park in New York City. One Park Service employee and resident of Vicksburg simply and emphatically stated, "We're proud of our park."

At the same time, it is more. Today the visitor to VNMP is presented with an intersection of an extravagant Beaux-Arts sculpture integrated with profuse aggregates of numbers and narrative inscribed on the tablets, plaques, and waysides—both are nineteenth-century legacies. This data on the landscape is consonant with efforts to come to terms with the war from an objective, positivist perspective—war as a science.

However, as secular, mundane, and warlike as the history of Vicksburg is, the landscape has been shaped in such a way that one experiences the battlefield grounds as a hallowed space more noticeably than on other NPS battlefields. Vicksburg, with a population of twenty-five thousand, has its central district enfolded by the siege line. To enter the Vicksburg battlefield park proper is to enter grounds that are fenced off, that are separated from the city—unlike the grounds of any other Civil War battlefield military park. To secure the grounds and enhance the experience of the park as a historic site, there is one gated main entrance, and a second gate to the national cemetery, park offices, and the USS *Cairo* museum.

There are practical reasons for shielding the park from the hazards of local traffic and as a matter of security, but there are at least two layers of symbolism to this as well. First, the Union monumentation marking the siege lines continues to encircle the city, perpetually surrounding the city of Vicksburg with commemorative Federal siege lines. Second, the landscape is held apart, sanctified. As it happens, most visitors enter the national military park through the 1917 arch on Union Avenue, and the arch serves as a point of entry to a kind of temple.

I intend neither irony nor cynicism by that assertion. All the elements of theater and drama are present. The participants—the dramatis personae—are commemorated in profuse narrative detail. Almost all of the dates and narratives terminate at 1863 as if the participants have no life afterward. The drama centers on the events leading to the siege, the siege itself, and the surrender.

The drama is multidimensional. The Mississippi and Alabama State Memorials, for example, offer defiant counterpoints to the Union victory, depicting embattled soldiers in valiant combat. There is no prospect of victory in these scenarios, but the legacy of the struggle is perpetuated.

The Vicksburg monument landscape is equally absolute: this was a Union victory—a triumph. Monuments such as the Massachusetts common soldier, the Rhode Island common soldier, and the New York obelisk offer clear testimony that in the end, the North—the Federals—won the victory.

There is another element to this space: temple sacrifice in the most literal sense. Architecturally speaking, several state and regimental monuments have an explicit temple form with a large stylobate—a temple floor, a place of sacrifice or sacrament. The state memorials of Missouri, Iowa, New York, Minnesota, and Pennsylvania, and, for that matter, the statues of Grant, Vilas, and Logan, have either extended plazas or exedra, are invariably on an elevated level, and thus all intimate the presence of sacred space. From Union Avenue, the Wisconsin monument looks like an impressive but simple large column surmounted by an eagle. However, visitors who walk up the marble steps find another temple floor—a stylobate—where bronze tablets display the names of over 9,075 Wisconsin soldiers who served at Vicksburg. The visitor walks up to a more visible sacred space at the Iowa monument. And one walks up to the state of Mississippi's monument, with its extended stylobate and presiding obelisk.

The Illinois monument is the largest and most elaborate of its genre: an enormous domed structure surmounting high ground at a key point of the battlefield. It may seem daunting to have to walk up the forty-seven steps to this monument on a hot summer day—one step for each day of the siege—but many visitors do. There they enter a recreation of the Roman Pantheon in which the names of 36,325 Illinois soldiers are displayed.

From this perspective, the collective effect of the monumentation at VNMP is to offer a kind of reenactable drama that gives the landscape a sacramental value. Lincoln was neither a priest nor a prophet, but he remains, if not the best exegete on the war, certainly the most prominent. The words of his Gettysburg Address, dedicating another Civil War cemetery, are posted at national cemeteries across the country, including Vicksburg's, and his observations are as applicable to Vicksburg and to all battlefields. As Lincoln declared, "we can not dedicate—we can not consecrate—we can not hallow—this ground. The brave men, living and dead, who struggled here, have consecrated it, far above our poor power to add or detract." The host of participants who are commemorated at Vicksburg represent a kind of American Eucharist. It is all the more appropriate that the site is in the middle of America, in the Mississippi Valley, and that the soldiers were engaged in the central life-and-death drama of the country's history.

Having said this, there may seem to be a contradiction in the fact that tours of the site of a forty-seven-day siege have been designed to be accomplished in a few hours, a day at most. From a cynic's perspective, the NPS's ability to swiftly move visitors across this landscape could seem as if the intention is to make history perfunctory, mechanical, or cursory—as a feat of mere efficiency. The nineteenth-century American writer Mark Twain may merit the last word in this regard. By his own admission, Twain's service in the war—as a Confederate soldier, as Samuel Clemens—was brief and undistinguished. However, he lived through the war and into the twentieth century—long enough to look back at the war with a measure of detachment. Twain articulated something of the restlessness in the American soul that is consonant with the idea of swift passage across the Vicksburg park. In the closing passage of his most famous novel, *Huckleberry Finn*, his title character professes a need to move elsewhere—away from the society that bore him and toward some other destiny—to "light out for the territory ahead of the rest." The impetus for movement across the park could be said to manifest a resonance with an American ideal of the pursuit of fulfillment, for better or worse, of a restlessness that propels a perpetual moving on. From this perspective, Vicksburg is not the consummate destination. The consolation of the horizon still awaits the living. Americans, in the words of Emily Dickinson, continue to dwell in possibility.

1.1 Subject: Visitor Center Monument: Surrender Site Monument
Location: 3201 Clay Street   N 32 20 39 33 / W 90 51 08 84
Installed or dedicated: 1864
Medium: Marble
Monument is a marble shaft.

Inscription

TAKEN FROM / THE SITE OF / INTERVIEW BETWEEN / MAJOR GENERAL / U S GRANT / & / LIEUT. GENERAL / PEMBERTON / JULY 4, / 1863.

This monument once marked the site where generals Grant and Pemberton met to discuss surrender terms of the Confederate army at Vicksburg. Grant and Pemberton conferred between the opposing lines at 3:00 p.m. on July 3, 1863—not July 4, as the monument has it. Reports indicate that the shaft was initially intended to be a grave marker or, alternatively, that it was meant to be a Mexican War memorial. Either way, it was confiscated by Federal troops occupying Vicksburg. In 1868 the monument was vandalized and was moved to the National Cemetery. It remained vulnerable to vandals and was placed in storage. Today it stands on display in the present-day visitor center. The surrender site is marked with a stele (2.3.48) and an upturned cannon barrel (2.3.47) on Pemberton Avenue, near the former visitor center (monument numbers here and below refer to site descriptions in text).

This is one of the earliest of Civil War battlefield monuments, preceded by only three others: the Barlow monument on the Manassas battlefield, erected on September 4, 1861; the 32nd Indiana VI stele erected in January 1862, after the battle of Rowlett's Station in Munfordville, Kentucky; and the Hazen monument on the Stones River battlefield, erected in the spring of 1863.

· The shaft is ten feet in height and was originally surmounted by a finial sphere. The figure of an American eagle in inscribed on it, with one claw holding a laurel and the other a shield; the eagle's beak grasps a pennant.

Memorial
Arch

Minnesota
State
Memorial

1.2 Subject: Memorial Arch   **WPA Index:** 367
Location: Union Avenue   N 32 20 37 31 / W 90 50 57 68
Dedicated: October 20, 1920
Medium: Marble

Inscription

MEMORIAL TO THE NATIONAL REUNION OF UNION AND CON / FEDERATE VETERANS
OF THE CIVIL WAR OCTOBER 16–19 1917

The arch is a legacy of the National Memorial Reunion and Peace Jubilee in 1917. With an appropriation of $150,000, the US Congress sponsored a four-day veterans' reunion at Vicksburg National Military Park. Approximately eight thousand veterans attended on the occasion. At its conclusion about $35,000 of the appropriation remained unspent, and the funds were used to erect this monument, an "arch with Doric order columns of grandeur and dignity," as Parker Hills observes. The arch was first erected to stand alongside Clay Street, the east–west main street in Vicksburg; it was moved to its present location in 1967, during the course of the Mission 66 redevelopment.

Charles L. Lawhon, of the Albert Weiblen Marble and Granite Company of New Orleans, designed the edifice, which was executed by the firm using Stone Mountain granite. Originally, the names of the states whose soldiers participated in the campaign were to be inscribed on the base. This was not done, but two obelisks presently located near the visitor center do so.

1.3 Subject: Minnesota State Memorial   **WPA Index:** 57
Location: Union Avenue, milepost 0.6   N 32 20 59 93 / W 90 50 42 94
Installed: 1906–7
Dedicated: May 24, 1907
Media: Bronze, granite
Monument is an obelisk, stylobate, and bronze *Statue of Peace*.

Inscriptions
[Front]

WILLIAM COUPER NEW YORK *[Left base of bronze statue:]* GORHAM CO. FOUNDERS

1ST BATTERY, LIGHT ARTILLERY, LIEUT. HENRY HURTER, CAPT. WILLIAM Z.
CLAYTON. 6TH DIV., 17TH CORPS. SERVED WITH THE 2D BRIGADE OF THE DIVISION
DURING THE INVESTMENT, MAY 18–JULY 4, 1863. 5TH INFANTRY. COL. LUCIUS F.
HUBBARD. 2D BRIG., 3D DIV., 15TH CORPS. CASUALTIES: JACKSON, MAY 14, 1863,
NONE REPORTED; ASSAULT, MAY 22, KILLED 2, WOUNDED 1, MISSING 7, TOTAL
10; MECHANICSBURG, JUNE 4, NONE REPORTED; RICHMOND, LOUISIANA, JUNE
15, WOUNDED 8; ON PENINSULA OPPOSITE VICKSBURG, JUNE 20–JULY 4, NONE
REPORTED. AGGREGATE: KILLED 2, WOUNDED 9, MISSING 7, TOTAL 18. / MINNESOTA

3D INFANTRY. COL. CHAUNCEY W. GRIGGS. MONTGOMERY'S BRIG., KIMBALL'S PROVISIONAL DIV., 16TH CORPS. SERVED AT HAYNES' AND SNYDER'S BLUFFS ON OUTPOST DUTY AND THE CONSTRUCTION OF DEFENSIVE WORKS AGAINST THE EXPECTED ATTACK OF GENERAL JOSEPH E. JOHNSTON'S ARMY FROM JUNE 8TH TO JULY 4TH, 1863. 4TH INFANTRY. LIEUT. COL. JOHN E. TOURTELLOTTE. 1ST BRIG., 7TH DIV., 17TH CORPS. CASUALTIES: RAYMOND, MAY 12, 1863, NONE REPORTED; JACKSON, MAY 4, WOUNDED 2; CHAMPION'S HILL, MAY 16, WOUNDED 2; ASSAULT, MAY 22, KILLED 12, WOUNDED 42, TOTAL 54, LIEUT. GEORGE G. SHERBROOK KILLED, LIEUT. CLARK TURNER MORTALLY WOUNDED; SIEGE, MAY 23-JULY 4. WOUNDED 4. AGGREGATE: KILLED 12, WOUNDED 50, TOTAL 62. THE COLONEL OF THE REGIMENT, JOHN B. SANBORN, COMMANDED 1ST BRIGADE, 7TH DIVISION, 17TH CORPS DURING THE SIEGE OF VICKSBURG. / MINNESOTA.

The Minnesota State Memorial consists of a granite obelisk with a bronze statue of a woman at its base. Standing less than a mile from the present-day main point of entry to the park, most visitors see this monument first among the state monuments on the automobile tour. It was erected at a cost of $24,500 and faces east on Union Avenue. Bronze tablets display a summary roster of Minnesota's units at Vicksburg, their role, and their leadership.

The obelisk, ninety feet in height, was executed in white granite quarried in Mount Airy, North Carolina. The Van Ambringe Granite Company of Boston constructed the obelisk; the bronze work was executed by the Gorham Manufacturing Company. For all its size, there is an understated elegance to the edifice not unlike that attributed to the New York monument. Even the word Minnesota has a modest presence: the word is found only at the base of the plinth on the north and south side.

Most prominent on the monument is sculptor William Couper's *Statue of Peace,* a bronze statue of a woman based on the Roman goddess of peace, Pax. Parker Hills describes Couper's sculpture as a "beautiful, radiant young woman." Like the figures of women on the Michigan or Mississippi monuments, she is a mediating figure: she bears a sword and shield from both armies, Union and Confederate, who have placed their weapons in her keeping.

1.4 Subject: Michigan State Memorial   **WPA Index:** 102
Location: Union Avenue, Battery De Golyer   N 32 21 13 48 / W 90 50 28 06
Dedicated: November 10, 1916
Medium: Granite
Monument is an obelisk with figure of a woman at the base.

Inscription
MICHIGAN'S / TRIBUTE OF HONOR / TO HER SOLDIERS WHO SERVED / IN THE CAMPAIGN / AND SIEGE / OF VICKSBURG.

State of Michigan Memorial

The obelisk of the Michigan State Memorial stands thirty-seven feet in height, but this is not the central feature of this monument. The statue of a woman stands at the base of the obelisk, facing east, modeled after the Greek goddess Athena. The monument is said to have been carved from a single forty-ton mass of White Bethel granite. The monument was sponsored by the state and erected at a cost of $10,000.

Hills describes the sculptor, Herbert Adams, as an "interpreter par-excellence of feminine grace and intellectual beauty" and the figure, *Spirit of*

Michigan, as having a "serene, serious, somewhat aloof, masculine beauty." The woman bears a palm frond in one hand, representing peace, as well as a gear wheel as a symbol of civilization and movement and progress. Symbols of peace are not uncommon on Civil War monumentation; the gear wheel is uncommon, however—perhaps unique. Parker Hills further observes that the gear wheel was in use in ancient Greek cultures, at least as far back as the time of Aristotle, ca. 330 BC. It is also consonant with the logistics and practical, day-to-day, grinding tasks that characterized the siege of Vicksburg.

Visual elements predominate. The inscription is modest and simple, and an adjacent granite-and-bronze stele displays a roster of Michigan regiments that served at Vicksburg: the 2nd, 12th, 15th, and 27th Infantries, and the 7th Light Artillery.

- Antonin Mercie influenced Adams's Beaux-Arts style when Adams was a student at the École des Beaux-Arts. Mercie had a direct influence on the American monument landscape with his 1890 statue of Robert E. Lee on Monument Avenue in Richmond, Virginia. Mercie's sculpture *Gloria Victis* (1890), a tribute to French soldiers who fought in the Franco-Prussian War, may be said to have parallels with Lost Cause mythology in the South by attributing glory to the men who fought in the war rather than the cause in and of itself.

1.5 Subject: Statue, Maj. Gen. John A. Logan   **WPA Index:** 144
Location: The old Jackson Road   N 32 21 32 95 / W 90 50 22 98
Installed or dedicated: 1919
Media: Bronze, granite
Monument is statue surmounting a base.

Inscription

JOHN A. LOGAN / COMMANDING / THIRD DIVISION / SEVENTEENTH ARMY CORPS
MAJOR GENERAL / JOHN A. LOGAN / ILLINOIS

JOHN A. LOGAN / MAJOR GENERAL, U.S. VOLS. / COMMANDING
3RD DIVISION / SEVENTEENTH ARMY CORPS / 2ND LIEUT. 1ST ILL. INF. MAY 29,
1847 / HONORABLY MUSTERED OUT OCT 16, 1848 / COLONEL, 31ST ILL. INF. SEPT
18, 1861 / BRIG. GEN., U.S. VOLS. MARCH 21, 1862 / MAJ. GENERAL OF VOLS. NOV 29,
1862 / RESIGNED AUGUST SEVENTEENTH, 1865.

Leonard Crunelle is the sculptor of the statue of Major General John A. "Black Jack" Logan, which surmounts a pedestal with exedra wings. It stands at a prominent place overlooking the old Jackson Road, east of the Shirley House, and is an example of the extensive and elaborate monumentation that the state of Illinois erected at Vicksburg. The state rendered the largest contribution of troops to the campaign of any state. In numbers alone, over thirty-six thousand men, it exceeded the size of the Confederate army at Vicksburg.

Maj. Gen. John A. Logan

Logan is regarded as one of the most able volunteer officers of the war. Unlike many other politician generals, "Black Jack" Logan excelled in combat leadership and won a degree of acceptance by professional officers that was not easily given. Entering service as colonel of the 31st Illinois VI, by March 1863, Logan had risen to the rank of major general commanding a division. He saw extensive service in the Western Theater and eventually rose to corps command during the Carolinas Campaign. Logan's public career after the war included a term as commander-in-chief of the veterans' organization, the Grand Army of the Republic. In that capacity, his General Order 11, published in 1868, is associated with the establishment of May 30 as Decoration Day— today Memorial Day—"for the purpose of strewing with flowers or otherwise decorating the graves of comrades who died in defense of their country during the late rebellion."

· Equestrian statues of Logan stand at the center of Logan Circle, Washington, DC, (Franklin Simmons, 1901) and in Grant Park in Chicago, Illinois (Augustus Saint-Gaudens, 1897).

1.6 Subject: The Illinois State Memorial and Temple   **WPA Index:** 282
Location: Union Avenue, milepost 1.8   N 32 21 35 85 / W 90 50 29 34
Dedicated: October 26, 1906
Media: Bronze, granite, marble
Monument is a rotunda with three medallion portraits.

Inscriptions

[Front]
ILLINOIS / WITH MALICE TOWARD NONE, WITH CHARITY FOR ALL, LET US HAVE PEACE.

[Three medallion portraits in Georgia marble:]

[Abraham Lincoln:]
THE MYSTIC CHORDS / OF MEMORY, STRETCHING / FROM EVERY / BATTLE-FIELD,
AND PATRIOT GRAVE, TO EVERY LIVING HEART / AND HEARTHSTONE / ALL OVER
THIS / BROAD LAND. / WILL YET SWELL THE CHORUS OF / THE UNION, / WHEN
AGAIN / TOUCHED, / AS SURELY / THEY WILL BE / BY THE BETTER / ANGELS OF /
OUR NATURE / A LINCOLN

[Ulysses Grant:]
WE HAVE BUT / LITTLE TO DO / TO PRESERVE / PEACE / HAPPINESS / AND
/ PROSPERITY / AT HOME AND / THE RESPECT / OF OTHER NATIONS. / OUR
EXPERIENCE / OUGHT TO / TEACH US THE / NECESSITY OF / THE FIRST; / OUR
POWER SECURES / THE LATTER. / U. S. GRANT

[Richard Yates:]
GOD FORBID / THAT I SHOULD / SAY AUGHT IN / MALICE AGAINST / THE SOUTH. / I
LOOK BEYOND / THE BLUE WAVES / OF THE OHIO / AND UPON THE / GREEN HILLS /
OF KENTUCKY / AND THERE / IS THE GRAVE / OF MY MOTHER. / R. YATES

Officially known as the Illinois State Memorial and Temple, this is the largest
and most prominent monument on the Vicksburg battlefield. It is also the
largest Union Civil War monument in the South and is comparable only to the
Pennsylvania monument at Gettysburg in size and scale of Union battlefield
monuments.

The edifice stands on high ground. In addition, forty-seven granite steps
lead up to the stylobate—the temple floor of the portico and rotunda. Each
step represents one day of the Siege of Vicksburg. The rotunda, modeled after the Roman Pantheon, is entered by way of a gabled portico with a carved
pediment relief of three female figures, surmounted by a bronze eagle in the
acroterium. Sixty bronze tablets adorn the interior walls, listing 36,325 Illinois
soldiers who participated in the campaign.

Sponsored by the state of Illinois, the temple stands sixty-two feet high
and originally cost $194,423.92. The monument is adjacent to the Shirley
House, facing south, in line of sight with the location where generals Grant
and Pemberton met to discuss surrender terms on July 3, 1863. It also stands
along the old Jackson Road, formerly the main road between Jackson and

The Illinois State Memorial and Temple

Vicksburg as well as the site of the May 19 and May 22 assaults by Union troops on Confederate lines. The NPS Mission 66 initiative led to the redesign of the layout of the park such that this monument is now even more prominent. Local traffic was rerouted around the monument, and the roadbed of the old Jackson road now serves as a park service artery. Visitors are frequently drawn to the high ground and the interior space.

The quotation on the medallion ascribed to Lincoln is taken from his First Inaugural Address; the quotation ascribed to U. S. Grant is excerpted from the *Personal Memoirs of Ulysses S. Grant*; the quotation by Richard Yates, the wartime governor of Illinois, is taken from an unsourced speech. Yates (1815–73) is one of four wartime governors either cited or given monuments on the field: the others are Samuel Kirkwood of Iowa, Andrew Curtin of Pennsylvania, and Oliver P. Morton of Indiana.

· A bronze plaque on the rear of the rotunda, interior declares:
"ILLINOIS ERECTS THIS MONUMENT IN GRATEFUL REMEMBRANCE OF THE SERVICES, THE SUFFERINGS, THE SACRIFICES AND THE DEVOTION OF HER SONS WHO PARTICIPATED ON LAND AND WATER IN THE CAMPAIGN AND SIEGE OF VICKSBURG FROM MARCH 29, TO JULY 4, 1863.

"THE NAMES ENROLLED WITHIN THIS STRUCTURE IN MARBLE AND BRONZE, ARE OF THE OFFICERS AND MEN OF ILLINOIS WHO SERVED IN THAT MEMORABLE CAMPAIGN AND SIEGE AND WHO FILLED THE RANKS OF THE SEVENTY-NINE ILLINOIS ORGANIZATIONS IN GENERAL GRANT'S ARMY.

"THE PEOPLE OF ILLINOIS, FREE OF MALICE, FULL OF CHARITY, DEDICATE THIS MONUMENT AS A MEMORIAL TEMPLE TO ENDURING HARMONY AND PEACE, AND AS A SHRINE AT WHICH ALL MAY AGAIN AND AGAIN RENEW THEIR CONSECRATION TO LOYAL CITIZENSHIP, AND GATHER INSPIRATION TO THE MOST UNSELFISH AND EXALTED PATRIOTISM.

"NOT WITHOUT THY WONDROUS STORY, ILLINOIS, ILLINOIS. CAN BE WRIT THE NATION'S GLORY, ILLINOIS, ILLINOIS. ON THE RECORDS OF THY YEARS, ABRAHAM LINCOLN'S NAME APPEARS, GRANT AND LOGAN, AND OUR TEARS, ILLINOIS, ILLINOIS."

- The exterior is white Georgia marble; the base and steps are Stone Mountain Georgia granite; the female figures are white marble; the eagle is bronze with gold leaf; the tablets are bronze. Stone Mountain Georgia granite forms the base and stairway. The edifice above the base is Georgia white marble. A marble mosaic of the Illinois State Seal is emplaced on the floor of the rotunda.

- Charles J. Mulligan and Frederick E. Triebel served as sculptors; Frederick C. Hibbard designed the surmounting bronze eagle. Parker Hills notes that it is eight feet, six inches wide, sculpted in gilded bronze, placed above the apex of the portico, to "represent the 'protecting wings of our nation'[; it] was also used by the Romans to indicate the location of a commanding officer on the field of battle."

- Dedicated on October 26, 1906, with elaborate ceremonies, the monument was transferred to the United States by Illinois Governor C. S. Deneen and accepted by the War Department.

- The edifice was erected by the Culver Construction Company; William B. Mundie was contractor. The architect was William L. B. Jenney, who served as Maj. Gen. William T. Sherman's chief engineer during the Vicksburg Campaign.

- The passage beginning "Not Without Thy Wondrous Story" is taken from the state song of Illinois.

1.7 Subject: Wisconsin State Memorial   **WPA Index:** 334
Location: Union Avenue, milepost 2.9   N 32 21 53 37 / W90 50 26 38
Dedicated: May 22, 1911
Media: Bronze, granite
Monument is an eagle surmounting a column, with bronze reliefs and two flanking soldiers on the plaza or stereobate at base.

Inscription
[Front (tablet at the base of the obelisk)]
THIS MEMORIAL / IS DEDICATED IN GRATEFUL / REMEMBRANCE OF THE FAITHFUL / SERVICE, UNSELFISH DEVOTION AND / EXALTED PATRIOTISM OF WISCONSIN /

Wisconsin State Memorial

SOLDIERS ENGAGED IN THE / CAMPAIGN AND SIEGE OF VICKSBURG, / MARCH 29–
JULY 4, 1863

BRONZE WORKS / ROMAN BRONZE WORKS

This is a soldier's monument. A sculpture of the "war eagle," "Old Abe," mascot of the 8th Wisconsin VI, surmounts the central column, which stands 123 feet high. Bronze reliefs displaying rosters of soldiers and statues of two flanking soldiers are located at the base. The monument stands on high ground, facing south, above Union Avenue. At car level on Union Avenue, the column seems to be the principal feature of the monument. One must walk up a flight of steps to the monument to see the monument's stylobate—temple floor—and the bronze tablets displaying the names of 9,075 Wisconsin soldiers who served at Vicksburg. In addition, a bronze relief tablet at the base of the column depicts a uniformed Union and Confederate soldier clasping hands in friendship. Flanking them are figures of two soldiers: one stands, bearing a rifle in both hands at waist level—albeit with a shortened right arm, as noted by Parker Hills. The other soldier is depicted in the act of firing his rifle. Beside him is his horse, fallen on hind legs, apparently shot, with head rearing back.

The monument was erected at a cost of $90,644. The contractors were the Harrison Granite Company and the Winnsboro Granite Company. The stonework is Winnsboro granite. The Roman Bronze Works, still active under the

State of West Virginia, Maj. Arza M. Goodspeed

name Roman Bronze Studios, did the foundry work. The sculptor was Julius C. Loester, of New York. Among Civil War monuments, Loester also sculpted the common soldier on the 77th Pennsylvania VI monument at Shiloh.

- The flanking soldiers are approximately 8 feet by 56 inches by 108 inches; the bronze reliefs are approximately 72 inches by 88 inches.

1.8 Subject: State of West Virginia, Maj. Arza M. Goodspeed
WPA Index: 416
Location: Union Avenue south of Graveyard Road   N 32 22 12 19 / W 90 50 25 58
Installed or dedicated: November 1922
Media: Bronze, granite
Monument is a bust surmounting a base.

Inscription

GOODSPEED. WEST VIRGINIA / 15TH ARMY CORPS / 2ND DIV., 2ND BRIGADE / BRIG. GEN. J. A. J. LIGHTBURN; 2ND DIV. / 3RD BRIGADE FOURTH INFANTRY COL. J. A. J. LIGHTBURN, COL. JAMES H. DAYTON. / KILLED 30, WOUNDED 126, TOTAL 156. / MAJOR ARZA M. GOODSPEED KILLED / LT. FINDLEY D. ONG / MORTALLY WOUNDED.

Aristide B. Cianfarani is the Italian-born American sculptor of this, the most modest Union state monument on the battlefield. It commemorates the 4th West Virginia VI's commander, Major Arza M. Goodspeed (1840–63), of Athens, Ohio, who was killed in action during the Union army's May 19 assault on the Confederate works.

The Kansas State Memorial

This was the only West Virginia unit on the Vicksburg battlefield, although many of its soldiers, including Goodspeed, were from Ohio. The 4th was placed in the advance of Lightburn's Brigade, as part of Sherman's 15th Corps. NPS notes record that with "lines neatly dressed and their battle flags blowing in the breeze above them, Sherman's troops surged across the rugged terrain at 2:00 p.m. . . . toward Stockade Redan." The attack was repulsed. The regiment suffered twenty-five men killed and ten mortally wounded in the assault that was "bloody and futile," according to historian Mark Snell, who records that "although a few of the regiment's soldiers climbed the parapet of the Stockade Redan and got inside the fort, all of them were either shot or captured."

1.9 Subject: The Kansas State Memorial   **WPA Index:** 727
Location: Grant Avenue   N 32 22 27 17 / W 90 50 01 66
Installed: June 1960
Media: Bronze, granite, marble
Monument is three circles, in bronze, surmounted by an eagle, surmounting a base.

Inscription
KANSAS

This is an utterly minimalistic abstract monument, uniquely so on NPS battle-fields, erected at a cost to the state of Kansas of $5,000. No formal dedication ceremony was held. The monument is merely three bronze circles—two whole and the middle one broken—representing the Civil War era and the periods that preceded and followed it. Strands of bronze shaped like an eagle surmount the circle. It was evidently deemed to be so abstract as to need an interpretive tablet, in pebbled marble and red granite, placed at the base of the sculpture by the Daughters of Union Veterans of the Civil War. The inscription reads as follows:

THE BOTTOM CIRCLE REPRESENTS THE UNITY / OF THE PRE-CIVIL WAR ERA. / THE BROKEN CIRCLE IN THE CENTER REPRESENTS THE / UNION TORN ASUNDER BY THE WAR 1861–1865 / THE PERFECT CIRCLE AT THE TOP DEPICTS THE / REGAINED UNITY OF THE POST-WAR ERA / AN EAGLE ATOP ALL TYPIFIES "THE GLORIUS [SIC] MAJESTY OF OUR COUNTRY" / THIS PLAQUE ERECTED 1973 BY / THE KANSAS DEPARTMENT DAUGHTERS OF UNION VETERANS / OF THE CIVIL WAR

- Kansas earned a name for its own civil war in the 1850s—"Bleeding Kansas." Thus, there is irony in inscription's reference to the "Unity / of the Pre-Civil War Era." Hostilities between proslavery and free-state advocates led to armed bands ranging across the state warring with one another as well as pillaging and committing mayhem. John Brown was among the perpetrators.

- Three Kansas units served in the Vicksburg Campaign: the 1st Kansas VI (mounted), and the 5th and 6th Kansas Cavalry. Sources indicate that "because of its internal divisions over the issue of slavery Kansas suffered the highest rate of casualties of any Union state."

1.10 Subject: State of Mississippi: The African American Monument
Location: Grant Avenue, mileposts 4.3–4.4   N 32 22 26 65 / W 90 50 00 28
Dedicated: February 4, 2004
Media: Bronze, granite
Monument is three bronze figures surmounting a base.

Inscription
COMMEMORATING THE / SERVICE OF THE / 1ST AND 3D MISSISSIPPI / INFANTRY REGIMENTS, / AFRICAN DESCENT AND / ALL MISSISSIPPIANS OF / AFRICAN DESCENT / WHO PARTICIPATED IN / THE VICKSBURG / CAMPAIGN

Three bronze male figures—two black Union soldiers and a field hand—surmount a base of black African granite. The field hand and one soldier support between them the second soldier, who is wounded. The first soldier "gazes toward a future of freedom secured by force of arms on the field of battle," as the NPS notes. The figure of the field hand on the right looks behind at a past of slavery, to the past as it were, but is young enough to look to a better future. The middle figure is the eldest: he is wounded and dazed, a symbol of

State of Mississippi: The African American Monument

the sacrifices made by black soldiers during the war. Notably, the wound may not be mortal, and he has the assistance of his comrades to move forward.

The monument was erected at a cost of $325,000, including $300,000 in support from the state of Mississippi and $25,000 contributed by the City of Vicksburg. The nine-foot tall bronze sculpture on a black granite base is the first monument placed in a National Park as a tribute to African American Civil War soldiers. The sculpture is the work of Dr. Kim Sessums, of Brookhaven, Mississippi. Sessums is also the sculptor of the state of Mississippi's monument to its soldiers who fought at the Battle of Shiloh, erected in 2015. Parker Hills avers that the civilian laborer in farm attire is resonant with the American initiative and volunteer spirit of Daniel Chester French's 1874 Minute Man statue. For his part, Sessums, as a twenty-first-century sculptor, credits the influence of twentieth-century realist painter Andrew Wyeth, noted by Michael Kimmelman for his "precise realist views of hardscrabble rural life."

- As a monument to "All Mississippians Of / African Descent," this is one of three Vicksburg monuments that commends the service of participants on both sides of the conflict. It is the only monument that is ethnically or racially specific. Historians John F. Marszalek and Clay Williams note that more than "17,000 black Mississippi slaves and freedmen fought for the Union"; in addition, as noted elsewhere, a "large but undetermined number of slaves served as body servants to white Confederate officers and soldiers, built fortifications, and did other manual labor for the Confederate Army."

· African Americans of the United States Colored Troops (USCT) are said to have proved their combat mettle in the midst of the Vicksburg Campaign at Port Hudson in May 1863; Milliken's Bend on June 7, 1863; and Goodrich's Landing on June 29–30, 1863. The "African Brigade" of Louisiana and Mississippi troops served at Milliken's Bend; African Americans of the 1st Arkansas and 10th Louisiana served at Goodrich's Landing.

1.11 Subject: Rhode Island State Memorial   **WPA Index:** 742
Location: Grant Avenue near Grant's Circle   N 32 22 33 54 / W 90 49 56 38
Installed: April 30, 1908; Dedicated: November 11, 1908
Media: Bronze, granite
Monument is a common soldier surmounting a base.

Inscription

RHODE ISLAND / 7TH INFANTRY /
COL. ZENAS R. BLISS / 1ST BRIG., 2ND DIV. / 9TH CORPS
FRANK EDWIN ELWELL SCULPTOR 1907

GORHAM CO. FOUNDERS *[Incised on base, left:]* JUDGE NATHA *[SIC]* B. LEWIS WILLIAM P. HOPKINS ELISHA KNIGHT / COMMISSION

HOPE

[With 9th Corps emblem]

The 7th Rhode Island VI served at Vicksburg with the 9th Corps. The 9th Corps participated in the investment of Vicksburg, but contrary to the image depicted in the statue, it played a supporting role on the exterior line of the siege and was not under fire. Its personnel losses were caused by disease, including Brig. Gen. Thomas Welsh, commanding the 1st Division of the Corps, who died of malaria shortly after the campaign's end. As a whole, the 9th Corps saw extensive action in the eastern and western theaters of war, and this dynamic monument is entirely appropriate to the corps' history; it was later engaged in the fighting for the state capitol at Jackson, where its losses were 34 men killed, 229 wounded, and 28 missing.

The Rhode Island State Memorial was erected at a cost of $5,000 and is the work of the sculptor Frank E. Elwell. The monument depicts a common soldier in action, an infantryman who has picked up the fallen colors and is advancing under fire. Emphasis is on the individual taking initiative, the citizen/

Rhode Island State Memorial

soldier defending the Union in the tradition of his presumed Revolutionary War forebears. He carries a weapon, but the flag—and the cause—he holds is especially prominent.

Elwell's figure is evidently influenced by Daniel Chester French's "The Minute Man" (1871–1875) which, as art historian Thayer Tolles observes, "depicts a farmer becoming a soldier, relinquishing his plow, raising his rifle, and stepping forward resolutely toward battle." French's figure in turn is regarded as being naturalistic in style but classic in pose, inspired by the Apollo Belvedere, a cast of which French studied at the Boston Athenaeum. More broadly, some see parallels between the weapon held by the soldier and the staff held by Moses as a symbol of authority as well as the responsibility residing with private citizens in a democratic republic.

1.12 Subject: The New York State Memorial   **WPA Index:** 747
Location: Grant Avenue, milepost 4.8   N 32 22 34 59 / W 90 49 59 96
Dedicated: October 17, 1917
Media: Bronze, granite
Monument is an obelisk surmounting a base.

Inscriptions

[Front]
[Circular bronze relief: New York coat of arms]

THIS MONUMENT IS ERECTED BY A GRATEFUL COMMONWEALTH IN
COMMEMORATION OF THE / SERVICES OF THE NEW YORK TROOPS IN THE NINTH
ARMY CORPS, MAJOR GENERAL JOHN G. PARKE, U.S.V., / COMMANDING, THAT TOOK
PART IN THE CAMPAIGN AND SIEGE OF VICKSBURG, JUNE 14–JULY 4, 1863 / 79TH
NEW YORK INFANTRY—"HIGHLANDERS"—COL. DAVID MORRISON / 3D BRIGADE
LEASURE'S, 1ST DIVISION—WELSH'S / 51ST NEW YORK INFANTRY COLONEL
CHARLES W. LEGENDRE / 2D BRIGADE—FERRERO'S, 2D DIVISION—POTTER'S /
46TH NEW YORK INFANTRY COLONEL JOSEPH GERHARDT / 3D BRIGADE—CHRIST'S,
2D DIVISION—POTTER'S; 2D NEW YORK LIGHT, BATTERY L CAPT. JACOB ROEMER.
/ BY GENERAL GRANT'S ORDER MAJ. GEN. PARKE WAS DIRECTED TO CAUSE THE
DIFFERENT REGIMENTS AND BATTERIES OF HIS COMMAND TO INSCRIBE ON THEIR
BANNERS AND GUIDONS "VICKSBURG" AND "JACKSON." / ERECTED BY THE STATE OF
NEW YORK, 1908.

[Circular bronze relief: artillery]
[Circular bronze relief: Ninth Corps insignia]

ON JUNE 3, 1863, GENERAL BURNSIDE, COMMAND- / ING DEPARTMENT OF THE
OHIO, RECEIVED ORDERS TO / SEND 8000 MEN TO GENERAL GRANT AT VICKSBURG.
/ THE NINTH ARMY CORPS, THEN IN KENTUCKY, / WAS DETACHED AND MOVED
DOWN THE OHIO AND / MISSISSIPPI RIVERS. POTTER'S DIVISION ARRIVED / ON
THE 14TH AND WELSH'S ON THE 15TH OF JUNE. / POTTER'S DIVISION LANDED AT
YOUNG'S POINT, / MARCHED OVER THE PENINSULA OPPOSITE VICKS- / BURG AND
CROSSED THE RIVER BELOW THE / TOWN TO TAKE POSITION ON THE EXTREME /
LEFT IN THE INVESTING LINE. THIS ORDER WAS SOON / COUNTERMANDED. THE
TROOPS RETURNED / AND WERE MOVED IN TRANSPORTS WITH THE RE- / MAINDER
OF THE CORPS UP THE YAZOO RIVER / TO SNYDER'S BLUFF, TAKING POSITION
UNDER / GENERAL SHERMAN'S COMMAND ALONG THE SKIL-LAKALIA VALLEY
BETWEEN MILLDALE AND BENTON ROAD, TO OPPOSE JOHNSTON'S ARMY, THEN /
THREATENING THE INVESTING FORCES. ENTRENCH / MENTS WERE CONSTRUCTED
ON THE HILLS. AFTER JULY 4 THE CORPS FORMED PART / OF SHERMAN'S ARMY
WHICH DROVE JOHNSTON / FROM HIS POSITION ON THE BIG BLACK RIVER /
INTO HIS ENTRENCHMENTS AT JACKSON, AND / AFTER A SIEGE OF EIGHT DAYS,
COMPELLED THE / CONFEDERATE FORCES TO RETREAT. / LEFT JACKSON ON JULY
20, AND REACHED ITS / MILLDALE CAMP ON JULY 23; ORDERED ON THE 24TH TO
RETURN / TO THE DEPARTMENT OF THE OHIO.

[Circular bronze relief, infantry]

The New York State Memorial

The forty-three-foot tall obelisk, constructed from Mount Airy, North Carolina, granite, displays two bronze inscription tablets commemorating the service of the 46th, 51st, and 79th New York VI and Company L, 2nd New York Light Artillery, all of the Ninth Corps.

The monument was erected at a cost $11,636.83, and it was formally dedicated on Wednesday, October 17, 1917, on the occasion of the National Memorial Reunion and Peace Jubilee. A. J. Zabriskie was the designer. An engineer by profession, Zabriskie also served on the monuments commission for the New York monuments at Gettysburg and Chattanooga. The New York monuments at these sites are characterized by extended narratives on bronze tablets and skillfully, precisely carved granite shafts and obelisks. Composed of three granite stones, the New York obelisk at Vicksburg looks like a simple monument, but there is an understated elegance to it. The monument reflects advancing technologies that, as Cynthia Mills notes, "made use of pneumatic tools, frequently employed by immigrants skilled in stonecutting, that made granite a much more usable medium, as opposed to the softer and less durable marble." Michael Panhorst also takes note of the balance between copious detail in the inscription and the monument's overall simplicity, observing that, "each panel reads as a single dark form in contrast with the light stone of the monument."

· Five state monuments are in the vicinity of Grant's headquarters: Ninth Corps memorials from Rhode Island, New York, Pennsylvania, Massachusetts, and New Hampshire. The corps' service at Vicksburg is cogently summarized on the New York monument.

The Massachusetts State Memorial: "The Volunteer"

1.13 Subject: The Massachusetts State Memorial **WPA Index:** 752
Location: Grant Avenue at Grant Circle   N 32 22 37 39 / W 90 49 59 62
Dedicated: November 14, 1903
Media: Bronze, granite
Monument is a common soldier surmounting a base.

Inscription

[Front]

ENSE PETIT-PLACIDAM-SUB LIBERTATE-QUIETEM

[state seal of Massachusetts]

MASSACHUSETTS TRIBUTE TO THE / 29TH, 35TH AND 36TH REGIMENTS
VOLUNTEER INFANTRY / 9TH ARMY CORPS

[Badge, Ninth Corps]

THEO ALICE RUGGLES-KITSON
SCULPTOR. BOSTON, MASS. / COPYRIGHT 1901–1903.

This, the first state memorial erected within Vicksburg NMP, commemorates the service of three Ninth Corps regiments from Massachusetts—the 29th, 35th, and 36th Infantry. The sculpture, known as the "Volunteer," depicts a soldier striding off to war in 1861. It was erected at a cost of $4,500. The sculptor was Theo Alice Ruggles Kitson; the figure of the soldier is mounted on a fifteen-ton boulder shipped from Massachusetts.

In ways that are similar to the Rhode Island common soldier (1907–8), the Iowa common soldier (1912) and, for that matter, the Texas common soldier (1962–63), the individuality of the soldier is emphasized, transcending the typecast commonality that is so frequently attributed to Civil War statues. Kitson offers an archetypical but distinctive depiction of this American figure: This figure looks confident in his place and his future. He is not bellicose, but he carries a weapon. He is in motion, looking purposeful, vigorous, relaxed but alert.

In her time, T. A. R. Kitson was one of the most prolific female bronze sculptors in America, and, as noted elsewhere, she is the most commonly represented artist at Vicksburg NMP. Kitson was born in 1876 in Brookline, Massachusetts; she studied under the English born American sculptor Henry Hudson Kitson, whose work is also represented at Vicksburg and with whom she collaborated on the Iowa monument. The two were married in Paris in 1893. The "Volunteer" was recast ten times for monument sites in New York, New England, and California.

- "Ense petit placidam sub libertate quiete," the official motto of the Commonwealth of Massachusetts, is translated from the Latin as, "By the sword we seek peace, but peace only under liberty."

- A period photograph indicates that ten yoke of oxen were necessary to haul the monument from the railroad siding delivery point to its present-day site.

The New Hampshire State Memorial

1.14 Subject: The New Hampshire State Memorial   **WPA Index:** 786
Location: Grant Circle   N 32 22 38 25 / W 90 50 01 24
Dedicated: n.a.
Medium: Granite
Monument is an obelisk surmounting a base.

Inscriptions
[Front]
[Relief: Ninth Corps emblem]

NEW HAMPSHIRE
SIXTH / NINTH / ELEVENTH / N. H. VOLUNTEER INFANTRY / 9TH ARMY CORPS

NEW HAMPSHIRE

[state seal of New Hampshire]
[Motto: Neo Hantoniensis Sigillum Reipublicae 1784.]

NEW HAMPSHIRE

NEW HAMPSHIRE

The New Hampshire State Memorial, a rough granite shaft standing twenty feet high, was erected in November 1904 at a cost of $5,000. There was no formal dedication; the federal government formally accepted the monument on

April 20, 1906. The shaft is inscribed with the names of the New Hampshire units at Vicksburg, the 6th, 9th, and 11th VI, all of the 9th Corps, commanded by Maj. Gen. John G. Parke. The corps arrived at Snyder's Bluff on June 16, 1863, eighteen days before the end of the campaign.

The monument's designer is unknown. It is spare but distinguished. Surmounting the column is a cannon ball finial.

1.15 Subject: The Pennsylvania State Memorial   **WPA Index:** 777
Location: Grant Circle, milepost 4.6   N 32 22 40 29 / W 90 50 01 00
Erected: 1905; Dedicated: March 24, 1906
Media: Bronze, granite
Monument is a curved stele and stylobate.

Inscriptions

HERE BROTHERS FOUGHT FOR THEIR / PRINCIPLES. HERE HEROS DIED FOR
THEIR COUNTRY AND A UNITED PEOPLE / WILL FOREVER CHERISH THE PRECIOUS /
LEGACY OF THEIR NOBLE MANHOOD

[Incised under medallions, left to right:]
CURTIN BRENHOLTZ HARTRANFT LEASURE DURELL / PENNSYLVANIA
FORTY-FIFTH, FIFTIETH, FIFTY-FIRST AND ONE-HUNDREDTH INFANTRY REGIMENTS
AND BATTERY D LIGHT ARTILLERY PENNSYLVANIA VOLUNTEERS. VIRTURE, LIBERTY
AND INDEPENDENCE. ERECTED BY THE COMMONWEALTH OF PENNSYLVANIA.

The Pennsylvania State Memorial

The Pennsylvania State Memorial consists of an inscribed and decorated granite stele facing an elliptical platform—a stylobate or temple floor—approached by a flight of three steps. The whole of the monument faces southwest, toward the siege lines. Albert B. Ross was the architect; the Lewiston Monumental Works, fabricator. Charles A. Lopez designed the bronze reliefs. The monument was erected at a cost of $12,500.

Reliefs of the Pennsylvania State Coat of Arms and the 9th Corps insignia are displayed on the stele. In addition, five bronze medallions portray the Pennsylvania unit commanders at Vicksburg: Lt. Col. John I. Curtin, a cousin of Governor Andrew G. Curtin, commanded the 45th Pennsylvania VI; Lt. Col. Thomas S. Brenholtz commanded the 50th Pennsylvania VI; Col. John F. Hartranft raised and commanded the 51st Regiment of Pennsylvania VI, served throughout the war and ended the war as a major general; Col. Daniel Leasure commanded the 100th Pennsylvania VI, was wounded during the 1864 Overland Campaign, survived, but was mustered out of the service on August 30, 1864; and Capt. George W. Durell raised and commanded Durell's Battery, also known as Company D, 1st Pennsylvania Light Artillery.

· Columns flanking the monument feature busts of Governor Andrew G. Curtin (WPA Index: 778) and another Pennsylvanian, Maj. Gen. John G. Parke, 9th Corps commander, from Coatsville, Chester County (WPA Index: 777). Governor Andrew Curtin was wartime governor of Pennsylvania.

· Not included on the monument but present at Vicksburg: Brig. Gen. Thomas Welsh, of Columbia, Pennsylvania, who raised and commanded the 45th Pennsylvania and commanded the 1st Division, 9th Corps. A bust of Welsh stands nearby (WPA Index: 775).

1.16 Subject: Maj. Gen. Ulysses S. Grant   **WPA Index:** 787
Location: Grant Circle   N 32 22 37 98 / W 90 50 04 16
Installed or dedicated: 1918
Media: Bronze, granite
Monument is an equestrian figure surmounting a base.

Inscriptions
[Front]
[emblem:]

NATIONAL UNION, / STATE SOVEREIGNTY, / 1868–1918.
BORN / APRIL 27 / 1822 / DIED JULY 23 / 1885

[Under plaque, engraved in granite]
MAJOR GENERAL / ULYSSES S. GRANT

Maj. Gen. Ulysses S. Grant

[Bronze plaque on front of upper base:]
[FREDERICK C. HIBBARD SC. / CHICAGO 1918]

[Engraved in granite:]
MAJOR GENERAL / ULYSSES S. GRANT / *[On lower base, engraved:]* ILLINOIS ULYSSES
S. GRANT / BRIG. GEN. U.S. VOLS. MAY 17 1861 / MAJOR GENERAL OF VOLS. FEB. 16,
1862 / MAJ. GEN. U.S. ARMY JULY 4 1863 / LIEUTENANT GENERAL MARCH 2 1864
/ GENERAL JULY TWENTY-FIFTH 1866 / COMMANDER-IN-CHIEF OF THE ARMY /
MARCH 12 1864–MARCH 4 1869

[Engraved in granite:]
VICKSBURG / CAMPAIGN / GRAND GULF / PORT GIBSON / RAYMOND / JACKSON /
CHAMPION'S HILL / BLACK RIVER BRIDGE / VICKSBURG HEADQUARTERS / ARMY OF
THE TENNESSEE / MAY 19–JULY 4,1863 / ULYSSES S. GRANT / MAJOR GENERAL U.S.
VOLS / COMMANDING
[Engraved in granite:]
ULYSSES S. GRANT / CADET, U.S. MILITARY ACADEMY 1839 / B.V.T. 2ND LT. 4TH INF.
JULY 1 1843 / 2ND LT. 7TH INF. SEPT. 30 1845 / TRANS. TO 4TH INF. NOV. 15 1845 /
FIRST LIEUTENANT SEPT 16, 1847 / CAPTAIN, AUGUST FIFTH 1853 / COL. 21ST ILL.
INF. JUNE 28 1861

Equestrian statues of Ulysses Grant are found at prominent places in major
cities across the north, but Frederick Hibbard's statue of Grant stands on
the grounds of the general's headquarters during the campaign and is the
only battlefield monument of the general. Grant's characteristic stolidity and

unruffled nature is evident in most monuments—"stolid and unemotional and relentless," is how historian Bruce Catton characterized him. Hibbard, however, chose to depict Grant with a more formal appearance than the general usually affected in public. Grant is dressed as a major general, "attired and equipped splendidly," as Hills describes him, with a brace of pistols and a sword at his left side, although Grant professed "a distaste for military uniform."

Grant is both stoic and heroic in Hibbard's depiction. The monument stands fifteen feet high, surmounting an inscribed granite base, with two fifteen-foot-long granite benches, in keeping with exedra traditions for monumentation and the fact that the site served as Grant's headquarters during the siege. Notwithstanding the scale and grandeur of the monument, elements of democratic ideals expressed in the nearby state monuments are also resonant here. The statue of Grant is aligned in elevated height and supporting distance of the statues of the Massachusetts volunteer and the Rhode Island volunteer. The three monuments are thematically similar. Biographer Jean Edward Smith characterized Grant as "an ordinary man gifted with an extraordinary talent for making war." Waldrep notes that, "Grant, the quintessential ordinary man . . . described himself as only nominally a military man; he was, by his own description, a citizen soldier."

- Notable statues of Grant include those at Chicago's Lincoln Park (1891; Louis Rebisso, sculptor); Washington, DC, at the base of Capitol Hill (1924; Henry M. Shrady, sculptor); and Fairmount Park, Philadelphia (1897; Daniel Chester French and Edward C. Potter, sculptors).

- Among other Civil War monuments, Hibbard also designed and produced the United Daughters of the Confederacy (UDC) monument at Shiloh (1917); the eagle surmounting the portico of the Illinois monument at Vicksburg, and the courthouse common soldier at Raymond, Mississippi (1908).

1.17 Subject: The Navy Memorial   **WPA Index:** 653
Location: Union Avenue   N 32 22 37 43 / W 90 51 50 28
Erected: 1911; Dedicated: 1917
Media: Bronze, granite
Monument is an obelisk with four sculpted figures at base.

Inscriptions

[Front]

[On plaque on Porter base:] DAVID DIXON PORTER / COMMANDED THE MISSISSIPPI SQUADRON / FROM OCTOBER 1862 TO SEPTEMBER 1864 / AS ACTING REAR ADMIRAL U.S. NAVY / ENGAGED IN OPERATIONS ON THE MISSISSIPPI / RIVER

The Navy Memorial

AND TRIBUTARIES LEADING UP TO AND / DURING THE CAMPAIGN AND SEIGE OF / VICKSBURG MARCH 29–JULY 4, 1863 *[On Porter base, right:]* LORADO TAFT SC

[Incised on plinth, front:] FARRAGUT *[On plaque on Farragut base:]* DAVID GLASGOW FARRAGUT / COMMANDED THE WEST GULF BLOCKADING / SQUADRON FROM FEBRUARY 1862 TO NOVEMBER / 1864 AS FLAG OFFICER AND REAR ADMIRAL / U.S. NAVY ENGAGED IN OPERATIONS ON THE / MISSISSIPPI RIVER AND TRIBUTARIES LEAD- / ING UP TO AND DURING THE / CAMPAIGN AND SIEGE OF VICKSBURG / MARCH 29–JULY 4, 1863 / *[On Farragut base, right:]* HENRY H. KITSON FECIT 1911

[On plaque on Foote base:] ANDREW HULL FOOTE / COMMANDED THE NAVAL FORCES ON / WESTERN WATERS AS FLAG OFFICER U.S. / NAVY FROM SEPTEMBER 1861 TO MAY 1862 / ENGAGED IN OPERATIONS ON THE MISSISSIPPI RIVER AND TRIBUTARIES LEADING UP TO THE / CAMPAIGN AND SIEGE OF VICKSBURG / MARCH 29–JULY 4, 1863 / *[On Foote base, right:]* WM. COUPER

[Incised on plinth, front:] DAVIS *[On plaque on Davis base:]* CHARLES HENRY DAVIS / COMMANDED THE NAVAL FORCES ON / WESTERN WATERS AS FLAG OFFICER U.S. / NAVY FROM MAY 1862 TO OCTOBER 1862 / ENGAGED IN OPERATIONS ON THE MISSISSIPPI / RIVER AND TRIBUTARIES LEADING UP TO THE / CAMPAIGN AND SIEGE OF VICKSBURG / MARCH 29–JULY 4, 1863

[On Davis base, left:] F. EDWIN ELWELL SC 1910

At 202 feet this is the tallest monument in Vicksburg NMP. It stands on high ground and may seem aloof to visitors, since it is at some distance from passersby on Union Avenue, unlike the host of relief portrait and rosters of infantry, artillery, and cavalry units that are at or near the roadsides of the park. Its placement, however, makes it visible from a large distance, and the height affords views of the river and the Louisiana low country, where the "Brown Water Navy" served. It is thus suggestive of the vast scale of the campaign for Vicksburg: it took place at locations that are far beyond the reach of the park's formal confines. Records do not indicate the designer or architect for this tribute to the officers and sailors of the US Navy, but clearly it was modeled after the Washington Monument.

At the base of the monument are four plinths surmounted by statues of the fleet commanders, Admirals David Glasgow Farragut and David Dixon Porter, and Flag Officers Charles Henry Davis and Andrew Hull Foote. The sculptors of the figures at the base were Frank E. Elwell (Davis, 1910); William Couper (Foote, 1917); Henry H. Kitson (Farragut, 1911); and Lorado Taft (Porter, 1917).

The US Navy's contribution to the Union victory at Vicksburg was critical. Further, the collaborative relationship between the army and navy—especially the amphibious role in support of the army—would find no parallel until the European and Pacific amphibious assaults of World War II. Historian Terrence J. Winschel notes that "Grant was the first to acknowledge the Navy's assistance. On 4 July, after having witnessed the Stars and Bars of the Confederacy lowered from the cupola of the Warren County Courthouse in

Vicksburg National Cemetery Arch

Vicksburg and replaced by the Star and Stripes, the general rode to the city's waterfront to exchange congratulations with and extend his heartfelt thanks to Acting Rear Admiral David Dixon Porter, whose powerful gunboats of the Mississippi Squadron had proved to be the decisive factor in the campaign."

1.18 Subject: Vicksburg National Cemetery Arch
Location: Cemetery grounds off Washington Street   N 32 22 23 49 31 / W 90 52 16 00
Installed or dedicated: 1880
Medium: Limestone
Monument is an arch.

Inscription

NATIONAL MILITARY CEMETERY / VICKSBURG, A.D. 1865

HERE REST IN PEACE 16,100 CITIZENS / WHO DIED FOR THEIR COUNTRY / IN THE YEARS 1861 TO 1865

This arch stands at the original entrance to the national cemetery, off Washington Street. That point of entry is no longer in use, but the arch remains. NPS notes record that it was built of at a cost of $7,000, and is formed by two Alatawa (fossiliferous) limestone columns seventeen feet in height.

Vicksburg National Cemetery was established by an act of Congress in 1866. The remains of seventeen thousand Union soldiers are interred here, more than at any other national cemetery. Of this number, thirteen thousand are listed as "Unknown." The inscription is a tribute to citizen soldiers.

Note the retrospective inscription, which makes no assumption that future generations of visitors or passersby will know who or why these "16,100 Citizens" are interred here on a bluff overlooking the present-day Yazoo Canal, which follows the former channel of the Mississippi River. There is a logic to that assumption. Vicksburg was not established as a military park when the national cemetery was established; a less renowned site might well have needed the reminder that the inscription offers.

This ground was held by the 15th Corps during the siege of Vicksburg; several Iowa position and unit markers are on the grounds. The bluffs of this 116-acre site made extensive landscaping of terraces necessary to accommodate the gravesites.

- Confederate soldiers were not eligible for burial in a national cemetery; their remains were not disinterred. Four soldiers are said to have been inadvertently interred here.

1.19 Subject: The Tennessee State Memorial   **WPA Index:** 876
Location: Confederate Avenue, east of Fort Hill
N 32 22 18 27 / W 90 51 43 18
Erected: June 1996; Dedicated: June 29, 1996
Medium: Granite
Monument is a granite stele shaped in the outline of the state of Tennessee.

Inscriptions

TENNESSEE

DEDICATED TO THE TENNESSEE CONFEDERATE SOLDIERS / WHO SERVED IN THE DEFENSE OF VICKSBURG / [UDC Seal]

HONOR TO THOSE WHO NEVER SOUGHT IT; / FAME TO THOSE WHO NEVER WISHED IT; GLORY TO THOSE WHO NEVER DREAMED IT; / IMMORTALITY, FOR THEY EARNED IT— THE CONFEDERATE SOLDIERS OF TENNESSEE. / M. K. GRISSOM

SPONSORED BY / TENNESSEE / DIVISION UDC

The Confederate Order of Battle lists twenty-eight units of infantry, cavalry, or artillery in the Vicksburg Campaign. There are no Tennessee units in the Union Order of Battle. Mrs. Evelyn Pool, chairman of the Monument Committee for the Tennessee Division of the UDC, is credited with initiating the project to erect this monument. The idea was endorsed and supported by Mrs. Nelma Crutcher, UDC Division President.

The Tennessee State Memorial

It is a simple, unadorned monument. The designer is uncited, but the tribute was written by Michael A. Grissom of Oklahoma. The inscription is clear and direct, without the adornment or extensive rosters of units or soldiers that earlier monuments display. UDC monuments tend to be more sentimental and commemorative; there is less didacticism than in the monuments sponsored by the Sons of Confederate Veterans (SCV) in recent decades, and there are no rosters, unlike most of the state monuments at Vicksburg. Park Service notes on this monument aver that it reflects the evolution of commemorations on the battlefield—that as "those who had first-hand memories of the war became fewer and fewer, the emphasis on commemorating the battle and its participants gave way to an interest in the historical significance of the battle in a larger cultural context."

The State of Missouri Memorial

1.20 Subject: The State of Missouri, Shaft, Statue, and Reliefs
WPA Index: 786
Location: Confederate Avenue, milepost 10.9   N 32 22 07 29 / W 90 50 42 12
Dedicated: October 17, 1917
Media: Bronze, granite
Monument is a "winged Angel of Peace" surmounting a ship's bow before a pylon / stele, flanked by exedra walls.

Inscriptions
[Front]
[Relief: Missouri coat of arms]

TO COMMEMORATE AND PERPETUATE / THE HEROIC SERVICES, / THE UNSELFISH
DEVOTION TO DUTY / AND THE EXALTED PATRIOTISM OF THE MISSOURI SOLDIERS /
UNION AND CONFEDERATE, / WHO WERE ENGAGED IN THE / CAMPAIGN, SIEGE AND
DEFENSE / OF VICKSBURG

VICTOR S. HOLM / MCMXIV CAST BY AMERICAN ART BRONZE FDRY CHICAGO ILL.
DESIGNED AND ERECTED BY VICTOR S. HOLM SCULPTOR / AND HELLMUTH &
HELLMUTH ARCHITECTS *[list of monument committee members]*

No roster of units is inscribed on the state of Missouri's memorial at Vicksburg, but the height of its central pylon or stele, forty-two feet, is symbolic of the forty-two Missouri units that served at Vicksburg—twenty-seven Union and fifteen Confederate.

The monument was erected at a cost of $40,000. It was designed by Harry I. Hellmuth of the architectural firm of Hellmuth & Hellmuth. The bronze reliefs are the work of sculptor Victor S. Holms.

Aesthetically speaking, this extravagant Beaux-Arts monument, facing southwest, is best viewed in reverse as one tours the park by automobile. That is, drivers first see the monument in reverse since Confederate Avenue was converted for one-way traffic in 1970–71. Evidently, the monument was intended to be approached from the opposite direction. As it stands now, visitors must pull to the side of the road and look backward for a good view.

The inscription is relatively terse: there are no rosters of units, but it is with unabashed irony that the inscription gives tribute to the "Exalted Patriotism Of" soldiers on both sides of the conflict, regardless of the side on which they fought. The monument is simply dedicated to "The Missouri Soldiers / Union And Confederate, / Who Were Engaged In The / Campaign."

Two bronze panels are displayed on the front of each of the exedra walls. The stele walls rise fifteen feet and are approached by a flight of three steps across a stylobate or temple floor. The bronze panels are approximately seven feet high and twelve feet long and depict the collision of combat between opposing Missouri soldiers. The relief on the left depicts Missouri Union soldiers assaulting the field works; the relief on the right depicts Missouri Confederate soldiers defending the works. Between the reliefs in the front of the pylon is a granite sculpture of the bow of a Roman galley. The bow is surmounted by the bronze statue of a female, symbolic of the "Spirit of the Republic," alternatively referred to as an "Angel of Peace." The forty-two-foot pylon or stele is inscribed with the coat of arms of the state of Missouri, including the state motto, "Salus populi suprema lex esto" ("The welfare of the people shall be the supreme law"), which is drawn from Cicero's *De Legibus* (On the Laws).

The monument stands near where Union and Confederate Missouri troops met in combat. During the Union assaults of May 19 and 22, Union troops, including the 6th and 8th Missouri VI, opposed Confederate troops under Col. Francis Cockrell, including five Missouri infantry regiments and three Missouri artillery batteries. Eight Missouri Union infantry regiments under Col. Francis Manter and Col. Charles Woods, supported the attacks north of the redans. The Union assaults were repulsed. Approximately four thousand Union and three thousand Confederate casualties (killed, wounded, missing) were incurred during the May 19 and 22 assaults, many of them Missourians.

State of Arkansas State Memorial

· The monument was a major attraction during its unveiling during the "Peace Jubilee" in 1917. More than fifty thousand Civil War veterans were said to be on hand.

· The monument was rededicated in 2017, after state-sponsored repairs were completed to the bronze work and granite.

1.21 Subject: State of Arkansas State Memorial   **WPA Index:** 781
Location: Confederate Avenue   N 32 22 06 43 / W 90 50 43 82
Dedicated: August 2, 1954
Media: Bronze, marble
Monument is twin shafts and a sword surmounting a base, with two adjoining stele.

Inscription

ARKANSAS / TO THE ARKANSAS / CONFEDERATE SOLDIERS / AND SAILORS, A PART OF / A NATION DIVIDED BY / THE SWORD AND REUNITED
AT THE ALTAR OF FAITH

This is a stark but elegant multimedia narrative set into an art deco design by the state of Arkansas. The monument depicts a force of conflict represented by the sword dividing the nation, but common values of faith—as inscribed—ultimately brought the opposing sides back together. The monument was erected at a cost of $50,000, which was appropriated by the state of Arkansas in 1947. William H. Deacy was the architect. The monument is 42.5 feet long, 8 feet wide in the center, with twin 22-foot marble pylons rising from the base representing the divided nation; and a 12-foot bronze sword between them, embedded like a cross in an altar, which unites the two parts.

Sculpted panels on each side of the altar depict the sacrifice and conflict. The left panel displays a relief of eleven Confederate soldiers, representing the state's fellow seceded Confederate states, advancing against a line of Union soldiers; the right panel depicts the ironclad ram CSS *Arkansas* in action on the Mississippi River. The monument stands on high ground and has obvious messianic-cross symbolism, but there is also a postmodern kind of minimalism to it: there is no stylobate, for example—no temple floor. It bears some of the same design elements as the state of Missouri's extravagant monument nearby, but austereness and simplicity prevail.

- Biblically speaking, the sword is not used as a symbol of unity, but of division, though it seems clear that the reunion was won at the point of a sword ("divine chastisement or judgment" described in Deut. 32:25; Psalm 7:12; 78:62; Judg. 7:20). The phrase "Reunited At The Altar Of Faith" may be a reference to the blood sacrifices referenced in Leviticus 4:7, 18, 25; Luke 22:20; Romans 3:26–28; or Hebrews 11:17. Prototypical in New Testament references is Philippians 2:17, where the Apostle Paul declares his willingness to sacrifice his life on behalf of others for the cause of Jesus Christ: "If I be offered upon the sacrifice and service of your faith . . . martyrs, since their bodies will not be reunited with their souls until the judgment day.

- Sources differ on the source of the marble. The NPS notes that it was erected by McNeel Company of Marietta, Georgia, in Georgia marble. The Smithsonian website indicates that it was fabricated of marble from Mount Airy, North Carolina.

State of Louisiana State Memorial

1.22 Subject: State of Louisiana State Memorial **WPA Index:** 721
Location: Confederate Avenue, milepost 11.9 N 32 21 25 68 / W 90 50 49 34
Installation begun: July 10, 1919; Dedicated: October 18, 1920
Media: Bronze, granite
Monument is a Doric column surmounted by a brazier finial.

Inscriptions
[Front]
[state seal of Louisiana]

LOUISIANA

LOUISIANA COMMANDS ENGAGED IN THE / CAMPAIGN AND DEFENSE OF VICKSBURG / ARTILLERY / ARTILLERY: BOND'S, BRUCE'S, BUTLER'S, CAPER'S, GRAYSON'S, ROBERTSON'S. / HAYNES & LAMONS COMPANIES OF THE FIRST HEAVY /; BARROW'S, GRANDPRE'S, HART'S AND MCCRORY'S COMPANIES / OF THE EIGHTH HEAVY BATTALION COMPANIES (A, B, & C / OF THE POINTE COUPEE); FIFTH COMPANY, WASHINGTON / FENNER'S BATTERY; DURRIVE'S BATTERY.

LOUISIANA COMMANDS ENGAGED IN THE / CAMPAIGN AND DEFENSE OF VICKSBURG / INFANTRY / 3RD, 4TH, 12TH, 13TH, 16TH 17TH, 19TH, 20TH, 21ST, 25TH, 26TH, 27TH, 28TH, 30TH / 31ST, 4TH BATTALION—14TH BATTALION OF SHARPSHOOTERS /—FLEITAS' ZOUAVE BATTALION, GOMEZ'S COMPANY, MARK'S / COMPANY,

MORLOT'S COMPANY, THEARD'S COMPANY / MARK'S AND MORLOT'S COMPANIES
SERVED AS ARTILLERY / CAVALRY / MARTIN'S INDEPENDENT COMPANY.

THIS MONUMENT ERECTED UNDER THE / PROVISIONS OF ACT NO 95 OF THE GEN-
/ ERAL ASSEMBLY OF THE STATE OF LOUIS- / AND APPROVED JULY 3RD 1918 /
GROUND BROKEN JULY 10 1919 / CORNER STONE LAID SEPT 18 1920 / MONUMENT
UNVEILED OCT 18 1920

The Louisiana monument stands on the highest point in the park—397 feet
above sea level—at a prominent location near the Old Jackson Road, opposite
the Illinois monument. It offers a striking counterpoint to the Illinois state
monument and the array of monuments—position markers, regimental and
battery obelisks or stelae—that illustrate the extent of the action that took
place on this ground, especially the Union assaults of May 19 and May 22. It is
near the site of the Great Redoubt, manned by the 21st Louisiana, the largest
Confederate fort at Vicksburg, and the Third Louisiana Redan.

The state of Louisiana erected this monument at a cost of $43,500, including
three off-site relief portraits of Louisiana officers. It was constructed by the
Albert Weiban Marble and Granite Company. The work was completed and
dedicated on October 18, 1920. Alfred E. Theard is credited as the architect.

The roster of Louisiana's contribution of units to the Confederate Army is
extensive and is not paralleled elsewhere on Southern state battlefield monuments, apart from the centennial-era Texas monument.

The records indicate elaborate ceremonies at the breaking of ground for
the monument on July 10, 1919. These included an address "on behalf of the
United States," by Captain T. G. Berries of the US Navy; a roll call reading of the
Louisiana commands in the Vicksburg Campaign; the singing of "Dixie" and
"The Star Spangled Banner" by the assembled crowd; and the playing of "The
Stars and Stripes Forever"; a Memorial Ode "written and read by Miss Ethel
May Gutmann," and remarks by "Capt. F. A. Rozziene, of Illinois, Chairman
of the National Association of Vicksburg Veterans." (Vicksburg participants
listed in the program were listed by their wartime titles.)

Among the speakers at the dedication was William T. Rigby, park commissioner and a key figure in the history of Vicksburg NMP. The ceremonies included the singing of "The Star Spangled Banner," and "The Vacant Chair" ("We
shall meet, but we shall miss them, there will be two vacant chairs"). "Dixie"
was also sung. The lyrics for "Dixie" were printed in dialect in the program
(e.g., "Den I wish was in Dixie . . . I'll take my stand, to lib an' die in Dixie").

· To the "Honor and Glory of Confederate Veterans, living and dead,"
  bears a resemblance to the doxology in 1 Timothy 1:17 ("Now unto the
  King eternal, immortal, invisible, the only wise God, be honour and
  glory for ever and ever. Amen").

Brig. Gen. Lloyd Tilghman

1.23 Subject: Brig. Gen. Lloyd Tilghman   **WPA Index:** 713
Location: Confederate Avenue   N 32 21 24 00 / W 90 50 53 60
Dedicated: May 19, 1926
Media: Bronze, granite
Monument is equestrian figures surmounting a base.

Inscription

BRIGADIER GENERAL LLOYD TILGHMAN CSA
COMMANDING FIRST BRIGADE OF LORING'S DIVISION / KILLED MAY 16 1863 /
NEAR THE CLOSE OF THE BATTLE OF CHAMPION'S HILL MISS

Lloyd Tilghman joined the Confederate Army in 1861. He was a Maryland native, a West Point graduate, and an engineer in Kentucky before the war. His military service was varied: it included command at Fort Henry on February 6, 1862, when he was taken prisoner after engaging four Union ironclad gunboats with only about a hundred men, although he was eventually exchanged and was given a combat command.

Tilghman was not at Vicksburg during the siege. This monument commemorates his service at the battle of Champion Hill, on May 16, 1863, where he was mortally wounded. Tilghman commanded a brigade in Maj. Gen. William Loring's Division, which formed the rear guard when the tide of the battle turned against the Confederates. He was personally sighting a cannon when he was mortally wounded. A fragment from a Union artillery shell—a parrot shell from a gun of the Chicago Mercantile Battery—struck him in the chest or midsection. By one account, Tilghman was taken to a makeshift hospital at the nearby Yeiser house by his son and aide, Lloyd Jr., where he was pronounced dead by attending surgeons. He was forty-seven years old.

The monument was funded by Frederick and Sidell Tilghman, sons of General Tilghman, who were teenagers when their father was killed. Historians Rebecca Blackwell Drake and Pattie Adams Snowball note that the "tragedy of his death haunt[ed] them for the remainder of their lives." After the war, Tilghman's widow, Augusta Boyd Tilghman, moved from Paducah, Kentucky, to New York City, where her two sons became Wall Street stockbrokers. Eventually, the brothers sponsored three monuments in memory of their father. The first, dedicated May 15, 1909, in Paducah, Kentucky, is a statue sculpted by Henry H. Kitson. The second, also designed by Kitson, was dedicated on May 18, 1909, on the Champion Hill battlefield where Tilghman was killed. This, the third and final monument, was erected seventeen years later, in 1926.

This is the only equestrian monument to a Confederate soldier in the park. Indeed, this is the only equestrian figure of a Confederate soldier in Mississippi. The figure of Tilghman, the work of F. William Sievers, shows him bearing a sword and holding it aloft as if he were rallying troops in a lost cause. The outspread arms, look of agony on the face, and the wound piercing his side give the figure of Tilghman a decidedly messianic appearance.

- By at least one account, Tilghman's eldest son, Lt. Lloyd Tilghman Jr., came to his father's aid when he was hit. "With grief and lamentations," the seventeen-year-old son "cast himself on his dying father." Troops who witnessed the "distressing scene" were moved to tears. (The younger Tilghman did not survive Tilghman Sr. long; two months later, he was thrown from the horse he was riding and was killed.)

- Brig. Gen. Tilghman was buried in the city cemetery, Cedar Hill, after the battle. His surviving sons, who lived in New York City and worked in the financial district, arranged the reinterment of Tilghman's remains to Woodlawn Cemetery, Bronx, New York, in 1901. The general's remains are buried beneath a granite obelisk beside the grave of his widow, Augusta Murray Boyd Tilghman.

State of Mississippi State Memorial

- The sculptor, F. William Sievers, was educated at the Royal Academy of Fine Arts in Rome and the Académie Julian in Paris. Sievers' Civil War sculptures include the Virginia monument at Gettysburg, the Thomas J. "Stonewall" Jackson and Matthew F. Maury figures on Monument Avenue in Richmond, and courthouse statues or reliefs of Confederate soldiers at Abingdon, Leesburg, Louisa, and Pulaski, Virginia.

1.24 Subject: State of Mississippi State Memorial   **WPA Index:** 675
Location: Confederate Avenue, milepost 12.3   N 32 21 09 74 / W 90 51 05 04
Dedicated: November 13, 1909; Completed: 1912
Media: Bronze, granite
Monument is a statue, obelisk, and stylobate.

Inscription
MISSISSIPPI *[state coat of arms]*
VIRTUTE ET ARMIS

A statue of Clio, muse of history in Greek and Roman mythology, presides over the stylobate and sacred space of the Mississippi state monument at Vicksburg—the largest Confederate battlefield monument ever erected.

The obelisk is seventy-six feet high and was constructed of North Carolina granite from Mount Airy; the bronze work was fabricated in Rome and shipped to New Orleans on April 20, 1912. The architect is R. H. Hunt of Chattanooga. The bronze work is credited to the American sculptor Frederick Ernest "Fritz" Triebel, who also sculpted the Iowa monument on the Shiloh battlefield. The bronze was cast at the G. Vignali Foundry in Florence, Italy. The monument was erected at a cost of $32,000, was dedicated by Governor F. E. Noel, and was accepted on behalf of the War Department by Blewett Lee.

Vivid images are displayed: the bronze reliefs depict Mississippi in combat, defending themselves against an unseen host, variously wounded, fighting, and dying, with flags, cannon, and broken gun carriages around them. The reliefs are mounted on three sides of the memorial but not the fourth side. An embattled color guard is displayed on the left—southeast—corner; an embattled artillery crew is on the right—northeast—side of the plinth. Detritus of the battle are depicted on the north and south sides of the plinth. A cavalry scene for the fourth side, facing the river, was proposed but discarded due to cost considerations and other factors that are further noted in the introduction. There is no inscription apart from that on the coat of arms of Mississippi, including the state motto: "Virtute et Armis," Latin for "By valor and arms."

- A statue of Jefferson Davis in the place of the muse was considered and rejected. Hills notes that the figure of Clio—modeled after Triebel's wife, Santina—has a serious, masculine beauty.

Lt. Gen. John C. Pemberton

1.25 Subject: Lt. Gen. John C. Pemberton   **WPA Index:** 669
Location: Confederate Avenue   N 32 21 06 15 / W 90 51 07 32
Installed or dedicated: 1917
Media: Bronze, granite
Monument is a statue surmounting a base.

Inscription

PEMBERTON

JOHN C. PEMBERTON / LT. GENERAL C.S. ARMY COMMANDING DEPARTMENT OF /
MISS. AND EAST LOUISIANA /—/ CADET U.S. MILITARY ACADEMY 1833 / 2ND LT. 4TH
ART. JULY FIRST 1837 / FIRST LT. MAR. NINETEENTH 1842 / CAPTAIN SEPTEMBER
SIXTEENTH 1850 / RESIGNED APRIL TWENTY-FOURTH 1861 / MAJOR GENERAL FEB.
13 1862 / TO RANK FROM JAN. FOURTEENTH 1862 / LT. GEN. OCT. THIRTEENTH 1862
/ TO RANK FROM JAN. FOURTEENTH 1862 / LT. GEN. OCT. THIRTEENTH 1862 / TO
RANK FROM OCTOBER TENTH 1862

QVINN SC 1917 ROMAN BRONZE WORKS NY

When the war came, John C. Pemberton, a West Point graduate and native of Philadelphia, Pennsylvania, resigned his commission in the US Army and sided with the Confederacy. The decision is attributed to the influence of his Virginia-born wife and his prewar service in the South. Promotion made Pemberton a Lieutenant General by 1862, and Jefferson Davis appointed him to command of the Department of Mississippi and Eastern Louisiana. Pemberton was compelled to surrender the Confederate army at Vicksburg on July 4, 1863. Following this defeat, he resigned his commission and served first as a lieutenant colonel of artillery in Virginia and then as inspector general of artillery for the remainder of the war.

Pemberton has the singular notoriety of commanding Confederate arms in what was arguably the decisive defeat of the war. For his part, his friend, Confederate President Jefferson Davis, excused Pemberton for the course of action his general took that led to the surrender, writing that, "I thought and still think you did right to risk an army for the purpose of keeping command of even a section of the Mississippi River. Had you succeeded, none would have blamed, had you not made the attempt few would have defended your course."

The figure of Pemberton looks dignified, but he looks north, toward the surrender site, toward Federal lines, toward Pennsylvania—one might imagine—with his back to the river. Like most monuments to individuals on the battlefield, the service record culminates at Vicksburg. No aftermath is described.

· Given the defeat suffered by the army under Pemberton's command, private funding for a Pemberton monument was not forthcoming. The monument was federally funded by dint of park commissioner William T. Rigby as part of his goal of commemorating all Union and Confeder-

Jefferson Davis

ate brigade or battery commanders. Rigby, foreseeing that Pemberton would have been conspicuous by his absence, used discretionary park funding for the monument. Edmund T. Quinn was the sculptor; the foundry work was done by the Roman Bronze Works of New York.

1.26 Subject: Jefferson Davis **WPA Index:** 636
Location: Confederate Avenue   N 32 20 50 49 / W 90 51 16 49
Installed or dedicated: 1927
Media: Bronze, marble
Monument is a statue surmounting a base.

Inscription

JEFFERSON DAVIS / PRESIDENT CONFEDERATE STATES / AND COMMANDER-IN-CHIEF / CADET U.S. MILITARY ACADEMY 1824 / 2ND. LT. 1ST U.S. INFANTRY JULY 1, 1828 / 1ST LIEUT. DRAGOONS MARCH 4, 1833 / ADJT. AUG. 30, 1833 TO FEB. 5, 1834 / RESIGNED JUNE 30, 1835 / COL. 1ST MISS. RIFLES JULY 18, 1846 / HON. MUSTERED OUT JULY 12, 1847 / SEC. OF WAR MARCH 7, 1853 MARCH 6, 1857 / IN HONOR OF / THE DEFENDERS OF VICKSBURG

HENRY H. KITSON SCULPTOR

Henry Kitson's depiction of Davis does not consign him to history: it is a dynamic figure. The inscription focuses on Davis's military service; it omits Davis's term as a US senator from Mississippi. Although Kitson's figure of Davis is depicted in period civilian garb, he has an unspecified but apparently bellicose mission, a legacy to bear to perpetuity. In his left hand, he grips a flagpole, with a billowing Confederate flag—the second national flag, known as the Stainless Banner. In his right hand he bears a copy of the Confederate constitution. The seals on the document are conspicuously unclasped, perhaps suggesting the document's perpetuity or legacy, and arguably a reference to Revelation 5:1–2. As depicted, Davis continues to espouse the cause he came to be associated with in life: an independent South fighting for a constitutionally defensible cause. Nevertheless, the cost of the monument, an estimated $34,000, was paid by the federal government, and the figure of Davis faces north, toward Lincoln on the Illinois monument.

- The dedication address by US Senator Hubert D. Stephens included the claim that the "three greatest men this nation has produced are George Washington, Abraham Lincoln and Jefferson Davis. . . . Stars may fall from the heavens. Eclipses may darken the sun. But as long as men and women shall respect, honor and revere purity, integrity, loyalty to conviction, and unselfish sacrifice for principle, the name of Jefferson Davis will be enrolled as one of America's greatest sons. And as the centuries pass, that name will shine with ever increasing lustre."

- The statue appears to have been placed off center on the pedestal, perhaps in the aftermath of Mission 66 changes to the park, when the monument was moved to its present site.

Lt. Col. William Vilas

1.27 Subject: Statue, Lt. Col. William Vilas   **WPA Index:** 590
Location: North of the Visitors Center on Confederate Avenue
N 32 20 39 63 / W 90 51 08 16
Dedicated: December 1912
Media: Bronze, granite
Monument is a statue surmounting a pedestal and plaza, with thirteen steps and cheek blocks ornamented by two Civil War–era cannon tubes.

Inscription
LIEUTENANT COLONEL WILLIAM F. VILAS. COMMANDING TWENTY-THIRD
WISCONSIN INFANTRY DURING THE LATTER PART OF THE SIEGE OF VICKSBURG IN
MDCCLXIII. PRESENTED BY MRS. WILLIAM F. VILAS AND THEIR DAUGHTER MARY
ESTER VILAS HANKS. MCMXII.

The Vilas monument is particularly notable for its aesthetic qualities. By nothing more than happenstance it has a prominent place in the park. It stands only one hundred yards north of the present-day visitor center, at the South Loop intersection, but this was also the site where Vilas's 23rd Wisconsin VI served during the siege.

Vilas has a striking appearance, a look of command and self-assurance; he has one foot set upon a rock, and his hat is set at an angle. Hills notes that it has an "exquisitely proportioned" pink granite plaza or stereobate, surmounting a staircase of thirteen broad, short steps. Even the serif lettering of the inscription is notable; it may reflect the influence of Augustus Saint-Gaudens and Stanford White's design of the Farragut monument in Madison Square, New York City (1881). Adolph A. Weinman was the sculptor; Albert Randolph Ross was the architect. The foundry work was performed by the Roman Bronze Works. The inscription was written by William T. Rigby.

Parker Hills observes that the monument "speak[s] volumes about the high quality of monument design and construction in the early twentieth century. Simplicity and attention to detail proved to be key criteria employed by [the designers] in the integration of this magnificent portrait with [the] pedestal and plaza." Weinman was at one time an assistant to Augustus Saint-Gaudens. It appears, too, that Weinman shares with his mentor, Saint-Gaudens, an ability to depict "a New World directness" in his figures, as Burke Wilkinson describes it.

The Vilas monument is also an example of the fact that Vicksburg NMP is as much a postwar site as it is a commemoration of the war. William F. Vilas (1840–1912) came from a wealthy family who provided this opulent edifice erected at a cost of $18,000. Vilas had an honorable but not especially noteworthy service record during the war. Indeed, Col. Joshua J. Guppey—who has no monument at Vicksburg—initially commanded the 23rd Wisconsin at Vicksburg, not Vilas. Vilas took command in the latter days of the siege, but he resigned from the army in July 1863. However, Vilas had a distinguished postwar career in public service as US postmaster general, secretary of the interior, and US senator. A scholarship is still given in his name at the University of Wisconsin–Madison, and he is the author of a book on the Wisconsin units' service at Vicksburg.

1.28 Subject: The Texas State Memorial
Location: South Loop, Confederate Avenue, the Railroad Redoubt   N 32 20
33 05 / W 90 51 23 26
Dedicated: November 4, 1961; Completed, winter of 1962–63
Media: Bronze, Texas red granite
Monument is a Greek-Doric temple structure with three panels, four Doric
columns, and a common soldier.

Inscriptions
[left panel]
THE SEALING OF THE BREACH
AT THIS LOCATION / THE LINES OF / THE CONFEDERACY / WERE BROKEN /
AND THE TEXANS / WERE CALLED IN / TO SEAL THE BREACH. THEY NOT / ONLY
ACCOMPLISHED / THEIR MISSION / BUT CAPTURED A / NUMBER OF THE / ENEMY
AND SEIZED / THEIR STANDARDS.

[center panel, with bronze wreath and star]
TEXAS / REMEMBERS THE VALOR / AND DEVOTION OF HER / SONS WHO SERVED
AT / VICKSBURG AND IN OTHER / THEATERS OF THE WAR / BETWEEN THE STATES.
FOR THOSE MEN BELIEVED IN SOMETHING. THEY COUNTED / LIFE A LIGHT THING
TO LAY / DOWN IN THE FAITH THEY BORE. / THEY WERE GENEROUS IN VICTORY.
THEY ROSE UP / FROM DEFEAT TO FIGHT / AGAIN AND WHILE THEY LIVED THEY
WERE FORMIDABLE . . . / THE HERITAGE THEY LEFT OF VALOR AND DEVOTION IS
TREASURED BY A UNITED COUNTRY." / JOHN W THOMPSON

[right panel] TEXAS UNITS ENGAGED IN THE /
VICKSBURG CAMPAIGN AND SEIGE / *[Roster of 60 units]*

This temple structure with a common soldier figure at its center was erected
near the Railroad Redoubt, which in turn is adjacent to the tracks of what is today the Southern Railroad. The Texas monument at Vicksburg was the first and
largest of a series of centennial monuments sponsored by the Texas Civil War
Centennial Commission and the Texas State Historical Survey Committee.

That Texas is indomitable is the apparent theme of this monument: the legacy of Texans who fought here is not only remembered but continues. Eleven
steps lead to the stylobate or temple floor of the memorial, honoring Texas's
eleven "sister states in the Confederacy." A live yucca plant, native to Texas and
the southwestern United States, is a unique addition to the site.

The left panel displays the sealing of the breach of Confederate lines during
the May 22 assault; the center panel displays a verbal tribute to the Texas soldiers who fought here; the right panel enumerates the Texas units engaged in
the Vicksburg campaign, including the siege line units, those who served
with Johnston's Army of Relief, and Walker's Texas Division, which served in
Jackson and Louisiana, respectively.

The Texas State Memorial

On May 22, 1863, after failing to carry the Confederate lines on May 19, Maj. Gen. Grant ordered a second assault against the Confederate lines. The wall at the redoubt's southeast angle was damaged and breached by the artillery barrage. During the assault, elements of the 22nd Iowa VI entered the redoubt; however, reinforcements, including Waul's Texas Legion, counterattacked, drove the Federals back, and "sealed the breach." As the inscription describes the episode, the nation was saved: "The *Lines Of / The Confederacy / Were Broken / And The Texans / Were Called In*" (italics added).

The representative figure of a common soldier, seven feet tall, is depicted as if Texas's soldiers are still ready if or when their opponents come again. The monument faces south, toward the tour road, but the figure of the common soldier faces east, toward Union lines. The figure is posed in front of the columned wall, with his left foot resting on a cannon barrel; he holds a rifle in both hands, diagonally across his lower body. The figure has the appearance of being homely, alert, down-to-earth—vernacular. He offers a vigilant counterpart to the equestrian soldier of the Iowa monument which stands across the opposing siege lines, some 575 yards to the east.

· The inscription "They Counted / Life A Light Thing To Lay / Down" bears comparison to John 15:13, "Greater love hath no man than this, that a man lay down his life for his friends." Perhaps this is the intended allusion in the otherwise ambiguous tribute, "For Those Men Believed In Something."

· The memorial, erected at a cost of $100,000, was dedicated on November 4, 1961; it was completed during the winter of 1962–63. The sculptor was M. Herring Coe; Lundgren and Maurer were the architects; the Texas Granite Corporation was the contractor.

1.29 Subject: Brig. Gen. Stephen D. Lee, C.S.A.   **WPA Index:** 299
Location: South Loop, Confederate Avenue   N 32 20 36 35 / W 90 51 31 90
Dedicated: n.a.
Media: Bronze, granite
Monument is a statue surmounting a base.

Inscription

STEPHEN DILL LEE / LIEUTENANT GENERAL / C · S · A / BRIGADIER-GENERAL / COMMANDING SECOND / BRIGADE STEVENSON'S / DIVISION MAY SECOND / JULY FOURTH 1863

Brig. Gen. Stephen D. Lee commanded the 2nd Brigade, Stevenson's Division, May 2–July 4 1863 (20th, 23rd, 30th, 31st, and 46th Alabama Infantry, along with Waddell's Alabama Battery). On the site of this monument, Lee observed the May 22 assault by Union troops, which was repulsed by Southern arms. Henry Kitson, the sculptor, depicts the figure of Lee looking confident about the outcome but alert to its circumstances: he stands with one foot on the parapet in front of the rifle pits. His sword is drawn, and with two gloved hands he bears it across his right thigh. His binoculars are cased, a measure of his status as an officer, and, implicitly, a sign of the general's poise in the presence of the advancing enemy in the fields ahead.

The monument was dedicated in ceremonies on June 9, 1909.

· Stephen Dill Lee (1833–1909) was born in South Carolina, was a graduate of West Point, had extensive service in war, and eventually rose to the rank of Lieutenant General in the Confederate army. After the war, Lee became the first president of what is today Mississippi State University; he also served as chairman of the Vicksburg Park Commission. A bust of Lee, in civilian garb, stands in the center of the Drill Field at Mississippi State. Another bust is at his grave in Columbus's Friendship Cemetery. Historian Ezra J. Warner summarizes Lee as an able and versatile corps commander, averring that "despite his youth and comparative lack of experience, Lee's prior close acquaintanceship with all three branches of the service—artillery, cavalry, and infantry— rendered him one of the most capable corps commanders in the army."

Brig. Gen. Stephen D. Lee, CSA

State of Alabama Memorial

1.30 Subject: State of Alabama Memorial   **WPA Index:** 294
Location: Confederate Avenue, milepost 13.6   N 32 20 22 71 / W 90 51 34 36
Dedicated: July 19, 1951
Media: Bronze, granite
Monument is a bronze sculpture of seven common soldiers and one presiding female, the whole surmounting a granite base.

Inscription

ALABAMA

A granite base surmounted by a bronze work depicts an embattled color guard of seven uniformed Alabama soldiers. A female figure representing the state of Alabama holds a Confederate flag aloft in their midst. Four of the soldiers are firing rifled muskets, two are wounded, and one is dead. The color guard is standing on high ground, to judge by the angle at which the soldiers are firing their weapons. In addition, the men fire in several directions, as if they are surrounded and about to be inundated. The sculptor captures the moment when the group continues to withstand the unseen onslaught, but one of them is dead, or nearly so, and one is wounded and disabled. The Alabamians will not last long, but they won't give up either, and the woman stands in their midst.

Erected some thirty years after the passing of the American Renaissance, the monument is the work of the more expressionistic, German-born sculptor Steffen Thomas. Like the Renaissance-era Mississippi monument, the figures of the Confederate soldiers are depicted as being embattled and surrounded, but the figure of Clio is above the action. Thomas depicts an intimate scene with a woman at the center, as if she is mediating the passage between life and death.

In contrast to the sculptures of the women depicted on the Michigan, Minnesota, and Mississippi monuments, the Alabama monument depicts a female figure who is not separated or detached from the action. The woman's face is particularly luminous: she is transcendent but not aloof. She holds the flag aloft, she gives succor to a dying soldier; and she is in the midst of the fighting.

· A German émigré who began his career working on Germany's World War I monuments, Steffen Thomas (1906–90) came to the United States in 1928 and spent most of his career in Georgia. Art historian Anthony F. Janson calls him "Georgia's German Expressionist" and notes that Thomas's vision was defined soon after he came to the United States, particularly by his "muses"—the "idealized women who populate his work throughout his career and form its core. . . . In their many guises they express an ideal not simply of femininity but of humanity as a whole."

· Erected at a cost of $150,000, the monument stands approximately 14 by 20 by 6 feet; the base is approximately 18 inches by 31 feet by 31 feet. The bronze surmounts a base of Weiblin gray granite from the Elberton City Quarries of Elberton, Georgia. Marble from this source was also used for the construction of the Memorial Arch at the entrance to Vicksburg NMP, as well as the Jefferson Memorial in Washington, DC.

1.31 Subject: Kentucky Confederate monument   **WPA Index:** 287
Location: Confederate Avenue   N 32 20 17 67 / W 90 51 37 24
Dedicated: May 8, 2010
Media: Bronze, granite, marble
Monument is a CS battle flag, in bronze, draped over a stele, surmounting a base.

Inscriptions
[Front]

KENTUCKY CONFEDERATE MONUMENT

[Left panel:]
BRIGADIER GENERAL LLOYD TILGHMAN OF PADUCAH, KENTUCKY / KILLED IN
ACTION MAY 16, 1863 AT THE BATTLE OF CHAMPION HILL (VICKSBURG CAMPAIGN) /
IN MEMORY / COLONEL EUGENE ERWIN, CSA, SIXTH MISSOURI INFANTRY / BORN IN
FAYETTE COUNTY, KENTUCKY / GRANDSON OF STATESMAN HENRY CLAY / KILLED
IN ACTION AT VICKSBURG, JUNE 25, 1863

[Center panels:]
KENTUCKY'S GOVERNOR SOUGHT A POSITION OF NEUTRALITY AFTER THE
FIGHTING BEGAN AT FORT SUMTER ON APRIL 12, 1861, BUT ELECTIONS THAT
SUMMER RESULTED IN PRO-UNION MAJORITIES IN THE STATE LEGISLATURE
AND CONGRESSIONAL DELEGATION. ON NOVEMBER 18, 1861, A CONVENTION OF
KENTUCKY'S SECESSIONIST LEADERS MEETING IN RUSSELLVILLE, KENTUCKY,
APPROVED AN ORDINANCE OF SECESSION AND PETITIONED THE CONFEDERATE
GOVERNMENT FOR KENTUCKY'S ADMISSION AS A STATE IN THE CONFEDERACY.
UPON APPROVAL BY THE CONFEDERATE CONGRESS, KENTUCKY WAS ADMITTED
TO THE CONFEDERATE STATES OF AMERICA AS ITS 13TH STATE ON DECEMBER 10,
1861. THE PROVISIONAL CONFEDERATE GOVERNMENT, HOWEVER, WAS COMPELLED
BY MILITARY AFFAIRS TO LEAVE THE STATE IN 1861. / DURING THE WAR, AN
ESTIMATED 25,000 TO 40,000 KENTUCKIANS ENLISTED FOR SERVICE IN THE
CONFEDERATE ARMY. EVENTUALLY, IN ADDITION TO A NUMBER OF ARTILLERY
BATTERIES AND NUMEROUS CAVALRY UNITS, NINE REGIMENTS OF INFANTRY WERE
RAISED, AND FROM SIX OF THESE REGIMENTS THE FIRST KENTUCKY BRIGADE WAS
FORMED. THE SOLDIERS OF THE FIRST KENTUCKY BRIGADE, KNOWN TO HISTORY
AS THE ORPHAN BRIGADE, SERVED THROUGHOUT THE WESTERN THEATER OF
OPERATIONS.

IN THE SUMMER OF 1862 THESE KENTUCKY REGIMENTS SERVED AT VICKSBURG
AS PART OF MAJ. GEN. JOHN C. BRECKINRIDGE'S DIVISION MANNING VARIOUS
POSITIONS DURING THE DEFENSE OF THE CITY. THE FOURTH KENTUCKY INFANTRY
REGIMENT WAS DETACHED FOR A TIME AND SENT FOURTEEN MILES SOUTH OF
VICKSBURG TO WARRENTON, TO GUARD AGAINST A POSSIBLE LAND ATTACK BY THE
FEDERALS. / THE KENTUCKIANS FOUGHT NO PITCHED BATTLES AT VICKSBURG, BUT
WERE CONSTANTLY ON GUARD AGAINST BOMBARDMENT PARTICULARLY FROM THE
MORTAR BOATS, IF THE FEDERAL RIVER FLEET ATTACKED. THE MOST EXCITING
MOMENTS FOR THE ORPHANS CAME WHEN THE IRONCLAD C.S.S. ARKANSAS,
COMMANDED BY FELLOW KENTUCKIAN LT. ISAAC NEWTON BROWN, MADE A
DARING RUN THROUGH THE FEDERAL FLEETS AND ANCHORED AT VICKSBURG IN

Kentucky Confederate Monument

MID-JULY. DURING THIS FAMOUS ACTION, KENTUCKIAN WILLIAM GILMORE WAS KILLED BY A 160-POUND BOLT FROM A FEDERAL BOAT THAT CAME THROUGH THE ARKANSAS' ARMOR JUST ABOVE THE WATERLINE AND INTO THE ENGINE ROOM.

[Right panel:]
MAJOR GENERAL JOHN C. BRECKINRIDGE
BRIGADIER GENERAL ABRAHAM BUFORD
BRIGADIER GENERAL GEORGE B. COSBY
BRIGADIER GENERAL BEN HARDIN HELM

Three monuments to the service of Kentucky Civil War soldiers were projected in planning the park: two are in place. The state of Kentucky's monument was erected in 2001; the Kentucky Confederate monument was erected here in 2010; and space for a Kentucky Union monument is reserved at Kentucky Avenue to the east, near Union Avenue.

The Kentucky Division of the SCV raised about $50,000 for the monument's design and construction. State dignitaries and members of the Kentucky SCV and the UDC attended the dedication services on May 8, 2010, which was hosted by the NPS. The Vicksburg *Post* reported that some fifty reenactors attended to represent the 3rd Kentucky Infantry. Others formed part of a Civil War–era brass band or fired muskets and cannons in ceremonial volleys. Those in attendance engaged in sing-alongs of "My Old Kentucky Home" and "Dixie."

In his remarks at the dedication ceremonies, Michael Maddell, VNMP superintendent, observed that "Kentucky's tribute to her gallant sons who served in Confederate gray in the Vicksburg campaigns of 1862 and 1863 adds to the luster [of the park], and will serve to remind future generations of the selfless devotion to duty that has come to characterize the citizen-soldiers who have served our nation throughout its rich and glorious history."

- In offering enhanced detail and narratives and a tribute to Kentucky Confederates, the monument is also a counternarrative of sorts to the 2001 state monument, and a symbol of continuing divisions and interpretations of the conflict.

- The monument is fourteen feet high and twenty feet long in gray granite, with a black marble insert inscribed with a narrative of the service of Kentucky Confederate soldiers during the battle; a bronze Confederate flag is draped across the top of the stele, and the Kentucky Confederate seal, in bronze, is displayed below the flag. Although Kentucky is regarded as the thirteenth and final state admitted to the Confederacy, the state's elected general assembly never officially seceded from the Union. Nevertheless, the monument displays the state seal of the Confederate state of Kentucky: a circle of twelve stars with a hand in the center inserting a thirteenth star into the circle.

1.32 Subject: State of Georgia State Shaft
Location: South loop of Confederate Avenue at milepost 14.1   N 32 20 10 87 / W 90 51 48 44
Dedicated: October 25, 1962
Medium: Granite
Monument is an inscribed shaft.

Inscriptions

GEORGIA

[state seal of Georgia]

GEORGIA CONFEDERATE / SOLDIERS / WE SLEEP HERE IN OBEDIENCE TO LAW; / WHEN DUTY CALLED, WE CAME, / WHEN COUNTRY CALLED, WE DIED.

GEORGIA

[state seal of Georgia]

GEORGIA CONFEDERATE / SOLDIERS / WE SLEEP HERE IN OBEDIENCE TO LAW; WHEN DUTY CALLED, WE CAME, / WHEN COUNTRY CALLED, WE DIED.

State of Georgia Confederate Shaft

Georgia sent seventeen units of infantry, four batteries of artillery, and one cavalry unit to serve in the Vicksburg campaign. The inscription on the Georgia state monument, however, is dedicated to the Georgia Confederate dead. In this regard, it offers a contrast to other centennial-era monuments erected during this time, such as the Alabama monument, also erected in 1962, or the Texas state monument erected in 1963.

The art deco–style shaft of the Georgia State Memorial was erected at a cost of $7,500. The medium is variously described as blue or gray granite. The monument, designed by Harry Sellers and executed by Marietta Memorials, features flutes—three sculpted grooves cut into the four sides of the column. In addition, forty grooves are cut into the square top of the column, also symbolic of an unfinished life. There is no capstone.

The monument stands approximately eighteen feet high, and is similar or identical to Georgia state memorials at Gettysburg, Pennsylvania; Sharpsburg, Maryland; and Kennesaw Mountain, Georgia. An earlier version of this inscription stands at Stonewall Cemetery, Winchester, Virginia. The obelisk, of granite, surmounting a base, plinth, and dado, was dedicated June 4, 1884, and was given "By the People of Georgia to 290 of Her Sons Who Lie in this Cemetery." With a conspicuous parallel to the epitaph for the Spartans killed at the battle of Thermopylae (480 BC), it concludes:

Inscription

GO, STRANGER, AND TELL IT
IN GEORGIA, THAT WE DIED HERE
IN OBEDIENCE TO HER LAWS.

1.33 Subject: Indiana State Memorial   **WPA Index:** 585
Location: Union Avenue, milepost 14.3   N 32 19 57 89 / W 90 51 45 42
Erected: April 1922; Dedicated: June 16, 1926
Media: Bronze, limestone
Monument is a statue surmounting a base.

Inscription

INDIANA / OLIVER PERRY MORTON / GOVERNOR, 1861–1866 / IN HONOR OF / THE / INDIANA SOLDIERS / ENGAGED IN THE / VICKSBURG OPERATIONS.

The Indiana State Memorial is a bronze statue of Governor Oliver Perry Morton (1823–77), the wartime governor of Indiana but is explicitly "in Honor of / the / Indiana Soldiers / Engaged in the / Vicksburg Operations." The statue, suggested as a state monument by Park Commissioner William T. Rigby, was erected at a cost of $14,000. The whole of the monument stands twelve feet high.

As a wartime governor, Morton was an energetic supporter of President Lincoln and the war effort as a whole. He was known as "the soldier's friend,"

Indiana State Memorial

in recognition of his support of Union soldiers in the field. Historian A. James Fuller writes that he was a complex figure who "remained a dedicated advocate of the war during the conflict's darkest days. His support for the Union cause and for President Abraham Lincoln became the stuff of legend, even as his constant badgering of the president exasperated Lincoln and other national leaders. Morton hated slavery and saw it as a central cause of the conflict."

· The sculptor is George T. Brewster; the Morton monument was the last of twenty-three statues, busts, or reliefs Brewster designed for Vicksburg NMP between 1911 and 1926.

State of Kentucky Memorial

1.34 Subject: State of Kentucky   **WPA Index:** 456
Location: Kentucky Avenue, between the Union and Confederate lines
N 32 20 13 67 / W 90 51 36 72
Dedicated: October 20, 2001
Media: Bronze, granite
Monument is a stylobate or plaza centered on statues of United States President Abraham Lincoln and Confederate President Jefferson Davis, with extended stele or walls.

Inscriptions
[Front: plinth]

UNITED STATES ARMY
19TH KENTUCKY VOLUNTEER INFANTRY REGIMENT
22ND KENTUCKY VOLUNTEER INFANTRY REGIMENT
PATTERSON'S INDEPENDENT COMPANY OF KENTUCKY ENGINEERS AND MECHANICS.
/ 7TH KENTUCKY VOLUNTEER INFANTRY REGIMENT

CONFEDERATE STATES ARMY
COBB'S KENTUCKY ARTILLERY BATTALION
FAULKNER'S KENTUCKY PARTISAN BATTALION
BOLEN'S & TERRY'S COMPANIES OF KENTUCKY CAVALRY
2ND KENTUCKY VOLUNTEER INFANTRY REGIMENT
3RD KENTUCKY VOLUNTEER INFANTRY REGIMENT (MOUNTED)

4TH KENTUCKY VOLUNTEER INFANTRY REGIMENT
6TH KENTUCKY VOLUNTEER INFANTRY REGIMENT
7TH KENTUCKY VOLUNTEER INFANTRY REGIMENT
8TH KENTUCKY VOLUNTEER INFANTRY REGIMENT (MOUNTED)
9TH KENTUCKY VOLUNTEER INFANTRY REGIMENT

COMMONWEALTH OF KENTUCKY
UNITED WE STAND / DIVIDED WE FALL

[Seal of State of Kentucky]

ABRAHAM LINCOLN WAS PRESIDENT OF THE UNITED STATES OF / AMERICA FROM
1861 TO 1865. HE WAS BORN NEAR HODGENVILLE, KENTUCKY, ON FEBRARY 12,
1809. IN 1865 HE SAID, "WITH MALICE TOWARD NONE; WITH CHARITY FOR ALL,
WITH FIRMNESS IN THE RIGHT AS GOD GIVES US TO SEE TO THE RIGHT. LET US
STRIVE ON TO FINISH THE WORK WE ARE IN; TO BIND UP THE NATION'S WOUNDS;
TO CARE FOR HIM WHO SHALL HAVE BORNE THE BATTLE AND FOR HIS WIDOW AND
HIS ORPHAN—TO DO ALL WHICH MAY ACHIEVE AND CHERISH A JUST AND LASTING
PEACE AMONG OURSELVES AND WITH ALL NATIONS."

JEFFERSON DAVIS WAS PRESIDENT OF THE CONFEDERATE STATES / OF AMERICA
FROM 1861 TO 1865. HE WAS BORN AT FAIRVIEW, / KENTUCKY ON JUNE 3, 1808. IN
1888 HE SAID. "THE PAST IS / DEAD. LET IT BURY ITS DEAD . . . LET ME BESEECH YOU
TO LAY / ASIDE ALL RANCOR, ALL BITTER SECTIONAL FEELING AND TO TAKE / YOUR
PLACES IN THE RANKS OF THOSE WHO WILL BRING ABOUT A / CONSUMMATION
DEVOUTLY TO BE WISHED—A REUNITED COUNTRY."

The Kentucky State Memorial features bronze statues of two native Kentuckians: United States President Abraham Lincoln and Confederate States President Jefferson Davis. In addition, a roster of Kentucky's Union and Confederate units in the Vicksburg Campaign is displayed on adjoining stelae or walls on the south side of the plaza.

The designer of the monument was Louisville-based Terry Joy. The monument stands between Union and Confederate lines along Kentucky Avenue, which was originally laid out to run from Union Avenue to Confederate Avenue, but has never been completed. The setting was chosen to reflect the partisan divisions within Kentucky during the war as well as the reunification of the state and country afterward. Reconciliation is a theme of the monument. Intended by the Kentucky Vicksburg Monument Association to be a "modern abstract memorial," as Hills notes, this is one of three Vicksburg NMP state monuments dedicated to soldiers from both sides: the Missouri State monument and the Mississippi African American monuments are the others.

Gary Casteel is the sculptor of the figures of Lincoln and Davis. The two presidents are standing together, posed in conversation, facing one another, although the two never met in real life. Michael Panhorst observes that "the bronze figures were set on a sunken, paved plaza enclosed on two adjacent sides by retaining walls . . . rather like the walls of the Vietnam Memorial" in Washington, DC. Hills notes that the monument is no higher than the figures of Davis and Lincoln, which are themselves "less than life-size . . . with curious proportions."

This is one of two full-figure statues of Davis, the other being the statue on Confederate Avenue, and one of two images of Lincoln: a medallion relief of Lincoln appears on the Illinois state monument. The excerpt from Davis beginning "The past is dead" is taken from a speech given at Mississippi City, Mississippi, in 1888. It was his last public address before his death and includes references to the New Testament ("Let it bury its dead" [Matt. 8:22; Luke 9:60]) and Shakespeare's Hamlet ("To die, to sleep—No more—and by a sleep to say we end the heartache and the thousand natural shocks that flesh is heir to—'tis a consummation devoutly to be wished!"). The larger context reads, "The past is dead; let it bury its dead, its hopes, and its aspirations. Before you lies the future, a future full of golden promise, a future of expanding national glory, before which all the world shall stand amazed. Let me beseech you to lay aside all rancor, all bitter sectional feeling, and to take your places in the ranks of those who will bring about a consummation to be wished—a reunited country."

The excerpt from Lincoln is taken from his Second Inaugural Address, on March 4, 1865, given just forty-five days before his assassination. Historian Mark Noll calls the address the "last defining utterance on the nation's ultimate defining experience." Sources indicate that on the same day as the inaugural, President Lincoln encountered Frederick Douglass. Lincoln inquired about Douglass's opinion of the address. "I saw you in the crowd today, listening to my inaugural address," the president remarked. "How did you like it?" Douglass answered, "Mr. Lincoln, that was a sacred effort."

· The state seal is displayed on the floor of the circular granite plinth on which the statues are placed. Panhorst observes that the low profile of the monument is in "keeping with twenty-first century historic preservation ethics, which strive to minimize the memorial's impact on the historic landscape." In fact, it is perhaps best viewed from overhead.

· Soil taken from the site of the graves of two Kentucky soldiers—one Union, one Confederate—was sprinkled on site so visitors would have the assurance that they are on Kentucky soil.

· Credit for the initiative to erect this monument is given to Kentucky resident Sarah Bowers, who noted the absence of a monument after visiting Vicksburg in 1998. Bowers enlisted the support of state representatives and the Kentucky Heritage Council, after which the Official Kentucky Vicksburg Monument Association was formed.

1.35 Subject: Iowa State Memorial   **WPA Index:** 519
Location: Union Avenue, milepost 15.3   N 32 20 21 36 / W 90 51 11 66
Dedicated: November 15, 1906; Completed: 1912
Media: Bronze, granite
Monument is a Greek-Doric semiellipsed temple structure with an equestrian figure of a common soldier.

Inscriptions

[Arch:]
IOWA'S MEMORIAL TO HER SOLDIERS WHO SERVED / IN THE CAMPAIGN AND SIEGE OF VICKSBURG

[Center plaque:]
IOWA / COMMANDS AND CASUALTIES
ARTILLERY, FIRST BATTERY, WOUNDED 1. / 2ND BATTERY, KILLED 1, WOUNDED 6, TOTAL 7. / CAVALRY / 3RD REGIMENT, COMPANIES A, B, C, D, I, K. / 4TH REGIMENT, KILLED 9, WOUNDED 16, MISSING 23, TOTAL 48. / INFANTRY / 3RD REGIMENT, KILLED 1, WOUNDED 18, TOTAL 19. / 4TH REGIMENT, WOUNDED 13. / 5TH REGIMENT, KILLED 22, WOUNDED 97, TOTAL 119. / 6TH REGIMENT. / 8TH REGIMENT, WOUNDED 5. / 9TH REGIMENT, KILLED 37, WOUNDED 82, TOTAL 119. / 10TH REGIMENT, KILLED 38, WOUNDED 157, TOTAL 195. / 11TH REGIMENT, KILLED 1, WOUNDED 1, TOTAL 2. / 12TH REGIMENT, KILLED 1, WOUNDED 2, TOTAL 3. / 13TH REGIMENT. / 15TH REGIMENT. / 16TH REGIMENT, WOUNDED 2. / 17TH REGIMENT, KILLED 24, WOUNDED 151, MISSING 4, TOTAL 179. / 19TH REGIMENT, WOUNDED 1. / 20TH REGIMENT. / 21ST REGIMENT, KILLED 29, WOUNDED 174, MISSING 10, TOTAL 213. / 22ND REGIMENT, KILLED 29, WOUNDED 141, MISSING 19, TOTAL 189. / 23RD REGIMENT, KILLED 45, WOUNDED 148, TOTAL 193. / 24TH REGIMENT, KILLED 36, WOUNDED 125, MISSING 34, TOTAL 195. / 25TH REGIMENT, KILLED 5, WOUNDED 27, MISSING 5, TOTAL 37. / 26TH REGIMENT, KILLED 7, WOUNDED 34, TOTAL 41. / 28TH REGIMENT, KILLED 24, WOUNDED 76, MISSING 17, TOTAL 117. / 30TH REGIMENT, KILLED 13, WOUNDED 43, MISSING 1, TOTAL 57. / 31ST REGIMENT, KILLED 3, WOUNDED 20, TOTAL 23. / 34TH REGIMENT, KILLED 4, WOUNDED 6, TOTAL 10. / 35TH REGIMENT, KILLED 1, WOUNDED 1, MISSING 1, TOTAL 3. / 38TH REGIMENT. / 40TH REGIMENT.

AGGREGATE, KILLED 330, WOUNDED 1347, MISSING 114, TOTAL 1791

This impressive Greek-Doric semiellipsed temple structure—a peristyle, or curved column—is sixty-four feet wide and twenty-nine feet high in the center. Five steps lead up to the stylobate or temple floor and the equestrian figure. The monument stands on high ground, looking west, toward the site of the May 22 assault on the Confederate works, in particular the charge of the 21st and 22nd Iowa infantry. Today it also faces the Texas monument, erected in 1962–63, standing in line of sight, 575 yards to the west, at the Railroad Redoubt.

The tablets list thirty-eight infantry, three artillery, and three cavalry units. Six bronze relief sculptures of Union soldiers in action adorn the temple space. From left to right they are the battles of Grand Gulf, Port Gibson, Jackson,

Iowa State Memorial

Champion Hill, Big Black River Bridge, and the May 22 assault at Vicksburg, which took place on the landscape in front of the monument. The reliefs are the work of Henry H. Kitson, who served as the designer of the whole of the monument; Guy Lowell was the architect; Mead, Mason and Company served as the builder.

Completing the monument is the 1912 equestrian statue "The Standard Bearer," the collaborative work of Kitson and his wife, Theo Alice Ruggles Kitson. The figure is a mounted color-bearer with unfurled flag, facing west, awaiting the order to advance. Parker Hills and Michael Panhorst comment on the extraordinary detail, accuracy, and artistry, noting the ripples in the billowing flag of the color-bearer, the bellicose pose of the eagle on the finial, and the courage and manifest resolution depicted in the reliefs, even among the Confederates, including the artillerymen of Waddell's Alabama Battery in the panel depicting the Battle of Champion Hill.

The monument was erected at a cost $150,000. A delegation of Iowans led by Governor Albert B. Cummins and General Grenville Dodge attended the ceremonies as part of their tour dedicating Iowa Southern monuments to its soldiers at Shiloh, Chattanooga, and Andersonville, Georgia.

Historian William C. Lowe writes that the "full slate of ceremonies took on a broadly reconciliationist character." He continues: "Musical selections included 'America,' 'Nearer, My God, To Thee,' 'Dixie' (twice, once by the 55th regimental band and once by a choir of Vicksburg schoolchildren), and 'The Star-Spangled Banner.' . . . In his speech, Governor Cummins reminded the audience, estimated at some 2,500, that 'the war of 1861 was fought, not to determine the status of the negro, but to establish the permanence of the Union.' The Iowa monuments were intended 'to commemorate . . . the courage and heroism of Iowa soldiers,' just as other monuments would be raised to the courage of Confederate soldiers."

Charles A. Clark, chief officer of Iowa Grand Army of the Republic (GAR), gave the main address. Lowe observes that Clark's remarks were directed to a description of the overall character of the war rather than the Vicksburg Campaign. Clark noted the war had been given various names; he rejected descriptions like "War of the Rebellion," "Civil War," and "War Between the States." It should, he reasoned, be called the "War for the Union." Slavery, he argued, had to be destroyed because it was a threat to the Union. The Union soldier "and his no less gallant adversary gave us the heroic era of American history to which future generations will look back as their most glorious heritage."

· The Iowa legislature appropriated $300,000 for the monument's restoration in 2012; a rededication ceremony was held on May 25, 2013.

1.36 Subject: Maj. Gen. John A. McClernand, US Vols.   **WPA Index:** 523
Location: Union Avenue, North of Iowa State monument
N 32 20 24 01 / W 90 51 10 60
Dedicated: 1919
Media: Bronze, granite
Monument is an equestrian statue.

Inscriptions

MAJOR GENERAL / JOHN A. MCCLERNAND / COMMANDING / THIRTEENTH ARMY
CORPS / ILLINOIS

E.C. POTTER SC *[On left side of plinth:]* GORHAM CO. FOUNDERS *[On lower front of base, incised:]*

JOHN A. MCCLERNAND / MAJOR-GENERAL U.S. VOLS. / COMMANDG *[SIC]* 13TH
ARMY CORPS /—/ PVT. ILL.INFT. JUNE TO AUG. 1832 / BRIG.-GEN. U.S. VOLS. MAY 17,
1861 / MAJ.-GENERAL OF VOLS. MAR. 21, 1862 / RESIGNED NOVEMBER THIRTIETH
1864

Maj. Gen. John A. McClernand (1812–1900) was a lawyer, politician, Union
general, and a personal friend of Abraham Lincoln. He was popular with his
men, a good fighter with physical courage, and a competent general even
though he was a volunteer soldier, but his political maneuvering earned the
disfavor of U. S. Grant, and he was relieved of his command of the 13th Corps
at Vicksburg on June 18, 1863. He was succeeded in command by Maj. Gen.
Edward O. C. Ord, whose statue is adjacent to this site.

Notwithstanding the controversy surrounding McClernand's military service and his dismissal, this equestrian monument to his memory was sponsored by the state of Illinois, with the general posed looking west toward the
field of assault on May 22, 1863. It was an honor that was not conferred to his
fellow corps commanders at Vicksburg such as Maj. Gen. James B. McPherson
or Maj. Gen. William T. Sherman.

· Edward C. Potter served as the sculptor. Much noted for his ability
to sculpt equestrian figures, Potter is credited with the statue of Maj.
Gen. Henry W. Slocum at Gettysburg (1902), that of Maj. Gen. Joseph
Hooker at Boston (1903), and of Ulysses S. Grant at Fairmount Park.
His most prominent work may be the marble lions in front of the New
York Public Library erected in 1911.

Maj. Gen. John A. McClernand

The Virginia State Botetourt Artillery Memorial

Confederate Avenue

1.37 Subject: The Virginia State Memorial: The Botetourt Artillery, Stele
WPA Index: 43
Location: Southeast corner of the North Frontage Road and Iowa Avenue
N 32 19 03 81 / W 90 53 22 10
Dedicated: November 23, 1907
Media: Bronze, granite
Monument is a bronze plaque mounted on a granite stele.

Inscription

BOTETOURT ARTILLERY, STEVENSON'S DIVISION, ARMY OF VICKSBURG. CAPT. JOHN
W. JOHNSTON, LIEUT. FRANCIS OBENCHAIN. THE BATTERY WAS CLOSELY ENGAGED
IN THE BATTLE OF PORT GIBSON, MAY 1; ITS CASUALTIES WERE SEVERE BUT NOT
FULLY REPORTED; LIEUTS. PHILIP PETERS, WILLIAM P. DOUTHAT AND WILLIAM H.
NORGROVE KILLED, BUT ONLY LIEUT. PHILIP PETERS SO REPORTED. IT WAS ALSO
CLOSELY ENGAGED IN THE BATTLE OF CHAMPION'S HILL, MAY 16, AT THE ANGLE
ON THE CONFEDERATE LINE; ITS CASUALTIES WERE SEVERE, BUT NOT REPORTED;
THE FIRST CAPTAIN OF THE BATTERY, MAJOR JOSEPH W. ANDERSON, DIVISION

CHIEF OF ARTILLERY, KILLED. THE BATTERY, WITHOUT GUNS, FELL BACK WITH THE ARMY TO VICKSBURG, WHERE IT RECEIVED TWO 6-POUNDER GUNS. MOST OF ITS ENLISTED MEN, UNDER CAPTAIN JOHN W. JOHNSTON TO JUNE 2, AND AFTER THAT DATE UNDER LIEUT. FRANCIS G. OBENCHAIN, WERE ARMED WITH ENFIELD RIFLES AND SERVED IN THE TRENCHES ON THE RIVER-FRONT LINE FROM SOUTH FORT ON THE LEFT TO THE FIRST WORK ON THE RIGHT OF THAT FORT, FROM MAY 18, TO THE END OF THE DEFENSE, JULY 4. CAPTAIN JOHN W. JOHNSTON SERVED AS INSPECTOR GENERAL OF LIGHT ARTILLERY, STEVENSON'S DIVISION, FROM JUNE 2, TO THE END OF THE DEFENSE, JULY 4, 1863

The only unit from Virginia on the Vicksburg battlefield—and thus the only Virginia monument—is to the Botetourt Artillery. Dedicated on November 23, 1907, it was the first Confederate unit monument tablet to be placed in the military park. Names and events are duly described, in the tradition of battlefield monuments. Note that the monument's narrative does not end with the word *surrender* but only with "the end of the defense."

The Botetourt Artillery served as infantry and artillery in several different theatres of the war, from service in Virginia, including the battle of First Manassas as Company I, 28th Virginia Infantry, then as the Botetourt Artillery in Kentucky and Vicksburg. The unit surrendered at Vicksburg, was reconstituted, served in western Virginia, and was disbanded at Christiansburg in 1865.

The monument was erected at a cost of $520, raised by private donations. A second monument to the Botetourt Artillery, a granite obelisk erected in 1902, stands on Main Street in Buchanan, Virginia.

1.38 Subject: State of South Carolina State Memorial   **WPA Index:** 86
Location: Confederate Avenue, in front of Vicksburg High School
N 32 19 15 46 / W 90 53 07 14
Dedicated: November 22, 1935
Medium: Granite
Monument is an inscribed stele.

Inscription

TO THE EVERLASTING MEMORY OF / THOSE SOUTH CAROLINIANS WHO / OFFERED THEIR LIVES UPON THE FIELDS OF / VICKSBURG FOR THE SOUTHERN CONFEDERACY. / THIS MONUMENT IS DEDICATED BY THE SOUTH CAROLINA DIVISION / UNITED DAUGHTERS OF THE CONFEDERACY, 1935.

"LET THE STRANGER / WHO MAY IN FUTURE TIMES / READ THIS INSCRIPTION, RECOGNIZE THAT THESE WERE MEN WHOM POWER COULD NOT CORRUPT, WHOM DEATH COULD NOT TERRIFY, WHOM DEFEAT COULD NOT DISHONOR; AND LET THEIR VIRTUES PLEAD FOR JUST JUDGMENT OF THE CAUSE IN WHICH THEY PER-ISHED; LET THE SOUTH CAROLINIAN OF ANOTHER GENERATION REMEMBER THAT THE STATE TAUGHT THEM HOW TO LIVE AND HOW TO DIE; AND FROM HER BROKEN FORTUNES SHE HAS PRESERVED FOR HER CHILDREN THE PRICELESS TREASURE OF THEIR MEMORIES TEACHING ALL WHO MAY CLAIM THE SAME BIRTH-RIGHT THAT TRUTH, COURAGE, AND PATRIOTISM, ENDURE FOREVER." WILLIAM HENRY TRESCOTT.

THE SOUTH CAROLINA TROOPS ENGAGED IN THIS CAMPAIGN WERE GIST'S BRIGADE: SIXTEENTH, TWENTY-FOURTH SOUTH CAROLINA REGIMENTS, FERGUSON'S BATTERY; EVAN'S BRIGADE: SEVENTEENTH, EIGHTEENTH, TWENTY-SECOND, TWENTY-THIRD, TWENTY-SIXTH SOUTH CAROLINA REGIMENTS. HOLCOMB LEGION.

The South Carolina units commemorated here served in Johnston's Army of Relief; there were no South Carolina troops at Vicksburg. The memorial, con-structed of Winnsboro granite, was sponsored by the South Carolina UDC at a cost of $4,900.

The inscription is attributed to nineteenth-century South Carolina diplo-mat and historian William Henry Trescot, and also appears on the state house grounds Confederate monument at Columbia, South Carolina, dedicated in 1878. The larger context reads:

> Let the stranger, who in future times read this inscription, recognize that
> these were men whom power could not corrupt, whom death could not
> terrify, whom defeat could not dishonor, and let their virtues plead for just
> judgment of the cause in which they perished. . . . Let the South Carolinian
> of another generation remember that the state taught them how to live
> and how to die, and that from her broken fortunes she has preserved for
> her children the priceless treasures of her memories, teaching all who
> may claim the same birthright that truth, courage and patriotism endure
> forever.

State of South Carolina Memorial

State of Maryland Memorial

1.39 Subject: State of Maryland Memorial   **WPA Index:** 105
Location: South Confederate Avenue, 0.2 miles south of Mulvihill Street
N 32 19 28 78 / W 90 52 54 16
Installed or dedicated: March 1914
Media: Bronze, granite
Monument is an inscribed stele.

Inscriptions

STEVENSON'S DIVISION, THIRD CONFEDERATE BATTERY. CAPTAIN FERD. O.
CLAIBORNE, CAPTAIN JOHN B. ROWAN. ENGAGED: CHAMPION'S HILL, MAY 16;
DEFENSE, MAY 18–JULY 4. CASUALTIES NOT FULLY REPORTED, CAPTAIN FERD. O.
CLAIBORNE KILLED, JUNE 24, ON DUTY AT GUNS IN FRONT OF THIS MONUMENT.
A DETACHMENT, WITH ONE GUN, UNDER LIEUT. WILLIAM L. RITTER SERVED ON
ROLLING FORK AND DEER CREEK FROM APRIL SECOND TO JUNE FIRST WHEN IT WAS
ORDERED TO YAZOO CITY AND ATTACHED TO WALKER'S DIVISION.

MARYLAND: FERD O. CLAIBORN, / CAPT. THIRD BATTERY, KILLED JUNE 24, 1863.

This is the only Maryland unit that served at Vicksburg. As Ritter's Battery, this unit was organized in Baltimore, in the fall of 1861; it mustered into the Confederate Army as the Third Maryland Battery on January 14, 1862. Most of the battery was surrendered at Vicksburg, though, as the inscription notes, one gun of the battery was on detached duty and was not engaged in the siege. The battery was reconstituted after the surrender and thereafter saw action in Alabama, Georgia, Kentucky, Louisiana, Mississippi, and Tennessee,

State of Florida Memorial

according to historian Gary Baker. The battery was under General Richard Taylor's authority when he surrendered his command—the Department of Alabama, Mississippi, and East Louisiana—on May 4, 1865. Members of the 3rd Maryland were paroled on May 10, 1865.

1.40 Subject: State of Florida State Memorial
Location: Confederate Avenue at the Mulvihill Street intersection
N 32 19 37 28 / W 90 52 49 56
Dedicated: April 17, 1954
Medium: Granite
Monument is a stele surmounting a base.

Inscription
[Front]
[state seal of Florida; motto: "In God We Trust"]

IN TRIBUTE TO / THE 1ST AND 3RD FLORIDA INFANTRY / REGIMENTS COMMANDED BY COL. W. S. / DILWORTH AND THE 4TH INFANTRY / REGIMENT COMMANDED BY LT. COL. / ED. BADGER, WHO PARTICIPATED IN / MISSISSIPPI DURING THE WAR BETWEEN / THE STATES AS A PART OF STOVALL'S / BRIGADE, OF BRECKENRIDGE'S DIVISION / OF GENERAL JOHNSTON'S ARMY IN 1863 / ERECTED BY / FLORIDA DIVISION / UNITED DAUGHTERS / OF THE CONFEDERACY / 1954

WHETHER SLEEPING / IN DISTANT PLACES, OR GRAVELESS, / THIS MONUMENT HAS BEEN ERECTED / TO THE MEMORY OF THE MEN WHO / SERVED THE CONFEDERATE STATES OF AMERICA

No Florida units served in the siege of Vicksburg. This stele commemorates the service of three Florida regiments who served in General Joseph E. Johnston's Army of Relief. It was sponsored by the Florida UDC and was erected at a cost of $5,000.

Note the irony of the use of the phrase "In God We Trust" on the seal of the state of Florida. The phrase may be said to be a rejoinder to the official Confederate motto, "Deo Vindice." "In God We Trust" has been the official motto of the United States since 1956. Sources indicate that the impetus behind the motto was coincident with the coming of the Civil War. The Reverend M. R. Watkinson, in a letter dated November 13, 1861, petitioned the Treasury Department to add a statement recognizing "Almighty God in some form in our coins" in order to "relieve us from the ignominy of heathenism." At least part of the motivation was to declare that God was on the Union side of the Civil War. Secretary of the Treasury Salmon Chase approved the request.

Abraham Lincoln famously offered a kind of final word on the matter. In answering a question about whether he thought God was on the side of the Union, Lincoln averred, "Sir, my concern is not whether God is on our side; my greatest concern is to be on God's side" (cf. Josh. 5:13–15).

1.41 Subject: State of North Carolina
Location: Confederate Avenue, south of Hall's Ferry Road   N 32 19 41 83 / W 90 52 40 86
Erected: 1924; Dedicated: May 18, 1925
Medium: Granite
Monument is an arch supported by two Doric columns with a central stele.

Inscription

[state seal of North Carolina]

JOHNSTON'S ARMY / FRENCH'S DIVISION, / MCNAIR'S BRIGADE / 29TH INFANTRY / LT. COL. WM. B. CREASMAN / 39TH INFANTRY / COL. DAVID COLEMAN / BRECKINRIDGE'S DIV. / STOVALL'S BRIGADE, / 60TH INFANTRY / COL. WASH. M. HARDY / LT. COL. JAS. M. RAY / BY THE STATE / IN HONOR OF / HER SOLDIERS / ENGAGED IN THE / VICKSBURG OPERATIONS

NORTH CAROLINA.

The North Carolina State Memorial is a tribute to the three North Carolina infantry regiments involved in the Vicksburg Campaign, all of which, as it happened, were in Johnston's Army of Relief. None was at Vicksburg.

Though modest in size, this example of late American Renaissance architecture has a simplicity and elegance anticipating the art deco forms of the 1930s. The memorial was cut from Stone Mountain granite and sculpted by Aristide B. Cianfarani (1895–1960), the Italian-born American who also sculpted the bust of Maj. Arza Goodspeed on the West Virginia State Memorial.

State of North Carolina Memorial

1.42 Subject: Louisiana, City Shaft
Location: Monroe and Crawford Streets   N 32 30 55 90 / W 90 52 48 18
Dedicated: June 11, 1887
Medium: Marble
Monument is a marble shaft surmounted by a brazier.

Inscription
[Front]

TO THE / LOUISIANANS / WHO DIED / IN DEFENSE OF / VICKSBURG 1862–1863

IN LIFE / THE SHOCK OF BATTLE
IN DEATH'S SLEEP: / PEACE / AND ENDLESS FAME

BY THEIR / SURVIVING / COMRADES

SEAL OF STATE OF LOUISIANA / UNION JUSTICE & CONFIDENCE
DEDICATED / JUNE 11TH 1887 / LOUISIANA

This is the first Southern monument in Vicksburg; it is the oldest Vicksburg monument that remains in its original place. Erected thirty-three years later, the 1920 monument erected by the state of Louisiana would justly commemorate all Louisianan Confederates who served at Vicksburg. This monument is decidedly funereal and more personal: surviving comrades remember their dead. The finial—a sculptured marble flame—surmounts the shaft, just as a

Louisiana, City Shaft

brazier of granite with an "eternal flame" surmounts the monument on the Vicksburg battlefield.

- The inscription "Union Jutice & Confidence" is taken from the motto on the state's seal from 1802 to 1876; in 1879, the motto was changed to "Union, Justice and Confidence." The relief of a pelican feeding its chicks, from the coat of arms of Louisiana, is a reference to the proverbial and mythical piety associated with the pelican.

1.43 Subject: "Soldiers' Rest," Common Soldier
Location: North end, Mission 66 Road: Cedar Hill Cemetery 326 Lovers Ln, 39183   N 32 21 58 87 / W 90 51 34 22
Dedicated: April 16, 1893
Media: Granite, marble
Monument is a common soldier surmounting a shaft and base.

Inscriptions
[Front]
1861–1865
IN MEMORY OF / THE MEN, FROM ALL STATES / OF THE SOUTH,
WHO FELL IN / THE DEFENSE OF VICKSBURG / DURING A SIEGE OF
47 DAYS—MAY 18 TO JULY 3, / 1863—A DEFENSE / UNSURPASSED IN THE ANNALS /
OF WAR FOR HEROISM, ENDURANCE / OF HARDSHIP AND PATRIOTIC DEVOTION.

"WE CARE NOT WHENCE THEY CAME, / DEAR IN THEIR LIFELESS CLAY, /
WHETHER UNKNOWN OR KNOWN TO FAME, / THEIR CAUSE AND COUNTRY STILL
THE SAME, / THEY DIED AND THEY WORE THE GRAY"

CONFEDERATE DEAD

[Relief of crossed swords]

1861–1865
HERE RESTS [SIC] SOME FEW OF THOSE / WHO VAINLY BRAVE [SIC] /
DIED FOR THE LAND THEY LOVED, / BUT COULD NOT SAVE.

OUR DEAD ARE MOURNED FOREVER / THROUGH ALL THE FUTURE AGES. /
IN HISTORY AND IN STORY / THEIR FAME SHALL SHINE, / THEIR NAME SHALL
'TWINE; / THEY NEED NO GREATER GLORY, / TENDERLY FALL OUR TEARS / OVER
THEIR LIFELESS CLAY / HERE LIE THE DEAD WHO FOUGHT AND BLED / AND FELL IN
GARB OF GRAY.

OURS THE FATE OF THE VANQUISHED / WHOSE HEARTACHES NEVER CEASE,
OURS THE TEARS, / REGRET AND TEARS, [SIC]
THEIRS THE ETERNAL PEACE.

BUILDING COMMITTEE

[Four Names]
[Cornerstone]

VICKSBURG CONFEDERATE CEMETERY ASSOCIATION.
ORGANIZED MAY 15, 1866.

"Soldiers' Rest," Common Soldier

With its railroad and river access as well as its status as a major city in Mississippi, Vicksburg served as a hospital center even before the siege: wounded or ill soldiers from as far away as Shiloh were brought here. In addition, Confederate soldiers who were killed or died of disease during the siege were collected from various sites on the siege grounds and battlefield and were buried here.

The website for Cedar Hill Cemetery identifies it as being one of the oldest and largest private cemeteries in the United States that is still in use. It is also the resting place for some five thousand Confederate soldiers who died during the Vicksburg campaign or whose graves were reinterred here from other sites, of whom some sixteen hundred are identified. During the war, J. Q. Arnold, a local undertaker working under contract with the Confederate government, selected Cedar Hill Cemetery to inter the dead. Historian William Mathews records that local women formed the Vicksburg Confederate Cemetery Association in 1866. They obtained the parcel that is now called Soldiers' Rest and contracted to gather the dead from beyond the cemetery grounds—"fields, forts, rifle pits, and trenches"—and reinter them here.

In 1892, the association raised funds to erect the presiding monument. Records indicate that it was unveiled with much ceremony. "Following a luncheon in the rotunda of the Vicksburg Hotel, a procession was formed and . . . marched from the Louisiana monument downtown to the cemetery. General Stephen Dill Lee spoke for an hour and a half, paying a splendid tribute to the defenders of Vicksburg." A. A. Meneze is credited as the sculptor; William A. Roane the contractor; Hill City Marble Works, fabricator. The entry in Bettie A. C. Emerson's 1911 memorial volume *Historic Southern Monuments* declares this:

> Dedicated to the soldiers from all the States who fell in defense of Vicksburg, it is a tribute to universal Southern manhood, for no Southern State, it is believed, is without representatives among those who sleep beneath it. The body of the monument is of white Italian marble adorned with four reversed cannon and as many piles of balls, of Tennessee marble. The statue of a Confederate soldier which crowns its summit was carved at Carrara, Italy, and is singularly lifelike in pose and feature. The hands rest on the old familiar rifle, the head is bent forward, the feet are placed somewhat apart as if firmly planted on a rugged surface. It is a typical figure and such a one as might have been seen on a thousand battlefields during the war. The statue faces the south.

· The inscription that contains "Dear in their lifeless clay" is taken from the poem "March of the Deathless Dead," by Father Abram Ryan.

- The markers, called headstones in the literature on the cemetery, are actually cenotaphs. Likewise, the state markers are representative; they do not mark specific sites of soldiers from particular states. Erecting the headstones has been a long-term project. Matthews writes that in 1977, there were fewer than fifty headstones erected in the area. However, the United Daughters of the Confederacy (UDC) and the Jackson camp of the Sons of Confederate Veterans (SCV) ordered and put in place about sixteen hundred stones with names based on the cemetery sexton's list. In addition, 77 stones were erected in the summer of 1998 by the UDC and SCV. Further research has uncovered a 1935 map of the cemetery indicating that six lots interring Confederate soldiers are also on the grounds but are not included within Soldier's Rest. Finally, the graves of a number of Confederate veterans are in private lots.

- The graves of at least four Union soldiers are believed to be here. In addition, the graves of at least four Confederate soldiers are believed to be at Vicksburg National Cemetery.

1.44 Subject: Connecticut State Memorial
Location: Delta, Louisiana, off I-20 West, Exit 186, east on US 80, to Grant's Canal Reservation of VNMP   N 32 19 15 67 / W 90 55 59 06
Dedicated: October 14, 2008
Media: Concrete, granite
Monument is a granite stele with adjoining exedra.

The Connecticut State Memorial is located in Louisiana, but it merits inclusion in this study as a monument in the Vicksburg NMP and as the most recent state monument erected in the park.

The 9th Connecticut VI, organized at New Haven, September 26, 1861, served throughout the war and is the only unit from that state to participate in the campaign. Their service at Vicksburg involved the ill-fated effort to dig a three-mile-long canal across DeSoto Point, a Louisiana peninsula formed by a twist in the Mississippi in front of Vicksburg. The project was led by Brig. Gen. Thomas Williams during the first Union campaign to capture Vicksburg in the spring and summer of 1862. The effort was unsuccessful. Disease afflicted the participants, including the 9th CVI, which lost 153 men within a four-month period following their arrival at the canal.

The 9th saw no further action at Vicksburg, but it participated in the battle of Baton Rouge in August, served in the defenses in the New Orleans area, and eventually returned to the east and saw action in the Shenandoah Valley and Bermuda Hundred in eastern Virginia before the war ended.

Connecticut State Memorial, Grant's Canal Reservation of VNMP

The monument was designed by Mathieu Memorial and Granite Works of Southington, Connecticut, in conjunction with Royal Melrose Granite of Cold Spring, Minnesota, at a cost of $50,000. The granite shaft and exedra stand on a concrete plaza displaying the outline of the state of Connecticut. Etched photographs of soldiers of the 9th CVI, and scenes of their participation in the campaign are displayed—the work of artists Stacy Mathieu and Kerry Sheldon.

·   A monument to the 9th CVI, a common soldier statue erected in 1903, stands in Bayview Park in New Haven, Connecticut.

THE
VICKSBURG
NATIONAL MILITARY PARK
LANDSCAPE

Introduction

THE VICKSBURG monument landscape is an extravagant archive of nine-teenth- and twentieth-century sculpture, inscriptions, and military commemoration. The archive is so large that an accurate accounting defies a final word. The archive far exceeds the park's geographical boundaries, which are themselves expansive, and it certainly exceeds the ability of the Park Service's personnel and budget to maintain. Although the vast majority are in plain site near park service roads, many are not and have been obscured, some for decades, and are no longer tended. Interstate highway development and the growth of the city and Warren County have changed the landscape. Loess hills soil erosion, the Deep South climate, and the Mississippi undergrowth have had their effects.

Notwithstanding these changes, conditions, and challenges, the archive largely remains intact and is represented in the pages that follow. There is no American Civil War battlefield that offers as much public, on-the-ground testimony as Vicksburg does. A close reading of this chapter will reveal that these 721 monuments offer extraordinarily suggestive detail. Each monument and marker has import; each represents an experience and legacy before, during, or after the Vicksburg Campaign, with particular emphasis on the landscape of the siege. The monuments and tablets record dead, wounded, and missing personnel here. Many specify the location of Union troops during the failed assaults of May 19 and May 22; some detail the casualties for each assault as well. The officers in command are inscribed. Others specify the defense lines of Confederate units in response to the assaults or their status in the Army of Relief. Still other monuments document the service of units in the front lines of the siege, and the daily, mundane work of the sharpshooters or sappers, and where the units were encamped. No monument offers the complete story, of course, but each offers the story in microcosm.

William T. Rigby had a foundational influence on the history of Vicksburg National Military Park (NMP). Commissioners such as Stephen D. Lee and John Festus Merry were influential figures, but Rigby was an indefatigable advocate for the establishment and development of the park. A Civil War veteran who served in the 24th Iowa VI during the Vicksburg Campaign, Rigby served as Vicksburg NMP commissioner from 1899 to 1902, and superintendent from 1902 to 1929. Rigby set a goal that each brigade and battery commander who served in the campaign in the park be represented with a relief portrait, bust, or statue near the site where they served. That goal was largely fulfilled. By 1916, federal funds had funded 7 statues, 49 busts, and 59 relief portraits in the park. Individual states paid for many monuments, and private individuals funded commemorations of friends or family who served in the campaign.

Eighteen state monuments were erected in the early 1900s, beginning with the Massachusetts common soldier (1906) among Northern monuments, and the Virginia stele (1907) among Southern states. In addition, approximately 270 small unit, regimental, or battery or brigade monuments were erected by various states to mark the sites where individual units served. These vary in size, design, and scale, but they often display copious details as to unit names, officers' names, casualties, and the service of various units in the campaign. Approximately 230 stelae or flat slabs or tablets mark the location of regiments or artillery batteries. All of the regimental monuments and markers and the state memorials were constructed by the states. Finally, the War Department sponsored approximately 750 iron wayside tablets—blue for Union, red for Confederate. (As wayside tablets, they are not included in this study.) Several of these narratives are included for the sake of context. The NPS Tour Stops are included as reference points.

Today there are thirteen statues of officers and men from Northern states and five from Southern states. Four equestrian sculptures stand in the park: figures of Union generals Maj. Gen. Ulysses S. Grant and Maj. Gen. John A. McClernand; Confederate Brig. Gen. Lloyd Tilghman, and the common soldier on the Iowa state monument. There are 177 portrait figure reliefs and busts, including 63 men portrayed in busts and 94 more in reliefs.

Prominent artists include Herbert Adams, Sorlun Borgland, William Couper, Frank E. Elwell, Frederick Hibbard, Henry Kitson, Theo Alice Ruggles Kitson, Frederick W. Sievers, Steffen Thomas, Frederick Triebel, and Adolph A. Weinman. "Theo. A. R." Kitson has the most monuments of any artist at Vicksburg. She designed 73 sculptures—52 portrait reliefs, 19 busts, and 2 state monuments (Iowa and Massachusetts). Until 2008, she was the only female artist whose work was represented in the park. The foundries include the Gorham Manufacturing Company; Roman Bronze Works; and Tiffany and Company.

This survey of Vicksburg's monumentation begins where most visitors begin, at the visitor center, and follows and quotes from the tour stops as it moves through the park. It follows the route of Union Avenue to the national cemetery, then turns south along Confederate Avenue to the South Loop. The survey then moves beyond the NPS grounds and turns to the south end of the siege line, by the river. It moves from south to north, largely along the line of Confederate Avenue, to Clay Street before returning to the visitor center.

Much of the work for this survey was accomplished on foot, as field research, in summers over a period of four successive years. Each monument listed here was either directly observed on the field or it was documented to have been placed, based on various sources. In this quest, the on-site archives of the NPS were invaluable. A federal Works Progress Administration (WPA) study completed in 1942 offers a still-useful and comprehensive survey of the Vicksburg battlefield's monument and wayside tablet holdings. The staff of VNMP was invariably courteous and extended much assistance. (Pat Strange, of the Vicksburg Visitor Center merits note for her expertise. Luke Howard offered much advice on locations of hard-to-find monuments.)

David B. Dumas published a detailed 2016 study of the monumentation based in some measure on a 1930s-era topographical map (*The Original Vicksburg National Military Park and Vicinity*). In his *Memorial Art and Architecture of Vicksburg National Military Park*, Michael W. Panhorst examines Vicksburg's monumentation from an art historian's perspective. Parker Hills' *Art of Commemoration: Vicksburg National Military Park* is also instructive, though it is more selective. Jeff Giambrone offers substantial background history in his book *An Illustrated Guide to Vicksburg Campaign and National Military Park*. Christopher Waldrep offers a significant history of Vicksburg and the war, as well as interpretive commentary in his *Vicksburg's Long Shadow: The Civil War Legacy of Race and Remembrance*.

The States: Confederate Monuments

All of the former states of the Confederacy eventually erected state monuments: Alabama, Arkansas, Florida, Georgia, Louisiana, Maryland, North Carolina, South Carolina, Tennessee, Texas, and Virginia.

The state of Mississippi commissioned the first Southern state monument in 1906. Mississippi also sponsored the most recent state monument, to Mississippi's African American participants, in 2004. The state also sponsored a series of individual unit monuments—granite stelae—erected in 1906.

Louisiana erected its state monument in 1920, in addition to ten relief portraits and thirteen unit monuments. Along with those erected for the state of Mississippi, these are the only such series of battlefield stelae to individual state units in the South. In addition, a marble shaft stands at Monroe and Crawford streets in downtown Vicksburg, which predates the establishment of the national park. Georgia and Arkansas each sponsored a state monument and have a unit roster monument in the form of a granite stele and bronze tablet. The state of Tennessee erected a monument to Confederate soldiers at Vicksburg in 1996. A unit roster monument in the form of a granite stele and bronze tablet lists Tennessee units that served in the CS Army. No Tennessee units are listed on the Union order of battle at Vicksburg.

Border states, such as Kentucky and Missouri, erected monuments to Union and Confederate soldiers. Missouri erected a central monument as well as fifty red granite Missouri stelae to Missouri Union or Confederate units as position markers. Maryland, South Carolina, Florida, and North Carolina each have one monument.

Union Monuments

In addition to the state of Illinois's pantheon, the most expansive monument on the field, in which each soldier's name is placed, the state placed monuments for its 79 combat units at Vicksburg: 54 of infantry, 15 artillery, and 10 cavalry, including position markers for sharpshooters lines, assault lines, and camps.

Indiana's state monument is a statue of its wartime governor, Oliver P. Morton. Indiana was represented by 24 infantry regiments, 2 artillery batteries, and 2 companies of cavalry at Vicksburg, all of which are marked with inscribed granite shafts. The state also sponsored granite tablets for sharpshooters lines, assault lines, and camp sites.

Iowa erected a central monument as well as 13 standardized unit monuments commemorating the service of 32 Iowa infantry regiments, cavalry units, and artillery batteries, as well as a bust of wartime governor Samuel J. Kirkwood. Iowa also placed 59 bronze tablets, mounted on granite posts, to mark the positions of units on the siege line.

Ohio did not sponsor a central monument. Instead, as was the case on the Shiloh battlefield, the state sponsored a variety of granite monuments for each unit that was present: 26 infantry regiments; 12 artillery batteries; 1 cavalry—39 in total. The Hughes Granite & Marble Company of Clyde, Ohio executed the monuments; they were dedicated in ceremonies on May 22, 1905. The state also sponsored scroll-form tablets—position markers, in granite— marking points of advance during the May 19 and May 22 assaults.

Wisconsin sponsored a state monument, and standardized unit monuments, as well as stelae—position markers, in granite—marking points of advance during the May 19 and May 22 assaults. In addition to a central monument on Union Avenue, Minnesota erected 6 standardized engraved bronze tablets emplaced on red granite stelae. West Virginia is represented by 4 monuments—1 bust and 3 bronze and granite stelae—all to commemorate the service of soldiers of the 4th West Virginia VI. Rhode Island has a single state monument (1 infantry regiment), as does Massachusetts (3 infantry regiments), New York (3 infantry regiments, 1 artillery battery), New Hampshire (3 infantry regiments), Pennsylvania (4 infantry regiments, 1 artillery battery), and Kansas (3 regiments).

Kentucky's state monument was erected in 2001; a monument to Kentucky's Confederate soldiers was erected in 2010. Kentucky Union soldiers—which, according to historian Terry Winschel, comprised about two-thirds of all Kentuckians who served in the war—still have no monument at Vicksburg, although space was allocated for one.

The most recent monument is the Connecticut State monument near Lake Providence, Louisiana, erected in 2008. The site was added to the national military park and thus is included here. At this writing, Vermont is the only state without a state monument at Vicksburg.

The service of the US Navy at Vicksburg is commemorated with the obelisk on Union Avenue. The federal government sponsored bronze tablets for the three units of regular army soldiers who served at Vicksburg.

Several important figures have not been commemorated but have spaces reserved for them. Gen. Joseph E. Johnston, who commanded the Army of Relief, has a place for a monument near the Davis and Pemberton monuments. Maj. Gen. William T. Sherman, who commanded the 15th Corps, has no monument, although a place was made and remains vacant near Sherman Avenue. Neither does Maj. Gen. James B. McPherson, who commanded the 17th Corps. Records indicate that the state of Ohio was reluctant to erect a monument to Sherman because of his notoriety and that, as a matter of equity, McPherson was excluded as well.

The Visitor Center: Interior

2.1.1 Marble Shaft, Surrender Site Monument, 1864. N 32 20 39 33 / W 90 51 08 84 (See chap. 1.)

2.5 Visitor Center Parking Lot and Point of Entry

2.1.2 Granite obelisk: Confederate Army. Maryland, Mississippi, North Carolina, South Carolina, Tennessee, Texas, Virginia / Alabama, Arkansas, Florida, Georgia, Kentucky, Louisiana, Missouri. N 32 20 38 34 / W 90 51 02 30; WPA Index: 366

2.1.3 Granite obelisk: Union Army. Missouri, New Hampshire, New York, Ohio, Pennsylvania, Rhode Island, Wisconsin, West Virginia/Illinois, Indiana, Iowa, Kansas, Kentucky, Massachusetts, Michigan, Minnesota. N 32 20 38 34 / W 90 51 01 48; WPA Index: 368

2.6 Union Avenue: Union Lines

2.1.4 Granite Tablet, 8th Indiana VI Sharpshooters Line, May 23–July 4. N 32 20 36 06 / W 90 51 06 20; WPA Index: 575

2.1.5 Unit Monument: Granite Stele, 17th Battery, Ohio Lt. Artillery; 10th Division; 13th Corps. N 32 20 36 37 / W 90 51 04 42; WPA Index: 1

2.1.6 Unit Monument: Granite Stele: Common Soldier Relief, 96th Ohio VI, 1st Brigade; 10th Division; 13th Corps. N 32 20 36 20 / W 90 51 06 20; WPA Index: 2

2.1.7 Unit Monument: Granite Stele, Bronze Tablets: 60th, 16th, 67th Indiana VI, 1st Brigade; 10th Division; 13th Corps. N 32 20 35 78 / W 90 51 01 06; WPA Index: 8

2.1.8 Granite Stele, 23rd Wisconsin VI, Camp, May 19–July 4. N 31 20 35 78 / W 90 51 00 70; WPA Index: 5

2.1.9 Unit Monument: Granite Tablet, Co. C, 4th Indiana Vol. Cavalry, 10th Division; 13th Corps. N 32 20 34 03 / W 90 51 00 46; WPA Index: 6

2.1.10 Unit Monument: Granite Stele, 23rd Wisconsin VI, 1st Brigade; 10th Division; 13th Corps. N 32 20 36 72 / W 90 50 58 46; WPA Index: 11

2.1.11 Granite Tablet, 60th Indiana VI, Sharpshooters Line, May 23–July 4. N 32 20 37 09 / W 90 50 57 72; WPA Index: 13

2.1.12 Granite Tablet, 67th Indiana VI, Camp, May 19–July 4, in first ravine east of marker. N 32 20 37 66 / W 90 50 57 33; WPA Index: 14

2.2.1 The Arch: Memorial to the National Reunion of Union and Confederate Veterans. N 32 20 37 31 / W 90 50 57 68; WPA Index: 367 (See chap. 1.)

2.2.2 Granite Tablet, 67th Indiana VI, Sharpshooters Line, May 23–July 4. N 32 30 38 02 / W 90 50 58 38; WPA Index: 13

2.2.3 Unit Monument: Granite Obelisk, Illinois: Chicago Mercantile Battery, 10th Division; 13th Corps. N 32 20 37 58 / W 90 50 57 14; WPA Index: 16

2.2.4 Bust, Brig. Gen Stephen G. Burbridge, US Vols., Col., 26th Kentucky VI, commanding 1st Brigade; 10th Division; 13th Corps (Sculptor: T. A. R. Kitson, n.d.). N 32 20 37 93 / W 90 50 55 52; WPA Index: 588

2.2.5 Unit Monument: Granite Shaft, with Greyhound Relief, 83rd Ohio VI, 1st Brigade; 10th Division; 13th Corps. N 32 20 38 09 / W 90 50 54 84; WPA Index: 20

2.2.6 Relief Portrait, Col. William J. Landram, US Vols., 19th Kentucky VI, commanding 2nd Brigade; 10th Division; 13th Corps (Sculptor: Victor Holm, Jules Bercham, 1914). N 32 20 45 82 / W 90 50 47 66; WPA Index: 25

2.2.7 Unit Monument: Granite Obelisk, 77th Illinois VI, 2nd Brigade; 10th Division; 13th Corps. N 32 20 48 28 / W 90 50 47 12; WPA Index: 29

2.2.8 Unit Monument: Granite Tablet, 16th Indiana VI, 1st Brigade; 10th Division; 13th Corps. N 32 20 48 97 / W 90 50 46 46; WPA Index: 31

2.2.9 Unit Monument: Granite Obelisk, 97th Illinois VI, 2nd Brigade; 10th Division; 13th Corps. N 32 20 50 11 / W 90 50 46 18; WPA Index: 32

2.2.10 Granite Tablet, 16th Indiana VI, Camp, May 19–July 4. N 32 20 48 84 / W 90 50 46 04; WPA Index: 31

2.2.11 Unit Monument: Granite Stele, 48th Ohio VI, 2nd Brigade; 10th Division; 13th Corps. N 32 20 51 52 / W 90 50 44 80; WPA Index: 34

2.2.12 Granite Tablet, 60th Indiana VI, Camp, June 1–June 22. N 32 20 51 73 / W 90 50 44 12; WPA Index: 35

2.2.13 Unit Monument: Granite Obelisk, 108th Illinois VI, 2nd Brigade; 10th Division; 13th Corps. N 32 20 53 86 / W 90 50 42 94; WPA Index: 130

2.2.14 Unit Monument: Granite Obelisk, 130th Illinois VI, 2nd Brigade; 10th Division; 13th Corps. N 32 20 54 91 / W 90 50 43 02; WPA Index: 39

2.2.15 Unit Monument: Granite Arch and Column Relief, Bronze Tablets, 48th and 59th Indiana VI, 1st Brigade; 7th Division; 17th Corps. N 32 20 57 00 / W 90 50 42 66; WPA Index: 51

2.2.16 Relief Portrait, Col. Jesse I. Alexander, US Vols., 59th Indiana VI, commanding 1st Brigade, 7th Division, 17th Corps (Sculptor: T. A. R. Kitson, 1918). N 32 20 57 70 / W 90 50 41 78; WPA Index: 52

2.2.17 Granite Tablet, 60th Indiana VI, Sharpshooters Line, June 1–June 22. N 32 30 54 46 / W 90 50 43 14; WPA Index: 48

2.2.18 Unit Monument: Granite Stele, 18th Wisconsin VI, 1st Brigade, 7th Division; 17th Corps. N 32 20 58 17 / W 90 50 42 48; WPA Index: 55

2.3.1 Obelisk and Statue, Minnesota State Memorial (Sculptor: William Couper, 1907). N 32 20 59 93 / W 90 50 42 94; WPA Index: 57 (See chap. 1.)

2.3.2 Relief Portrait, Col. John B. Sanborn, US Vols., 4th Minnesota VI, commanding 1st Brigade, 7th Division; 17th Corps (Sculptor: T. A. R. Kitson, 1914). N 32 20 59 95 / W 90 50 42 06; WPA Index: 58

2.3.3 Unit Monument: Granite Stele, 4th Minnesota VI; 1st Brigade, 7th Division; 17th Corps. N 32 21 00 93 / W 90 50 42 20; WPA Index: 59

2.3.4 Relief Portrait, Col. Green B. Raum, US Vols., 56th Illinois VI, commanding 2nd Brigade, 7th Division; 17th Corps (Sculptors: George E. Ganiere, Jules Berchem, 1915). N 32 21 02 63 / W 90 50 42 04; WPA Index: 62

2.3.5 Unit Monument: Granite Obelisk with Exedra, 80th Ohio VI, 2nd Brigade, 7th Division; 17th Corps. N 32 21 02 63 / W 90 50 42 12; WPA Index: 63

2.3.6 Relief Portrait, Col. Samuel A. Holmes, US Vols., 10th Missouri VI, commanding 2nd Brigade, 7th Division; 17th Corps (Sculptor: T. A. R. Kitson, 1915). N 32 21 03 54 / W 90 50 41 90; WPA Index: 65

2.3.7 Unit Monument: Granite Stele, Bronze Tablet: 1st Missouri Lt. Artillery, 4th Missouri Vol. Cavalry, Co. F; 10th, 24th, 26th Missouri VI, 7th Division; 17th Corps. N 32 21 04 05 / W 90 50 41 90; WPA Index: 66

2.3.8 Unit Monument: Granite Tablet, 2nd Illinois Vol. Cavalry, Company E, 7th Division; 17th Corps. N 32 21 05 24 / W 90 50 41 24; WPA Index: 74

2.3.9 Unit Monument: Granite Obelisk, 56th Illinois VI, 2nd Brigade, 7th Division; 17th Corps. N 32 21 05 65 / W 90 50 40 88; WPA Index: 75

2.3.10 Relief Portrait, Col. George B. Boomer, US Vols., 26th Missouri VI. Killed May 22, 1863 (Sculptor: T. A. R. Kitson, n.d.). N 32 21 04 62 / W 90 50 38 88; WPA Index: 77

2.3.11 Bronze Tablet, 17th Iowa VI, Camp, May 20–July 4. N 32 21 03 46 / W 90 50 37 04; WPA Index: 78

2.3.12 Unit Monument: Granite Stele, 6th and 12th Wisconsin Lt. Artillery, 7th Division; 17th Corps. N 32 21 05 80 / W 90 50 37 64; WPA Index: 80

2.3.13 Bust, Brig. Gen. Isaac F. Quinby, US Vols., commanding 7th Division; 17th Corps (Sculptor: William Couper, 1911). N 32 21 07 16 / W 90 50 37 18; WPA Index: 81

2.3.14 Relief Portrait, Brig. Gen. Charles L. Matthies, US Vols., Col., 5th Iowa VI, commanding 3rd Brigade 3rd Division; 15th Corps (Sculptor: T. A. R. Kitson, 1913). N 32 21 09 47 / W 90 50 37 30; WPA Index: 85

2.3.15 Granite Stele, Bronze Tablet: 10th Missouri VI, May 22 Assault (W 3). N 32 21 09 51 / W 90 50 38 04; WPA Index: 86

2.3.16 Granite Tablet, 56th Illinois VI, May 22 Assault (K 1, W 3, T 4). N 32 21 10 66 / W 90 50 38 04; WPA Index: 88

2.3.17 Unit Monument: Granite Obelisk, 93rd Illinois VI, 3rd Brigade; 7th Division; 17th Corps. N 32 21 12 31 / W 90 50 37 94; WPA Index: 91

2.3.18 Relief Portrait, Col. Holden Putnam, US Vols., 93rd Illinois VI, commanding 3rd Brigade, 7th Division; 17th Corps (Sculptor: T. A. R. Kitson, 1919). N 32 21 13 22 / W 90 50 39 02; WPA Index: 93

2.3.19 Unit Monument: Granite Columns and Arch with Bronze Tablets: 5th, 10th, 17th Iowa VI, 2nd and 3rd Brigade, 7th Division; 17th Corps. N 32 21 14 52 / W 90 50 39 02; WPA Index: 95

2.7 Mowed Bay 3, West of Union Avenue, Near Pemberton Circle on Confederate Avenue

2.3.20 Granite Tablet, 130th Illinois VI, Sharpshooters Line, June 15–July 4. N 32 20 55 74 / W 90 50 58 96; WPA Index: 194

2.3.21 Granite Tablet, 16th Indiana VI, Sharpshooters Line, June 15–July 4. N 32 20 56 12 / W 90 50 58 38; WPA Index: 195

2.3.22 Granite Tablet, 97th Illinois VI, Sharpshooters Line, June 15–July 4. N 32 20 56 66 / W 90 50 58 04; WPA Index: 196

2.3.23 Granite Tablet, 60th Indiana VI, Sharpshooters Line, June 15–June 22. N 32 20 57 11 / W 90 50 57 96; WPA Index: 197

2.3.24 Granite Tablet, 77th Illinois VI, Sharpshooters Line, June 15–July 4. N 32 20 57 73 / W 90 50 58 32; WPA Index: 198

Granite Tablet, 56th Illinois VI; 2nd Brigade; 7th Division; 17th Corps. Sharpshooters Line, June 5–July 4. Many monuments between the siege lines are accessed by mowed avenues—bays—between extensive woods and undergrowth.

Union Line, Mowed Bay 2, Opposite the Mississippi State Monument and 35th Mississippi Stele

2.3.25 Bronze Tablet, 17th Iowa VI, Sharpshooters Line, June 5–July 4. N 32 21 06 45 / W 90 50 54 26; WPA Index: 202

2.3.26 Granite Tablet, 56th Illinois VI, Sharpshooters Line, June 5–July 4. N 32 21 07 18 / W 90 50 53 98; WPA Index: 204

2.3.27 Granite Stele, Bronze Tablet: 10th Missouri VI, Sharpshooters Line, June 5–July 4. N 32 21 07 64 / W 90 50 54 34; WPA Index: 206

2.3.28 Granite Tablet, 93rd Illinois VI, Picket and Sharpshooters Line, May 26–June 22. N 32 21 08 28 / W 90 50 54 26; WPA Index: 207

Union Monuments, Mowed Bay 1, Opposite Louisiana State Monument

2.3.29 Granite Tablet, 81st Illinois VI, May 22 Assault: Col. James J. Dollins KIA. N 32 21 22 48 / W 90 50 46 86; WPA Index: 232

2.3.30 Granite Tablet, 81st Illinois VI, May 22 Assault (K 18, W 80, T 98). N 32 21 24 12 / W 90 50 47 14; WPA Index: 233

2.3.31 Granite Tablet, 17th Illinois VI, May 22 Assault (K 3, W 23, T 26). N 32 21 24 47 / W 90 50 45 82; WPA Index: 234

2.3.32 Granite Stele, 32nd Ohio VI, May 22 Assault, Marks Farthest Advance. N 32 21 22 10 / W 90 50 44 64; WPA Index: 237

2.3.33 Granite Stele, 18th Wisconsin VI, May 22 Assault, Marks Farthest Advance. N 32 21 22 48 / W 90 50 46 86; WPA Index: 228

ABOVE Granite Tablet, 8th Illinois VI, May 22 Assault (K 4, W 19, T 23). Looking west, with Louisiana State monument and Confederate lines in background.

BELOW Bronze Tablet, 5th Iowa VI, 3rd Brigade, 7th Division, 17th Corps, Sharpshooters Line, June 5–June 22, west of Union Avenue. The extensive woods and undergrowth are a product of CCC efforts in the 1930s to control erosion.

2.3.34 Granite Tablet, 8th Illinois VI, May 22 Assault (K 4, W 19, T 23).
     N 32 21 18 84 / W 90 50 46 04; WPA Index: 230
2.3.35 Granite Tablet, 8th Illinois VI, Sharpshooters Line, June 5–July 4.
     N 32 21 20 14 / W 90 50 20 45 62; WPA Index: 231
2.3.36 Granite Stele, Bronze Tablet: 26th Missouri VI, Sharpshooters Line,
     June 5–June 22. N 32 21 11 12 / W 90 50 48 70; WPA Index: 225
2.3.37 Bronze Tablet, 5th Iowa VI, Sharpshooters Line, June 5–June 22.
     N 32 21 15 79 / W 90 50 47 16; WPA Index: 216

Granite Tablet, 17th Illinois VI, Sharpshooters Line, looking west toward Confederate lines from Pemberton Avenue. The landscape has been cleared to bear a closer resemblance to its wartime appearance.

2.3.38 Granite Tablet, 48th Indiana VI, Sharpshooters Line, June 23–July 4.
N 32 21 15 24 / W 90 50 47 14; WPA Index: 223

2.3.39 Granite Tablet, 59th Indiana VI, Sharpshooters Line, June 23–July 4.
N 32 21 13 14 / W 90 50 44 54; WPA Index: 219

2.3.40 Granite Tablet, 93rd Illinois VI, May 22 Assault (K 4, W 51, T 55).
N 32 21 12 52 / W 90 50 48 52; WPA Index: 217

2.3.41 Granite Stele, Bronze Tablet, 4th Minnesota VI, Sharpshooters Line,
June 23–July 4. N 32 21 11 12 / W 90 50 48 70; WPA Index: 214

2.3.42 Bronze Tablet, 10th Iowa VI, Sharpshooters Line, June 5–June 22.
N 32 21 10 36 / W 90 50 48 56; WPA Index: 213

Pemberton Avenue, Transverse to Confederate Avenue

2.3.43 Granite Tablet, 17th Illinois VI, Sharpshooters Line, June 5–July 4.
N 32 21 21 67 / W 90 50 40 42; WPA Index: 238

2.3.44 Granite Tablet, 81st Illinois VI, Sharpshooters Line, June 5–July 4.
N 32 21 22 61 / W 90 50 39 58; WPA Index: 240

2.3.45 Relief Portrait, Brig. Gen. John D. Stevenson, US Vols., commanding
3rd Brigade, 3rd Division; 17th Corps (Sculptor: T. A. R. Kitson, 1911).
N 32 21 22 61 / W 90 50 39 58; WPA Index: 242

2.3.46 Granite Stele, Bronze Tablet: 7th Missouri VI, Sharpshooters Line, June 5–July 4. N 32 21 26 36 / W 90 50 38 68; WPA Index: 243

2.3.47 Upturned Cannon Barrel, "Site of Interview between Maj. Gen. U.S. Grant, U.S.A. and Lt. Gen. Pemberton [CS Army], July 3rd, 1863." N 32 21 26 95 / W 90 50 40 24; WPA Index: 249.5

2.3.48 Granite Stele, "General Pemberton's Flag of Truce was met here, July 3, 1863." N 32 21 27 46 / W 90 50 42 26; WPA Index: 249

Pemberton and Union Avenue, Looking North

2.3.49 Granite Stele, with field artillery gun barrels, Yost's Ohio Battery, 3rd Division; 17th Corps. N 32 21 13 04 / W 90 50 27 78; WPA Index: 101

2.3.50 Bronze Tablet, 10th Iowa VI, Camp, May 20–June 6. N 32 21 13 27 / W 90 50 27 56; WPA Index: 103

2.4.1 Michigan State Memorial (Sculptor, Herbert Adams, 1916). N 32 21 13 48 / W 90 50 28 06; WPA Index: 102 (See chap. 1.)

2.4.2 Granite Stele, Bronze Tablet: Michigan, Unit Roster. N 32 21 13 59 / W 90 50 26 78; WPA Index: 105

2.4.3 Bronze Tablet, 5th Iowa VI, Camp, May 20–June 6. N 32 21 13 22 / W 90 50 27 56; WPA Index: 106

Tour Stop 1: Battery De Golyer:

The Union lines contained numerous artillery emplacements. Battery De Golyer was established on May 25, and contained the largest concentration of cannon (22) in the Union siege lines. This emplacement was representative of the Federal cannon that were positioned at important locations. The battery . . . was named after its commander, Capt. Samuel De Golyer, who was mortally wounded during the siege, and faces the Great Redoubt, a Confederate fortification constructed to guard the Jackson Road entrance to the city.

2.4.4 Unit Monument: Twin Columns Surmounted by Arch with Central Tablet, in Granite: 32nd Ohio VI, 3rd Brigade; 3rd Division; 17th Corps. N 32 21 15 88 / W 90 50 26 78; WPA Index: 108

2.4.5 Unit Monument: Granite Stele, 3rd Ohio Battery Lt. Artillery, 3rd Division; 17th Corps. N 32 21 17 44 / W 90 50 26 24 WPA Index: 111

2.4.6 Unit Monument: Granite Obelisk, 17th Illinois VI, 3rd Brigade; 3rd Division; 17th Corps. N 32 21 19 12 / W 90 50 25 44; WPA Index: 112

2.4.7 Unit Monument: Granite Obelisk, 2nd Illinois Lt. Artillery, Battery L, 3rd Division; 17th Corps. N 32 21 19 84 / W 90 50 25 08; WPA Index: 114

2.4.8 Site for monument to Maj. Gen. James B. McPherson, US Vols., commanding 17th Corps: Not installed. WPA Index: 115

2.4.9 Unit Monument: Granite Obelisk, 81st Illinois VI, 3rd Brigade; 3rd Division; 17th Corps. N 32 21 21 67 / W 90 50 24 90; WPA Index: 117

2.4.10 Unit Monument: Granite Obelisk, 8th Illinois VI, 3rd Brigade; 3rd Division; 17th Corps. N 32 21 25 02 / W 90 50 24 86; WPA Index: 120

2.4.11 Unit Monument: Granite Stele, Bronze Tablet: 7th Missouri VI, 3rd Brigade; 3rd Division; 17th Corps. N 32 21 26 05 / W 90 50 24 76; WPA Index: 121

2.4.12 Unit Monument: Granite Stele, 32nd Ohio VI, May 19 Assault, Marks Farthest Advance. N 32 21 30 25 / W 90 50 25 90; WPA Index: 125

Jackson Road, Moving East from Union Avenue

2.5.1 Statue, Maj. Gen. John A. Logan, US Vols., commanding 3rd Division; 17th Corps (Sculptor: Leonard Crunelle, 1919). N 32 21 32 95 / W 90 50 22 98; WPA Index: 144 (See chap. 1.)

2.5.2 Unit Monument: Granite Stele, 20th Ohio VI, 2nd Brigade; 3rd Division; 17th Corps. N 32 21 32 86 / W 90 50 23 86; WPA Index: 147

2.5.3 Unit Monument: Granite Stele, 78th Ohio VI, 2nd Brigade; 3rd Division; 17th Corps. N 32 21 32 23 / W 90 50 22 84; WPA Index: 143

2.5.4 Unit Monument: Granite Stele, 68th Ohio VI, 2nd Brigade; 3rd Division; 17th Corps. N 32 21 32 64 / W 90 50 22 14; WPA Index: 142

2.5.5 Unit Monument: Granite Stele, 11th Ohio Lt. Artillery, 7th Division; 17th Corps. N 32 21 32 17 / W 90 50 21 32; WPA Index: 141

2.5.6 Unit Monument: Granite Obelisk, 30th Illinois VI, 2nd Brigade; 3rd Division; 17th Corps. N 32 21 32 20 / W 90 50 20 48; WPA Index: 139

2.5.7 Unit Monument: Granite Tablet, 2nd Illinois Vol. Cavalry, Co. A, 3rd Division; 17th Corps. N 32 21 31 83 / W 90 50 19 82; WPA Index: 138

2.5.8 Unit Monument: Bronze Tablet, 1st United States (Siege Guns), Co. A, B, C, D, H, and I. N 32 21 31 24 / W 90 50 18 02; WPA Index: 132

Old Jackson Road—Off NPS Grounds, Present-Day Culkin Road

2.5.9 Unit Monument: Granite Obelisk, 2nd Illinois Lt. Artillery, Battery G, 3rd Division; 17th Corps. N 32 21 27 20 / W 90 50 13 94; WPA Index: 128

2.5.10 Unit Monument: Granite Stele, 4th Ohio Vol. Cavalry Company, 17th Corps. N 32 21 32 27 / W 90 50 14 96; WPA Index: 130

Old Jackson Road, Looking West From Union Avenue, Toward the Illinois State Monument, the May 22 Assault Lines, and the Great Redoubt

2.5.11 Unit Monument: Granite Obelisk, 45th Illinois VI, 1st Brigade; 3rd Division; 17th Corps. N 32 21 33 48 / W 90 50 25 72; WPA Index: 155

2.5.12 Bust, Brig. Gen. John E. Smith, US Vols., commanding 1st Brigade, 3rd Division; 17th Corps (Sculptor: George E. Ganiere, 1919). N 32 21 33 54 / W 90 50 26 10; WPA Index: 156

2.5.13 Unit Monument: Granite Obelisk, 1st Illinois Lt. Artillery, Battery D, 3rd Division; 17th Corps. N 32 21 33 91 / W 90 50 26 66; WPA Index: 157

2.5.14 Relief portrait, Col. Manning F. Force, US Vols., 20th Ohio Infantry, commanding 2nd Brigade, 3rd Division; 17th Corps (Sculptor: T. A. R. Kitson, 1912). N 32 21 33 87 / W 90 50 27 28; WPA Index: 159

2.5.15 Granite Tablet, 30th Illinois VI, 2nd Brigade; 3rd Division; 17th Corps, May 22 Assault, in reserve to assaulting columns of the 3rd and 1st Brigades. N 32 21 34 08 / W 90 50 28 10; WPA Index: 160

Tour Stop 2: Shirley House:

The Shirley House . . . is the only wartime structure remaining inside Vicksburg National Military Park, and was referred to as the "white house" by Federal soldiers during the siege. . . . It was near the Shirley House that mining operations against the Confederate forts guarding Jackson road were initiated. . . . West of the Shirley House lies the Third Louisiana Redan, a triangular earthwork, where Federal soldiers dug trenches to near the base of the redan. This avenue was known as Logan's Approach, since troops digging the trenches were commanded by Major General John A. Logan.

Jackson Road: Position Markers: Illinois State and Picket and Sharpshooter Lines and May 22 Assault Lines

2.6.1 The Illinois State Memorial and Temple (Architect: William L. B. Jenney; Sculptors: Charles J. Mulligan, Frederick E. Triebel, Frederick C. Hibbard, 1906). N 32 21 35 85 / W 90 50 29 34; WPA Index: 282 (See chap. 1.)

2.6.2 Granite Tablet, 124th Illinois VI, May 22 Assault (K 3, W 21, T 24). N 32 21 39 44 / W 90 50 32 36; WPA Index: 292

2.6.3 Granite Tablet, 31st Illinois VI, May 22 Assault (K 3, W 21, T 24). N 32 21 39 09 / W 90 50 32 42; WPA Index: 289

2.6.4 Granite Tablet, 124th Illinois VI, Co. A, Sharpshooters Line, May 23–July 4. N 32 21 39 09 / W90 50 32 42; WPA Index: 294

2.6.5 Granite Stele, 78th Ohio VI, May 22 Assault, Marks Farthest Advance. N 32 21 34 29 / W 90 50 30 52; WPA Index: 283

2.6.6 Granite Tablet, 72nd Illinois VI, Advanced Picket Line, Night of May 18–19. N 32 21 34 42 / W 90 50 30 58; WPA Index: 284

2.6.7 Granite Stele, 68th Ohio VI, May 22 Assault, Marks Farthest Advance. N 32 21 33 46 / W 90 50 31 86; WPA Index: 281

2.6.8 Granite Stele, 20th Ohio VI, May 22 Assault, Marks Farthest Advance. N 32 21 32 61 / W 90 50 34 36; WPA Index: 270

2.6.9 Granite Stele, 23rd Indiana VI, May 22 Assault (K 3, W 7, T 10). N 32 21 34 33 / W 90 50 34 48; WPA Index: 273

2.6.10 Granite Tablet, 30th Illinois VI, Sharpshooters Line, June 6–July 4. N 32 21 33 37 / W 90 50 34 06; WPA Index: 272

2.6.11 Granite Tablet, 20th Illinois VI, Sharpshooters Line, June 6–July 4. N 32 21 32 75 / W 90 50 34 70; WPA Index: 269

2.6.12 Granite Tablet, 31st Illinois VI, Sharpshooters Line, June 6–July 4. N 32 21 32 50 / W 90 50 35 02; WPA Index: 268

2.6.13 Granite Tablet, 45th Illinois VI, Sharpshooters Line, June 6–July 4. N 32 21 32 31 / W 90 50 35 44; WPA Index: 267

2.6.14 Granite Tablet, 124th Illinois VI, Sharpshooters Line, June 6–July 4. N 32 21 31 96 / W 90 50 35 44; WPA Index: 266

2.6.15 Relief Portrait, Brig. Gen. Mortimer D. Leggett, US Vols., 78th Ohio VI, commanding Second and, later, 1st, Brigade, Logan's Division (Sculptor: Henry Kitson, 1911). N 32 21 31 88 / W 90 50 36 02; WPA Index: 265

2.6.16 Granite Tablet, 23rd Indiana VI, Sharpshooters Line, June 6–July 4. N 32 21 31 81 / W 90 50 36 40; WPA Index: 264

2.6.17 Statue, Capt. Andrew Hickenlooper, US Vols., 5th Ohio Battery Lt. Artillery; Chief Engineer, 17th Corps (Sculptor: William Couper, 1912). N 32 21 31 44 / W 90 50 37 44; WPA Index: 261

2.6.18 Relief Portrait, Lt. Col. Melancthon Smith, 45th Illinois VI (Sculptor: George T. Brewster, 1916). N 32 21 31 03 / W 90 50 39 10; WPA Index: 257

Tour Stop 3: Third Louisiana Redan:

The Third Louisiana Redan was built to help guard the Jackson Road entrance into the city of Vicksburg. The redan was named after the regiment that garrisoned it, the 3rd Louisiana Infantry. The Confederates were aware of the Union approach trench and mine digging, but despite efforts of sharpshooters, were unable to stop the Federals. On June 24, 1863, the Union mine reached 40 feet under the redan. It was filled with 2,200 of black powder, and at 3:30 p.m. on June 25, fuses were prepared and the mine was exploded. Simultaneously, Northern artillery and infantry began firing all along the line. The 45th Illinois Infantry spearheaded the attack against the redan, where a huge crater (12 feet deep and 40 feet wide) was made. The assault was unsuccessful, however, as the Confederates positioned at the rear of the redan held their ground and the attacking Union soldiers could not advance out of the crater. The next day, Union soldiers withdrew after it was decided that the men could make no further progress and too many lives would be lost if they remained in the open crater.

2.6.19 Relief Portrait, Col. Eugene Erwin, 6th Missouri Infantry, CS Army, Killed in action, June 25, 1863 (Sculptor: George T. Brewster, 1916). N 32 21 30 85 / W 90 50 39 56; WPA Index: 256

2.6.20 Relief Portrait, Lt. Col. Pembroke S. Senteny, 2nd Missouri Infantry, CS Army; Killed in action, July 1, 1863 (Sculptor: T. A. R. Kitson, 1920). N 32 21 30 72 / W 90 50 39 78; WPA Index: 257

2.6.21 Granite Tablet, 45th Illinois VI, Assault May 22 (K 1, W 22, M 2, T 22). N 32 21 30 10 / W 90 50 39 78; WPA Index: 252

2.6.22 Granite Obelisk, 20th Illinois VI, Assault May 22 (W 23). N 32 21 30 23 / W 90 50 39 28; WPA Index: 253

2.6.23 Granite Tablet, 23rd Indiana VI: "Afternoon of June 25, 1863, Lieut. H.C. Foster and 100 men." N 32 21 30 51 / W 90 50 38 68; WPA Index: 254

2.6.24 Granite Stele, Bronze Tablet, Tyree Wooden Mortars. N 32 21 30 14 / W 90 50 36 16; WPA Index: 246

Union Avenue, North of the Shirley House

2.6.25 Unit Monument: Granite Obelisk, 124th Illinois VI, 1st Brigade; 3rd Division; 17th Corps. N 32 21 35 88 / W 90 50 25 44; WPA Index: 165

2.6.26 Unit Monument: Granite Obelisk, 31st Illinois VI, 1st Brigade; 3rd Division; 17th Corps. N 32 21 36 83 / W 90 50 24 26 WPA Index: 167

2.6.27 Unit Monument: Granite Obelisk, 20th Illinois VI, 1st Brigade; 3rd Division; 17th Corps. N 32 21 38 41 / W 90 50 22 98; WPA Index: 170

2.6.28 Unit Monument: Granite Stele, 23rd Indiana VI, 1st Brigade; 3rd Division; 17th Corps. N 32 21 40 40 / W 90 50 22 42; WPA Index: 172

2.6.29 Granite Tablet, 23rd Indiana VI, Camp, May 20–July 4. N 32 21 40 07 / W 90 50 21 78; WPA Index: 173

East of Confederate Avenue, North of the Glass Bayou Bridge

2.6.30 Granite Tablet, 72nd Illinois VI, Sharpshooters Line, May 23–July 4. N 32 21 50 21 / W 90 50 42 84; WPA Index: 320

2.6.31 Granite Tablet, 95th Illinois VI, Sharpshooters Line, May 23–July 4. N 32 21 51 86 / W 90 50 42 41; WPA Index: 321

2.6.32 Granite Tablet, 95th Illinois VI, May 19 Assault (K 8, W 54, T 62) (250 feet east of Confederate Avenue midway between Park Tour Stop 10 and the Glass Bayou Bridge [NPS]). WPA Index: 308

Ransom's Gun Path, Off Union Avenue

Tour Stop 4: Ransom's Gun Path:

The hilly terrain made it difficult for the Union commanders to establish adequate artillery emplacements. Along this part of the line, the Federal infantry, commanded by Brigadier General Thomas E. G. Ransom, required additional support. To provide it, artillerymen belonging to the 2nd Illinois Light Artillery dismantled two of their cannon (12-pounders) and, with the assistance of some of Ransom's infantrymen, dragged the guns over the hills to an earthwork about 100 yards from the Confederate trenches. Once reassembled, the cannon resumed bombarding the Southern lines.

2.6.33 Unit Monument: Granite Stele, Bronze Tablet: 1st Minnesota Lt. Artillery, 6th Division; 17th Corps. N 32 21 48 86 / W 90 50 29 42; WPA Index: 322

2.6.34 Bust, Brig. Gen. John McArthur, US Vols., Colonel, 12th Illinois VI, commanding 6th Division; 17th Corps (Sculptor: George E. Ganiere, 1919). N 32 21 49 57 / W 90 50 29 16; WPA Index: 323

2.6.35 Bust, Brig. Gen. Thomas E. G. Ransom, US Vols., commanding 2nd Brigade, 6th Division; 17th Corps (Sculptor: George T. Brewster, 1916). N 32 21 51 05 / W 90 50 30 16; WPA Index: 325

2.6.36 Unit Monument: Granite Obelisk, 11th Illinois VI, 2nd Brigade; 6th Division; 17th Corps. N 32 21 52 41 / W 90 50 30 30; WPA Index: 326

Ransom's Gun Path, Union Trench Line, South to North

2.6.37 Granite Tablet, 11th Illinois VI, Sharpshooters Line, June 16–July 4. N 32 21 50 39 / W 90 50 33 29; WPA Index: 300

2.6.38 Granite Tablet, 11th Illinois VI, May 19 Assault (W 12). N 32 21 51 95 / W 90 50 32 78; WPA Index: 318

2.6.39 Granite Tablet, 72nd Illinois VI Sharpshooters Line, June 18–July 4. N 32 21 52 80 / W 90 50 31 22; WPA Index: 310

2.6.40 Granite Obelisk, Battery F, 2nd Illinois Lt. Artillery. Capt. John W. Powell. 6th Division; 17th Corps. N 32 21 53 94 / W 90 50 29 34; WPA Index: 327

2.6.41 Unit Monument: Granite Obelisk, 14th Wisconsin VI, 2nd Brigade; 6th Division; 17th Corps. N 32 21 54 61 / W 90 50 28 88; WPA Index: 329

2.6.42 Unit Monument: Granite Obelisk, 17th Wisconsin VI, 2nd Brigade; 6th Division; 17th Corps. N 32 21 55 30 / W 90 50 28 52; WPA Index: 330

2.6.43 Granite Tablet, 72nd Illinois VI, May 22 Assault (K 22, W 73, M 5, T 96). N 32 21 55 93 / W 90 50 28 24; WPA Index: 349

Union Avenue

2.7.1 Wisconsin State Memorial (Sculptor: Julius C. Loester, 1911). N 32 21 53 37 / W 90 50 26 38; WPA Index: 334 (See chap. 1.)

2.7.2 Unit Monument: Granite Stele, 10th Ohio Lt. Artillery, 6th Division; 17th Corps. N 32 21 53 27 / W 90 50 24 26; WPA Index: 335

2.7.3 Bust, Brig. Gen. Marcellus M. Crocker, US Vols., commanding 3rd Brigade, 6th Division /7th Division (Sculptor: T. A. R. Kitson, 1913). N 32 21 53 62 / W 90 50 22 88; WPA Index: 336

2.7.4 Unit Monument: Granite Columns and Arch with Bronze Tablets: 11th, 13th, 15th, 17th Iowa VI: 3rd Brigade; 6th Division; 17th Corps. N 32 21 54 51 / W 90 50 21 52; WPA Index: 338

2.7.5 Relief Portrait, Col. Alexander Chambers, US Vols., 16th Iowa VI, commanding 3rd Brigade, 6th Division; 17th Corps (Sculptor: T. A. R. Kitson, 1918). N 32 21 53 99 / W 90 50 21 32; WPA Index: 343

2.7.6 Relief Portrait, Col. William Hall, US Vols., 11th Iowa VI, commanding 3rd Brigade, 6th Division; 17th Corps, May 2–June 5 (Sculptor: T. A. R. Kitson, 1915). N 32 21 54 61 / W 90 50 21 32; WPA Index: 342

2.7.7 Unit Monument: Granite Stele, Bronze Tablet: 1st Missouri Lt. Artillery, Battery C, US 6th Division; 17th Corps. N 32 21 55 64 / W 90 50 21 10; WPA Index: 346

2.7.8 Unit Monument: Granite Obelisk, 11th Illinois Vol. Cavalry, Co G, 6th Division; 17th Corps (Escort at Division Headquarters). N 32 21 57 99 / W 90 50 19 24; WPA Index: 347

Granite Tablet, 113th Illinois VI (Detachments); 1st Brigade; 2nd Division; 15th Corps, Sharpshooters Line, May 23–July 4. Erosion control work by the federal government's Civilian Conservation Corps in the 1930s led to the planting of thousands of tree seedlings that dominate much of the landscape today.

2.7.9 Unit Monument: Granite Obelisk, 95th Illinois VI, 2nd Brigade; 6th Division; 17th Corps. N 32 21 59 83 / W 90 50 16 58; WPA Index: 348

2.7.10 Unit Monument: Granite Obelisk, 72nd Illinois VI, 2nd Brigade; 6th Division; 17th Corps. N 32 22 03 51 / W 90 50 17 20; WPA Index: 349

2.7.11 Granite Tablet, 11th Illinois VI, May 22 Assault (K 3, W 30, M 9, T 42). N 32 21 58 50 / W 90 50 44 16; WPA Index: 351

2.7.12 Granite Tablet, 113th Illinois VI (Detachments), Sharpshooters Line, May 23–July 4. N 32 22 58 82 / W 90 50 37 53; WPA Index: 359

2.7.13 Granite Stele, 17th Wisconsin VI, May 19 Assault, Marks farthest advance. N 32 22 37 57 / W 90 50 59 58; WPA Index: 361

2.7.14 Granite Tablet, 116th Illinois VI, May 22 Assault (K 1, W 8, T 9) N 32 22 06 47 / W 90 50 38 23; WPA Index: 384

2.7.15 Granite Tablet, 113th Illinois VI, Companies A, B, E, G and H, May 22 Assault (K 7, W 20, T 27) (east of Confederate Avenue near the Missouri Memorial) N 32 22 06 07 / W 90 50 38 56; WPA Index: 389

Wooded Ravine, South of Graveyard Road

2.7.16 Granite Tablet, 116th Illinois VI, Campground during siege. N 32 22 06 07 / W 90 50 33 28; WPA Index: 394

2.7.17 Granite Tablet, 113th Illinois VI (Detachment), Companies A, B, E, G, and H, Campground during siege. N 32 22 07 29 / W 90 50 32 92; WPA Index: 391

2.7.18 Granite Stele, Bronze Tablet: 4th West Virginia VI, Camp, May 22–July 4. N 32 22 06 32 / W 90 50 32 70; WPA Index: 396

Union Avenue

2.7.19 Unit Monument: Granite Obelisk, 116th Illinois VI, 1st Brigade; 2nd Division; 15 Corps. N 32 22 06 32 / W 90 50 23 08; WPA Index: 410

2.7.20 Unit Monument: Granite Obelisk, 113th Illinois VI, Detachment, 1st Brigade; 2nd Division; 15th Corps. N 32 22 07 84 / W 90 50 23 44; WPA Index: 411

2.7.21 Bust, Col. Giles A. Smith, US Vols., 8th Missouri VI, commanding 1st Brigade, 2nd Division; 15th Corps (Sculptor: Solon Borglum, 1913). N 32 22 08 91 / W 90 50 23 90; WPA Index: 412

2.7.22 Granite Stele, Bronze Tablet: 6th, 8th Missouri VI; 10th Missouri Vol. Cavalry, 2nd Division; 15th Corps. N 32 22 09 59 / W 90 50 25 28; WPA Index: 413

2.7.23 Unit Monument: Granite Stele, Bronze Tablet, 1st Battalion, 13th US Infantry; 1st Brigade; 2nd Division; 15th Corps. N 32 22 10 99 / W 90 50 25 90; WPA Index: 414

2.8.1 Bust, State of West Virginia, Maj. Arza M. Goodspeed, 4th West Virginia VI, 2nd Brigade, 2nd Division; 15th Corps (Sculptor: Aristide B. Cianfarani, 1922). N 32 22 12 19 / W 90 50 25 58; WPA Index: 416 (See chap. 1.)

2.8.2 Unit Monument: Granite Obelisk, 1st Illinois Lt. Artillery, Battery H. N 32 22 11 75 / W 90 50 25 68; WPA Index: 418

2.8.3 Relief Portrait, Brig. Gen. Hugh Ewing, US Vols., commanding 3rd Brigade, 2nd Division; 15th Corps (Sculptor: T. A. R. Kitson, 1911). N 32 22 13 30 / W 90 50 23 90; WPA Index: 422

2.8.4 Unit Monument: Granite Stele: Relief of Common Soldier Bearing Rifle: 47th Ohio VI, 3rd Brigade; 2nd Division; 15th Corps. N 32 22 13 40 / W 90 50 26 18; WPA Index: 421

2.8.5 Granite Tablet, 33rd Indiana VI, May 19 Assault (K 1, W 5, T 6). N 32 22 14 04 / W 90 50 26 52; WPA Index: 423

2.8.6 Unit Monument: Granite Stele: Relief of Crossed Muskets and Laurel Wreath: 37th Ohio VI, 3rd Brigade; 2nd Division; 15th Corps. N 32 22 15 07 / W 90 50 27 06; WPA Index: 426

2.8.7 Unit Monument: Granite Stele: Common Soldier Bearing Flag, in High Relief, 30th Ohio VI, 3rd Brigade; 2nd Division; 15th Corps. N 32 22 16 12 / W 90 50 27 62; WPA Index: 435

2.8.8 Relief Portrait, Col. Joseph Cockerill, US Vols., 70th Ohio VI, commanding 3rd Brigade; 1st Division; 16th Corps (Sculptor: T. A. R. Kitson, 1918). N 32 22 16 62 / W 90 50 27 42; WPA Index: 696

2.8.9 Unit Monument: Granite Obelisk, Battery B, 1st Illinois Lt. Artillery. N 32 22 17 27 / W 90 50 26 12; WPA Index: 436

2.8.10 Bust, Maj. Gen. Francis P. Blair, US Vols., commanding 2nd Division; 15th Corps (Sculptor: William Couper, 1911). N 32 22 17 45 / W 90 50 25 04; WPA Index: 437

2.8.11 Unit Monument: Granite Obelisk, Thielemann's Vol. Cavalry Battalion, Companies A and B, 2nd Division, 15th Corps. N 32 22 17 89 / W 90 50 23 38; WPA Index: 532

2.8.12 Bronze Tablet, 35th Iowa VI, May 22 Assault (casualties not listed). N 32 22 18 41 / W 90 50 22 80; WPA Index: 535

2.8.13 Bronze Tablet, 8th Iowa VI, Sharpshooters Line, May 22–June 1. N 32 22 18 75 / W 90 50 22 40; WPA Index: 538

2.8.14 Unit Monument: Granite Stele with Common Soldier Relief, 57th Ohio VI, 2nd Brigade; 2nd Division, 15th Corps. N 32 22 19 58 / W 90 50 21 84; WPA Index: 536

2.8.15 Unit Monument: Granite Stele and Bronze Tablet with Surmounting Arch, 83rd Indiana VI, 2nd Brigade; 2nd Division; 15th Corps. N 32 22 20 26 / W 90 50 21 44; WPA Index: 537

Unit Monument: Granite Stele, with Common Soldier Relief, 54th Ohio VI, 2nd Brigade; 2nd Division; 15th Corps; Lieut. Col. Cyrus W. Fisher. (Reported casualties in regiment during the campaign and siege, K 3, W 17, T 20).

2.8.16 Unit Monument: Granite Stele with Common Soldier Relief, 54th Ohio VI, 2nd Brigade; 2nd Division; 15th Corps. N 32 22 21 06 / W 90 50 20 50; WPA Index: 539

2.8.17 Unit Monument: Granite Obelisk, 127th Illinois VI, 2nd Brigade; 2nd Division; 15th Corps. N 32 22 23 43 / W 90 50 20 14; WPA Index: 541

2.8.18 Unit Monument: Granite Obelisk, 55th Illinois VI, 2nd Brigade; 2nd Division; 15th Corps. N 32 22 24 84 / W 90 50 19 94; WPA Index: 542

Corner: Union Avenue and Grant Avenue

2.8.19 Site for monument to Maj. Gen. William T. Sherman: Not installed. WPA Index: 542

Grant Avenue

2.8.20 Unit Monument: Granite Minié Bullet, 53rd Ohio VI, 3rd Brigade; 1st Division; 16th Corps. N 32 22 28 02 / W 90 50 18 56; WPA Index: 698

2.8.21 Unit Monument: Granite Column, 70th Ohio VI, 3rd Brigade; 1st Division; 16th Corps. N 32 22 28 19 / W 90 50 17 86; WPA Index: 697

2.8.22 Statue, Maj. Gen. Cadwallader C. Washburn, US Vols., 2nd Wisconsin Vol. Cavalry, commanding detachment, 16th Corps (Sculptor: George T. Brewster, 1919). N 32 22 28 41 / W 90 50 16 70; WPA Index: 716

2.8.23 Unit Monument: Granite Stele: Shaft with Twin Columns in High Relief and Surmounting Arch: 58th Ohio VI, 1st Brigade; 1st Division; 15th Corps. N 32 22 28 67 / W 90 50 16 36; WPA Index: 718

2.8.24 Relief Portrait, Col. Milton Montgomery, US Vols., 25th Wisconsin VI, commanding Brigade, Provisional Division; 16th Corps (Sculptor: T. A. R. Kitson, 1913). N 32 22 28 96 / W 90 50 14 78; WPA Index: 719

2.8.25 Unit Monument: Granite Stele, 16th, 25th, 27th Wisconsin VI, 2nd Wisconsin Vol. Cavalry: outposts and exterior lines, 16th and 17th Corps (Sculptor: Roland H. Perry, 1916). N 32 22 28 87 / W 90 50 14 04; WPA Index: 720

2.8.26 Relief Portrait, Col. George W. Neely, US Vols., 131st Illinois VI, commanding detached brigade, District of Northeast Louisiana (Sculptor: R. Hinton Perry, 1916). N 32 22 28 61 / W 90 50 12 50; WPA Index: 721

2.8.27 Bust, Brig. Gen., Elias S. Dennis, US Vols., commanding District of Northeast Louisiana (Sculptor: George T. Brewster, 1915). N 32 22 29 44 / W 90 50 07 46; WPA Index: 722

2.8.28 Unit Monument: Granite Obelisk, 10th Illinois Vol. Cavalry, Detached Brigade; District of Northeast Louisiana. N 32 22 29 02 / W 90 50 06 14; WPA Index: 723

2.8.29 Relief Portrait, Col., Isaac F. Shepard, US Vols., 3rd Missouri VI, commanding African Brigade, District of Northeast Louisiana (Sculptor: Roland H. Perry, 1916). N 32 22 28 82 / W 90 50 05 66; WPA Index: 724

2.8.30 Relief Portrait, Brig. Gen. Hugh T. Reid, US Vols., commanding 1st Brigade, 6th Division; 17th Corps (Sculptor: Anton Schaaf, 1915). N 32 22 27 79 / W 90 50 03 94; WPA Index: 725

2.9.1 State of Kansas Monument (Sculptor: unknown, 1960). N 32 22 27 17 / W 90 50 01 66; WPA Index: 727 (See chap. 1.)

2.10.1 State of Mississippi: African American Monument (Sculptor: Kim Sessums, 2004). N 32 22 26 65 / W 90 50 00 28; WPA Index: n.a. (See chap. 1.)

2.10.2 Unit Monument: Granite Obelisk, 131st Illinois VI, Detached Brigade; District of Northeast Louisiana. N 32 22 26 79 / W 90 50 59 40; WPA Index: 729

2.10.3 Relief Portrait, Col. Cyrus Bussey, US Vols., 3rd Iowa Vol. Cavalry, commanding unattached cavalry, Army of the Tennessee (Sculptor: Francis E. Elwell, 1911). N 32 22 26 90 / W 90 50 57 62; WPA Index: 730

2.10.4 Unit Monument: Granite Obelisk, 120th Illinois VI, Detached Brigade; District of Northeast Louisiana. N 32 22 26 99 / W 90 50 57 08; WPA Index: 731

Close-up of the civilian in the trio of figures on the state of Mississippi's African American Monument: moving forward, as it were, but mindful of the past.

2.10.5 Bust, Brig. Gen. Robert B. Potter, US Vols., commanding 2nd Division, 9th Corps (Sculptor: R. Hinton Perry, 1914). N 32 22 27 51 / W 90 50 55 84; WPA Index: 732

2.10.6 Bust, Brig. Gen. William S. Smith, US Vols., commanding 1st Division; 16th Corps (Sculptor: Solon Borglum, 1913). N 32 22 28 37 / W 90 50 55 20; WPA Index: 733

2.10.7 Bust, Brig. Gen. Nathan Kimball, US Vols., commanding Provisional Division; 16th Corps (Sculptor: George T. Brewster, 1915). N 32 22 28 66 / W 90 50 54 68; WPA Index: 734

2.10.8 Unit Monument: Granite Obelisk, 18th Illinois VI, Richmond's Brigade; Provisional Division; 16th Corps. N 32 22 29 02 / W 90 50 54 32; WPA Index: 686

2.10.9 Unit Monument: Granite Obelisk, 48th Illinois VI, 4th Brigade; 1st Division; 16th Corps. N 32 22 29 15 / W 90 50 54 10; WPA Index: 694

2.10.10 Unit Monument: Granite Obelisk, 63rd Illinois VI, Detached Brigade; District of Northeast Louisiana. N 32 22 30 04 / W 90 50 53 72; WPA Index: 736

2.10.11 Bust, Brig. Gen. Edward Ferrero, US Vols., commanding 2nd Brigade; 2nd Division; 9th Corps (Sculptor: T. A. R. Kitson, 1915). N 32 22 30 38 / W 90 50 53 28; WPA Index: 737

2.10.12 Unit Monument: Granite Stele, Bronze Tablet, 2nd US Lt. Artillery, Battery E, 9th Corps. N 32 22 31 29 / W 90 50 53 78; WPA Index: 738

2.10.13 Unit Monument: Granite Obelisk, 5th Illinois Vol. Cavalry, Unattached Unit. N 32 22 32 03 / W 90 50 54 38; WPA Index: 739

2.10.14 Relief Portrait, Capt. Cyrus B. Comstock, US Vols., Chief Engineer, Army of the Tennessee (Sculptor: T. A. R. Kitson, 1910). N 32 22 32 87 / W 90 50 55 62; WPA Index: 740

2.10.15 Unit Monument: Granite Obelisk, 29th Illinois VI (Detachment), Companies D and K, Army of the Tennessee. N 32 22 32 86 / W 90 50 56 20; WPA Index: 741

2.11.1 The Rhode Island State Memorial (Sculptor: Frank E. Elwell, 1908). N 32 22 33 54 / W 90 49 56 38; WPA Index: 742 (See chap. 1.)

2.11.2 Unit Monument: Granite Stele, Bronze Tablet: Missouri Engineer Regiment of the West. N 32 22 33 45 / W 90 49 57 94; WPA Index: 743

2.11.3 Relief Portrait, Col. William W. Sanford, US Vols., 48th Illinois VI, commanding 4th Brigade; 1st Division; 16th Corps (Sculptor: T. A. R. Kitson, 1918). N 32 22 33 76 / W 90 49 57 84; WPA Index: 695

2.11.4 Relief Portrait, Capt. Frederick Prime, US Vols., Chief Engineer, Army of the Tennessee (Sculptor: T. A. R. Kitson, 1911; stolen and re-placed, 1971; Gary Predit, sculptor of replacement). N 32 22 33 93 / W 90 49 58 26; WPA Index: 744

2.11.5 Relief Portrait, 1st Lieut. James H. Wilson, US Vols., Topographical Engineer, Army of the Tennessee (Sculptor: T. A. R. Kitson, 1910). N 32 22 34 02 / W 90 49 58 58; WPA Index: 745

2.12.1 The New York State Memorial (Designer: A. J. Zabriskie, 1917). N 32 22 34 59 / W 90 49 59 96; WPA Index: 747 (See chap. 1.)

2.12.2 Relief Portrait, Lt. Col. John A. Rawlins, US Vols.; Assistant Adjutant General, Army of the Tennessee (Sculptor: T. A. R. Kitson, 1911). N 32 22 36 02 / W 90 49 59 46; WPA Index: 749

2.12.3 Unit Monument: Granite Obelisk, 101st Illinois VI, Companies A, D, G, H and K, various commands, Army of the Tennessee. N 32 22 36 98 / W 90 49 59 40; WPA Index: 750

2.12.4 Unit Monument: Granite Stele, 4th Illinois Vol. Cavalry, Co A. Escort at Headquarters, Army of the Tennessee. N 32 22 37 02 / W 90 49 59 54; WPA Index: 751

2.13.1 The Massachusetts State Memorial (Sculptor: T. A. R. Kitson, 1903). N 32 22 37 39 / W 90 49 59 62; WPA Index 752 (See chap. 1.)

The Massachusetts Memorial: Close-up of T. A. R. Kitson's 1903 sculpture.

2.13.2 Relief Portrait, Col. Simon G. Griffin, US Vols., 6th New Hampshire VI, commanding 1st Brigade, 2nd Division, 9th Corps (Sculptor: Anton Schaaf, 1915). N 32 22 38 35 / W 90 49 00 14; WPA Index: 782

2.14.1 New Hampshire State Memorial (Sculptor: unknown, 1904). N 32 22 38 25 / W 90 50 01 24; WPA Index: 786 (See chap. 1.)

2.15.1 State of Pennsylvania Memorial (Designers: Albert B. Ross, Charles A. Lopez, 1906). N 32 22 40 29 / W 90 50 01 00; WPA Index: 777 (See chap. .)

2.15.2 Bust, Andrew Gregg Curtin, Pennsylvania Governor, 1861–1867 (Sculptor: R. Tait McKenzie, 1930). N 32 22 40 29 / W 90 50 01 00; WPA Index: 778

2.15.3 Bust, Maj. Gen. John Grubb Parke, US Vols., commanding 9th Army Corps (Sculptor: R. Tait McKenzie, 1930). N 32 22 38 44 / W 90 50 01 56; WPA Index: 776

2.15.4 Bust, Brig. Gen. Thomas Welsh, US Vols., commanding 1st Division, 9th Corps (Sculptor: Roland H. Perry, 1913). N 32 22 38 69 / W 90 50 01 06; WPA Index: 775

2.15.5 Maj. Gen. Ulysses S. Grant (Sculptor: Frederick Hibbard, 1918). N 32 22 37 98 / W 90 50 04 11; WPA Index: 742 (See chap. 1.)

Sherman Circle

WPA Index: 711: "U.S. Headquarters 15th Corps; Army of the Tennessee. Maj. Gen. William T. Sherman. May 19–June 23, 1863. From June 23 to July 4 General Sherman was in command of the force deployed on the exterior line from Big Black River Bridge on the right to Haynes' Bluff on the left and headquarters of the 15th Corps were near Bear Creek."

2.15.6 Unit Monument: Stele with Granite Columns and Arch, with Bronze Tablets: 6th, 40th Iowa VI, 4th Brigade; 1st Division; 16th Corps. N 32 22 35 78 / W 90 50 15 88; WPA Index: 708

2.15.7 Unit Monument: Four-Sided Granite Shaft, with Bronze Tablets and Surmounting Capstone: 12th, 99th, 100th, 97th Indiana VI, 16th Corps. N 32 22 35 33 / W 90 50 14 18; WPA Index: 709

2.15.8 Unit Monument: Granite Stele, Bronze Tablet, 6th Battery Indiana Lt. Artillery, 1st Division; 16th Corps. N 32 22 35 05 / W 90 50 13 64; WPA Index: 710

2.15.9 Unit Monument: Granite Columns and Arch with Bronze Tablets: 3rd Iowa Vol. Cavalry, Unattached; 4th Iowa Vol. Cavalry, 15th Corps. N 32 22 46 88 / W 90 50 15 52; WPA Index: 707

Four-Sided Granite Shaft, with Bronze Tablets and Surmounting Capstone: 12th, 99th, 100th, 97th Indiana VI, 16th Corps. These regiments served on the exterior line at various locations from about June 12 to the end of the siege, July 4, 1863.

2.15.10 Unit Monument: Granite Obelisk, 26th Illinois VI, 1st Brigade; 1st Division; 16th Corps. N 32 22 27 25 / W 90 50 15 47; WPA Index: 704

2.15.11 Relief Portrait, Col., John M. Loomis, 26th Illinois VI, commanding 1st Brigade; 1st Division; 16th Corps (Sculptor: T. A. R. Kitson, 1918). N 32 22 37 09 / W 90 50 15 42; WPA Index: 705

Short Sherman, off Sherman Avenue: Off NPS Grounds

The road formerly extended to the park at Sherman Circle. The property was quitclaimed to the county in the 1960s. Monuments formerly located on Sherman Avenue were moved to Union Avenue; a portion of the road was closed and is now given over to woods and undergrowth.

2.15.12 Relief Portrait, Col. Stephen G. Hicks, US Vols., 40th Illinois VI (Sculptor: Bruce W. Saville, 1916). N 32 22 49 01 / W 90 50 19 18; WPA Index: 701

2.15.13 Unit Monument: Stele, 40th Illinois VI, 2nd Brigade; 1st Division; 16th Corps. N 32 22 48 14 / W 90 50 19 26; WPA Index: 702

Union Avenue, Corner of Grant Avenue—Traveling West

2.15.14 Unit Monument: Granite Obelisk, Battery F, 1st Illinois Lt. Artillery, 1st Division; 16th Corps. N 32 22 29 92 / W 90 50 21 74; WPA Index: 693

2.15.15 Unit Monument: Granite Obelisk, 103rd Illinois VI, 2nd Brigade; 1st Division; 16th Corps. N 32 22 29 92 / W 90 50 22 14; WPA Index: 699

2.15.16 Unit Monument: Column Surmounted by Eagle, 22nd Ohio VI, Richmond's Brigade; Kimball's Provisional Division, 16th Corps. N 32 22 29 70 / W 90 50 23 08; WPA Index: 682

2.15.17 Unit Monument: Granite Obelisk, 90th Illinois VI, 1st Brigade; 1st Division; 16th Corps. N 32 22 29 56 / W 90 50 23 38; WPA Index: 703

2.15.18 Unit Monument: Granite Obelisk, Cogswell's Battery, Illinois Lt. Artillery; 1st Division; 16th Corps. N 32 22 29 35 / W 90 50 23 44; WPA Index: 691

2.15.19 Unit Monument: Granite Obelisk, 8th Wisconsin VI, 2nd Brigade; 3rd Division; 15th Corps. N 32 22 27 64 / W 90 50 25 90; WPA Index: 548

2.15.20 Unit Monument: Granite Stele, Bronze Tablet: 5th Minnesota VI, 2nd Brigade; 3rd Division; 15th Corps. N 32 22 27 89 / W 90 50 28 66; WPA Index: 549

2.15.21 Unit Monument: Granite Obelisk, 47th Illinois VI, 2nd Brigade; 3rd Division; 15th Corps. N 32 22 28 41 / W 90 50 31 62; WPA Index: 552

2.15.22 Unit Monument: Granite Stele, Bronze Tablet: 11th Missouri VI, 2nd Brigade; 3rd Division; 15th Corps. N 32 22 28 98 / W 90 50 32 84; WPA Index: 553

2.15.23 Bust, Brig. Gen. James M. Tuttle, US Vols., commanding 3rd Division; 15th Corps (Sculptor: T. A. R. Kitson, 1912). N 32 22 31 14 / W 90 50 35 52; WPA Index: 555

2.15.24 Bust, Brig. Gen. Ralph P. Buckland, US Vols., commanding 1st Brigade, 3rd Division, 15th Corps (Sculptor: Henry Kitson, 1915). N 32 22 30 93 / W 90 50 37 40; WPA Index: 556

2.15.25 Unit Monument: Granite Obelisk, 114th Illinois VI, 1st Brigade; 3rd Division; 15th Corps. N 32 22 30 33 / W 90 50 38 68; WPA Index: 559

2.15.26 Unit Monument: Granite Tablet, 93rd Indiana VI, 1st Brigade; 3rd Division; 15th Corps. N 32 22 30 54 / W 90 50 38 62; WPA Index: 557

2.15.27 Granite Tablet, 114th Illinois VI, Sharpshooters Line, May 23–June 4. N 32 22 29 57 / W 90 50 39 18; WPA Index: 560

2.15.28 Unit Monument: Granite Tablet, 93rd Indiana VI, Sharpshooters Line, May 23–June 22. N 32 22 29 02 / W 90 50 41 84; WPA Index: 562

2.15.29 Unit Monument: Granite Stele, 93rd Indiana VI; 1st Brigade; 3rd Division; 15th Corps. N 32 22 29 23 / W 90 50 40 42; WPA Index: 564

2.15.30 Unit Monument: Granite Stele, 72nd Ohio VI, 1st Brigade; 3rd Division; 15th Corps. N 32 22 27 34 / W 90 50 44 72; WPA Index: 567

2.15.31 Relief Portrait, Col. William McMillan, US Vols., 95th Ohio VI, commanding 1st Brigade, 3rd Division; 15th Corps (Sculptor: T. A. R. Kitson, 1915). N 32 22 26 99 / W 90 50 46 70; WPA Index: 572

Granite Stele, Relief of Common Soldier as Sharpshooter, 72nd Ohio VI, 1st Brigade; 3rd Division; 15th Corps. Engaged on the siege line and in the assaults of May 19 and May 22. Aggregate reported casualties in regiment during the campaign and siege, K 1, W 16, T 17.

2.15.32 Unit Monument: Granite Stele, 95th Ohio VI, 1st Brigade; 3rd Division; 15th Corps. N 32 22 26 95 / W 90 50 47 12; WPA Index: 571

2.15.33 Granite Stele, 30th Ohio VI, May 19 Assault, Marks Farthest Advance. N 32 22 24 82 / W 90 50 47 45; WPA Index: 574

2.15.34 Unit Monument: Granite Obelisk, 1st Illinois Lt. Artillery, Battery I, 1st Division; 16th Corps. N 32 22 26 86 / W 90 50 47 56; WPA Index: 692

2.15.35 Unit Monument: In Granite: Three Upturned Cannon Barrels Surmounting Base, 4th Ohio Battery, Lt. Artillery, 1st Division; 15th Corps. N 32 22 26 14 / W 90 50 49 44; WPA Index: 576

2.15.36 Unit Monument: Granite Obelisk, 43rd Illinois VI, Engelmann's Brigade; Provisional Division; 16th Corps. N 32 22 26 07 / W 90 50 50 08; WPA Index: 689

2.15.37 Bronze Tablet, 30th Iowa VI, Sharpshooters Line, May 23–July 4. N 32 22 25 44 / W 90 50 52 55; WPA Index: 579

2.15.38 Unit Monument: Granite Columns and Arch with Bronze Tablets: 4th, 9th, 26th, 30th Iowa VI, 3rd Brigade; 1st Division; 15th Corps. N 32 22 26 62 / W 90 50 53 78; WPA Index: 580

2.15.39 Granite Stele, Bronze Tablet: 31st Missouri VI, May 22 Assault (K 1, W 1, T 2). N 32 22 27 64 / W 90 50 53 53 62; WPA Index: 585

2.15.40 Granite Stele, Bronze Tablet: 30th Missouri VI, May 22 Assault (W 3). N 32 22 28 75 / W 90 50 53 55 30; WPA Index: 586

2.15.41 Relief Portrait, Maj. Gustavus Lightfoot, US Vols., 12th Missouri VI, Killed in action, May 22, 1863 (Sculptor: Henry Kitson, 1914). N 32 22 27 10 / W 90 50 59 22; WPA Index: 589

Thayer's Approach

Tour Stop 6: Thayer's Approach:

Union soldiers commanded by Brig. Gen. John M. Thayer, took part in unsuccessful assaults on May 19 and May 22. During those attacks, Thayer's men advanced up the hill only to be driven back by Confederates positioned at the top. After the second repulse, the Federals began digging a six-foot-deep approach trench. To prevent Thayer's men from exposure to Confederate fire, a short tunnel was excavated through the ridgeline protecting the Union forces. Once the Federals broke through the ridge, under cover of darkness, they were able to begin digging the approach trench toward the Southern position. Once close enough to the Confederate works atop the hill, the intent was to start a mine under the defensive position, similar to the one being dug under the Third Louisiana Redan. The men digging the approach trench were protected from Confederate fire by bundles of cane called *fascines*, which served as a roof over the trench. Thayer's soldiers had nearly completed the mine when Vicksburg surrendered.

2.15.42 Bronze Tablet, 9th Iowa VI, May 19 Assault (K 4, W 12, T 16). N 32 22 25 52 / W 90 50 58 78; WPA Index: 594

2.15.43 Granite Tablet, 13th Illinois VI, May 22 Assault (K 1, W 1, T 2). N 32 22 25 23 / W 90 50 59 36; WPA Index: 592

2.15.44 Bronze Tablet, 26th Iowa VI, Sharpshooters Line, May 23–July 4. N 32 22 25 32 / W 90 50 00 44; WPA Index: 583

Union Avenue

2.15.45 Relief Portrait, Col. Adolph Engelmann, US Vols., 43rd Illinois VI, commanding Brigade, Prov. Division; 16th Corps (Sculptor: Bruce W. Saville, 1916). N 32 22 29 84 / W 90 51 09 08; WPA Index: 690

2.15.46 Bust, Brig. Gen. John Thayer, US Vols., 3rd Brigade, 1st Division, 15th Corps (Sculptor: T. A. R. Kitson, 1915). N 32 22 30 56 / W 90 51 10 34; WPA Index: 612

2.15.47 Granite Obelisk, 106th Illinois VI, Engelmann's Brigade; Provisional Division; 16th Corps—exterior line. N 32 22 32 65 / W 90 51 15 16; WPA Index: 687

2.15.48 Bronze Tablet, Iowa 1st Battery, 1st Division; 15th Corps. N 32 22 36 58 / W 90 51 20 52; WPA Index: 625

2.15.49 Relief Portrait, Col. Bernard C. Farrar, US Vols., 30th Missouri VI, commanding 1st Brigade; 1st Division; 15th Corps (Sculptor: George E. Ganiere, 1914). N 32 22 36 99 / W 90 51 20 16; WPA Index: 624

2.15.50 Granite Stele, Bronze Tablet: 32nd Missouri VI, Sharpshooters Line, June 5–July 4. N 32 22 36 84 / W 90 51 20 56; WPA Index: 626

2.15.51 Bronze Tablet, 4th Iowa VI, Sharpshooters Line, May 23–July 4. (Atop Bell Smith Ridge 1,800 feet past Park Tour Stop 6,250 feet north of Union Avenue [NPS]); WPA Index: 615

2.15.52 Bronze Tablet, 4th Iowa VI, May 19 Assault (W 13). (Atop Bell Smith Ridge 1,800 feet past Park Tour Stop 6,250 feet north of Union Avenue [NPS]); WPA Index: 617

2.15.53 Unit Monument: Stele, 46th Ohio VI, 2nd Brigade; 1st Division; 16th Corps. N 32 22 37 77 / W 90 51 21 44; WPA Index: 700

2.15.54 Granite Stele, Bronze Tablet: 31st Missouri VI, Sharpshooters Line, June 5–July 4. N 32 22 42 79 / W 90 51 29 72; WPA Index: 629

2.15.55 Unit Monument: Granite Obelisk, Illinois: Kane County Independent Vol. Cavalry. N 32 22 43 98 / W 90 51 31 06; WPA Index: 632

2.15.56 Granite Stele, Bronze Tablet: 30th Missouri VI, Companies B and K, May 19 Assault (K 1, W 6, T 7) [location coordinates n.a.]; WPA Index: 667

2.15.57 Granite Tablet, 3rd Illinois Vol. Cavalry, Company D, Headquarters Escort; 1st Division; 15th Corps. N 32 22 44 23 / W 90 51 31 48; WPA Index: 633

2.15.58 Relief Portrait, Col. Francis Manter, US Vols., 32nd Missouri VI, commanding 1st Brigade; 1st Division; 15th Corps (Sculptor: Allan G. Newman, 1916). N 32 22 44 06 / W 90 51 31 82; WPA Index: 634

2.15.59 Granite Stele, Bronze Tablet: 30th Missouri VI, Sharpshooters Line, June 5–July 4. N 32 22 44 06 / W 90 51 31 88; WPA Index: 630

2.15.60 Unit Monument: Granite Obelisk, 13th Illinois VI, 1st Brigade; 1st Division; 15th Corps. N 32 22 45 50 / W 90 51 37 38; WPA Index: 638

2.15.61 Granite Stele, 29th Missouri VI, Sharpshooters Line, June 5–July 4. N 32 22 44 67 / W 90 51 38 20; WPA Index: 639

2.15.62 Granite Stele, 27th Missouri VI, Sharpshooters Line, June 5–July 4. N 32 22 44 41 / W 90 51 38 92; WPA Index: 641

2.15.63 Granite Stele, Bronze Tablet: 17th Missouri VI, Sharpshooters Line, May 23–July 4. N 32 22 44 46 / W 90 51 39 88; WPA Index: 648

2.15.64 Unit Monument: Granite Obelisk, 54th Illinois VI, Richmond's Brigade; Provisional Division; 16th Corps. N 32 22 45 01 / W 90 51 40 62; WPA Index: 685

Granite Stele, Relief of Common Soldier in Camp, 46th Ohio VI, 2nd Brigade; 1st Division; 16th Corps. Regiment served on the exterior line from about June 12, 1863, until the end of the siege, July 4.

2.15.65 Relief Portrait, Col. Jonathan Richmond, 126th Illinois VI, commanding Brigade, Provisional Division; 16th Corps (Sculptor: Bruce W. Saville, 1916). N 32 22 44 89 / W 90 51 41 94; WPA Index: 684

2.15.66 Unit Monument: Granite Obelisk, 61st Illinois VI, Engelmann's Brigade; Provisional Division; 16th Corps—exterior line. N 32 22 42 28 / W 90 51 45 48; WPA Index: 688

2.15.67 Granite Stele, Bronze Tablet: 12th Missouri VI, Sharpshooters Line, May 23–July 4. N 32 22 38 53 / W 90 51 49 74; WPA Index: 651

2.15.68 Unit Monument: Granite Obelisk, 126th Illinois VI, Richmond's Brigade; Provisional Division; 16th Corps. N 32 22 38 56 / W 90 51 49 90; WPA Index: 683

2.16.1 The Navy Memorial (Designer: unknown; Sculptors: various; Dedicated: 1917). N 32 22 37 43 / W 90 51 50 28; WPA Index: 653 (See chap. 1.)

NPS tablet regarding US Campaign, Siege and Defense of Vicksburg, 1863:

Operations of the Union Navy, March 29–July 4. The Vicksburg campaign would not have been planned and could not have been conducted on the lines on which it was successfully made without the assistance of the U.S. Navy. About 26 gunboats and light-draughts of the Mississippi Squadron, with necessary attendants, Acting Rear Admiral David D. Porter commanding, and, during part of the time, the Mississippi Marine Brigade, Brig. Gen. Alfred W. Ellet commanding, co-operated with the army in the operations of the campaign and siege.

2.16.2 Unit Monument: Granite Stele, Bronze Tablet, US, Battery Selfridge: two eight-inch columbiads. N 32 22 34 96 / W 90 51 50 64; WPA Index: 654

Granite Stele, Relief of Common Soldier in Mourning: 76th Ohio VI, 2nd Brigade; 1st Division; 15th Corps. Engaged May 19 assault, May 22 assault; casualties during the campaign and siege, K 1, W 5, T 6.

Tour Stop 7: Battery Selfridge:

Battery Selfridge was the only battery containing cannon manned exclusively by sailors. The position, named after its commander, Lieutenant Commander Thomas O. Selfridge, Jr., now overlooks the current display and museum of the U.S.S. *Cairo*.

2.16.3 Unit Monument: Granite Stele, 76th Ohio VI, 2nd Brigade; 1st Division; 15th Corps. N 32 22 34 71 / W 90 51 52 42; WPA Index: 656

2.16.4 Unit Monument: Granite Stele, 8th Ohio Lt. Artillery, 2nd Division; 15th Corps. N 32 22 34 48 / W 90 51 53 04; WPA Index: 658

2.16.5 Bust, Lieutenant Commander Thomas O. Selfridge Jr., USN, commanding Battery Selfridge (Sculptor: Henry Kitson, 1913). N 32 22 34 13 / W 90 51 54 12; WPA Index: 661

2.16.6 Bust, Brig. Gen. Alfred W. Ellet, US Vols., commanding Marine Brigade (Sculptor: T. A. R. Kitson, 1915). N 32 22 32 97 / W 90 51 55 78; WPA Index: 664

2.16.7 Granite Stele, Bronze Tablet: 3rd Missouri VI, Sharpshooters Line, May 23–July 4. N 32 22 32 44 / W 90 51 56 18; WPA Index: 665

2.16.8 Bust, Col. Charles R. Woods, US Vols., 76th Ohio VI (Sculptor: T. A. R. Kitson, 1911). N 32 22 29 23 / W 90 51 58 88; WPA Index: 666

2.16.9 Statue, Maj. Gen. Frederick Steele, US Vols., commanding 1st Division; 15th Corps (Sculptor: Francis E. Elwell, 1908). N 32 22 29 01 / W 90 51 59 30; WPA Index: 669

2.16.10 Unit Monument: Granite Stele, Bronze Tablet: 30th Missouri VI, 1st Brigade; 1st Division; 15th Corps. N 32 22 28 68 / W 90 51 59 30; WPA Index: 667

2.16.11 Unit Monument: Granite Stele, Bronze Tablet: Missouri: Roster of units: 15th Corps; 1st Division; 1st Brigade: 2nd Lt. Artillery, Battery F, 27th, 29th, 30th, 31st, 32nd Missouri VI, 2nd Brigade: 3rd, 12th, 17th Missouri VI. N 32 22 28 37 / W 90 51 58 46; WPA Index: 668

Vicksburg National Cemetery

2.17.1 Arch, Vicksburg National Cemetery. N 32 22 23 49 31 / W 90 52 16 00 (See chap. 1.)

2.17.2 Unit Monument: Granite Columns and Arch with Bronze Tablets: 25th, 31st Iowa VI, 2nd Brigade; 1st Division; 15th Corps. N 32 22 24 08 / W 90 52 11 44; WPA Index: 677

2.17.3 Bronze Tablet, 31st Iowa VI, Sharpshooters Line, May 27–July 4. N 32 22 23 93 / W 90 52 11 16; WPA Index: 675

2.17.4 Bronze Tablet, 25th Iowa VI, Sharpshooters Line, May 27–July 4. N 32 22 24 75 / W 90 52 08 30; WPA Index: 676

2.17.5 Cannon: Self–Described Monument: Upturned Cannon Barrel. N 32 21 58 87 / W 90 51 34 22; WPA Index: n.a.

Fort Hill: Confederate Avenue, Looking South

Tour Stop 9: Fort Hill:

Fort Hill was the anchor of the left flank of the rear Confederate defense line. The fort's position was so strong that the Union Army did not even attempt an attack during the assaults of May 19 and 22. Overlooking the Mississippi River and the water battery located on the bank below, Fort Hill commanded the bend in the river north of the city.

Grant required naval assistance to carry out his plan to capture Vicksburg. Admiral David Dixon Porter assembled a fleet of seven ironclad gunboats, a ram, and three transports for his attempt to pass the city. The transports were fortified with bales of cotton and hay, while the ironclads, with coal barges lashed to their sides, would provide additional protection for the vulnerable vessels. These transports would be used to transfer the Union infantry from the west bank to the east bank of the Mississippi River. From Fort Hill you can observe the area where Admiral Porter's fleet began its run past the Vicksburg batteries.

On the night of April 16, the fleet steamed down the Mississippi River in single file, hugging the western shore in an effort to sneak by without being detected. But Confederate lookouts spotted the boats and sounded the alarm. Quickly, Southern batteries went into action. To aid the Confederate gunners, tar barrels were lit along the city's river bank and houses in the village of De Soto, LA, across the river, were set on fire. With that assistance, the Confederate artillery fire pounded the Union ships, but despite numerous hits, only one transport was sunk. The remainder of the fleet met Grant's infantry near Hard Times, LA, as planned.

During the siege, the Union ironclad and sister ship to the U.S.S. *Cairo*, the USS *Cincinnati*, was sunk by the combined fire of the water battery and other river batteries. The *Cincinnati* was eventually raised, refitted, and returned to service.

NPS notes further observe that the fort "was the northern anchor of the Confederate defense lines. As a Confederate fort, it was open to the rear, but after Union occupation, the earthwork was enclosed. The earthwork is square in shape, and the line of the parapet is easily determined. At the center of the fort was an excavation, probably a bombproof or a magazine. The depression left by the collapse of this excavation is still visible," but NPS sources describe the extant fort as being largely "a reconstruction, precise details are lacking."

2.17.6 Unit Monument: Granite Stele, Bronze Tablet: Tennessee River Batteries, Heavy Artillery. N 32 22 11 65 / W 90 52 10 34; WPA Index: 916

2.17.7 Unit Monument: Granite Stele, 14th Mississippi Lt. Artillery, Company C (Engaged, campaign and defense: casualties not listed). N 32 22 13 26 / W 90 52 07 04; WPA Index: 912

2.17.8 Unit Monument: Granite Stele, 6th Mississippi Infantry (Engaged, campaign and defense: casualties not listed). N 32 22 13 92 / W 90 52 06 36; WPA Index: 910

2.17.9 Relief Portrait: Brig. Gen. Jeptha V. Harris, CS Army, commanding Mississippi State Troops (Engaged, defense: casualties not listed) (Sculptor: George E. Ganiere, 1915). N 32 22 14 73 / W 90 52 03 34; WPA Index: 903

2.17.10 Unit Monument: Granite Stele, 3rd Battalion, Mississippi State Troops, Smith's Division (Engaged, defense: casualties not listed). N 32 22 14 93 / W 90 52 03 28; WPA Index: 902

2.17.11 Unit Monument: Granite Stele, 14th Mississippi Lt. Artillery, Company B, Smith's Division (Engaged, defense: casualties not listed). N 32 22 15 32 / W 90 52 02 04; WPA Index: 901

2.17.12 Unit Monument: Granite Stele, 5th Mississippi Infantry (Engaged, defense: casualties not listed). N 32 22 15 69 / W 90 52 00 26; WPA Index: 898

2.17.13 Relief Portrait, Brig. Gen. John G. Vaughn, CS Army, commanding brigade, Smith's Division (Sculptor: T. A. R. Kitson, 1911). N 32 52 15 87 / W 90 51 47 08; WPA Index: 886

2.17.14 Unit Monument: Granite Stele, Bronze Tablet: Smith's Division; Tennessee Battery; 60th, 61st, 62nd Infantry. N 32 22 16 45 / W 90 51 46 88; WPA Index: 885

2.17.15 Granite Stele, Bronze Tablet: CS 6th Missouri Infantry, Repulse of Union assault, May 19. N 32 22 16 83 / W 90 51 45 70; WPA Index: 883

2.17.16 Unit Monument: Granite Stele, 14th Mississippi Lt. Artillery, Company A, Smith's Division (Engaged, defense: casualties not listed). N 32 22 16 80 / W 90 51 45 02; WPA Index: 882

2.17.17 Bust, Brig. Gen. John Adams, CS Army, commanding 1st Brigade, Loring's Division, Johnston's Army (Sculptor: Anton Schaaf, 1915). N 32 22 16 83 / W 90 51 43 58; WPA Index: 878

2.17.18 Relief Portrait, Col. Randall W. McGavock, CS Army, 10th Tennessee Infantry, Killed in action, May 12 (Sculptor: George T. Brewster, 1919). N 32 22 16 80 / W 90 51 43 14; WPA Index: 887

2.18.1 Granite Stele, The Tennessee State Memorial (Sculptor: n.a., 1996). N 32 22 18 27 / W 90 51 43 18; WPA Index: 876 (See chap. 1.)

2.18.2 Unit Monument: Granite Stele, Bronze Tablet: Tennessee. Johnston's Army; Breckinridge Division. Johnston Artillery; 3rd Infantry (Vols.) (K 27, W 90, M 70, T 187); 10th and 30th Infantry (K 15, W 65, M 8, T 88); 41st Infantry (K 2, W 7, M 14, T 23); 50th Infantry (K 4, W 7, M 5, T 16. 1st Infantry Battalion (K 3, W 9, M 30, T 42). Also engaged: 42nd, 46th, 48th, 49th, 53rd, 55th Infantry; 7th Cavalry, Company A. N 32 22 17 49 / W 90 51 41 50; WPA Index: 877

2.18.3 Unit Monument: Granite Stele, 46th Mississippi Infantry (Engaged campaign and defense: casualties not listed). N 32 22 20 51 / W 90 51 32 46; WPA Index: 868

2.18.4 Unit Monument: Granite Stele, 1st Mississippi Lt. Artillery, Co. D (Engaged, campaign and defense: casualties not listed). N 32 22 19 48 / W 90 51 26 82; WPA Index: 864

2.18.5 Bust, Brig. Gen. William E. Baldwin. CS Army, commanding brigade, M.L. Smith's Division (Sculptor: T. A. R. Kitson, 1915). N 32 22 19 12 / W 90 51 23 36; WPA Index: 861

2.18.6 Granite Stele, 4th Mississippi Infantry (Engaged, campaign and defense: casualties not listed). N 32 22 18 52 / W 90 51 20 92; WPA Index: 858

NPS, Confederate Position Tablet; WPA Index: 749:

Third Louisiana Redan, on Left of Jackson Road. This redan was held, May 22, 1863, and the assaults of the Union force repulsed, by the Third

Louisiana, with the 43rd Mississippi on its left. The casualties cannot be accurately stated. A Union mine was fired under the redan the afternoon of June 25, almost destroying its front parapet, making a crater in its terreplain, but not injuring a parapet across its gorge. It was then held by the 3rd Illinois, supported by the 6th Missouri, with the 38th Mississippi on the right and the 43rd Mississippi on the left. The Union force assaulted immediately after the mine was fired, occupied the crater and attempted to carry the parapet across the gorge of the redan, but was repulsed. Col. Erwin, 6th Missouri, at the head of some of his men, attempted a counter-charge and was killed on top of the parapet. The Union force in the crater was successively relieved by fresh troops, the fighting continued all night and most of the next day, and the position was firmly held. Hand grenades, and shells with lighted fuses in place of grenades, were freely used on both sides. After dark of the 25th, the 5th Missouri reinforced this position. Casualties: 3rd Louisiana, killed 6, wounded 21, total 27; 38th Mississippi, killed 1, wounded 3, total 4; 43rd Mississippi, killed 6 (buried by firing of mine), wounded 5, total 11; 5th Missouri, killed 1, wounded 7, total 8; 6th Missouri, killed 3, wounded 22, total 25, Col. Eugene Erwin and Lieut. W. S. Lipscomb killed; aggregate, killed 17, wounded 58, total 75.

2.18.7 Unit Monument: Granite Stele, Bronze Tablet: Guibor's Battery, CS Missouri Lt. Artillery (Engaged campaign and defense: K 3, W 6, M 2, T 11). N 32 22 17 90 / W 90 51 13 50; WPA Index: 850

2.18.8 Relief Portrait, Lt. Col. Madison Rogers, CS Army, 17th Louisiana Infantry; killed in action, May 20, 1863 (Sculptor: George T. Brewster, 1919). N 32 22 18 38 / W 90 51 10 60; WPA Index: 848

2.18.9 Unit Monument: Granite Stele, Bronze Tablet, 17th, 31st Louisiana Infantry (Engaged defense, May 18–July 4: casualties not fully reported). N 32 22 18 37 / W 90 51 10 46; WPA Index: 847

2.18.10 Relief Portrait, Lt. Col. S. H. Griffin, CS Army, 31st Louisiana Infantry; killed in action, June 27, 1863 (Sculptor: George T. Brewster, 1919). N 32 22 18 30 / W 90 51 10 12; WPA Index: 846

2.18.11 Relief Portrait, Col. Robert Richardson, CS Army, 17th Louisiana Infantry, commanding brigade (Sculptor: T. A. R. Kitson, 1910). N 32 22 17 54 / W 90 51 08 90; WPA Index: 845

2.18.12 Relief Portrait, Maj. William W. Martin, CS Army, 26th Louisiana Infantry. Killed June 22, 1863 (Sculptor: T. A. R. Kitson, 1911). N 32 22 18 85 / W 90 51 02 72; WPA Index: 842

Thayer's Approach, Below Confederate Lines, Union Monuments
NPS, Wayside Tablet; WPA Index: 590:

Thayer's Approach. The trench for Thayer's Approach to the Confederate work [o]n [t]his front was started about May 30, 1863, on the north side of this ridge, through which it was carried by a tunnel, preserved by the brick arch. The trench across the ravine to the foot of the spur south of this marker, about six feet wide and six feet deep, was covered by a blinding of bundles of cane laid across it and affording protection against rifle balls. The Confederates did not use artillery against this blinding. When the trench reached cover at base of spur two lines of approach were started and these lines united on top of the spur to form one approach.

2.18.13 Granite Stele, Bronze Tablet: US 12th Missouri VI, May 22 Assault (K 26, W 82, T 108). N 32 22 18 04 / W 90 51 02 79; WPA Index: 603

2.18.14 Granite Stele, Bronze Tablet: US 17th Missouri VI, May 22 Assault (Casualties not listed). N 32 22 21 33 / W 90 51 00 60; WPA Index: 597

2.18.15 Granite Stele, Bronze Tablet: US 3rd Missouri VI, May 22 Assault (K 3, W 12, M 3, T 18). N 32 22 21 61 / W 90 51 00 18; WPA Index: 596

2.18.16 Bronze Tablet, 26th Iowa VI, May 22 Assault (K 4, W 23, T 27). N 32 22 18 01 / W 90 51 01 98; WPA Index: 602

2.18.17 Bronze Tablet, 31st Iowa VI, May 22 Assault (K 3, W 19, T 22). N 32 22 22 80 / W 90 50 59 88; WPA Index: 596

2.18.18 Bronze Tablet, 25th Iowa VI, May 22 Assault (K 5, W 27, M 5, T 37). N 32 22 21 36 / W 90 51 03 40; WPA Index: 607

2.18.19 Unit Monument: Granite Stele, CS 3rd Missouri Lt. Artillery Battery. N 32 22 16 60 / W 90 50 58 82; WPA Index: 839

2.18.20 Unit Monument: Granite Stele, Bronze Tablet: 26th Louisiana Infantry (Engaged defense, May 18–July 4: K 28, W 44, T 72). N 32 22 16 17 / W 90 50 58 24; WPA Index: 835

2.18.21 Relief Portrait, Capt. Lewis Guion, CS Army, 26th Louisiana Infantry (Sculptor: T. A. R. Kitson, 1920). N 32 22 15 17 / W 90 50 58 24; WPA Index: 836

2.18.22 Relief Portrait, Brig. Gen. Francis A. Shoup, CS Army, Louisiana, commanding brigade, Smith's Division (Sculptor: T. A. R. Kitson, 1910). N 32 22 14 40 / W 90 50 51 56; WPA Index: 833

2.18.23 Relief Portrait, Col. Allen Thomas, CS Army, 28th Louisiana Infantry, commanding Baldwin's Brigade (Sculptor: T. A. R. Kitson, 1919). N 32 22 14 08 / W 90 50 57 00; WPA Index: 832

2.18.24 Unit Monument: Granite Stele, Bronze Tablet: 28th Louisiana Infantry, Shoup's Brigade (Engaged defense, May 18–July 4: K 16, W 57, T 73). N 32 22 11 09 / W 90 50 54 98; WPA Index: 828

2.18.25 Granite Stele, Bronze Tablet: CS Army Headquarters, Forney's-Bowen's Division; Army of Vicksburg, Maj. Gen. John S. Bowen. N 32 22 11 31 / W 90 50 49 36; WPA Index: 824

2.18.26 Bust, Maj. Gen. John S. Bowen, commanding Division, CS Army of Vicksburg (Sculptor: Anton Schaaf, 1916). N 32 22 11 54 / W 90 50 49 12; WPA Index: 823

2.18.27 Relief Portrait, Col. William Wade, CS Chief of Artillery, Bowen's Division. Killed April 29, 1863 (Sculptor: Francis E. Elwell, 1912). N 32 22 11 71 / W 90 50 48 70; WPA Index: 821

2.18.28 Unit Monument: Granite Stele, Bronze Tablet: Missouri, Bledsoe's Battery, Clark Artillery, CS Army. N 32 22 11 57 / W 90 50 48 16; WPA Index: 822

2.18.29 Bust, Maj. Gen. Martin L. Smith, commanding Division, CS Army of Vicksburg, March 29–July 4 (Sculptor: Henry Kitson, 1911). N 32 22 13 58 / W 90 50 47 12; WPA Index: 819

2.18.30 Granite Stele, Bronze Tablet: 2nd CS Missouri Infantry, May 22 Repulse of Union assault (Casualties not separately reported). N 32 22 13 81 / W 90 50 45 54; WPA Index: 816

2.18.31 Granite Stele, Bronze Tablet: 2nd CS Missouri Infantry, May 19 Repulse of Union assault (Casualties not separately reported). N 32 22 13 97 / W 90 50 44 86; WPA Index: 817

2.18.32 Relief Portrait, Col. Francis M. Cockrell, CS Missouri Infantry, commanding brigade, Bowen's Division (Sculptor: Allen G. Newman, 1915). N 32 22 13 36 / W 90 50 44 12; WPA Index: 813

2.18.33 Relief Portrait, Col. Leon D. Marks, CS Army, 27th Louisiana Infantry. Mortally wounded, June 28, 1863 (Sculptor: T. A. R. Kitson, 1910). N 32 22 13 28 / W 90 50 43 82; WPA Index: 812

2.18.34 Unit Monument: Granite Stele, Bronze Tablet: 27th Louisiana Infantry, Shoup's Brigade. N 32 22 13 74 / W 90 50 43 68; WPA Index: 811

2.18.35 Relief Portrait, Lieut. Col. L.L. McLaurin, CS Army, 27th Louisiana Infantry. Killed in action, June 21, 1863 (Sculptor: George T. Brewster, 1921). N 32 22 13 84 / W 90 50 43 36; WPA Index: 810

Slope North of Graveyard Road: Union Monuments

2.18.36 Granite Stele, Bronze Tablet: 4th West Virginia VI, May 19 Assault (K 27, W 110, T 137). N 32 22 15 29 / W 90 50 44 22; WPA Index: 485

2.18.37 Granite Stele, 83rd Indiana VI Sharpshooters, June 23–July 4. N 32 22 16 73 / W 90 50 43 70; WPA Index: 479

2.18.38 Granite Stele, 47th Ohio VI, May 19 Assault, Marks Farthest Advance. N 32 22 14 04 / W 90 50 43 02; WPA Index: 487

2.18.39 Granite Stele, Bronze Tablet: 6th Missouri VI, May 19 Assault (K 3, W 25, T 28). N 32 22 13 33 / W 90 50 42 20; WPA Index: 488

Tour Stop 5: Stockade Redan Attack:

Stockade Redan was a Confederate fortification guarding the Graveyard Road approach to Vicksburg. On May 19, General Grant thought Southern morale to be so low after the defeats at Champion Hill and Big Black River Bridge, he ordered General Francis P. Blair Jr.'s division to attack the redan. Blair's three brigades advanced over rough terrain obstructed by dozens of felled trees cut by the Confederates to impede Federal advances. Fresh Southern troops defended the redan, however, and Blair's operation was unsuccessful. A few Federal soldiers got close to the redan, but Confederate fire pinned them down, and under cover of darkness, the Union soldiers withdrew.

Grant still thought that his army could successfully storm the Vicksburg defenses, and three days later, on May 22, he ordered another attack along the entire line. Sherman ordered his men to attack straight down the Graveyard Road to avoid the difficult terrain and Southern obstructions. Additionally, 150 volunteers, carrying wooden planks to bridge the ditch in front of the redan and ladders to climb the wall, went ahead of the Federal infantry.

The Confederates held their fire until the assaulting wave neared the redan, then opened with a devastating volley. Still, Union soldiers were able to bridge the ditch, and two color-bearers planted flags on the redan's exterior slope. But Southern fire was so intense that the Federals soon retreated. Following this repulse of his troops, Grant did not order any additional frontal assaults after May 22.

2.18.40 Bronze Tablet, 12th Iowa VI, May 22 Assault (Casualties not listed). N 32 22 18 13 / W 90 50 25 30; WPA Index: 439

Union Monuments: As Emplaced, Moving East to West, from the Corner of Graveyard Road and Union Avenue, West along Graveyard Road to Confederate Avenue and the Stockade Redan.

2.18.41 Bronze Tablet, 12th Iowa VI, 3rd Brigade; 3rd Division; 15th Corps, Camp, May 22–June 11. N 32 22 18 11 / W 90 50 25 16; WPA Index: 442

2.18.42 Relief Portrait, Col. Joseph J. Woods, CS Army, 12th Iowa VI, commanding 3rd Brigade, 3rd Division; 15th Corps (Sculptor: T. A. R. Kitson, 1910). N 32 22 18 27 / W 90 50 25 56; WPA Index: 440

2.18.43 Granite Tablet, 55th Illinois VI, Campground during siege, June 11–July 4. (North of Graveyard Road); WPA Index: 441

2.18.44 Granite Columns and Arch, with Bronze Tablets: 8th, 12th, 35th Iowa VI, 3rd Brigade; 3rd Division; 15th Corps. N 32 22 18 62 / W 90 50 26 54; WPA Index: 444

Relief Portrait, Col. Joseph J. Woods, 12th Iowa VI, commanding 3rd Brigade, 3rd Division, 15th Corps. (Sculptor: T. A. R. Kitson, 1910). Donated by Woods's son, O. E. Woods: $300 for bronze, $92.30 granite pedestal. Joseph J. Woods (b. 1823) was a West Point graduate with service in the War with Mexico; he also served at Fort Donelson and at Shiloh where he was wounded; after Vicksburg he served in operations against Price in Arkansas, Missouri. Woods survived the war and died in 1889.

2.18.45 Relief Portrait, Brig. Gen., J. A. J. Lightburn, US Vols., 4th West Virginia VI, commanding 2nd Brigade, 2nd Division; 15th Corps (Sculptor: Victor S. Holm, 1915). N 32 22 18 45 / W 90 50 27 20; WPA Index: 445

2.18.46 Stele, with Cannon Barrel Arch and Bronze Tablet, 2nd Battery Iowa Lt. Artillery; 3rd Division; 15th Corps. N 32 22 17 90 / W 90 50 28 66; WPA Index: 450

2.18.47 Granite Stele, 95th Ohio VI, May 19 Assault, Marks Farthest Advance. N 32 22 17 90 / W 90 50 28 66; WPA Index: 451

2.18.48 Granite Tablet, 114th Illinois VI, May 19 Assault (K 2, W 10, T 12). N 32 22 17 20 / W 90 50 28 54; WPA Index: 454

2.18.49 Unit Monument, Granite Obelisk, Battery E, 1st Illinois Lt. Artillery. N 32 22 17 15 / W 90 50 28 84; WPA Index: 452

2.18.50 Granite Stele, 72nd Ohio VI, May 19 Assault, Marks Farthest Advance. N 32 22 17 35 / W 90 50 29 38; WPA Index: 456

2.18.51 Relief Portrait, Capt. William L. G. Jenney, US Vols., Chief Engineer, 15th Corps (Sculptor: T. A. R. Kitson, 1911). N 32 22 14 19 / W 90 50 32 28; WPA Index: 493

2.18.52 Unit Monument, Granite Obelisk, Battery A, 1st Illinois Lt. Artillery, 2nd Division; 15th Corps. N 32 22 12 64 / W 90 50 34 48; WPA Index: 408

2.18.53 Granite Tablet, 55th Illinois VI, May 19 Assault (K 4, W 22, T 26). N 32 22 12 02 / W 90 50 64 76; WPA Index: 406

2.18.54 Granite Stele, 47th Ohio VI, May 22 Assault, Marks Farthest Advance. N 32 22 10 82 / W 90 50 34 70; WPA Index: 402

2.18.55 Granite Stele, 54th OVI, May 19 Assault, Marks Farthest Advance. N 32 22 10 24 / W 90 50 34 86; WPA Index: 400

2.18.56 Granite Stele, 57th OVI, May 19 Assault, Marks Farthest Advance. N 32 22 10 06 / W 90 50 34 76; WPA Index: 399

2.18.57 Granite Stele, Bronze Tablet, 4th West Virginia VI, May 22 Assault (K 3, W 16, T 19). N 32 22 09 85 / W 90 50 34 76; WPA Index: 398

2.18.58 Granite Stele, Bronze Tablet, 4th West Virginia VI, Trench line. N 32 22 09 69 / W 90 50 34 78; WPA Index: 397

2.18.59 Granite Stele, Bronze Tablet, 5th Minnesota VI, May 22 Assault (K 2, W 1, M 7, T 10). WPA Index: 495

2.18.60 Relief Portrait, Col. Thomas Kilby Smith, US Vols., 54th Ohio VI, commanding 2nd Brigade, 2nd Division; 15th Corps (Sculptor: Louis Milione, 1912). N 32 22 13 53 / W 90 50 35 52; WPA Index: 496

2.18.61 Relief Portrait, Brig. Gen. Joseph Mower, US Vols., commanding 2nd Brigade, 3rd Division; 15th Corps (Sculptor: Solon Borglum, 1911). N 32 22 12 46 / W 90 50 25 80; WPA Index: 502

2.18.62 Granite Stele, 37th Ohio VI, May 22 Assault, Marks Farthest Advance. N 32 22 12 37 / W 90 50 36 20; WPA Index: 503

2.18.63 Granite Stele, 8th Wisconsin VI, May 22 Assault, Marks Farthest Advance. N 32 22 12 30 / W 90 50 36 82; WPA Index: 504

2.18.64 Granite Tablet, 127th Illinois VI, May 19 Assault (K 8, W 31, M 1, T 40). N 32 22 12 20 / W 90 50 38 62; WPA Index: 508

2.18.65 Granite Tablet, 83rd Indiana VI, May 19 Assault (K 10, W 46, T 56). N 32 22 12 16 / W 90 50 39 18; WPA Index: 518

NPS, Union Position Tablet, Ewing's Brigade, Assault, May 22, 1863; WPA Index: 526:

Blair's Division was massed for the assault, the morning of May 22, on the left of the Graveyard Road and about 900 yards from the Confederate Stockade Redan. A volunteer storming party of 150 men from the regiments of the Division, under command of Capt. John H. Groce, 30th Ohio, advanced at 10:00 a.m., by the flank, on the Graveyard Road, followed by Ewing's Brigade—the 30th Ohio leading. The headquarters flag was placed on the parapet of the Confederate Redan, and the storming party

Placed at the base of Confederate Stockade Redan is this granite stele to the 30th Ohio VI, marking its effort during the May 22 Assault: "Marks Farthest Advance."

took position in the ditch and on the north face of the parapet. The 30th Ohio advanced close to the angle of the redan but was compelled to seek shelter from the Confederate fire, and the Brigade was reformed behind the crest of the ridge, at the left of the road, and about 140 yards from the Confederate line. This position was held continuously, and that night the dead, the wounded and the colors were brought back to it, and entrenchments were begun. (Casualties: 30th Ohio, K 6, W 43, M 2, T 51; 37th Ohio, K 10, W 31, T 41; 47th Ohio, K 6, W 26, M 1, T 33; 4th West Virginia, K 3, W 16, T 19; aggregate, K 25, W 116, M 3, T 144.)

2.18.66 Granite Stele, 30th Ohio VI, May 22 Assault, Marks Farthest Advance. N 32 22 11 93 / W 90 50 39 18; WPA Index: 528

2.18.67 Granite Stele, Bronze Tablet: 11th Missouri VI, May 22 Assault (K 7, W 85, T 92). N 32 22 11 82 / W 90 50 39 58; WPA Index: 524

2.18.68 Granite Stele, 6th Missouri VI, May 22 Assault (K 2, W 13, T 15). N 32 22 10 17 / W 90 50 39 18; WPA Index: 529

2.18.69 Granite Tablet, 47th Illinois VI, May 22 Assault (K 5, W 33, T 38). N 32 22 12 16 / W 90 50 37 86; WPA Index: 505

2.18.70 Relief Portrait, Capt. Edward C. Washington, 13th US Infantry. Mortally wounded May 19, 1863 (Sculptor: T. A. R. Kitson, 1910). N 32 22 12 53 / W 90 50 32 40 00; WPA Index: 522

2.18.71 Granite Tablet, 116th Illinois VI, May 19 Assault (K 6, W 64, M 1, T 71). N 32 22 13 03 / W 90 50 32 39 08; WPA Index: 523

2.18.72 Bronze Tablet, 1st Battalion 13th US Infantry, May 19 Assault (K 21, W 49, T 70). N 32 22 12 53 / W 90 50 39 76; WPA Index: 521

Buckland's Approach: Union Monuments

2.18.73 Granite Tablet, 93rd Indiana VI, Sharpshooters Line, June 5–June 22. N 32 22 17 34 / W 90 50 35 58; WPA Index: 471

2.18.74 Granite Stele, Bronze Tablet: 8th Missouri VI, May 19 Assault (K 10, W 16, T 26). N 32 22 21 13; / W 90 50 39 15; WPA Index: 483

2.18.75 Granite Tablet, 55th Illinois VI, Sharpshooters Line, June 23–July 4, WPA Index: 481

NPS, Union Position Tablet, WPA Index: 486:

Ewing's Brigade; Assault, May 19, 1863. This Brigade, with skirmishers in advance, was formed behind the crest of the ridge immediately north of Mint Spring Bayou, in order from right to left as follows: 37th Ohio, 4th West Virginia, 47th Ohio, in line, and the 30th Ohio in reserve. The Brigade connected closely with Steele's Division on its right, and with Giles A. Smith's Brigade on its left. This Brigade moved promptly at the appointed time, 2:00 p.m. Its left two regiments advanced close to the Confederate intrenchment, where their colors remained until after dark. The right regiment was unable to cross the ravine in its front, on account of obstacles, but covered the left in its advanced position by a heavy fire. When the line moved forward, the reserve regiment advanced to the crest of the hill and began firing. After dark the brigade retired, under orders, to the position where it formed for the assault. This tablet marks the farthest advance of the 4th West Virginia.

2.18.76 Granite Tablet, 83rd Indiana VI, Sharpshooters Line, June 23–July 4. N 32 22 17 48 / W 90 50 35 72; WPA Index: 479

2.18.77 Granite Tablet, 93rd Indiana VI, Sharpshooters Line, June 5–June 22. [Location coordinates n.a.] WPA Index: 471

2.18.78 Bronze Tablet, 12th Iowa VI, Sharpshooters Line, June 5–June 22. N 32 22 17 68 / W 90 50 35 80; WPA Index: 469

2.18.79 Bronze Tablet, 35th Iowa VI, Sharpshooters Line, June 5–June 22. N 32 22 17 82 / W 90 50 35 86; WPA Index: 468

2.18.80 Bronze Tablet, 8th Iowa VI, Sharpshooters Line, June 5–June 22. N 32 22 17 96 / W 90 50 35 94; WPA Index: 467

2.18.81 Granite Tablet, 55th Illinois VI, Sharpshooters Line, June 1–July 4. N 32 22 18 16 / W 90 50 36 02; WPA Index: 466

2.18.82 Granite Tablet, 114th Illinois VI, Sharpshooters Line, June 5–June 9. N 32 22 18 31 / W 90 50 36 20; WPA Index: 465

A series of Missouri Confederate stelae stand on the Confederate side of the Stockade Redan. At the center is the unit monument Bowen's Division, 1st Brigade. The remaining four unit monuments commemorate Missouri Confederate infantry in the repulse of successive Union assaults, May 19 and May 22: 1st and 4th Missouri (May 22); 5th Missouri; Bowen's Division; 3rd Missouri; 1st and 4th Missouri (May 19).

Confederate Avenue Near Missouri Monument

2.18.83 Granite Stele, 1st and 4th Missouri Infantry, CS Army, Repulse of Union assault, May 22 (Casualties not reported). N 32 22 12 13 / W 90 50 41 38; WPA Index: 800

2.18.84 Granite Stele, Bronze Tablet: 5th Missouri Infantry, CS Army, Repulse of Union May 19 assault (Casualties not reported). N 32 22 11 98 / W 90 50 41 42; WPA Index: 801

2.18.85 Granite Stele, Bronze Tablet: Arkansas: Johnston's Army, Roster of units: French's Division, McNair's Brigade: 1st Rifles (Dismounted), 2nd Rifles (Dismounted); 4th, 25th, 31st Infantry, Loring's Division, 3rd Brigade: 9th Infantry; Walker's Division, Ector's Brigade, McNally's Battery (Section); Cavalry Division, 2nd Brigade, Bridges' Battalion. WPA Index: 799 (Removed, date unknown.)

2.18.86 Unit Monument: Granite Stele, Bronze Tablet: CS Missouri: Bowen's Division. 1st Brigade, 1st and 4th—consolidated Infantry (K 47, W 164, M 52, T 263); 2nd Infantry (K 27, W 124, M 38, T 189); 3rd Infantry (K 31, W 146, M 44, T 221); 5th Infantry (K 28, W 101, M 37, T 163); 6th Infantry (K 28, W 182, M 67, T 369); Guibor's Battery: (K 3, W 6, M 2, T 11); Landis' Battery: K 8, W 7, T 15. Wade's Battery: (K 2, W 17, M 2 T 21); 2nd Brigade: 1st Cavalry—Dismounted: 3rd Cavalry Battalion—Dismounted: 3rd

Battery: (K 3, W 5, M 4, T 12); Lowe's Battery: (K 4, W 9, T 13); Bledsoe's Battery. N 32 22 11 91 / W 90 50 41 38; WPA Index: 807

2.18.87 Unit Monument: Granite Stele, Bronze Tablet: 3rd Missouri Infantry, CS Army, Repulse of Union assault, May 19 (Casualties not reported). N 32 22 11 72 / W 90 50 41 30; WPA Index: 804

2.18.88 Granite Stele, Bronze Tablet: 1st and 4th Missouri Infantry, CS Army, Repulse of Union assault, May 19 (Casualties not reported). N 32 22 11 52 / W 90 50 41 30; WPA Index: 805

NPS, Stockade Redan on Graveyard Road, Confederate Position Tablet; WPA Index: 803:

This redan, the line immediately to its right, and part of the stockade to its left were held, the afternoon of May 19, 1863, and the assaults of the Union force repulsed, by the 36th Mississippi, with the 5th Missouri in support, on its East face; and the 1st and 4th Missouri (consolidated) on its north face and part of the line of the Stockade. The 3rd Missouri was in reserve. Casualties: in 36th Mississippi, cannot be accurately stated; in Cockrell's Brigade, killed 8, wounded 62, total 70, nearly all in this position. The position was held, May 22, and the assaults of the Union force repulsed by the 36th Mississippi and six companies of the 1st and 4th Missouri on its east face, and the 3rd Missouri on its north face and part of the line of the stockade. Three companies of the 1st and 4th Missouri in reserve, were moved from point to point, as required. Casualties: in Hebert's Brigade, killed 21, wounded 39, total 60; not distributed between this redan and other points on the Brigade line, Major Alexander Yates, 36th Mississippi, killed; in Cockrell's Brigade, killed 28, wounded 95, total 123, nearly all in this position; in 3rd Missouri, of that brigade, killed 12, wounded 52, total 64. The stockade and the north face of the redan were held, after May 25, by the 27th Louisiana. The east face of the redan was held, after June 2, by the left regiment of Green's Brigade. Two countermines against the Union approach, from the ditch of the redan, were fired the night of June 26; another was prepared but not fired.

2.18.89 Granite Tablet, 113th Illinois VI, Companies A, B, E, G and H, May 19 Assault (W 7) (Graveyard Road opposite the north face of the Stockade Redan). [Location coordinates n.a.]. WPA Index: 490

2.18.90 Relief Portrait, Maj. Alexander Yates, CS Army, 36th Mississippi Infantry. Killed in action, May 22 (Sculptor: George T. Brewster, 1917). N 32 22 10 97 / W 90 50 41 38; WPA Index: 489.5

2.18.91 Relief Portrait, Col. Thomas P. Dockery, CS Army, 19th Arkansas Infantry, commanding 2nd Brigade, Bowen's Division, June 27–July 4 (Sculptor: Victor S. Holm, 1915). N 32 22 10 86 / W 90 50 41 30; WPA Index: 794

Panel Relief: Missouri Confederate soldiers, the Siege Line. The State of Missouri Monument (1917).

2.18.92 Brig. Gen. Martin L. Green, commanding brigade, Bowen's Division. Killed June 27, 1863 (Sculptor: T. A. R. Kitson, 1911). N 32 22 08 01 / W 90 50 41 30; WPA Index: 787

2.18.93 Granite Stele, Bronze Tablet: 5th Missouri Infantry, CS Army, Repulse of Union May 22 assault (Casualties not reported). N 32 22 07 40 / W 90 50 41 16; WPA Index: 790

2.19.4 The State of Missouri Memorial, Shaft, Statue and Reliefs (Design: Hellmuth & Hellmuth; Sculptor: Victor S. Holms, 1917). N 32 22 07 29 / W 90 50 42 12; WPA Index: 786 (See chap. 1.)

Mowed Bay East of Missouri Monument

2.19.2 Granite Tablet, 113th Illinois VI (Companies A, B, E, G, and H), May 22 Assault (K 7, W 20, T 27). N 32 22 08 01 / W 90 50 39 14; WPA Index: 389

2.19.3 Granite Stele, Bronze Tablet: 8th Missouri VI, May 22 Assault (K 10, W 40, M 1, T 51). N 32 22 05 67 / W 90 50 40 38; WPA Index: 375

2.19.4 Granite Tablet, 55th Illinois VI, May 22 Assault (K 5, W 13, T 18). N 32 22 04 22 / W 90 50 40 20; WPA Index: 373

2.19.5 Granite Tablet, 116th Illinois VI, Sharpshooters Line, May 23–July 4. N 32 22 59 69 / W 90 50 37 30; WPA Index: 362

2.19.6 Granite Stele, 17th Wisconsin VI, May 22 Assault, Marks Farthest Advance. N 32 22 59 39 / W 90 50 37 40; WPA Index: 353

2.19.7 Granite Tablet, 113th Illinois VI, Sharpshooters Line, May 23–July 4. N 32 22 58 81 / W 90 50 37 72; WPA Index: 359

Confederate Avenue

2.19.8 Unit monument: Granite Stele, Bronze Tablet: Lowe's (Missouri) Battery, CS Army; Forney's-Bowen's Division; Army of Vicksburg. N 32 22 06 90 / W 90 50 42 44; WPA Index: 784

2.20.1 The State of Arkansas Memorial (Designer: William H. Deacy, 1954). N 32 22 06 43 / W 90 50 43 82; WPA Index: 781 (See chap. 1.)

2.20.2 Granite Tablet, 72nd Illinois VI, May 22 Assault (K 20, W 71, M 5, T 96). N 32 22 03 76 / W 90 50 44 58; WPA Index: 357

2.20.3 Granite Stele, 14th Wisconsin VI, May 22 Assault, Marks Farthest Advance. N 32 22 02 71 / W 90 50 46 54; WPA Index: 356

2.20.4 Unit monument: Granite Stele, Bronze Tablet: 1st Missouri CS Cavalry. N 32 22 01 66 / W 90 50 45 42; WPA Index: 773

2.20.5 Granite Tablet, 11th Illinois VI, May 22 Assault (K 3, W 30, M 9, T 42). (100 feet east of Confederate Avenue past the Missouri Memorial) N 32 21 58 50 / W 90 50 44 18; WPA Index: 351

2.20.6 Unit monument: Granite Stele, Bronze Tablet: 3rd Missouri CS Cavalry, dismounted detachment. N 32 22 00 38 / W 90 50 45 06; WPA Index: 771

2.20.7 Granite Tablet, 95th Illinois VI, May 22 Assault (K 18, W 86, M 8, T 109) (100 feet east of Confederate Avenue, south of the Missouri Memorial). N 32 22 00 35 / W 90 50 44 72; WPA Index: 352

North of Bridge, above Jackson Road

2.20.8 Unit monument: Granite Stele, 37th Mississippi Infantry, Engaged defense, May 18–July 4 (K 17, W 56, M 7, T 80). N 32 22 55 57 / W 90 50 44 80; WPA Index: 767

Ransom's Approach, East of Confederate Avenue, Mowed Bay

2.20.9 Granite Tablet, 95th Illinois VI, Sharpshooters Line, June 18–July 4. N 32 21 51 73 / W 90 50 42 20; WPA Index: 307

2.20.10 Granite Tablet, 72nd Illinois VI, Sharpshooters Line, June 18–July 4. N 32 21 51 53 / W 90 50 43 02; WPA Index: 310

2.20.11 Granite Tablet, 11th Illinois VI, Sharpshooters Line, May 23–July 4. N 32 21 46 37 / W 90 50 41 08; WPA Index: 314

2.20.12 Unit monument: Granite Stele, Company C, 1st Mississippi Lt. Artillery, engaged May 18–July 4 (K 3, W 13, M 2, T 80). N 32 21 36 08 / W 90 50 43 02; WPA Index: 761

2.20.13 Unit monument: Granite Stele, 43rd Mississippi Infantry, engaged May 18–July 4 (K 3, W 13, M 2, T 18). N 32 21 34 57 / W 90 50 42 26; WPA Index: 758

2.20.14 Unit monument: Granite Stele, Bronze Tablet: 3rd Louisiana Infantry, engaged May 18–July 4 (K 49, W 119, M 7, T 175). N 32 21 31 62 / W 90 50 41 56; WPA Index: 752

2.20.15 Unit monument: Granite Stele, Bronze Tablet: 6th Missouri, 5th Missouri, 2nd Missouri, 1st and 4th consolidated Missouri Infantry, CS Army, supporting 6th Louisiana Infantry. N 32 21 31 28 / W 90 50 39 92; WPA Index: 747

2.20.16 Relief Portrait, Col. James H. Jones, CS Army, 38th Mississippi, Engaged defense, May 18–July 4 (K 3, W 13, M 2, T 18) (Sculptor: T. A. R. Kitson, 1912). N 32 21 21 29 04 / W 90 50 42 44; WPA Index: 743

2.20.17 Unit monument: Granite Stele, 38th Mississippi Infantry: Engaged defense, May 18–July 4 (K 35, W 37, M 2, T 74). N 32 21 28 05 / W 90 50 43 54; WPA Index: 739

2.20.18 Relief Portrait, Brig. Gen. Louis Hebert, CS Army, commanding brigade, Forney's Division (Sculptor: T. A. R. Kitson, 1910). N 32 21 27 69 / W 90 50 46 04; WPA Index: 732

2.20.19 Granite Stele, Bronze Tablet: 7th Missouri VI, US, May 22 Assault (K 9, W 93, T 102). N 32 21 27 02 / W 90 50 46 92; WPA Index: 733

Tour Stop 11: The Great Redoubt:

The Great Redoubt (a four-sided, rectangular fortification), along with the Third Louisiana Redan (Tour Stop 3), was constructed to protect the Jackson Road entrance to Vicksburg. It was the largest and most formidable defensive work in the Confederate line. The redoubt was fiercely attacked by Union soldiers on May 22, and Federal color-bearers planted flags on the redoubt's walls. But after savage fighting, the blue-clad infantry was repulsed with heavy losses. During the ensuing siege operations, Union artillery bombarded the Great Redoubt until the surrender of Vicksburg on July 4, 1863.

Old Jackson Road, West of Confederate Avenue and the Louisiana Memorial at Beulah Cemetery (off NPS grounds)

2.20.20 Unit monument: Granite Stele, Bronze Tablet: Louisiana, Forney's Division; Pointe Coupee Artillery, Company B; 21st Louisiana Infantry, 22nd Louisiana Infantry, Companies C and D. N 32 21 31 13 / W 90 50 50 40; WPA Index: 729

Confederate Avenue

2.21.1 State of Louisiana Memorial, Doric Column (Alfred E. Theard, Architect, 1920). N 32 21 25 68 / W 90 50 49 34; WPA Index: 721

2.21.2 Unit monument: Granite Stele, Bronze Tablet: Louisiana, Johnston's Army, Breckinridge's Division, Washington Artillery, 5th Company; 13th, 16th, 19th, 20th, 25th Infantry; 14th Battalion, Sharpshooters; French's

Bust, Brig. Gen. Daniel Adams, CS Army, 1st Louisiana Infantry, commanding brigade, Breckinridge's Division (Sculptor: T. A. R. Kitson, 1912). The state of Louisiana's monument is in the background. Adams (b. 1821) was wounded at the battles of Shiloh, Stones River, and Chickamauga. He survived the war, however, and lived until 1872; his remains were interred at Greenwood Cemetery in Jackson. His grave is adjacent to that of his brother William W. Adams, who also served as a brigadier general in the CS Army.

Brig. Gen. Lloyd Tilghman, CS Army. Mortally wounded, Battle of Champion Hill, May 16, 1863. Sculpture by Frederick W. Sievers. The spread arms, the look of agony on the visage, and the wound in the side may be a messianic allusion.

Division, Fenner's Battery, 4th, 30th Infantry; Loring's Division, 12th Infantry, Pointe Coupee Artillery; Walker's Division, 4th Battalion, Cavalry Division, Independent Company, Reserve Artillery, Durrive's Battery. N 32 21 24 54 / W 90 50 50 90; WPA Index: 717

2.21.3 Unit monument: Granite Stele, Bronze Tablet: 7th Battalion, Mississippi Infantry, engaged defense, May 18–July 4 (K 17, W 33, T 50). N 32 21 23 62 / W 90 50 52 78; WPA Index: 710

2.21.4 Bust, Brig. Gen. Daniel W. Adams, CSA, 1st Louisiana Infantry, commanding brigade, Breckinridge's Division (Sculptor: T. A. R. Kitson, 1912). N 32 21 24 30 / W 90 50 53 38; WPA Index: 714

2.21.5 Equestrian monument, Brig. Gen. Lloyd Tilghman, CS Army (Sculptor: Frederick W. Sievers). N 32 21 24 00 / W 90 50 53 60; WPA Index: 713 (See Chap. 1)

2.21.6 Unit monument: Granite Stele, 7th Battalion, Mississippi Infantry. Engaged: Defense, May 18–July 4 (K 28, W 72, M 1, T 101). N 32 21 23 62 / W 90 50 53 78; WPA Index: 704

2.21.7 Granite Stele, Bronze Tablet: Brig. Gen. Lloyd Tilghman, CS Army, commanding 1st Brigade, Loring's Division, Johnston's Army. N 32 21 23 27 / W 90 50 53 32; WPA Index: 708

Clio, Muse of History, Mississippi State Memorial. Sculptor: Frederick E. Triebel, sculpture completed 1912.

2.21.8 Unit monument: Granite Stele, 36th Mississippi Infantry: Engaged Defense, May 18–July 4 (K 17, W 33, T 50). N 32 21 19 01 / W 90 51 56 68; WPA Index: 710

2.21.9 Relief Portrait, Col. W. W. Witherspoon, CS Army, 36th Mississippi, Hebert's Brigade, Forney's Division (Sculptor: George E. Ganiere, 1915). N 32 21 17 44 / W 90 50 59 88; WPA Index: 705

2.21.10 Unit monument: Granite Stele, Bronze Tablet: Missouri, Landis' Battery, CS Army. N 32 21 16 03 / W 90 51 59 92; WPA Index: 701

2.21.11 Statue, Maj. Gen. John H. Forney, CS Army, Divisional Commander (Sculptor: Steffen Thomas, 1951). N 32 21 14 04 / W 90 51 59 70; WPA Index: 699

2.21.12 Unit monument: Granite Stele, 35th Mississippi Infantry: Engaged Defense, May 18–July 4 (K 20, W 82, T 102). N 32 21 11 94 / W 90 51 59 22; WPA Index: 697

2.21.13 Relief Portrait, Maj. Samuel H. Lockett, Chief Engineer, CS Army of Vicksburg (Sculptor: T. A. R. Kitson, 1911). N 32 21 10 57 / W 90 51 02 08; WPA Index: 693

2.22.1 Mississippi State Memorial (Architect: R. E. Hunt; Sculptor: Frederick E. Triebel. Dedicated 1909; completed 1912). N 32 21 09 74 / W 90 51 05 04; WPA Index: 675 (See chap. 1.)

2.22.2 Unit monument: Granite Stele, 40th Mississippi Infantry: Engaged Defense, May 18–July 4 (K 12, W 38, T 50). N 32 21 09 37 / W 90 51 05 24; WPA Index: 673

2.22.3 Statue, Lt. Gen. John C. Pemberton. CS Army, commanding Department of Mississippi and East Louisiana (Sculptor: Edward T. Quinn, 1917). N 32 21 06 15 / W 90 51 07 32; WPA Index: 669 (See chap. 1.)

2.22.4 Relief Portrait, Maj. Robert S. Campbell, Jr., CS Army, 40th Mississippi Infantry. Died June 28, 1863, from wounds received during defense. (Sculptor: George T. Brewster, 1920). N 32 21 04 94 / W 90 51 06 56; WPA Index: 654

2.22.5 Bust, Maj. Gen. Dabney H. Maury, CS Army, commanding Division, Army of Vicksburg (Sculptor: George T. Brewster, 1915). N 32 21 02 23 / W 90 51 08 02; WPA Index: 651

2.22.6 Bust, Col. William Temple Withers, CS Army, Commander of Artillery, Army of Vicksburg (Sculptor: Albert G. Rieker, 1929). N 32 20 58 00 / W 90 51 16 80; WPA Index: 647

2.22.7 Unit monument: Granite Stele, 1st Mississippi Lt. Artillery, Co. G (W 2). N 32 20 54 54 / W 90 51 16 80; WPA Index: 640

2.22.8 Statue, Jefferson Davis, "President, Confederate States, Commander-in-Chief" (Sculptor: Henry Kitson, 1927). N 32 20 50 49 / W 90 51 16 49; WPA Index: 636 (See chap. 1.)

2.22.9 Granite Stele, 3rd Missouri Cavalry Battalion, CS Army, May 22 Sortie (Casualties not reported). N 32 20 47 32 / W 90 51 14 44; WPA Index: 633

2.22.10 Granite Stele, 1st Missouri Cavalry, CS Army, dismounted detachment, May 22 Sortie (Casualties not reported). N 32 20 46 78 / W 90 51 14 34; WPA Index: 622

2.22.11 Relief Portrait, Brig. Gen. John C. Moore, CS Army, commanding brigade, Forney's Division (Sculptor: T. A. R. Kitson, 1911). N 32 20 46 65 / W 90 51 15 16; WPA Index: 624

2.22.12 Granite Stele, Moore's Brigade, 2nd Texas Infantry (K 38, W 73, M 15, T 126). N 32 20 46 37 / W 90 51 14 86; WPA Index: 623

2.22.13 Site for monument to Gen. Joseph E. Johnston, commanding the CS Army of Relief at Jackson: not installed. WPA Index: 637

Tour Stop 12: Second Texas Lunette:

The Second Texas Lunette (a crescent-shaped fortification) was the Confederate defensive work constructed to guard the Baldwin Ferry Road entering Vicksburg. In 1863, the road approached the city from the southeast, passed in front of the lunette, and then entered the city. The lunette is named after the Second Texas Volunteer Infantry which held the position throughout the siege.

The lunette was the subject of tremendous artillery bombardment and repeated, furious Union assaults on May 22. However, the determination and bravery of the attacking Federals was matched by the Confederates, whose withering defensive fire consistently forced the Union soldiers to retire. After the assaults, the commander of the Second Texas stated, "along the road [Baldwin Ferry] for more than 200 yards the bodies lay so thick that one might have walked the whole distance without touching the ground."

With so many casualties, the Federals changed their strategy of attack against the Second Texas Lunette, and commenced mining operations by digging approach trenches. At the time of the Vicksburg surrender, one of the trenches was within 10 yards of the outer ditch of the fortification.

This tract of land is now partly occupied by the Jewish Anshe Chesed Cemetery. Deeded to the synagogue in 1864, a year after the siege, the land became the re-interment site for original congregation members. The first new burial in the cemetery most likely took place in May 1865, when a man named Mayer was interred in grave No. 1. This shows the cemetery's creation to be almost 40 years prior to the establishment of Vicksburg National Military Park, which now surrounds the cemetery.

Baldwin's Ferry Road, Union Monuments off Confederate Avenue

2.22.14 Granite Tablet, 59th Indiana VI, May 22 Assault (K 11, W 99, M 1, T 111). N 32 20 45 62 / W 90 50 11 84; WPA Index: 621

2.22.15 Granite Stele, 83rd Ohio VI, May 22 Assault, Marks Furthest Advance. N 32 20 45 41 / W 90 50 12 14; WPA Index: 620

2.22.16 Granite Tablet, 48th Indiana VI, May 22 Assault (K 8, W 24, M 1, T 33). N 32 20 44 41 / W 90 50 11 50; WPA Index: 617

2.22.17 Granite Stele, 4th Minnesota VI, May 22 Assault (K 12, W 42, T 54). N 32 20 44 14 / W 90 50 11 88; WPA Index: 615

2.22.18 Granite Stele, Flag of Truce, Lt. Gen. Pemberton, July 3. N 32 20 43 72 / W 90 50 11 10; WPA Index: 176

2.22.19 Granite Tablet, 67th Indiana VI, Sharpshooters Line, June 15–July 4. N 32 20 44 09 / W 90 50 10 60; WPA Index: 178

2.22.20 Granite Tablet, 67th Indiana VI, May 22 Assault (K 6, W 23, T 29). N 46 65 54 44 / W 90 51 10 76; WPA Index: 186

Between Clay Street and the Anshe Chesed Jewish Cemetery

2.22.21 Granite Tablet, 99th Illinois VI, May 22 Assault ("National colors of regiment were carried across Confederate parapet by Sgt. Thomas J. Higgins"). N 32 20 43 86 / W 90 50 12 88; WPA Index: 372

Foreground: Granite Tablet: 99th Illinois VI, May 22 Assault, placed at the threshold of Anshe Chesed Cemetery. In the distance (*left*) are relief portraits of Peter C. Hains, 1st Lieut., US Vols., Chief Engineer, 13th Corps; Brig. Gen. Thomas J. Lucas, US Vols., Col., 16th Indiana VI; and Capt. Patrick H. White, US Vols., Chicago Mercantile Battery. The landscape is much altered since the war, of course, with the overgrowth and the addition of the asphalt road, but the cemetery and upslope of the ground are wartime geographical features of an area marking the limit of the Union advance of May 22.

Confederate Avenue, near the Anshe Chesed Jewish Cemetery

2.22.22 Granite Tablet, 99th Illinois VI, May 19 Assault (K 19, W 77, M 6, T 102) N 32 20 43 69 / W 90 51 16 58; WPA Index: 614

2.22.23 Granite Tablet, 18th Indiana VI, May 22 Assault (K 7, 39, M 1, T 46). N 32 20 44 30 / W 90 51 12 88; WPA Index: 610

2.22.24 Granite Stele, 23rd Wisconsin VI, May 22 Assault, Marks Furthest Advance. N 32 20 44 48 / W 90 51 12 82; WPA Index: 611

2.22.25 Granite Tablet, 16th Indiana VI, May 22 Assault (K 2, W 12, T 14). N 32 20 44 65 / W 90 51 12 80; WPA Index: 612

2.22.26 Granite Tablet, 99th Illinois VI, May 22 Assault (K 19, W 77, M 6, T 102). N 32 20 46 37 / W 90 51 02 80; WPA Index: 596

2.2.27 Relief Portrait, Peter C. Hains. 1st Lieut., US Vols., Chief Engineer, 13th Corps (Sculptor: T. A. R. Kitson, 1911). N 32 20 40 63 / W 90 51 10 88; WPA Index: 600

2.22.28 Relief Portrait, Brig. Gen. Thomas J. Lucas, US Vols., Col., 16th Indiana VI (Sculptor: Allan G. Newman, 1916). N 32 20 40 74 / W 90 51 11 10; WPA Index: 601

2.22.29 Relief Portrait, Capt. Patrick H. White, US Vols., Chicago Mercantile Battery (Sculptor: George T. Brewster, 1917). N 32 20 40 91 / W 90 51 11 32; WPA Index: 602

Lt. Col. William F. Vilas, 23rd Wisconsin VI, US Volunteers, close-up. Like the figure of Stephen D. Lee, the Vilas statue, by Adolph A. Weinman, depicts a figure who is confident, down-to-earth, fearless, even cocky.

Close up of the state of Texas's common soldier. The figure is frank, unmartial, unmilitary, but vigilant, confident and ready if "they" come again.

2.22.30 Statue, Lt. Col. William F. Vilas, 23rd Wisconsin VI (Sculptor: Adolph A. Weinman, 1912). N 32 20 39 63 / W 90 51 08 16; WPA Index: 590

South Loop: South of the Railroad, East of the Texas Monument

2.22.31 Granite Stele, 48th OVI, May 22 Assault, Marks Farthest Advance. N 32 20 31 09 / W 90 51 20 76; WPA Index: 338

2.22.32 Granite Tablet, 18th Indiana VI, Sharpshooters Line, June 19–July 4. N 32 20 31 95 / W 90 51 19 66; WPA Index: 341

2.22.33 Granite Tablet, 130th Illinois VI, May 22 Assault (K 10, W 31, T 41). N 32 20 32 87 / W 90 51 20 91; WPA Index: 325

2.22.34 Granite Tablet, 77th Illinois VI, May 22 Assault (K 19, W 85, M 26, T 130). N 32 20 32 53 / W 90 51 21 20; WPA Index: 327

2.22.35 Bronze Tablet, 22nd Iowa VI, May 22 Assault (K 27, W 118, M 19, T 164). N 32 20 32 53 / W 90 51 21 62; WPA Index: 323

2.22.36 Bronze Tablet, 21st Iowa VI, May 22 Assault (K 16, W 87, M 10, T 113). N 32 20 32 67 / W 90 51 21 18; WPA Index: 326

2.23.1 Texas State Monument (Designers: M. Herring Coe; Lundgren and Maurer 1961–63). N 32 20 33 05 / W 90 51 23 26 (See chap. 1.)

Tour Stop 13: The Railroad Redoubt:

The Railroad Redoubt was a Confederate fortification built to protect a vital entrance to the city—in this case the Southern Railroad of Mississippi. On May 22, General Grant ordered a second major assault against the formidable Confederate positions. Union forces began their carefully planned attack with a fierce artillery bombardment, followed by the advance of the infantry. Unlike other points along the Confederate defense line, the blue-clad soldiers found that the redoubt's southeast angle had been partially destroyed by the artillery bombardment. Union soldiers commanded by Sgt. Joseph E. Griffith of the 22d Iowa were able to exploit this brief breakthrough and quickly entered the redoubt in an attempt to storm the Confederate earthworks. The Confederates counterattacked and called up reinforcements. Waul's Texas Legion arrived to drive out the Federals and 'seal the breach.' Although Union forces sustained heavy losses, Griffith managed to withdraw, taking a dozen prisoners with him. By evening, the Federals had returned to their lines. There were no further attacks on the Railroad Redoubt, and mining operations commenced. By the time of the surrender on July 4, 1863, approach trenches had reached the redoubt's outer ditch.

NPS records observe that the Railroad Redoubt stands south of the railroad line running into Vicksburg, which is still active. The location is clearly marked, but this is regarded as being largely a CCC-era reconstruction.

NPS, Union Position Tablet; WPA Index: 328

Landram's Brigade; Assault, May 22, 1863. This brigade was formed, in support of Lawler's, for the assault of the Confederate railroad redoubt, behind the crest of the ridge about 380 yards in front of that redoubt, in lines of battle—the 77th Illinois on the right supported by the 48th Ohio, the 19th Kentucky on the left, and the 130th Illinois in support of both right and left. The 97th Illinois was temporarily attached to Lawler's brigade and formed with it, in support of the 11th Wisconsin, on the left of that brigade. This brigade advanced about 10 A.M.; some men of the 77th Illinois reached the ditch of the redoubt and the flag of that regiment was placed on its parapet; the brigade took position on the slope in front of the redoubt, and the flag of the 130th Illinois was placed close to that work. About 5:30 P.M., the Confederates made a sortie from the intrenchment in the rear of the redoubt and reoccupied it; later in the evening, about 30 men of the brigade were captured in the ditch of the redoubt. Col. Sullivan, in his report, states that the flag of the 48th Ohio was also placed on the parapet and was brought off just before the sortie was made. This brigade held its position on the slope in front of the redoubt until after dark and then retired, under orders. This tablet marks the place on the parapet of the redoubt where the flag of the 77th Illinois was placed. Casualties: 77th

Illinois, killed 19, wounded 85, missing 26, total 130; 97th Illinois, wounded 12, missing 2, total 14; 130th Illinois, killed 10, wounded 31, total 41, Capt. William M. Colby killed; 19th Kentucky, killed 5, wounded 57, missing 2, total 64, Major Morgan V. Evans killed; 48th Ohio, killed 10, wounded 25, total 35, Major Virgil H. Moats mortally wounded; aggregate, killed 44, wounded 210, missing 30, total 284.

NPS, Confederate Position Tablet, The Railroad Redoubt; WPA Index: 329:

This salient redoubt was occupied, May 22, 1863, by a detachment of the 30th Alabama, supported by two companies, under Major O. Steele, of Waul's Texas Legion. The entrenchment in rear was held by the 30th Alabama, reinforced during the day, by the 46th Alabama under command of Lieut. Col. E. W. Pettus, 20th Alabama—a large part of the 46th, including all its field officers, having been captured, May 16, in the battle of Champion's Hill. About 11 a.m., a detachment of the Union assaulting force reached the ditch of the Redoubt and placed flags on its parapet; a small party entered this work at its salient angle, where a breach had been made by the Union artillery, captured a Lieut. and a few enlisted men, held the redoubt a short time and then retired to its ditch, after sustaining severe loss. This work was retaken about 5:30 p.m. by a detachment of Capt. Bradley's and Lieut. Hogue's companies of Waul's Texas Legion, led by Lieut. Col. E. W. Pettus, 20th Alabama; later in the evening, a Lieut. Col. and about 58 men were captured in the ditch.

The casualties in the commands defending and recapturing the redoubt on that day cannot be accurately stated. This tablet marks the salient angle at which the assaulting party entered this redoubt on May 22. Casualties in the 46th Alabama during the defense: killed 15, wounded 45, total 60.

2.23.2 Unit monument: Granite Stele, Texas: Waul's Legion: Roster. N 32 20 34 25 / W 90 51 23 92; WPA Index: 316

2.23.3 Granite Stele, Bronze Tablet, Texas: Johnston's Army of Relief: Gregg's Brigade, 7th Infantry; Ector's Brigade, 9th Infantry 10th, 14th, 32nd Cavalry, Dismounted; Maxey's Brigade, 1st Battalion Sharpshooters; 2nd Cavalry Brigade, 3rd, 6th, 9th Infantry, 1st Legion. N 32 20 33 26 / W 90 51 23 92; WPA Index: 317

2.23.4 Granite Stele, 11th Wisconsin VI, May 22 Assault, Marks Farthest Advance. N 32 20 32 02 / W 90 51 26 80; WPA Index: 309

2.23.5 Granite Tablet, 97th Illinois VI, May 22 Assault (W 12, M 2, T 14). N 32 20 29 88 / W 90 51 24 68; WPA Index: 310

2.23.6 Granite Stele, Bronze Tablet: Waul's Texas Legion, Dupeir's Louisiana Zouaves (Battalion). N 32 20 32 60 / W 90 51 28 06; WPA Index: 313

Confederate Line: Granite Stele, 1st Mississippi Lt. Artillery, Co. E. Unit monument: Stele, 1st Mississippi Lt. Artillery, Co. E: Engaged: Defense, May 18–July 4 (W 2).

2.23.7 Unit monument: Granite Stele, Mississippi: Hudson's Battery, Engaged: Defense, May 18–July 4 (K 1, W 22, T 22). N 32 20 32 02 / W 90 51 28 64; WPA Index: 311

2.23.8 Bust, Col. Thomas N. Waul, CS Army, Commanding Texas Legion (Sculptor: T. A. R. Kitson, 1912). N 32 20 29 30 / W 90 51 30 40; WPA Index: 306

2.23.9 Statue, Brig. Gen. Stephen D. Lee, CS Army, commanding 2nd Brigade, Stevenson's Division (Sculptor: Henry Kitson, 1909). N 32 20 36 35 / W 90 51 31 90; WPA Index: 299 (See chap. 1.)

2.23.10 Unit monument: Stele, 1st Mississippi Lt. Artillery, Co. E: Engaged: Defense, May 18–July 4 (W 2). N 32 20 25 21 / W 90 51 32 16; WPA Index: 298

2.25.1 State of Alabama Memorial (Sculptor: Steffen Thomas, 1951). N 32 20 22 71 / W 90 51 34 36; WPA Index: 294 (See chap. 1.)

2.26.1 State of Kentucky, Confederate monument (Sculptor: n.a.). N 32 20 17 67 / W 90 51 37 24; WPA Index: 287 (See chap. 1.)

2.26.2 Bust, Brig. Gen. Edward D. Tracy, CS Army, commanding 2nd Brigade, Stevenson's Division, Killed in action, May 1, 1863 (Sculptor: Solon Borglum, 1913). N 32 20 17 60 / W 90 51 39 98; WPA Index: 284

2.26.3 Granite Stele, Brig. Gen. Edward D. Tracy, CS Army, killed in the battle of Port Gibson, May 1, 1863. N 32 20 17 44 / W 90 51 39 26; WPA Index: 273

2.26.4 Unit monument: Granite Stele, Vaiden Battery, Mississippi, River Batteries, Engaged May 18–July 4. N 32 20 17 35 / W 90 51 38 56; WPA Index: 283

2.26.5 Bust, Brig. Gen. Isham W. Garrott, CS Army, Colonel, 20th Alabama, commanding second brigade, Stevenson's Division, May 1–2, 1863 (Sculptor: William Couper, 1909). N 32 20 11 45 / W 90 51 47 94; WPA Index: 269

2.27.1 Shaft, Georgia State Memorial (Designer: Harry Sellers, 1962). N 32 20 10 87 / W 90 51 48 44; WPA Index: n.a. (See chap. 1.)

Tour Stop 14: Fort Garrott:

Situated to protect a significant overland route into Vicksburg, Fort Garrott was named after the courageous commander of the 20th Alabama Volunteer Infantry, Colonel Isham W. Garrott. As one of the regiments that garrisoned the fort, the 20th Alabama was, like all other Southern troops, subjected to the constant sniping fire of Federal sharpshooters. Finally frustrated over conditions in the fort—particularly the annoying sharp-shooters—Col. Garrott decided to return the compliment. He obtained a musket and prepared to return a sharpshooter's fire when he was hit and killed instantly by a Union minié ball. He died without learning that he had been promoted to the rank of Brigadier General.

Union Lines

2.27.2 Unit monument: Four-Sided Granite Shaft, with Bronze Tablets and Surmounting Capstone: 11th, 24th, 34th, 46th Indiana VI, 1st Brigade; 12th Division; 13th Corps. N 32 20 06 60 / W 90 51 46 32; WPA Index: 409

2.27.3 Unit monument: Granite Obelisk, 29th Wisconsin VI, 1st Brigade; 12th Division; 13th Corps. N 32 20 03 94 / W 90 51 47 56; WPA Index: 410

2.27.4 Relief Portrait, Brig. Gen. George F. McGinnis, US Vols., commanding 1st Brigade; 12th Division; 13th Corps (Sculptor: T. A. R. Kitson, 1911). N 32 20 01 35 / W 90 51 47 48; WPA Index: 412

Tour Stop 15: Hovey's Approach:

The Union forces opposite Fort Garrott were commanded by Brigadier General Alvin Hovey. It was Hovey's infantrymen who dug two approach trenches which merge just before Fort Garrott. Here you can obtain an excellent view of how siege operations were conducted. The approach trench is zig-zag, a design to minimize Northern casualties by reducing the effectiveness of Southern enfilading fire.

2.28.1 Indiana State Monument, Statue of Governor Oliver P. Morton, 1861–1866 (Sculptor: George T. Brewster, 1926). N 32 19 57 89 / W 90 51 45 42; WPA Index: 585 (See chap. 1.)

ABOVE Granite Tablet, 11th Indiana VI Sharpshooters, looking west toward Confederate lines.

BELOW Granite Tablet, 46th Indiana VI, Sharpshooters Line. Looking northwest across the landscape between the siege lines. Union Avenue can be seen on the right. The ridge where the Kentucky State Monument stands is in the distance to the left.

2.28.2 Granite Tablet, 11th Indiana VI, Sharpshooters Line, June 4–July 4.
   N 32 20 02 56 / W 90 51 42 34; WPA Index: 418

2.28.3 Granite Tablet, 46th Indiana VI, Sharpshooters Line, June 4–July 4.
   N 32 20 02 96 / W 90 51 42 12; WPA Index: 420

2.28.4 Granite Tablet, 24th Indiana VI, Sharpshooters Line, June 4–July 4.
   N 32 20 03 24 / W 90 51 41 26; WPA Index: 422

US Union Trench

2.28.5 Granite Tablet, 11th Indiana VI, Camp, June 4–July 4. In first ravine east of marker. N 32 20 58 61 / W 90 51 38 56; WPA Index: 414

2.28.6 Granite Tablet, 24th Indiana VI, Camp, June 4–July 4. In first ravine east of marker. N 32 20 20 01 45 / W 90 51 26 59; WPA Index: 416

2.28.7 Granite Tablet, 46th Indiana VI, Camp, June 4–July 4. In first ravine east of marker. N 32 20 58 95 / W 90 51 37 54; WPA Index: 415

Hovey's Approach

Union Trench; WPA Index: 377: "Hovey's Approach. First angle in left line of Hovey's approach. From this marker to where the right and left lines of the approach united this trench was a zigzag with eight angles."

2.28.8 Granite Tablet, 8th Indiana VI, Camp, May 23-July 4. N 32 20 33 04 / W 90 51 08 16; WPA Index: 570

2.28.9 Bust, Brig. Gen. Alvin P. Hovey, US Vols., commanding 12th Division; 13th Corps (Sculptor: George T. Brewster, 1915). N 32 20 50 89 / W 90 51 36 44; WPA Index: 426

Bust, Brig. Gen. Alvin P. Hovey, US Vols. (1821–1891), commanding 12th Division; 13th Corps at Vicksburg. Monument is on the South Loop of Union Avenue, facing west toward Confederate lines. Hovey was colonel of the 24th Indiana VI at Shiloh, a brigade commander at Champion Hill, a division commander in the Atlanta Campaign. He was a US congressman and governor of Indiana after the war.

Granite Obelisk, Bronze Tablet, with Company C, 1st Indiana Vol. Cavalry, Union Avenue, South Loop. Cavalry had a limited role in the siege of Vicksburg, but all units from the state of Illinois present for duty at Vicksburg were accorded separate stand-alone monuments. The monument to Company C, 1st Indiana Volunteer Cavalry is a granite obelisk faced with a bronze tablet and a bronze seal of the state of Indiana. Adjacent slabs are decorated with crossed sword reliefs; the whole surmounts a gran-ite plinth. This unit served as headquarters escort to Brig. Gen. Alvin P. Hovey's 12th Division; 13th Corps. It had no reported casualties in the campaign.

2.28.10 Bust, William T. Rigby, 2nd Lt., Co. B, 24th Iowa VI; Park Commissioner (Sculptor: Henry Kitson, 1928). N 32 20 05 98 / W 90 51 36 20; WPA Index: 427

2.28.11 Granite Obelisk, Bronze Tablet, Company C, 1st Indiana Vol. Cavalry; 12th Division; 13th Corps, Escort at Division Headquarters. N 32 20 06 12 / W 90 51 35 62; WPA Index: 428

2.28.12 Bronze Tablet, 28th Iowa VI, Sharpshooters Line, June 5–July 4. N 32 20 06 53 / W 90 51 35 46; WPA Index: 429

2.28.13 Bronze Tablet, 28th Iowa VI, Camp, June 4–July 4. N 32 20 06 56 / W 90 51 35 96; WPA Index: 432

2.28.14 Unit monument: Granite Columns and Arch with Bronze Tablets: 24th, 28th Iowa VI, 2nd Brigade; 12th Division; 13th Corps. N 32 20 06 96 / W 90 51 36 14; WPA Index: 433

2.28.15 Bronze Tablet, 24th Iowa, Camp, June 4–July 4. N 32 20 07 99 / W 90 51 35 88; WPA Index: 434

Bronze Tablet: 28th Iowa VI, 2nd Brigade; 12th Division; 13th Corps, Advanced Sharpshooters Line, west of Union Avenue, siege line, looking southwest, with Fort Garrott in background. Engaged, battle of Port Gibson, May 1, 1863, battle of Champion's Hill, May 16. Aggregate reported casualties during the campaign and siege: K 24, W 76, M 17, T 117.

Field East of Square Fort, also Known as Fort Garrott

2.28.16 Bronze Tablet, 28th Iowa VI, Advanced Sharpshooters Line, June 5– July 4. N 32 20 10 66 / W 90 51 39 56; WPA Index: 394

2.28.17 Bronze Tablet, 24th Iowa VI, Advanced Sharpshooters Line, June 5– July 4. N 32 20 11 49 / W 90 51 38 92; WPA Index: 398

Union Avenue

2.28.18 Bronze Tablet, 24th Iowa VI, Sharpshooters Line, June 5–July 4. N 32 20 11 49 / W 90 51 38 92; WPA Index: 435

2.28.19 Relief Portrait, Col. James R. Slack. 47th Indiana VI, commanding Second Brigade; 12th Division; 13th Corps (Sculptor: Adolf A. Weinman, 1912). N 32 20 08 80 / W 90 51 34 66; WPA Index: 440

2.28.20 Unit Monument: Granite Stele, 56th Ohio VI, 2nd Brigade; 12th Division; 13th Corps. N 32 20 09 00 / W 90 51 90 51 34 80; WPA Index: 441

2.28.21 Granite Tablet, 47th Indiana VI, Camp. N 32 20 09 69 / W 90 51 34 16; WPA Index: 443

2.28.22 Granite Tablet, 118th Illinois VI May 22 Assault (K 2, W 3, T 5). N 32 20 09 84 / W 90 51 34 62; WPA Index: 444

The Siege Line: Granite Stele, 56th Ohio VI, 2nd Brigade; 12th Division; 13th Corps. Engaged, battle of Port Gibson, May 1, 1863; skirmish on Fourteen Mile Creek; battle of Champion's Hill. Aggregate reported casualties during the campaign and siege, K 26, W 113, M 35, T 175.

2.28.23 Unit Monument: Granite Stele, Bronze Tablet: 47th Indiana VI, 2nd Brigade; 12th Division; 13th Corps. N 32 20 10 25 / W 90 51 34 22; WPA Index: 445

2.28.24 Granite Stele, 120th Ohio VI, May 22 Assault. N 32 20 10 67 / W 90 51 34 22; WPA Index: 446

2.28.25 Granite Tablet, 47th Indiana VI, Sharpshooters Line, June 5–July 4. N 32 20 10 94 / W 90 51 33 96; WPA Index: 447

2.28.26 Granite Tablet, 87th Illinois VI, Sharpshooters Line, June 5–July 4. N 32 20 11 08 / W 90 51 33 62; WPA Index: 448

2.28.27 Unit Monument: Granite Stele, Bronze Tablet: 1st Missouri Lt. Artillery. N 32 20 11 34 / W 90 51 33 06; WPA Index: 450

2.28.28 Unit Monument: Granite Stele, 2nd Ohio Battery, Lt. Artillery, 12th Division; 13th Corps. N 32 20 10 56 / W 90 51 31 36; WPA Index: 452

Kentucky Avenue

2.29.1 State of Kentucky Memorial (Designer: Terry Joy, 2001). N 32 20 13 67 / W 90 51 36 72; WPA Index 456

2.29.2 Bust, Brig. Gen. George B. Cosby, CS Army, commanding 1st Brigade, Cavalry, Division, Johnston's Army (Sculptor: Anton Schaaf, 1915). N 32 20 14 03 / W 90 51 36 86; WPA Index: 455

The Kentucky Memorial: Close-up of the two wartime presidents, each born in Kentucky, in apparent conversation.

2.29.3 Bust, Maj. Gen. John C. Breckinridge, CS Army, commanding Division, Johnston's Army (Sculptor: T. A. R. Kitson, 1915). N 32 20 13 23 / W 90 51 35 68; WPA Index: 457

2.29.4 Bust, Brig. Gen., William Vandever, US Vols., commanding 1st Brigade, Herron's Division (Sculptor: George T. Brewster, 1915). N 32 20 13 07 / W 90 51 55 40; WPA Index: 67

2.29.5 Bust, Brig. Gen. Jacob G. Lauman, US Vols., commanding 4th Division; 16th Corps (Sculptor: Roland H. Perry, 1914). N 32 20 12 99 / W 90 51 35 20; WPA Index: 226

2.29.6 Granite Tablet, 54th Indiana VI, Sharpshooters Line, June 4–June 22. N 32 20 12 99 / W 90 51 35 20; WPA Index: 458

2.29.7 Bust, Brig. Gen. Benjamin H. Helm. CS Army, commanding Kentucky Brigade, Breckinridge's Division, Johnston's Army (Sculptor: Anton Schaaf, 1914). N 32 20 12 71 / W 90 51 34 98; WPA Index: 460

Granite Tablet, 69th Indiana VI, May 22 Assault. Image looks west, toward Confederate Avenue—at the tree line—showing the nature of the terrain between the siege lines.

The Ridge Extending Northwest from Kentucky Avenue, 400 Feet West of Union Avenue

2.29.8 Granite Stele, 16th Ohio VI, May 22 Assault, Marks Farthest Advance. N 32 20 13 71 / W 90 51 31 90; WPA Index: 465

2.29.9 Granite Tablet, 69th Indiana VI, May 22 Assault (K 2, W 10, T 12). N 32 20 13 14 / W 90 51 31 90; WPA Index: 464

2.29.10 Granite Stele, 114th Ohio VI, May 22 Assault, Marks Farthest Advance. N 32 20 12 71 / W 90 51 32 24; WPA Index: 462

Union Avenue/ Kentucky Avenue

2.29.11 Relief Portrait, Brig. Gen. T. T. Garrard, US Vols., commanding 1st Brigade, 9th Division; 13th Corps (Sculptor: T. A. R. Kitson, 1912). N 32 20 10 42 / W 90 51 31 22; WPA Index: 466

2.29.12 Unit Monument, Granite Obelisk, 87th Illinois VI, 2nd Brigade; 12th Division; 13th Corps. N 32 20 10 14 / W 90 51 31 06; WPA Index: 454

2.29.13 State of Kentucky, Site for Union monument—not installed. WPA Index: 470

2.29.14 Unit Monument: Granite Stele, 1st Wisconsin Lt. Artillery; 19th Division; 13th Corps. N 32 20 09 05 / W 90 51 30 38; WPA Index: 471

2.29.15 Granite Tablet, 49th Indiana VI, May 22 Assault (K 2, W 13, T 15). N 32 20 15 52 / W 90 51 31 25; WPA Index: 478

2.29.16 Unit Monument: Granite Obelisk, 118th Illinois VI; 1st Brigade, 9th Division; 13th Corps. N 32 20 15 88 / W 90 51 21 40; WPA Index: 488

2.29.17 Relief Portrait, Col. James Keigwin, 49th Indiana VI, commanding 1st Brigade, 9th Division; 13th Corps (Sculptor: T. A. R. Kitson, 1914). N 32 20 16 98 / W 90 51 19 94; WPA Index: 491

2.29.18 Unit Monument: Granite Stele, 120th Ohio VI, 1st Brigade; 9th Division; 13th Corps. N 32 20 17 77 / W 90 51 19 56; WPA Index: 492

Union Avenue: Relief Portrait, Col. James Keigwin, 49th Indiana VI. The relief portraits in the park could be a study in itself. Col. James Keigwin is one example. Keigwin (1829–1904) was lieutenant colonel of the 49th until October 18, 1862, when he was promoted to colonel of the regiment. He led the regiment, as well as holding interim brigade and division commands, until 1864, when the enlistment term of the 49th expired. The portrait was funded by the federal government at a cost of $275.

The Siege Line, Union Avenue: Granite Obelisk, 120th Ohio VI, 1st Brigade; 9th Division; 13th Corps. "Aggregate reported casualties in regiment during the campaign and siege, killed 2, wounded 22, missing 2, total 26." Note the laurel wreaths, muskets, state seal, canteen, and cartridge box, all in high relief, in granite.

2.29.19 Unit Monument: Granite Stele with Bronze Tablets and Surmounting Capstone: 54th, 49th, 69th Indiana VI, 2nd Brigade, 9th Division, 13th Corps VI. N 32 20 18 27 / W 90 51 19 06; WPA Index: 493

2.29.20 Relief Portrait, Col. Daniel W. Lindsey, 22nd Kentucky VI, commanding 2nd Brigade, 9th Division; 13th Corps, May–July 4 (Sculptor: T. A. R. Kitson, 1915). N 32 20 18 27 / W 90 51 19 06; WPA Index: 494

2.29.21 Unit Monument: Granite Stele, Bronze Tablet: 6th Missouri Vol. Cavalry, 9th Division; 13th Corps. N 32 20 18 93 / W 90 51 18 50; WPA Index: 497

2.29.22 Bust, Brig. Gen. Peter J. Osterhaus, 9th Division; 13th Corps (Sculptor: T. A. R. Kitson, 1913). N 32 20 19 10 / W 90 51 18 32; WPA Index: 498

The Siege Line, Union Avenue: Granite Stele with Bronze Tablets and Surmounting Cap, 49th, 54th, 69th Indiana VI, 2nd Brigade, 9th Division, 13th Corps. Union regimental monuments provide copious detail of the service of individual units at Vicksburg NMP. The regiment was a foundational unit of organization in the war, and regimental histories are a significant if underutilized genre of American literature. As an example, this monument displays the following data: the 54th VI, engaged at Port Gibson, Raymond, Big Black River Bridge and for prisoners, May 17–June 4; siege, June 4–June 22; 49th VI, engaged at Port Gibson, Champion's Hill, Big Black River Bridge, Vicksburg: May 19 assault, May 22 assault; duty at Big Black River Bridge, May 24–July 4. Casualties: K 10, W 52, M 2, T 64. 69th VI, engaged at Port Gibson, Champion's Hill, Big Black River Bridge; Vicksburg: May 19 assault; May 22 assault; duty at Big Black River Bridge, May 24–July 4. Casualties: K 16, W 72, M 7, T 95.

2.29.23 Unit Monument: Granite Obelisk, 3rd Illinois Vol. Cavalry, Companies A, D, E, G, and K. N 32 20 19 52 / W 90 51 17 90; WPA Index: 500

2.29.24 Unit Monument: Granite Obelisk, 2nd Illinois Vol. Cavalry, Companies F, G, H, I, and K, 9th Division; 13th Corps. N 32 20 19 78 / W 90 51 17 68; WPA Index: 502

2.29.25 Relief Portrait: Col. Lionel A. Sheldon, 42nd Ohio VI, commanding 2nd Brigade, 9th Division; 13th Corps (Sculptor: Victor S. Holm [date n.a.]). N 32 20 19 19 / W 90 51 17 50; WPA Index: 503

2.29.26 Unit Monument: Granite Stele, 114th Ohio VI, 2nd Brigade, 9th Division; 13th Corps. N 32 20 20 44 / W 90 51 16 94; WPA Index: 505

Granite Stele, 42nd Ohio VI, farthest advance, May 22 assault, looking west. Located between Union Avenue and Confederate Avenue on a ridge southeast of the Alabama Memorial. The monument is intact, but the area between the lines receives minimal maintenance, and in this image may only just be discernible. Several monuments have no trails or other means of access and appear to be seldom visited.

2.29.27 Unit Monument: Granite Stele, 42nd Ohio VI, 2nd Brigade, 9th Division; 13th Corps. N 32 20 20 61 / W 90 51 16 04; WPA Index: 506

2.29.28 Granite Tablet, 49th Indiana VI, May 22 Assault (K 2, W 13, T 15). N 32 20 15 52 / W 90 51 31 25; WPA Index: 478

2.29.29 Granite Stele, 42nd Ohio VI, Sharpshooters Line, June 4–June 22. N 32 20 17 66 / W 90 51 30 41; WPA Index: 479

2.29.30 Granite Stele, 42nd Ohio VI, farthest advance, May 22 assault. N 32 20 17 88 / W 90 51 30 38; WPA Index: 483

2.29.31 Unit Monument: Granite Stele, 16th Ohio VI, 2nd Brigade, 9th Division; 13th Corps. N 32 20 20 97 / W 90 51 15 30; WPA Index: 512

2.29.32 Bust, Samuel J. Kirkwood, Iowa Governor 1860–1864 (Sculptor: Henry Kitson, 1927). N 32 20 20 76 / W 90 51 14 16; WPA Index: 514

2.29.33 Unit Monument: Granite Stele, Ohio 16th Battery, 12th Division; 13th Corps. N 32 20 20 88 / W 90 51 13 20; WPA Index: 515

2.29.34 Bronze Tablet, 23rd Iowa VI, 2nd Brigade; 14th Division; 13th Corps, Camp, June 18–July 4. N 32 20 21 41 / W 90 51 12 14; WPA Index: 517

2.29.35 Bronze Tablet, 22nd Iowa VI, Sharpshooters Line, May 23–July 4. N 32 20 21 86 / W 90 51 11 72; WPA Index: 508

2.29.36 Bronze Tablet, 22nd Iowa VI, Camp, May 21–July 4. N 32 20 20 48 / W 90 51 10 34; WPA Index: 520

The Siege Line: Union Avenue: Bust, Samuel J. Kirkwood, Iowa Governor 1860–64 (Sculptor: Henry Kitson, 1927). Kirkwood, like other wartime governors commemorated on the field, was a staunch supporter of Lincoln and the Union war effort.

2.30.1 Iowa's State Memorial (Henry H. Kitson, T. A. R. Kitson, 1906, 1912). N 32 20 21 36 / W 90 51 11 66; WPA Index: 519 (See chap. 1.)

2.30.2 Statue, Maj. Gen. Edward O. C. Ord, US Vols., commanding 13th Corps, June 19–July 4 (Sculptor: Anton Schaaf, 1916). N 32 20 23 29 / W 90 51 10 88; WPA Index: 587

2.30.2 Equestrian Statue, Maj. Gen. John A. McClernand, US Vols., Illinois, commanding 13th Corps (relieved June 19, 1863) (Sculptor: Edward C. Potter, 1919). N 32 20 24 01 / W 90 51 10 60; WPA Index: 523 (See chap. 1.)

2.30.3 Unit Monument: Granite Tablet, 3rd Illinois Vol. Cavalry, Company L, 13th Corps. Escort at Corps Headquarters. N 32 20 24 56 / W 90 51 10 12; WPA Index: 525

2.30.4 Bronze Tablet, 21st Iowa VI, Camp, May 21–July 4, 1863 (in first ravine east of marker). N 32 20 25 21 / W 90 51 09 50; WPA Index: 528

2.30.5 Bronze Tablet, 21st Iowa VI, Sharpshooters Line, May 23–July 4. N 32 20 25 28 / W 90 51 09 72; WPA Index: 542

2.30.6 Bust, Brig. Gen. Michael Lawler, US Vols., commanding 2nd Brigade; 14th Division; 13th Corps (Sculptor: Anton Schaaf, 1915). N 32 20 25 76 / W 90 51 09 49; WPA Index: 543

Statue, Maj. Gen. Edward O. C. Ord, US Vols., commanding 13th Corps, June 19–July 4 (Sculptor: Anton Schaaf, 1916). Ord (1818–83) was a West Point graduate and was serving in the regular army at the outbreak of war. He had extensive service in the eastern and western theaters of the conflict and rose to command of the Army of the James by war's end. He died in Havana, Cuba, of yellow fever in 1883.

2.30.7 Unit Monument: Granite Columns and Arch with Bronze Tablets: 21st, 22nd, 24th Iowa, 2nd Brigade; 14th Division; 13th Corps. N 32 20 25 91 / W 90 51 09 90; WPA Index: 544

2.30.8 Unit Monument: Granite Obelisk, 11th Wisconsin VI, 2nd Brigade; 14th Division; 13th Corps. N 32 20 26 65 / W 90 51 08 62; WPA Index: 545

2.30.9 Relief Portrait, Col. Charles L. Harris, US Vols., 11th Wisconsin VI, commanding 2nd Brigade; 14th Division; 13th Corps, May 29–April 30 (Sculptor: T. A. R. Kitson, 1913). N 32 20 27 09 / W 90 51 08 13; WPA Index: 545

2.30.10 Unit Monument: Granite Tablet, 3rd Illinois Vol. Cavalry, Company G, 13th Corps. Escort at Division Headquarters. N 32 20 27 56 / W 90 51 07 66; WPA Index: 555

2.30.11 Relief Portrait, Col. Henry Washburn, US Vols., 18th Indiana VI, commanding 1st Brigade; 14th Division; 13th Corps Sculptor: T. A. R. Kitson, 1915). N 32 20 27 90 / W 90 51 08 02; WPA Index: 553

2.30.12 Granite Tablet, 18th Indiana VI, Camp, May 23–July 4. N 32 20 29 10 / W 90 51 08 28; WPA Index: 551

2.30.13 Granite Tablet, 18th Indiana, Sharpshooters Line, May 23–July 4. N 32 20 29 10 / W 90 51 08 28; WPA Index: 552

2.30.14 Bust, Brig. Gen. Eugene A. Carr, US Vols., commanding 14th Division; 13th Corps (Sculptor: Roland H. Perry, 1916). N 32 20 29 67 / W 90 51 08 48; WPA Index: 554

2.30.15 Unit Monument: Granite Obelisk, 33rd Illinois VI, 1st Brigade; 14th Division; 13th Corps. N 32 20 30 10 / W 90 51 08 68; WPA Index: 557

2.30.16 Granite Obelisk, 99th Illinois VI, 1st Brigade; 14th Division; 13th Corps. N 32 20 30 22 / W 90 51 08 70; WPA Index: 569

2.30.17 Relief Portrait, Brig. Gen. William P. Benton, US Vols., commanding 1st Brigade; 14th Division; 13th Corps (Sculptor: T. A. R. Kitson, 1911). N 32 20 30 63 / W 90 51 08 70; WPA Index: 558

2.30.18 Relief Portrait, Col. David Shunk, US Vols., 8th Indiana VI, commanding 1st Brigade; 14th Division; 13th Corps (Sculptors: Victor S. Holm, Jules Berchem, 1915). N 32 20 30 95 / W 90 51 08 68; WPA Index: 550

2.30.19 Granite Tablet, 99th Illinois VI, Campground during siege. N 32 20 30 08 / W 90 51 08 66; WPA Index: 560

2.30.20 Unit Monument: Granite Obelisk, Battery A, 2nd Illinois Lt. Artillery. N 32 20 31 13 / W 90 51 08 68; WPA Index: 561

2.30.21 Granite Tablet, 33rd Illinois VI, Campground during siege. N 32 20 30 56 / W 90 51 07 38; WPA Index: 566

2.30.22 Granite Tablet, 8th Indiana VI, Camp, May 23–July 4, 1863. WPA Index: 570

South End of Vicksburg lines, at Navy Circle, of Bus. US 61, Visitors Center

2.30.1 Unit Monument: Granite Obelisk, 37th Illinois VI, Col John C. Black, 1st Brigade, Herron's Division. N 32 18 42 38 / W 90 53 57 90; WPA Index: 3

2.30.2 Granite Tablet, 26th Indiana VI, 1st Brigade, Herron's Division, Sharpshooters Line, June 24–July 4; WPA Index: 56 (Presently in storage.)

South Fort

2.30.3 Bronze Tablet, 11th, 13th, 15th, and 16th Iowa VI (Skirmishers), 3rd Brigade; 6th Division 17th Corps, May 22 Assault (K 1, W 2, T 3). N 32 18 55 75 / W 90 53 54 38; WPA Index: 9

Louisiana Circle, Mississippi River Overlook

2.30.4 Unit Monument: Granite Stele, Bronze Tablet: 8th Louisiana Heavy Artillery. N 32 19 10 54 / W 90 53 49 84; WPA Index: 29

2.30.5 Relief Portrait, Capt. Toby Hart, CS Army, Company E, 8th Heavy Artillery Battalion (Sculptor: George T. Brewster, 1921). N 32 19 10 34 / W 90 53 49 70; WPA Index: 28

2.30.6 Relief Portrait, Col. Edward Higgins, CS Artillery, commanding river batteries (Sculptor: T. A. R. Kitson, 1915). N 32 19 10 23 / W 90 53 49 56; WPA Index: 27

2.30.7 Relief Portrait, Maj. Fred H. Ogden, CS Army, 8th Heavy Artillery Battalion (Sculptor: George T. Brewster, 1921). N 32 19 09 10 / W 90 53 49 38; WPA Index: 26

2.30.8 Unit Monument: Granite Stele, Bronze Tablet: 22nd Louisiana Infantry. N 32 19 09 99 / W 90 53 49 30; WPA Index: 25

2.30.9 Unit Monument: Granite Stele, Bronze Tablet: Louisiana River Batteries. N 32 19 09 90 / W 90 53 49 10; WPA Index: 24

Vicksburg, West End: Frontage Road, Corner of Washington Street

2.30.10 Bust, Brig. Gen. John W. Whitfield CS Army, 2nd Brigade, Cav. Division Johnston's Army (Sculptor: George T. Brewster, 1917). N 32 19 06 67 / W 90 53 47 32; WPA Index: 33

2.30.11 Bust, Brig. Gen. William H. Jackson, CS Army, Commanding Cavalry Division, Johnston's Army (Sculptor: R. Hinton Perry, 1913). N 32 19 08 24 / W 90 53 48 06; WPA Index: 22

2.30.12 Relief Portrait, Col. Lawrence S. Ross, CS Army, 6th Texas Cavalry, commanding 2nd Brigade, Cavalry Division, Johnston's Army (Sculptor: Anton Schaaf, 1915). N 32 19 03 37 / W 90 53 41 46; WPA Index: 34

Stouts Bayou Railroad Bridge

2.30.13 Bust, Brig. Gen. Samuel B. Maxey, CS Army, commanding brigade, French's Division, Johnston's Army (Sculptor: T. A. R. Kitson, 1915). N 32 19 05 64 / W 90 53 29 60; WPA Index: 37

2.30.14 Bust, Maj. Gen. Samuel French, CS Army, commanding Division, Johnston's Army (Sculptor: R. Hinton Perry, 1914). N 32 19 06 12 / W 90 53 27 88; WPA Index: 38

2.30.15 Statue, Brig. Gen. Evander McNair, CS Army, 4th Arkansas Infantry, commanding brigade, French's Division, Johnston's Army (Sculptor: Anton Schaaf, 1915). N 32 19 05 50 / W 90 53 25 12; WPA Index: 39

Confederate Avenue and Frontage Road, Vicksburg Theater Guild

2.30.16 Granite Stele, Bronze Tablet: Louisiana Pointe Coupee Artillery, Company C, Stevenson's Division. N 32 19 04 09 / W 90 53 25 04; WPA Index: 41

2.31.1 Granite Stele, Bronze Tablet: The Virginia State Memorial, Botetourt Artillery. N 32 19 03 81 / W 90 53 22 10; WPA Index: 43 (See chap. 1.)

2.31.2 Relief Portrait, Lt. Francis Obenchain, CS Army, commanding Botetourt Artillery (Sculptor: Frederick Hibbard, 1915). N 32 19 04 36 / W 90 53 20 54; WPA Index: 44

Iowa Avenue

There is no public access to the monuments at Iowa Circle. They stand on former park property in the City of Vicksburg, south of Interstate 20 and modern Iowa Avenue

2.31.3 Unit Monument: Granite Stele, 26th Indiana VI, 1st Brigade, Herron's Division. WPA Index: 60 (Presently in storage)

2.31.4 Unit Monument: Granite Stele, Column and Bronze Tablet: 19th, 20th, 34th, 38th Iowa VI. N 32 18 34 81 / W 90 53 34 81; WPA Index: 65

Confederate Avenue

2.31.5 Relief Portrait, Brig. Gen. Seth Barton, CS Army, commanding brigade, Stevenson's Division, March 29–July 4 (Sculptor: T. A. R. Kitson, 1911). N 32 19 07 69 / W 90 53 15 64; WPA Index: 75

2.31.6 Relief Portrait, Col. Skidmore Harris, CS Army, 43rd Georgia Infantry. Killed in action, May 16, 1863 (Sculptor: George T. Brewster, 1919). N 32 19 10 09 / W 90 53 11 52; WPA Index: 77

2.31.7 Unit Monument: Granite Stele, Bronze Tablet: Louisiana, Point Coupee Artillery, Co A. N 32 19 09 65 / W 90 53 10 30; WPA Index: 78

2.30.8 Bust, Brig. Gen. Nathan Evans, CS Army, commanding brigade, French's Division, Johnston's Army (Sculptor: Louis Millione, 1914). N 32 19 13 15 / W 90 53 09 00; WPA Index: 82

2.32.1 Granite Stele, State of South Carolina Memorial (1925). N 32 19 15 46 / W 90 53 07 14; WPA Index: 86 (See chap. 1.)

2.32.2 Bust, Brig. Gen. States Rights Gist, CS Army, commanding brigade, Walker's Division, Johnston's Army. Killed in action, Nov. 30, 1864 (Sculptor: George T. Brewster, 1915). N 32 19 16 59 / W 89 53 05 90; WPA Index: 89

2.32.3 Bust, Maj. Gen William Loring, CS Army, commanding Division, Army of Relief (Sculptor: T. A. R. Kitson, 1911). N 32 19 17 37 / W 90 53 02 10; WPA Index: 90

2.32.4 Relief Portrait, Brig. Gen. Abraham Buford, CS Army, commanding 3rd Brigade, Loring's Division (Sculptor: T. A. R. Kitson, 1911). N 32 19 17 59 / W 90 53 59 78; WPA Index: 92

2.32.5 Relief Portrait, Col. Arthur E. Reynolds, CS Army, 26th Mississippi, commanding brigade, Loring's Division (Sculptor: George E. Ganiere, 1915). N 32 19 18 85 / W 90 53 57 86; WPA Index: 96

2.32.6 Unit Monument: Granite Stele, Mississippi, 1st Lt. Artillery, Company I. N 32 19 21 21 / W 90 52 57 94; WPA Index: 98

2.32.7 Bust, Brig. Gen. W. S. Featherston, CS Army, commanding brigade, Loring's Division (Sculptor: Edmund T., 1915). N 32 19 21 56 / W 90 52 58 42; WPA Index: 99

2.33.1 Granite Stele, Bronze Tablet: State of Maryland Memorial (1914). N 32 19 28 78 / W 90 52 54 16; WPA Index: 105 (See chap. 1.)

2.33.2 Unit Monument: Granite Stele, Tennessee, Stevenson's Division, CS Army: 1st Cavalry; 3rd, 31st, 43rd, 59th Infantry. N 32 19 33 48 / W 90 52 52 86; WPA Index: 108

2.33.3 Relief Portrait, Col. Alexander W. Reynolds, CS Army, commanding brigade, Stevenson's Division (Sculptor: T. A. R. Kitson, 1911). N 32 19 36 46 / W 90 52 50 60; WPA Index: 111

2.34.1 Granite Stele, State of Florida Memorial. N 32 19 37 28 / W 90 52 49 56; WPA Index: 113 (See chap. 1.)

2.35.1 Granite Stele, State of North Carolina Memorial. N 32 19 41 83 / W 90 52 40 86; WPA Index: 122 (See chap. 1.)

2.35.2 Relief Portrait, Maj. Joseph W. Anderson, CS Artillery, killed in action, May 16, 1863 (Sculptor: George T. Brewster, 1919). N 32 19 44 05 / W 90 52 36 88; WPA Index: 125

2.35.3 Bust, Maj. Gen. Carter L. Stevenson, CS Army, commanding Division, Army of Vicksburg (Sculptor: T. A. R. Kitson, 1914). N 32 19 44 23 / W 90 52 35 74; WPA Index: 128

Union Monuments East of Hall's Ferry Road, between the Georgia Salient and John Allen Street (350 feet east of Hall's Ferry Road, 150 feet north of John Allen Street)

NPS, Lauman's Approach; WPA Index: 183

"On the line of Lauman's third parallel and beginning of his left approach to the salient Confederate work on east side of Hall's Ferry Road. Work on the approach commenced June 25, 1863."

2.35.4 Granite Tablet, 76th Illinois VI, Sharpshooters Line, June 25–July 4. W 32 19 35 98 / N 90 52 27 78; WPA Index: 178

2.35.5 Granite Stele, Bronze Tablet, 3rd Iowa VI, Sharpshooters Line, June 25–July 4. W 32 19 35 92 / N 90 52 27 36; WPA Index: 179

2.35.6 Granite Tablet, 46th Illinois VI, Sharpshooters Line, June 25–July 4. W 32 19 36 18 / N 90 52 27 46; WPA Index: 180

2.35.7 Granite Tablet, 15th Illinois VI, Sharpshooters Line, June 25–July 4. W 32 19 36 39 / N 90 52 27 58; WPA Index: 181

2.35.8 Granite Tablet, 14th Illinois VI, Sharpshooters Line, June 25–July 4. W 32 19 37 32 / N 90 52 27 36; WPA Index: 182

Halls Ferry Road, Illinois Circle Beginning 280 yards south of Confederate Ave overpass, including Illinois Circle

2.35.9 Relief Portrait, Col. Cyrus Hall, 14th Illinois VI, commanding 2nd Brigade, 4th Division; 16th Corps (Sculptor: Anton Schaaf, 1915). N 32 19 34 71 / W 90 52 32 12; WPA Index: 136

2.35.10 Relief Portrait, Col. George E. Bryant, 12th Wisconsin VI, commanding 3rd Brigade, 4th Division; 16th Corps (Sculptor: T. A. R. Kitson, 1913). N 32 19 35 08 / W 90 52 32 12; WPA Index: 137

2.35.11 Unit Monument: Granite Tablet, 53rd Indiana VI, 2nd Brigade, 4th Division; 16th Corps. N 32 19 32 63 / W 90 52 33 96; WPA Index: 138

2.35.12 Unit Monument: Granite Obelisk, 76th Illinois VI, 2nd Brigade, 4th Division; 16th Corps. N 32 19 32 58 / W 90 52 33 84; WPA Index: 139

2.35.13 Unit Monument: Granite Obelisk, 46th Illinois VI, 2nd Brigade, 4th Division; 16th Corps. N 32 19 31 62 / W 90 52 33 76; WPA Index: 140

2.35.14 Relief Portrait, Col. Amory K. Johnson, 26th Illinois VI, commanding 3rd Brigade, 4th Division; 16th Corps (Sculptors: George E. Ganiere, Jules Berchem, 1915). N 32 19 31 62 / W 90 52 33 98; WPA Index: 141

2.35.15 Unit Monument: Granite Obelisk, 15th Illinois VI, 2nd Brigade, 4th Division; 16th Corps. N 32 19 30 80 / W 90 52 33 84; WPA Index: 142

2.35.16 Unit Monument: Granite Obelisk, 14th Illinois VI, 2nd Brigade, 4th Division; 16th Corps. N 32 19 31 32 / W 90 52 33 76; WPA Index: 143

ABOVE Granite Obelisk, 28th Illinois VI, 3rd Brigade, 4th Division, 16th Corps "Entered campaign at Young's Point, Louisiana, about May 15, 1863; investment line about June 11."

BELOW Looking southeast from Illinois Circle: Granite Obelisk, 12th Wisconsin VI, 3rd Brigade, 4th Division; 16th Corps. Commanding officers: Colonel George E. Bryant, Lieut. Colonel Dewitt C. Poole, Major William E. Strong. Engaged: Siege, June 11–July 4.

2.35.17 Unit Monument: Granite Stele, with Relief of Eagle, 15th Ohio Battery, 4th Division; 16th Corps. N 32 19 30 77 / W 90 52 34 26; WPA Index: 145

2.35.18 Unit Monument: Granite Obelisk, 28th Illinois VI, 3rd Brigade, 4th Division; 16th Corps. 32 19 30 18 / W 90 52 34 31; WPA Index: 147

2.35.19 Unit Monument: Granite Obelisk, 12th Wisconsin VI, 3rd Brigade, 4th Division; 16th Corps. N 32 19 29 89 / W 90 52 34 36; WPA Index: 148

2.35.20 Unit Monument: Granite Obelisk, 32nd Illinois VI, 3rd Brigade, 4th Division; 16th Corps. N 32 19 29 25 / W 90 52 34 56; WPA Index: 149

2.35.21 Unit Monument: Granite Stele, 7th Ohio Battery, 4th Division; 16th Corps. N 32 19 29 01 / W 90 52 33 98; WPA Index: 153

Vicksburg Mall, off Hall's Ferry Road

Monuments at Vicksburg Mall (N 32 18 51 77 / W 90 52 48 60; formerly Pemberton Mall) were collected at one location when the area was developed as a retail site in the late 1960s

2.35.22 Relief Portrait, Brig. Gen William W. Orme, US Vols., 2nd Brigade, Herron's Division, Provisional Elements (Sculptor: T. A. R. Kitson, 1917). WPA Index: 171

2.35.23 Unit Monument: Granite Obelisk, 20th Wisconsin VI, 2nd Brigade, Herron's Division. WPA Index: 163

2.35.24 Bust, Brig. Gen. Francis J. Herron, US Vols., commanding Herron's Division, Provisional Elements (Sculptor: Solon Borglum, 1914). WPA Index: 170

2.35.25 Unit Monument: Granite Obelisk, 15th Illinois Vol. Cavalry Co. F and I, 4th Division; 16th Corps. WPA Index: 159

2.35.26 Unit Monument: Granite Obelisk, 94th Illinois VI, 2nd Brigade, Herron's Division. WPA Index: 165

2.35.27 Unit Monument: Granite Obelisk, 2nd Illinois Lt. Artillery, Battery K, 4th Division; 16th Corps. WPA Index: 158

Confederate Avenue, North of Hall's Ferry Road

2.35.28 Relief Portrait, Col. Claudius C. Wilson, CS Army, 25th Georgia Infantry, commanding brigade, Walker's Division, Johnston's Army (Sculptor: T. A. R. Kitson, 1915). N 32 19 45 91 / W 90 52 32 29; WPA Index: 191

2.35.29 Granite Stele, Bronze Tablet: Georgia: Roster of units. Johnston's Army, Breckinridge's Division, Stovall's Brigade, 47th Infantry; Walker's Division, Ind. Cav. Company; 25th, 29th, 30th Infantry; 1st Battalion Sharpshooters; Martin's Battery; Gist's Brigade, 46th Infantry; 8th

Battalion; Reserve Artillery, Columbus Artillery. N 32 19 45 91 / W 90 52 32 60; WPA Index: 192

2.35.30 Bust, Brig. Gen. Marcellus A. Stovall, CS Army, commanding brigade, Breckinridge's Division, Johnston's Army (Sculptor: T. A. R. Kitson, 1915). N 32 19 46 29 / W 90 52 32 52; WPA Index: 193

Wisconsin Avenue, Looking South to North

2.35.31 Unit Monument: Granite Obelisk, 33rd Wisconsin VI, 1st Brigade, 4th Division; 16th Corps. N 32 19 19 24 62 / W 90 52 12 54; WPA Index: 225

Wisconsin Avenue and John Allen Street

2.35.32 Unit Monument: Granite Stele, Column and Bronze Tablet: 3rd Iowa VI, 1st Brigade; 4th Division; 16th Corps. N 32 19 29 01 / W 90 52 11 02; WPA Index: 222

2.35.33 Unit Monument: Granite Sculpture of Light Artillery Piece surmounting base, 5th Ohio Lt. Artillery, 4th Division; 16th Corps. N 32 19 29 54 / W 90 52 09 68; WPA Index: 220

2.35.34 Granite Obelisk, 53rd Illinois VI, 1st Brigade, 4th Division; 16th Corps. N 32 19 19 32 49 / W 90 52 15 22; WPA Index: 217

2.35.35 Granite Tablet, 41st Illinois VI, Sharpshooters Line, June 9–July 4. N 32 19 42 09 / W 90 52 17 48; WPA Index: 212

2.35.36 Granite Tablet, 53rd Illinois VI, Sharpshooters Line, June 5–June 22. N 32 19 19 32 58 / W 90 52 15 22; WPA Index: 213

Corner of Adams Street and Wisconsin Avenue

2.35.37 Unit Monument: Granite Obelisk, Battery E, 2nd Illinois Lt. Artillery, 4th Division; 16th Corps. N 32 19 45 33 / W 90 52 15 82; WPA Index: 206

2.35.38 Relief Portrait, Col. Isaac C. Pugh. 41st Illinois VI, commanding 1st Brigade, 4th Division; 16th Corps (Sculptor: T. A. R. Kitson, 1916). N 32 19 45 70 / W 90 52 15 78; WPA Index: 204

2.35.39 Unit Monument: Granite Obelisk, 41st Illinois VI, 1st Brigade, 4th Division; 16th Corps. N 32 19 45 60 / W 90 52 15 30; WPA Index: 203

Confederate Avenue, North of Wisconsin Avenue

2.35.40 Unit Monument: Granite Stele, Bronze Tablet: Wades Battery, Artillery Missouri, CS Army. N 32 19 53 18 / W 90 52 16 24; WPA Index: 230

2.35.41 Unit Monument: Granite Stele, Bronze Tablet: Georgia, Stevenson's Division. N 32 19 53 42 / W 90 52 15 56; WPA Index: 108

2.35.42 **Relief Portrait,** Brig. Gen. Alfred Cumming, CS Army, commanding brigade, Stevenson's Division (Sculptor: T. A. R. Kitson, 1911). N 32 19 53 35 / W 90 52 15 04; WPA Index: 233

Indiana Avenue, Corner of Indiana and Churchill Drive

2.35.43 **Granite Tablet,** 34th Indiana VI, Sharpshooters Line, June 20–July 4. N 32 19 54 67 / W 90 52 04 16; WPA Index: 241

Northeast Corner of Indiana Avenue and North Frontage Road

2.35.44 **Granite Tablet,** 34th Indiana VI, Camp, June 4–July 4. N 32 19 50 00 / W 90 51 46 98; WPA Index: 247

Confederate Avenue, Corner of Military Avenue

2.35.45 **Bust,** Brig. Gen. Thomas H. Taylor, CS Army, commanding 3rd Brigade, Stevenson's Division (Sculptor: T. A. R. Kitson, 1915).. N 32 20 04 55 / W 90 52 01 44; WPA Index: 260

South of Clay Street, Vicinity of Melborn Place

2.35.46 **Granite Tablet,** 33rd Illinois VI, Sharpshooters Line, June 18–July 4. N 32 20 36 06 / W 90 51 14 46; WPA Index: 346

2.35.47 **Bronze Tablet,** 10th Iowa VI, May 22 Assault (afternoon position) (W 12). N 32 20 36 92 / W 90 51 13 64; WPA Index: 347

2.35.48 **Granite Tablet,** 93rd Illinois VI, May 22 Assault (afternoon position) (K 4, W 51, T 55). N 32 20 36 92 / W 90 51 13 73; WPA Index: 348

2.35.49 **Granite Tablet,** 99th Illinois VI, Sharpshooters Line, June 18–July 4. N 32 20 37 40 / W 90 51 13 50; WPA Index: 349

2.35.50 **Granite Tablet,** 8th Indiana VI, May 22 Assault (K 22, W 95, T 117). N 32 20 38 85 / W 90 51 20 92; WPA Index: 359

2.35.51 **Granite Tablet,** 33rd Illinois VI, May 22 Assault (K 13, W 59, T 72). N 32 20 40 32 / W 90 51 20 16; WPA Index: 360

Corner of Grove and Hope, formerly Baldwin's Ferry Road

2.35.52 **Granite Stele, Bronze Tablet:** Company A, 1st Mississippi Lt. Artillery. N 32 20 51 23 / W 90 51 20 02; WPA Index: 638

2.35.53 **Granite Stele,** 1st Mississippi Lt. Artillery, Company A, Camp, May 19–July 4. N 32 20 51 66 / W 90 51 20 76; WPA Index: 639

North Side of Clay Street at Melborn Place

2.35.54 **Bust,** Maj. Gen. William H. T. Walker, CS Army, commanding division, Johnston's Army (Sculptor: T. A. R. Kitson, 1913). N 32 20 43 62 / W 90 51 19 38; WPA Index: 369

South Side of Clay and Melborn Streets

2.35.55 Bust, Brig. Gen. John Gregg, CS Army, commanding brigade, Walker's Division, Johnston's Army (Sculptor: Solon Borglum, 1914). N 32 20 43 45 / W 90 51 20 78; WPA Index: 365

2.35.56 Bust, Brig. Gen. Matthew D. Ector, CS Army, commanding brigade, Walker's Division, Johnston's Army (Sculptor: Anton Schaaf, 1915). N 32 20 43 28 / W 90 51 20 84; WPA Index: 364

South Loop above the Clay Street Bridge

2.35.57 Granite Stele, 26th Missouri VI, May 22 Assault (K 5, W 5, T 10). N 32 20 38 32 / W 90 51 11 92; WPA Index: 352

2.35.58 Bronze Tablet, 5th Iowa VI, May 22 Assault (K 2, W 16, T 18). N 32 20 38 54 / W 90 51 11 72; WPA Index: 353

2.35.59 Granite Tablet, 8th Indiana VI, Sharpshooters Line, June 18–July 4. N 32 20 39 64 / W 90 51 10 68; WPA Index: 355

South Side of Clay Street, Across from Visitor Center

2.35.60 Bust, Brig. Gen. Andrew J. Smith, US Vols., commanding 10th Division; 13th Corps (Sculptor: Frank E. Elwell, 1911). N 32 20 34 07 / W 90 51 04 28; WPA Index: 578

2.35.61 Unit Monument: Granite Stele, Bronze Tablets: 8th, 18th Indiana VI, 1st Brigade; 14th Division; 13th Corps. N 32 20 34 00 / W 90 51 05 00; WPA Index: 572

2.35.62 Unit Monument: Granite Stele, Bronze Tablet: 1st Battery, Indiana Lt. Artillery, 14th Division; 13th Corps. N 32 21 34 00 / W 90 51 05 00; WPA Index: 573

City of Vicksburg

2.36.1 Louisiana, Marble shaft, Monroe and Crawford streets (Sculptor: n.a., 1887). N 32 30 55 90 / W 90 52 48 18; WPA Index: n.a. (See chap. 1.)

2.37.1 Common Soldier, Cedar Hill Cemetery, granite, marble (Sculptor: A. A. Meneze, 1893). N 32 21 58 87 / W 90 51 34 22; WPA Index: n.a. (See chap. 1.)

Grant's Canal Reservation, VNMP, Louisiana

2.38.1 Connecticut State Memorial, concrete, granite (Designer: various, 2008). N 32 19 15 67 / W 90 55 59 06; WPA Index: n.a. (See chap. 1.)

North Mississippi

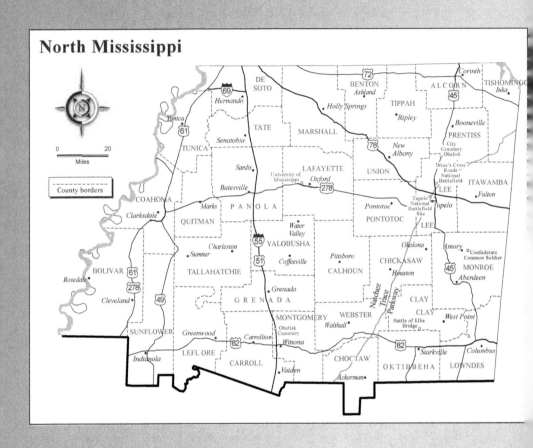

3

NORTHERN
MISSISSIPPI

Introduction

NORTHERN MISSISSIPPI was a battlefield, a staging ground, a refuge, a strategic crossroads, and the area where many hospitals and cemeteries were established during the war. In addition, after it was occupied by Union forces, Corinth became a location for freed African Americans to establish their own community.

Corinth's significance as a rail crossroads led to its being compared to Richmond, Virginia, in importance to the life of the Confederacy. The battle of Brice's Corner is a veritable textbook example of Southern arms in victory, and the battle of Tupelo/Harrisburg has been called a valiant last stand of Confederate arms in Mississippi. Corinth's Civil War Interpretive Center is part of the Shiloh National Military Park. Brice's Corner and Tupelo/Harrisburg sites are marked with federal monuments. A series of state-sponsored monuments also stands on the battlefield at Brice's Corner.

Corinth served as the base of operations for the advance of Confederate troops on the Union army encamped at Pittsburg Landing, near Shiloh Church, twenty-two miles to the north, in Tennessee. The two-day battle that took place there, April 6–7, 1862, was a major engagement: some forty-five thousand Confederates under Gen. Albert Sidney Johnson were opposed by some sixty-five thousand Union soldiers commanded by Maj. Gen. Ulysses S. Grant. The battle was a defeat for Confederate forces and killed some seventeen hundred men on the battlefield and left some eight thousand wounded. The Confederates withdrew to Corinth, and the aftermath of the battle became a life-and-death struggle for the wounded. The medical facilities at Corinth were overwhelmed; moreover the city came under siege by advancing Union forces. As a result, the army loaded many of the wounded onto trains that were sent along the north-to-south Mobile & Ohio and the east-to-west Memphis & Charleston. The trains traveled to successive towns across northern and central Mississippi as authorities looked to see how many of the wounded could be cared for at each stop. Today monuments at Corinth, Okolona, Macon, Iuka, Booneville, Columbus, Oxford, and points south mark the sites of hospitals and cemetery grounds where the wounded were cared for and the dead were buried.

Eighteen courthouse monuments would be erected across northern Mississippi in the postbellum era, and Corinth became a site for commemorations and interments: the Corinth National Cemetery was dedicated directly after the war under federal auspices, along with burials and commemorations of the Confederate dead under private auspices. The courthouse monument was dedicated in 1896; various monuments on the site of Fort Robinette early in the twentieth century; and the Corinth Interpretive Center and associated Contraband Camp at Corinth early in the twenty-first century.

Alcorn County

Corinth

3.1.1 Subject: Courthouse Common Soldier, Confederate
Location: Courthouse square, Franklin and Waldron   N 34 56 05 39 / W 88 31 10 02
Installed April 1896; relocated October 1916
Media: White bronze, concrete, limestone, marble
Monument is figure of a Confederate common soldier, surmounting a base.

Inscription

[Front]
BRAVE
ERECTED AS A / TRIBUTE TO THE MEMORY / OF THE CONFEDERATE
PATRIOTS WHO FELL AT / THE BATTLE OF CORINTH / ON OCTOBER 1862
"ON FAME'S ETERNAL CAMPING GROUND / THEIR SILENT TENTS ARE SPREAD,
AND GLORY GUARDS WITH SOLEMN ROUND / THE BIVOUAC OF THE DEAD.["]

OUR DEAD
THEY WERE / THE KNIGHTLIEST OF THE KNIGHTLY RACE / WHO SINCE THE DAY OF
OLD / HAVE KEPT THE LAMPS OF CHIVALRY / ALIGHT IN HEARTS OF GOLD.

HONORABLE

PATRIOTS
COL. W. P. ROGERS / 2ND TEXAS REG'T. / KILLED AT FT. ROBINETTE / OCT. 4, 1862.
AS LONG AS COURAGE, MANLINESS AND / PATRIOTISM EXIST, THE NAME OF
ROGERS WILL BE HONORED AMONG / MEN. HE FELL IN THE CENTER OF THE
ENEMIES [SIC] STRONGHOLD. [SIC] HE SLEEPS / AND GLORY IS HIS SENTINEL.

Corinth is twenty-two miles southwest of Pittsburg Landing, on the Tennessee River, where, on April 6–7, 1862, the Battle of Shiloh was fought. The Battle of Shiloh was fought over control of the railroads running through Corinth. Corinth served as the Confederates' staging ground and base of operations for the campaign that led to the battle. Shiloh was a defeat for the Confederates, however. They returned to Corinth and fortified the area, but withdrew after coming under siege by Union forces.

"Take and hold Corinth," historian Peter Cozzens writes, "and Union armies would sever the most viable Confederate line of communications . . . between the eastern seaboard and the vast trans-Mississippi region. Maj. Gen. Henry

Corinth, Courthouse Common Soldier, Confederate

Halleck . . . counted the seizure of Corinth more important than the destruction of the Confederacy's western armies."

This monument was sponsored by the A. S. Johnson Camp of the United Confederate Veterans (UCV) and is specifically dedicated to Confederate soldiers who were killed during the battle of Corinth. Special mention is given to Col. William P. Rogers of the 2nd Texas Infantry, who was killed in action at Fort Robinette during the battle. The figure of a Confederate soldier—in zinc—stands at parade rest, surmounting an inscribed shaft and base of mixed media, including marble, limestone, and granite. The base in turn surmounts a concrete foundation with a pea-gravel surface.

The monument was relocated to its present site in October 1916. It stands southwest of the county courthouse completed in 1918, by E. G. Parish, from designs by N. W. Overstreet.

· The excerpt beginning "On Fame's Eternal Camping Ground" is taken from the first stanza of "The Bivouac of the Dead," by Theodore O'Hara, a Kentuckian who fought on the Confederate side in the war. The poem extends to nine stanzas, dates from 1847, and was written in commemoration of Americans killed at the battle of Buena Vista during the US–Mexican War. Stanzas of the poem are also posted in national cemeteries, including the Corinth National Cemetery.

· The Monumental Bronze Company of Connecticut manufactured statues of Civil War soldiers of various patterns and types like this one across the North and South. The medium is called white bronze but is composed of zinc.

Corinth Civil War Interpretive Center: Tableau Relief, Six Soldiers

Corinth Civil War Interpretive Center

3.1.2 Subject: Tableau Relief, Six Soldiers
Location: 501 West Linden Street, 38834   N 34 55 37 62 / W 88 30 37 06
Installed or dedicated: July 2004
Medium: Bronze

A high relief depiction of six soldiers, marching east, in column, adorns the main entryway to the Corinth Civil War Interpretive Center, part of the Shiloh NMP. The figures, life-size in scale, are based on six employees of the park at the time of its opening, and is the work of sculptor Andrea Lugar of Memphis.

The twenty-two-acre site is on a hill overlooking Corinth's downtown and railroad junction and is the site of Battery Robinette, a Federal earthwork redoubt. Battery Robinette was the scene of major fighting on October 4, 1862, during the Second Battle of Corinth. The earthworks were destroyed after the war, but the city and the United Daughters of the Confederacy (UDC) preserved the grounds as a park. Ultimately, the site was donated to the Park Service after the center proposal was approved by dint of federal legislation on November 12, 1996. In 1999, the fort's outlines were surveyed and partially restored when the foundations of the interpretive center were laid.

Today the west side of the hill displays a symbolic representation of what was in 1862 a killing field of the battle of Corinth. Here, bronze replicas of the

The Fountain, Corinth Civil War Interpretive Center

"detritus of war"—the work of Andrea Lugar—are embedded in the walk, such as a broken sword, a bent bayonet, or a knapsack spilling its contents.

· Former superintendent of Shiloh NMP Haywood S. "Woody" Harrell, collaborated with the firm of Overland Partners Architects on this site's design. The initiative for the interpretive center is credited to Rosemary Williams and the Siege and Battle of Corinth Commission.

3.1.3 Subject: The Fountain, Corinth Civil War Interpretive Center
Location: 501 West Linden Street, 38834
Dedicated: July 2004
Media: Bronze, granite
Monument is a fountain and black obelisk, with series of inscribed granite blocks, a walkway, and pool.

Inscription
[Declaration of Independence and the Preamble to the Constitution]
[Granite blocks, individually inscribed with the names of 56 battles]

This arrangement of waterfalls, pools, and granite blocks presents a symbolic narrative flow of American history from 1770 to 1870.

A fountain and black obelisk are at the north end. Union, disunion, and reunion are the themes of this fountain. The obelisk is inscribed with quotations from the Declaration of Independence and the Preamble to the Constitution. The water, representing the course of the "American ideal of freedom and liberty," flows over a wall with thirteen tiers, representing the thirteen original states. It flows south, following a course in which every 3.5 inches represents a year. The stream widens in accordance with new states joining the union: the names of slaveholding and free states are inscribed on separate sides of the stream. Two waterfalls represent the 1820 Missouri Compromise and the Compromise of 1850. The water volume then accelerates into a second level of turbulent water, representing the onset of the war.

Thereafter the water divides into two streams—North and South. Granite shafts in the stream stand for fifty-six battles between north and south; each shaft is inscribed with the Confederate and Union names of each engagement (A.D., Antietam vis-à-vis Sharpsburg); the size of the blocks is proportional to the number of casualties.

The two streams unite at Appomattox; the turbulence is "brought to calm by three stones representing the 13th, 14th and 15th Amendments," as the NPS notes on the site declare. A reflecting pool represents the nation today; however, thirty-six bronze leaves are embedded in the walkway surrounding the pool: they represent the state trees of the states in the Union during the war to symbolize the sacrifice necessary—fallen leaves—to bring about the reunion of the states.

3.1.4 Subject: Col. William P. Rogers, Obelisk
Location: 501 West Linden Street, 38834   N 34 56 15 44 / W 88 31 44 02
Dedicated: August 15, 1912
Medium: Granite
Monument is an obelisk surmounting a base and stele front.

Inscription
A TRIBUTE FROM / CORINTH CHAPTER
U.D.C. NO. 333 TO THE / MEMORY AND VALOR OF / COL. WM. P. ROGERS
WILLIAM P. ROGERS / A NATIVE OF ALABAMA / CAPTAIN OF MISSISSIPPI RIFLES /
1845–47

FIRST MAN TO MOUNT WALLS / AT MONTEREY FORMERLY KNOWN AS MICHIE
U.S. COUNSEL TO MEXICO 1849 / SIGNED ORDINANCE OF SECESSION / OF TEXAS,
FEBRARY 1, 1861 / COL. 2ND TEXAS INFANTRY / BREVET BRIGADE COMMANDER

FELL LEADING MOORE'S BRIGADE / FORT ROBINETTE OCT. 4, 1862. / "HE WAS ONE
OF THE BRAVEST MEN / THAT EVER LED A CHARGE. / BURY HIM WITH MILITARY
HONORS."
MAJ. GEN. W. S. ROSECRANS, / COMMANDER ARMY OF / CUMBERLAND U.S.A.

ERECTED BY THE TEXAS DIV. / UNITED DAUGHTERS OF THE / CONFEDERACY.
THE SURVIVING MEMBERS OF THE / FAMILY / AND ADMIRING FRIENDS /
AUGUST 15, A.D. 1912. / ROGERS

Col. William P. Rogers, Obelisk

THE GALLANTRY WHICH / ATTRACTED THE ENEMY AT
CORINTH WAS IN KEEPING WITH / THE CHARACTER HE ACQUIRED
IN THE FORMER SERVICE / HIS LAST WORDS WERE: "MEN!
SAVE YOURSELVES, OR SELL / YOUR LIVES AS DEAR AS POSSIBLE."

A climactic moment of the battle of Corinth occurred here when Confederate troops commanded by Brig. Gen. John C. Moore stormed the earthwork redoubt of Battery Robinette. The men also assaulted and seized Battery Powell, which stood south of Battery Robinette. They were repulsed from Battery Robinette at least three times: on their third attempt they carried the ditch, as well as the outside of the work. The Federals were driven from their guns, and only the earth wall separated the combatants.

Hand-to-hand fighting ensued, but the battery did not fall. Timely reinforcements arrived, charging to the right and left of the battery walls; cannon fire from Battery William, to the north, also contributed. In the course of the third assault, Col. William P. Rogers of the 2nd Texas Infantry was killed.

Some Confederates—including Texans commemorated on the adjacent monument—fought their way into Corinth, but the Federals repelled them. The Federals then recaptured Battery Powell. Ultimately, the Confederates ceded the ground and withdrew. Rogers's conspicuous bravery caused the Federals to bury his remains upon the embankment as something of a tribute. An extant period photograph shows the aftermath of the battle and Rogers's body among the dead.

Historian Peter Cozzens observes that the "Confederate assaults on Batteries Robinette and Powell . . . stand among the fiercest of the war and among the few in which the fighting became hand to hand."

3.1.5 Subject: Brig. Gen. Joseph L. Hogg, Stele
Location: 501 West Linden Street, 38834   N 34 56 14 89 / W 88 31 44 16
Installed or dedicated: 1918
Medium: Granite
Monument is a stele surmounting a base.

Inscription
BRIGADIER-GENERAL / JOSEPH LEWIS HOGG, / OF TEXAS, BORN IN 1809, / DIED NEAR HERE / MAY 16, 1862.

ERECTED BY HIS / GRANDCHILDREN / OF TEXAS / 1918.

Joseph Lewis Hogg was one of many victims of disease during the war. He was born on September 13, 1806—apparently the above inscription is an error—in Georgia but was raised in Texas. Elected captain of the Lone Star Defenders, which became Company C of the 3rd Texas Cavalry, he was soon promoted to brigadier general in the Confederate Army. However, before he could undertake active combat service with the army, he was stricken with dysentery and died.

Hogg's remains were buried near the Mount Holly School House in nearby Washington County, but his grave was removed to this site in 1918.

Brig. Gen. Joseph L. Hogg, Stele

State of Texas Monument, Stele

3.1.6 Subject: State of Texas Monument, Stele
Location: 501 West Linden Street, 38834   N 34 56 16 37 / W 88 31 44 76
Installed or dedicated: 2010
Media: Bronze, granite
Monument is a granite stele decorated with a bronze star surmounting a base.

Inscription

TEXAS

REMEMBERS THE VALOR AND DEVOTION OF ITS SONS / WHICH SERVED AT CORINTH AND ITS SURROUNDING / ENVIRONS DURING THE WESTERN CAMPAIGN OF 1862.

HERE IN THE DAYS FOLLOWING THE RETREAT OF / SOUTHERN FORCES FROM THE BATTLEFIELD OF / SHILOH, TWO CONFEDERATE ARMIES COMBINED TO / DEFEND THE STRATEGIC RAILROAD CROSSING AT / CORINTH. TEXANS FROM 18 DIFFERENT UNITS / ASSISTED IN THE DEFENSE UNTIL, HEAVILY OUT- / NUMBERED, THE CONFEDERATES WERE COMPELLED / TO ABANDON THE CITY ON THE 30TH OF MAY. / BY MID-SEPT., THE CONFEDERATE ARMY OF THE / WEST UNDER MAJOR GENERAL STERLING PRICE / MANEUVERED TO PREVENT UNION REENFORCEMENTS / FROM LEAVING THE THEATER OF OPERATIONS. / ON SEPT. 19, THE BATTLE OF IUKA WAS FOUGHT 23 / MILES SOUTH EAST OF CORINTH. THERE TEXANS OF / LOUIS HEBERT'S BRIGADE MADE REPEATED CHARGES / ON THE UNION FORCES. THE FIGHTING WAS INCON- / CLUSIVE AND PRICE WAS ABLE TO EXTRICATE HIS / ARMY AND RENDEVOUS WITH MAJOR GENERAL EARL / VAN DORN IN RIPLEY (MS) TO CARRY

OUT A BOLD PLAN / TO DRIVE THE UNION ARMY FROM WEST TENNESSEE / BY FIRST ATTACKING THEIR GARRISON AT CORINTH.

HERE THE BATTLE OF CORINTH, FOUGHT ON THE / 3RD AND 4TH OF OCT., CULMINATED IN THREE CHARGES / AGAINST THIS SITE LED BY COL. WILLIAM P. ROGERS / OF THE 2ND TEXAS INFANTRY. THE ATTACKS FAILED / AND ROGERS WAS KILLED. TEXANS FROM BRIGADIER / GENERAL CHARLES PHIFER'S BRIGADE ADVANCED / SOUTHEAST BEYOND THIS POINT, BRIEFLY CAPTURING THE RAILROAD CROSSROADS AT THE HEART OF THE / CITY BEFORE COMPELLED TO RETIRE. VAN DORN'S / SHATTERED ARMY RETREATED WEST AND ON THE FOLLOWING DAY, WHILE ATTEMPTING TO CROSS THE / HATCHIE RIVER AT DAVIS BRIDGE (TN), THE SONS OF / TEXAS WERE AGAIN CONSPICUOUS IN HOLDING BACK ATTACKING UNION FORCES UNTIL A RIVER CROSSING / COULD BE SECURED UPSTREAM / ERECTED BY THE STATE OF TEXAS 2010

TEXAS UNITS INVOLVED DURING / THE CORINTH CAMPAIGN / APRIL—OCTOBER 1862

SIEGE OF CORINTH MS
2ND TEXAS INFANTRY / 6TH TEXAS INFANTRY / 9TH TEXAS INFANTRY
GOOD'S BATTERY / TEAL'S BATTERY / 1ST TEXAS CAVALRY (DISMOUNTED)
3RD TEXAS CAVALRY (DISMOUNTED) / 6TH TEXAS CAVALRY (DISMOUNTED)
9TH TEXAS CAVALRY (DISMOUNTED) / 10TH TEXAS CAVALRY (DISMOUNTED)
11TH TEXAS CAVALRY (DISMOUNTED) / 14TH TEXAS CAVALRY (DISMOUNTED)
15TH TEXAS CAVALRY (DISMOUNTED) / 16TH TEXAS CAVALRY (DISMOUNTED)
17TH TEXAS CAVALRY (DISMOUNTED) / 27TH TEXAS CAVALRY (DISMOUNTED)
32ND TEXAS CAVALRY (DISMOUNTED) / WHARTON'S TEXAS RANGERS
BATTLE OF IUKA MS
1ST TEXAS LEGION / 3RD TEXAS CAVALRY DISMOUNTED
BATTLE OF CORINTH MS
2ND TEXAS (INFANTRY) / 3RD TEXAS CAVALRY (DISMOUNTED) / 6TH TEXAS CAVALRY (DISMOUNTED) / 9TH TEXAS CAVALRY (DISMOUNTED)
BATTLE OF DAVIS BRIDGE
1ST TEXAS LEGION / 2ND TEXAS INFANTRY / 6TH TEXAS CAVALRY (DISMOUNTED) 9TH TEXAS CAVALRY (DISMOUNTED)

TEXAS REMEMBERS AND HONORS HER SONS / THEY SLEEP THE SLEEP OF THE BRAVE.

This state monument to Texans who fought in the campaigns of 1862 offers a vivid tribute and summary narrative of four separate actions: the siege of Corinth, the battle of Corinth, the battle of Iuka, and the battle of Davis Bridge, Tennessee. The inscription is, in effect, a summary of Confederate military operations in northeastern Mississippi and is reproduced here in full.

Eleven markers of this design were sponsored by the state of Texas and erected across the South between 1963 and 1965. "Texas Remembers" is a prominent theme of these monuments. The Texas monument at Vicksburg is a particularly elaborate variation on this series erected at the same time.

Four Texas monuments stand in Mississippi, more than from any other state. A third Texas monument was erected in Mississippi on the Raymond battlefield in 2002; a fourth, at Meridian, was erected in 2010.

Corinth, Unknown Confederate Dead, inscribed granite shaft

3.1.7 Subject: Unknown Confederate Dead
Location: 501 West Linden Street, 38834   N 34 56 14 70 / W 88 31 43 52
Installed or dedicated: n.a.
Medium: Granite
Monument is a shaft surmounting a base.

Inscription

UNKNOWN— / WE CARE NOT WHENCE THEY CAME, / DEAR IN THEIR LIFELESS CLAY:

WHETHER UNKNOWN OR KNOWN TO FAME, / THEIR CAUSE AND COUNTRY STILL THE SAME. / THEY DIED AND WORE THE GRAY / CONFEDERATE DEAD

REMEMBER / THE UNKNOWN HEROES / THEY THAT ARE EQUAL TO THE SAME THING ARE EQUAL TO THE OTHER.

This monument unveiling date and sponsors are unknown. At one time the gravestones were believed to be headstones for six Confederate color-bearers killed in the assault on Battery Robinette, but recent archaeological ground scans showed no current evidence of any graves at this site, although known and unknown graves of Confederate soldiers are understood to be located at numerous sites in the Corinth area.

- The excerpt beginning "We care not" is taken from "March of the Deathless Dead" by Father Abraham Ryan, a Roman Catholic priest, poet, and Confederate soldier. The larger context reads:

  > Gather the corpses strewn O'er many a battle plain;
  > From many a grave that lies so lone,
  > Without a name and without a stone,
  > Gather the Southern slain.

- The expression beginning "They that are equal" is taken from Euclid's "Common Notion 1": "Things which are equal to the same thing are also equal to one another."

3.1.8 Subject: Corinth Contraband Camp, Union soldier (USCT) and female civilian
Location: 501 West Linden Street, 38834   N 34 56 05 80 / W 88 30 08 16
Installed or dedicated: 2009
Medium: Bronze
Monuments are bronze figures.

Inscription

SITE OF THE / CORINTH CONTRABAND CAMP / NOVEMBER 1862–DECEMBER 1863

HERE A NEWLY FREED PEOPLE TOOK / THEIR UNSWERVING FIRST STEPS ON / THE LONG ROAD TO FULL CITIZENSHIP.

Corinth Contraband Camp, Union soldier (USCT)

Many local African American slaves who were freed by Federal troops or who made their own escape to Union lines first settled here, in a "contraband camp," just east of Corinth in 1862. Under Union occupation—commanded by Brig. Gen. Grenville M. Dodge—Corinth was a secure sanctuary, and the camp developed as an independent community. The camp was disbanded in 1864 when Federal troops withdrew from the area; the remaining residents moved to Memphis. The campsite was demolished after the war, but the ground was purchased by Friends of the Siege and Battle of Corinth, then surveyed and restored in the process of developing the Corinth Interpretive Center.

Presented here are a common soldier, Union (USCT), and a female civilian. Six additional life-size bronze sculptures stand on the grounds, representing the men, women, and children who inhabited the camp and who were considered to be "contraband" of war—former slaves. Andrea Lugar's sculptures emphasize the individuality, humanity, independence, and aspirations of those who lived here. The Union soldier, fully outfitted, bears a musket and holds a book, inscribed "Hardee's Tactics," representing *Hardee's Rifle and Light Infantry Tactics*, the standard instructional manual for the US Army, manifesting the soldier's initiative, literacy, and willingness to fight. This is one of four figures of Civil War–era African American men in Mississippi. The African American female, a young woman, may be considered a counterpart to white females depicted in sculptures on a host of monuments across the South as a woman of initiative and independence. The figure is modeled on a period photograph.

- Andrea Lugar, the sculptor, also designed and executed the bronze sculptures at the Corinth Interpretive Center.

- Brig. Gen. Dodge is credited with enlisting freedmen into the army as teamsters, cooks, and laborers. Dodge also recruited male refugees, armed them, and placed them in charge of security at the camp. Dodge's pragmatic administrative initiatives led to the formation of the 1st Alabama Regiment of African Descent, consisting of approximately one thousand men. The unit was later redesignated the 55th United States Colored Troops (USCT).

3.1.9 Subject: SCV Chamber of Commerce Stele
Location: 810 Tate Street, 38834   N 34 55 52 11 / W 88 31 05 80
Installed or dedicated: October 4, 1992
Medium: Granite
Monument is a stele surmounting a base.

Inscription
IN MEMORY OF / CONFEDERATE / SOLDIERS / APRIL–MAY 1862 / WHO DIED FROM / WOUNDS OR DISEASE / IN THE SIEGE OF CORINTH

SCV Chamber of Commerce Stele

DEDICATED OCTOBER 4, 1992

SPONSORED BY / CORINTH CHAPTER / UNITED DAUGHTERS OF / THE CONFEDERACY

COL. WILLIAM P. ROGERS / CAMP #321 / SONS OF CONFEDERATE / VETERANS

This monument, standing twenty-four by thirty-six inches, is easily over-looked. It has an unobtrusive place amid the landscaping in front of Corinth's Chamber of Commerce building. However, it is the only commemoration of the wounded or those who died of disease during the siege of Corinth. Although there are hundreds of monuments at Shiloh and several commemorating the battle of Corinth, this is the only monument erected to remember the siege, the success of which effectively fulfilled the ambitions and completed the victory of the Federal forces who fought at Shiloh. It also offers a modest Confederate rejoinder to the formal commemoration and interment of the Union dead at Corinth National Cemetery a few blocks away. Many Confederate dead are buried in unknown and unmarked mass graves in Corinth and vicinity.

Corinth National Cemetery

3.1.10 Subject: The Corinth National Cemetery
Location: 1551 Horton Street, 38834   N 34 55 35 / W 88 30 36
Installed or dedicated: 1864
There is no central monument at Corinth National Cemetery, but the graves of 1,793 known and 3,895 unknown soldiers are interred here, representing 273 regiments from fifteen states. The grounds were established as a cemetery in September 1864. Interments came from at least fifteen battlefields or skirmishes, including Corinth, Iuka, Holly Springs, Guntown, and Farmington. By 1870, Corinth had 5,688 interments, including several Confederate soldiers.

Tishomingo County

3.2.1 Subject: Iuka, Old Tishomingo County Courthouse Museum, Stele
Location: Fulton and Quitman Streets, 38852   N 34 48 32 93 / W 88 11 23 84
Dedicated: May 1902
Media: Marble, fieldstone
Monument is a cross, in marble, shaped as two wooden beams, surmounting a shaft and base.

Inscription

[Front]
[Relief of Star, Dove, Gate]

HEROES OF A LOST CAUSE / REST IN HONOR AND IN / GRATEFUL MEMORY
ERECTED BY / JOHN MARSHALL STONE / CHAPTER U.D.C[.] / MAY 1902 /
CONFEDERATE / HEROES
MISSOURI

[blank]

TEXAS

A rare mention of the Lost Cause is inscribed on this late funereal monument, which appears to have been intended to stand at Shady Grove Cemetery nearby. The graves of unknown Confederate soldiers killed in the battle of Iuka are interred in a mass grave there.

There are no direct references to the battle of Iuka, but this is the largest monument in the county, and the graves nearby offer a testimony to the history that took place. The battle was fought on September 19, 1862, on grounds that are now largely occupied by the intersection of US 72 and MS 25. It was an unexpected and particularly bloody clash. Elements of Maj. Gen. William S. Rosecrans's Army of the Mississippi—some forty-five hundred Union troops—fought thirty-two hundred Confederates of the CS Army of the West commanded by Maj. Gen. Sterling Price in what is regarded as a "meeting engagement"—nothing less than a collision. They took some 780 and 799 casualties, respectively. Historian Peter Cozzens writes that "Federal and a Confederate brigade collided in march column, and the ensuing three-hour struggle was over before either army commander understood what had happened." This was a Union victory; however, contemporaries and historians alike regard the engagement as a missed opportunity: the Federals might have destroyed or captured Price's army; instead, the Confederates joined with Van Dorn's forces and assaulted Corinth in October.

- This is one of only a few crosses on a Confederate monument in Mississippi. Crosses were destined to be common features of tombstones in the twentieth century, especially of military tombstones during the world wars, but are uncommon among Civil War monuments.

- The image of the dove may derive from Genesis 6:8, when a dove returned to Noah's ark with a sprig in its beak after the flood, heralding the end of the deluge, symbolic of peace and the Holy Spirit, and a symbol of hope and renewal after a storm. It is found only twice among the one thousand monuments this writer has researched across Northern and Southern states. The other is at Pontotoc. This is the older example.

Iuka, Courthouse Stele

Tippah County

3.3.1 Subject: Ripley, Courthouse Common Soldier, Confederate
Location: Commerce Street, courthouse grounds, northeast corner, 38663
N 34 43 50 98 / W 86 56 56 50Dedicated: September 21, 1911
Media: Carrara marble, granite
Monument is a figure of a private soldier, Confederate, surmounting a shaft
and base.

Inscription
[Front]
C.S.A.

[Unfurled C.S. Battle Flag]

1861–1865

IN MEMORY OF THE / CONFEDERATE / SOLDIERS OF / TIPPAH COUNTY / OUR HEROIC
DEAD AND / THE CHIVALROUS LIVING / WHO WORE THE GRAY, / 1861–1865.

C.S.A. / ERECTED BY THE THOMAS SPIGHT CHAPTER, UNITED DAUGHTERS / OF THE
CONFEDERACY / AUGUST 1911 / "LEST WE FORGET".

C.S.A. / "SLEEP SOLDIERS! / STILL IN HONORED REST / YOUR TRUTH AND VALOR
WEARING; / THE BRAVEST ARE / THE TENDEREST, / THE LOVING ARE THE DARING."

C.S.A. / ON EVERY GREAT BATTLE / FIELD OF THE WAR, / THEIR VALOR WAS
ILLUSTRATED, / THEY WON IMPERISHABLE RENOWN, FOR THEY WILL / LIVE
IN HISTORY AND IN / THE HEARTS OF THEIR / DESCENDENTS TO THE / LATEST
GENERATION.

This UDC monument, erected at a cost of $1,500, stands about twenty-seven
feet high and has a prominent place adjacent to the north entrance of the
Tippah County courthouse.

The statue of the soldier is about six feet high. It was imported in twelve
sections from Italy and erected near the corner of Main and Jefferson streets
circa 1911, about two hundred yards from its current site. The monument was
struck and toppled by a passing truck in May 1970 or 1971. The figure's head
was severed, and the rifle was damaged. Repairs were done, and the monument
was re-erected at its present location in 1984. Evidence of the damage remains,
however. The body of the soldier is posed facing east; the head faces northeast:
the two elements are not in symmetry. The gunstock is missing. Because the
monument no longer surmounts a base or mound, the inscriptions are only
inches from the ground—as if the monument was planted there. However,
as of 2015, the county and the city approved funding for a restoration of the
monument.

- A statue of Colonel William Clark Falkner stands in City Cemetery off
  MS 15, north of the courthouse square (N 34 44 15 33 / W 88 56 46 32).
  Falkner, great-grandfather of author William Faulkner, was a Confed-

Ripley, Courthouse Common Soldier

erate veteran and a resident of Ripley. Falkner's exploits served as a model for Faulkner's character of Colonel John Sartoris.

- A compelling, albeit fictional and somewhat caustic account of the unveiling of the monument appears in William Faulkner's novel *Requiem for a Nun*:

> On Confederate Decoration Day, Mrs. Virginia DuPre, Colonel Sartoris's sister, twitched a lanyard and the spring-restive bunting collapsed and flowed, leaving the marble effigy—the stone infantryman on his stone pedestal on the exact spot where forty years ago the Richmond officer and the local Baptist minister had mustered in the Colonel's regiment, and the old men in gray and braided coats (all officers now, none less in rank than captain) tottered into the sunlight and fired shotguns at the bland sky and raised their cracked, quavering voices in the shrill hackle-lifting yelling which Lee and Jackson and Longstreet and the two Johnsons . . . had listened to amid the smoke and the din; epilogue and epitaph, because apparently neither the U.D.C. ladies who instigated and bought the monument, nor the architect who designed it nor the masons who erected it, had noticed that the marble eyes under the shading marble palm stared not toward the north and the enemy, but toward the south, toward (if anything) his own rear . . . the wits said (could say now, with the old war thirty-five years past and you could even joke about it—except the women, the ladies, the unsurrendered, the irreconcilable, who even after another thirty-five years would get up and stalk out of picture houses showing *Gone With the Wind*).

- The excerpt beginning "Sleep Soldiers" is taken from American poet and journalist Bayard Taylor's "The Song of the Camp," published in 1863.
- Figures of four soldiers of World War I—infantrymen, doughboys— surmount decorated column reliefs on the courthouse, erected in 1929 from a design by N. W. Overstreet. An earlier courthouse, erected in 1838, was burned by Federal troops in August 1864.

Booneville, City Cemetery shaft

Prentiss County

3.4.1 Subject: Booneville, City Cemetery shaft
Location: King Street, south of Marietta Street
N 34 38 57 82 / W 88 33 32 88
Installed or dedicated: n.a.
Medium: Marble
Monument is a shaft surmounting a base.

Inscription

IN MEMORY OF / CONFEDERATE DEAD.
FOR A JUST CAUSE YOU DIED—/ YET THAT CAUSE WAS LOST.
FOR LOVE OF COUNTRY / ONE JUSTLY DIES. / REST IN PEACE

Direct, explicit references to the Lost Cause are uncommon in Confederate monumentation. The modest Booneville city cemetery monument is one of the few exceptions. It is also unusual in offering a consoling word of direct address to the dead: "For A Just Cause You Died—/ Yet That Cause Was Lost. For Love Of Country / One Justly Dies."

The graves of many Confederate veterans are evident on this ground, but this modest shaft and the adjacent graves of several unknown soldiers are near the entrance. Contemporary records on this site appear to be incomplete. However, a 1904 publication of the Mississippi Historical Society observes that "two of the soldiers buried here were killed in General Chalmers's Booneville fight [fought on July 1, 1862]; the others are principally from Bragg's army at Corinth. The patriotic spirit of the people of Prentiss county is happily illustrated by the fact that they took steps a few years ago to locate all the Confederate graves in the county. The bodies were then carefully removed, re-coffined and re-interred in this cemetery"

Lee County

3.5.1 Subject: Tupelo, Courthouse Common Soldier
Location: Courthouse grounds, 200 Jefferson Street at West Broadway
N 34 15 30 17 / W 88 42 18 86
Dedicated: May 3, 1906
Media: Marble, limestone, concrete
Monument is a figure of a private soldier, Confederate, surmounting a shaft and base.

Inscription
[Front]
[Relief of CS National Flag] [Relief of crossed musket, sword and belt]

CSA
ERECTED IN HONOR OF, / AND TO THE MEMORY OF / CONFEDERATE SOLDIERS,
BY THEIR / COMRADES, THEIR / SONS, AND DAUGHTERS[.]
THE LOVE, GRATITUDE / AND MEMORY OF THE / PEOPLE OF THE SOUTH, / SHALL
GILD THEIR / FAME IN ONE ETERNAL / SUNSHINE / UNVEILED MAY 3RD, 1906.

THOSE WHO DIE / FOR A RIGHT / PRINCIPLE, DID / NOT DIE IN VAIN

[roster of soldiers]

"OH! GRIEVE NOT HEARTS / HER MATCHLESS SLAIN, CROWNED WITH THE
WARRIOR'S WREATH / FROM BEDS OF FAME THEIR PROUD REFRAIN / WAS LIBERTY
OR DEATH

THEIR NAMES, / GLOW ON THE ROLL WHICH DUTY KEEPS FOR FAME, / THAT
GOLDEN ROLL, WITH IRON PEN ENGRAVED / DIPPED IN THE HEART / BLOOD OF THE
NOBLE DEAD."

[roster of soldiers]

THE LOYAL AND TRUE, / THEIR FAITH SEALED
WITH THEIR MOST / PRECIOUS BLOOD / *[roster of soldiers]*

The Confederate monument is the foremost structure on the courthouse grounds as one approaches the Tupelo courthouse grounds from the west off the highway. The statue surmounting the Lee County monument is said to be

Tupelo, Courthouse Common Soldier

"granite or Italian marble; base: concrete or marble," according to Smithsonian records. The monument as a whole stands thirty feet high. The surmounting figure faces southwest from the corner of the courthouse grounds, looking in the direction of the Tupelo/Harrisburg battlefield. John Stinson is cited as the sculptor; however, the Columbus Marble Works erected the monument, and the statue is likely an Italian import, the work of an unknown craftsman.

This monument is a lofty edifice, but the marble is much weathered and discolored by age, and the inscribed rosters are no longer entirely legible. It is also grim and funereal but staunch in its claims: the references to blood— "Blood of The Noble Dead. . . . Most Precious Blood"—are unusual but intimate martyrdom of a kind ascribed to the faithful in the New Testament book of Hebrews 11:28 ("By faith he kept the Passover and sprinkled the blood, so that the Destroyer of the firstborn might not touch them.").

· The exhortation beginning "Those who die for a right," may be a reference to the Gettysburg Address and Lincoln's declaration that "we here highly resolve that these dead shall not have died in vain." The excerpt beginning "Oh! Grieve Not Hearts Her Matchless Slain" is taken from the poem, "The Southern Republic," by "Miss Thomas, of Mississippi."

· The excerpt beginning 'Their Names, Glow" is taken from the poem "The Confederate Dead," by A. J. Beresford Hope (1820–1887), English politician and author.

Tupelo, Battlefield Shaft, Triptych

Tupelo National Battlefield

3.5.2 Subject: Tupelo, Battlefield Shaft, Triptych
Location: West Main Street (MS 178) and Monument Drive   N 34 15 20 86 / W 88 44 14 30
Installed or dedicated: 1929
Medium: Granite
Monument is a shaft surmounted by an eagle; adjoining stelae form a kind of triptych.

Inscription

[Eagle] [U.S. emblem, with wreath]

IN MEMORY / OF THE MEN OF THE / FEDERAL AND / THE CONFEDERATE / ARMIES WHO TOOK PART IN THE / BATTLE OF TUPELO OR HARRISBURG / JULY 14–15, / 1864 / WHICH RESULTED IN / A VICTORY FOR THE FEDERAL FORCES UNDER / MAJOR GENERAL / ANDREW J. SMITH

The Tupelo National Battlefield monument presides over a one-acre site on Main Street west of downtown Tupelo on a heavily trafficked four-lane highway. The last major Civil War battle fought in Mississippi took place on these grounds on July 14–15, the battle of Harrisburg, also known as the battle of

Tupelo. Note the neutrality of the commemoration on this federal monument: the inscription does not purport to take sides: "In Memory of the Men"

- Near here Maj. Gen. A. J. Smith, commanding a force of fourteen thousand men, engaged eight thousand Confederate troops under the command of Lt. Gen. Nathan Bedford Forrest and Lt. Gen. Stephen D. Lee on the morning of July 14, 1864, in what came to be known as the battle of Tupelo. Smith's troops withstood several attacks from the Southerners, forced the Confederates from the field, and then withdrew toward Memphis. The Confederates sustained thirteen hundred casualties, including Forrest, who was wounded. Federal losses numbered 648. Historian Ben Wynne observes that the "battle of Tupelo was a major defeat for the Confederates." In its aftermath, it became "painfully apparent that Sherman's movements across the South would not be checked."

- Harrisburg was the town at the time. In 1859, many residents of the small town of Harrisburg moved two miles to the east, adjacent to the line of the newly completed Mobile & Ohio Railroad, and Harrisburg was abandoned in favor of Tupelo, which arose near the railroad.

Tupelo, Confederate Dead—Battlefield Stele

3.5.3 Subject: Confederate Dead—Battlefield Stele
Location: 2005 Main St.
Installed or dedicated: 1918
Medium: Granite
Monument is a stele surmounting a base.

Inscription

TO OUR / CONFEDERATE DEAD / THAT GAVE THEIR
LIVES IN BATTLE / HERE ON / JULY 14, 1864
FOR THEIR RIGHTS / ERECTED 1918.

No sponsorship is claimed on this subdued stele, which stands near the federal monument on this modest site. Understating claims of sponsorship may well be matters of deference—that is, the dead are of import, not those who remember them. In this instance, even the battle is not named. No victory is asserted either, only the granite-inscribed assertion that "Our Confederate Dead Gave Their Lives In Battle . . . For Their Rights."

It is terse but affecting, especially given the fact that when it was erected it was the only monument on the field and might have remained so, had it not been for the federal initiative in the 1920s to establish this one-acre site and the adjacent monument and commemoration.

Brice's Cross Roads Battlefield Shaft

Brice's Cross Roads National Battlefield Site

3.5.4 Subject: Battlefield Shaft Main, Triptych
Location: Exit off US 45 on MS 370, west of Baldwyn   N 34 30 21 56 / W 88 43 45 18
Installed or dedicated: 1929
Media: Bronze, granite
Monument is a shaft surmounted by an eagle; adjoining steles form a kind of triptych.

Inscription

IN MEMORY / OF THE MEN OF THE / CONFEDERATE / AND THE / FEDERAL ARMIES / WHO TOOK PART IN THE BATTLE OF / BRICE'S CROSS ROADS OR TISHOMINGO CREEK / JUNE 10, 1864 / WHICH RESULTED IN / A VICTORY FOR THE / CONFEDERATE FORCES / UNDER BRIGADIER / GENERAL N. B. FORREST.

Near here troops commanded by Maj. Gen. Samuel D. Sturgis were moving southeast on the morning of June 10, 1864, when they encountered Confederate cavalry commanded by Maj. Gen. N. B. Forrest about half a mile east of this crossroads.

Forrest's troops pressed the Federals back, but reinforcements arrived and formed an arcing battle line around the crossroads. Action ensued over the next four hours, but by 5:00 p.m., after enveloping both Federal flanks and launching a frontal attack, Forrest broke the Union lines and forced their withdrawal. An overturned wagon at the bridge over Tishomingo Creek obstructed the Federal line of retreat; disaster seemed imminent. However, a series of intervening defensive stands by United States Colored Troops allowed the army to escape complete defeat and possible capture.

- Mississippi's Last Stands Visitor and Interpretive Center in Baldwyn is east of the intersection of exit US 45 at MS 370. The center offers facilities, interpretations, exhibits, and archives related to the battle of Brice's Cross Roads and the battle of Tupelo/Harrisburg.
- Maj. Gen. N. B. Forrest is misidentified as "Brigadier General N. B. Forrest."
- Half of the 223 Union soldiers reported as killed at Brice's Cross Roads were members of Bouton's Brigade of United States Colored Troops. Most served in the 55th and 59th USCT.

3.5.5 Subject: Morton's Battery, Obelisk, Confederate
Location: Intersection of Bethany Road and CR 833   N 34 30 18 62 / W 88 43 46 00
Dedicated: June 11, 2005
Medium: Granite
Monument is an inscribed obelisk.

Inscription

[Relief of six cannon balls]

DEDICATED TO / MORTON'S BATTERY

[Etching of four artillerists tending a field piece]

FORREST'S ARTILLERY / AND / JOHN W. MORTON, JR. / GEN. N. B. FORREST'S / CHIEF OF ARTILLERY AND / THE CONFEDERACY'S / YOUNGEST ARTILLERY CAPTAIN / MORTON'S BATTERY FOUGHT HERE / DURING THE BATTLE OF BRICE'S / CROSSROADS JUNE 10, 1864, WITH / FOUR THREE INCH RIFLED CANNON.

BROUGHT AT A GALLOP FOR SOME EIGHT MILES, / MORTON'S AND RICE'S BATTERIES WERE SENT / FORWARD TO A HILL AND OPENED WITH SPIRIT AND EXECUTION. / GEN. FORREST ORDERED HIS ARTILLERY TO BE DOUBLE-SHOTTED / WITH CANISTER AND MOVED TO WITHIN SIXTY YARDS OF THE / FEDERAL LINES; ABOUT A FOURTH MILE NORTHEAST OF BRICE'S / HOUSE, OPENING WITH GREAT DESTRUCTION. AS THE FEDERALS / WERE DRAWING BACK TOWARD TISHAMINGO CREEK,

MORTON'S AND RICE'S BATTERIES FIRED WITH FEARFUL CARNAGE. / THEY CHARGED THEIR BATTERIES UP TO THE ENEMY AND / POURED A DEADLY TIDE OF CANISTER WITH GHASTLY / EFFECT. AS THE FEDERALS EMERGED FROM THE CREEK, FORREST'S / ARTILLERY PLAYED UPON THEM FOR HALF A MILE, / KILLING OR DISABLING LARGE NUMBERS. / ERECTED BY FREEMAN'S BATTERY FORREST'S ARTILLERY CAMP 1939 / SONS OF CONFEDERATE VETERANS

Morton's Battery, Obelisk

Freeman's Battery Camp 1939 of the Sons of Confederate Veterans (SCV) erected this granite obelisk with a vigorous, detailed narrative of this battery's service here: for example, "Fearful Carnage . . . Deadly Tide of Canister. . . . Fearful Effect." Other SCV monuments to Freeman's Battery stand at Parker's Crossroads and Franklin, Tennessee. This is the only battlefield monument to a Confederate unit in the state apart from Vicksburg.

Historian Derek W. Frisby writes:

Having fought for over three hours in the sweltering heat, Grierson's cavalry began to waver as the Federal infantry went into position, with Sturgis forming a semicircular line just east of Brice's Crossroads. After two hours of continuous fighting along this position, Forrest decided to strike. He directed his chief of artillery, Capt. John W. Morton, to advance his battery to within point-blank range of McMillen's line and open fire with double rounds of canister. Forrest knew that he was risking the loss of Morton's rifled guns, but his gamble paid off. Morton's four cannons inflicted heavy casualties on the Federals and spread fear and confusion in their ranks. Then he sent detachments sweeping around each of the Union flanks.

3.5.6 Subject: 114th Illinois Volunteer Infantry, Stele
Location: Intersection of CR 833 and MS 370   N 34 30 19 44 / W 88 43 45 55
Dedicated: June 8, 2019
Media: Granite
Monument is a stele surmounting a base.

Inscription

ILLINOIS / 114TH INFANTRY / STURGIS' EXP. FORCE 1ST DIV. 1ST BRIG. / LTC JOHN
F KING COMMANDING / LINE OF BATTLE JUNE 10, 1864 / IN THIS AREA THE 114TH
REGIMENT, ILLINOIS VOLUNTEER INFANTRY ENGAGED CONFEDERATE FORCES /
THIS MONUMENT IS DEDICATED IN HONOR OF MEMBERS OF THE 114TH REGIMENT
WHO SERVED, SUFFERED, OR / DIED ON JUNE 10, 1864 DURING THE BATTLE OF
/ BRICE'S CROSS ROADS / 18 OFFICERS AND 397 ENLISTED MEN ENGAGED / 265
KILLED, WOUNDED, AND MISSING

MONUMENT FUNDED BY THE / 114TH REGIMENT, VOLUNTEER / INFANTRY
REACTIVATED TO MARK ITS 50TH ANNIVERSARY. / 1969–2019

MONUMENT DEDICATED / 8 JUNE 2019

This is the only Union battlefield monument in Mississippi that is not on the Vicksburg battlefield. It was sponsored by members of the 114th Regiment, Illinois Volunteer Infantry Reactivated in honor the fiftieth anniversary of the unit's reactivation. It was placed here to commemorate the 155th anniversary of the battle of Brice's Cross Roads and, at this writing, is the most recent Civil War monument erected in Mississippi.

A state-sponsored unit monument, a granite obelisk (2.15.26), commemorates the 114th's service at Vicksburg, as do three granite tablets (2.15.28, 2.18.50, 2.18.84).

· The 114th organized at Camp Butler, Illinois, and mustered in September 18, 1862. In addition to its service in the Vicksburg Campaign and at Brice's Crossroads, the regiment's service included participation in Grant's Central Mississippi Campaign, the "Tallahatchie March," and in the battle of Nashville. The regiment mustered out and was discharged in August 1865. The 114th lost 210 men killed, mortally wounded, or by disease.

Brice's Cross Roads Battlefield: "First Shots," Shaft, Narrative Stele

3.5.7 Subject: First Shots, Narrative Stele
Location: MS 370   N 34 30 3262 / W 88 42 11 52
Installed: 1957
Media: Bronze, granite
Monument is a stele.

Inscription

FIRST SHOTS OF / THE BATTLE OF / BRICE'S CROSSROADS
WERE FIRED HERE / AT 9:30 / MORNING OF / JUNE 10, 1864

SCOUTS FROM GENERAL NATHAN BEDFORD FORREST'S / 7TH TENNESSEE
(CONFEDERATE) / MET SCOUTS FROM GENERAL / SAMUEL D. STURGIS' 4TH /
MISSOURI (FEDERAL). / ERECTED BY ACT OF THE LEGISLATURE OF / THE STATE OF
MISSISSIPPI

J. P. COLEMAN GOVERNOR / 1957

A Baldwyn native, Claude Gentry—"Mr. Claude"—was involved in organizing
several anniversary commemorations of the battle in the 1950s and 1960s;
he is also credited with an instrumental role in establishing the present-day
Mississippi's Last Stands Visitor and Interpretive Center as well as this series
of eight granite markers erected by the State of Mississippi in the 1950s, which

are placed across the breadth of the battlefield along MS 370, and which successively describe the action here. The landscape retains its rural character, and Brice's Cross Roads ranks with Vicksburg and Corinth among Mississippi battlefields for the extent of its monumentation. The events of the battle are more readily envisioned here than elsewhere.

3.5.8 Subject: Advance Forces
Location: MS 370   N 34 30 32 59 / W 88 42 28 20
Installed: 1957
Media: Bronze, granite

Inscription

ADVANCE FORCES OF / GENERAL FORREST / AND / GENERAL STURGIS' CAVALRY MET IN / SKIRMISH HERE. / THE 3RD, 7TH, 8TH AND 12TH / KENTUCKY (CONFEDERATE) MET THE 4TH MISSOURI, 3RD, / 9TH ILLINOIS AND 2ND NEW JERSEY SHORTLY BEFORE / FORMING FIRST BATTLE / LINE. ERECTED BY ACT OF THE LEGISLATURE OF THE STATE OF MISSISSIPPI / J. P. COLEMAN GOVERNOR / 1957

3.5.9 Subject: Federal Cavalry
Location: MS 370   N 34 30 30 01 / W 88 43 20 28
Erected: 1957
Media: Bronze, granite

Inscription

FEDERAL CAVALRY / AND ARTILLERY / FORMED FIRST BATTLE LINE HERE FROM 500 HUNDRED YARDS NORTH / AND EXTENDING MORE THAN A MILE / SOUTH, ACROSS THE GUNTOWN ROAD, / THIS LINE, BEHIND RAIL FENCES AND / DENSE SCRUB-OAK THICKETS FOUGHT / STUBBORNLY AS THE CONFEDERATES / PUSHED ON TO THE CROSSROADS. HAND / TO HAND FIGHTING [OCCURRED] ALONG THIS LINE. / FEDERAL CAVALRY AND ARTILLERY / ENGAGED IN THIS LINE / FROM THE NORTHERN END OF THE / LINE: COMPANY H OF 7TH INDIANA; / 4TH MISSOURI; 4TH MISSOURI BATTERY. / ON NORTH SIDE OF ROAD: 14TH INDIANA / BATTERY ON SOUTH SIDE OF ROAD: / 7TH INDIANA; 2ND NEW JERSEY; 3RD / IOWA BATTALION;

4TH IOWA AND 3RD / IOWA BATTALION.

ERECTED BY ACT OF THE LEGISLATURE OF / THE STATE OF MISSISSIPPI

J. P. COLEMAN GOVERNOR / 1957

3.5.10 Subject: Confederates' Second Battle Line
Location: MS 370   N 34 30 28 92 / W 88 43 29 58
Installed: 1957
Media: Bronze, granite

Inscription

CONFEDERATES' SECOND BATTLE LINE

PUSHING THE UNION FORCES BACK, GENERAL FORREST SLOWLY CLOSED HIS
PINCERS MOVEMENT, FORCING GENERAL STURGIS NEARER THE CROSSROADS. THIS
LINE WAS ANCHORED ON THE BLACKLAND ROAD 400 YARDS NORTHWEST. THE
SOUTHERN END ACROSS THE GUNTOWN ROAD. [SIC]

CONFEDERATE UNITS FORMING THIS LINE

WARREN'S AND WILLIAMS' BATTALIONS; 4TH ALABAMA; MORELAND'S 7TH
KENTUCKY; 12TH KENTUCKY; MORTON'S AND RICE'S BATTERIES; 7TH TENNESSEE;
18TH MISSISSIPPI; 16TH TENNESSEE; 15TH TENNESSEE; 19TH TENNESSEE; 8TH
MISSISSIPPI; GENERAL FORREST'S ESCORT AND CO'S A AND C OF 12TH KENTUCKY.

ERECTED BY ACT OF THE LEGISLATURE OF / THE STATE OF MISSISSIPPI

J. P. COLEMAN GOVERNOR / 1957

3.5.11 Subject: Federal's Second Battle Line
Location: MS 370   N 34 30 24 83 / W 88 43 39 00
Installed: 1957
Media: Bronze, granite

Inscription

FEDERAL'S [SIC] / SECOND BATTLE LINE / GENERAL STURGIS WAS ABLE TO USE /
HIS INFANTRY HERE FOR THE FIRST / TIME IN THE BATTLE. GENERAL FORREST
HAD BEATEN THE UNION CAVALRY / BEFORE THE INFANTRY REACHED THE /
BATTLEFIELD. INFANTRY AND CAVALRY / FORMED THIS LINE.

INFANTRY UNITS / ENGAGED IN THIS LINE / 95TH OHIO, 113TH ILLINOIS, 120TH
MISSOURI, 109TH ILLINOIS, 35TH / ILLINOIS, 81ST ILLINOIS, 114TH ILLINOIS, 93RD
INDIANA AND 9TH MINNESOTA

CAVALRY UNITS / ENGAGED IN THIS LINE / GENERAL STURGIS, PERSONAL ESCORT /
THE 19TH PENNSYLVANIA BLOCKING THE / BALDWYN ROAD, 3RD IOWA BATTALION
/ AND 4TH IOWA.

ERECTED BY ACT OF THE LEGISLATURE OF / THE STATE OF MISSISSIPPI

J. P. COLEMAN, GOVERNOR / 1957

3.5.12 Subject: General Sturgis's Supreme Effort
Location: MS 370   N 34 30 22 06 / W 88 43 43 06
Installed: 1957
Media: Bronze, granite

Inscription

GENERAL STURGIS' / SUPREME EFFORT / TO HOLD / THE CROSSROADS

PLACING THE 93RD ILLINOIS, 8TH /
ILLINOIS AND 114TH ILLINOIS INFANTRY / HERE AND IMMEDIATELY BEHIND, HE /
PLACED HIS ARTILLERY CONSISTING / OF BATTERY B OF 2ND ILLINOIS; 7TH /
WISCONSIN BATTERY; 14TH INDIANA / BATTERY; BATTERY E OF 1ST ILLINOIS /
AND JOYCE'S BATTERY. ORDERS WERE / GIVEN TO FIRE OVER HEADS OF INFANTRY
INTO ADVANCING CONFEDERATES. /

ERECTED BY ACT OF THE LEGISLATURE OF THE STATE OF MISSISSIPPI /
J. P. COLEMAN, GOVERNOR / 1957

3.5.13 Subject: The Brice Home
Location: MS 370, Crossroads   N 34 30 20 64 / W 88 43 44 44
Installed: 1957
Media: Bronze, granite

Inscription

THE BRICE HOME / STOOD / WHERE MONUMENT IS LOCATED /
THE BATTLE-SCARRED / TWO-STORY HOUSE WITH / ITS BLOOD STAINED FLOORS /
AND WALLS WAS USED BY / WOUNDED OF BOTH ARMIES / TO ESCAPE SHOT AND
SHELL / AS THE BATTLE RAGED / ERECTED BY ACT OF THE LEGISLATURE OF /
THE STATE OF MISSISSIPPI / J. P. COLEMAN GOVERNOR / 1957

3.5.14 Subject: General Barteau's Flank Movement
Location: Southeast of the Tishomingo Creek bridge on MS 370   N 34 30 39
70 / W 88 43 58 74 42
Installed: 1957
Media: Bronze, granite

Inscription

GENERAL BARTEAU'S FLANK MOVEMENT

ALONG THE RIDGE NORTH- / EAST, GENERAL BARTEAU'S / 2ND TENNESSEE
FLANKED / THE UNION FORCES, CREATING HAVOC / AMONG WHITE AND NEGRO
/ SOLDIERS OF GENERAL STURGIS' COMMAND. / ERECTED BY ACT OF THE
LEGISLATURE OF / THE STATE OF MISSISSIPPI

J. P. COLEMAN GOVERNOR / 1957

3.5.15 Subject: Tishomingo Creek Bridge
Location: Southeast of the Tishomingo Creek bridge on MS 370
N 34 30 39 70 / W 88 43 58 52 42
Erected: 1957
Media: Bronze, granite

Inscription

TISHOMINGO / CREEK BRIDGE / RETREATING WAGONS / BLOCKED BRIDGE.
GENERAL FORREST / CAPTURED 200 / WAGONS, 14 PIECES OF / ARTILLERY
AND HUNDREDS / OF MEN. ARTILLERY FIRE / FROM THE CROSSROADS / KILLED
HUNDREDS OF / FEDERALS HERE. / ERECTED BY ACT OF THE LEGISLATURE OF / THE
STATE OF MISSISSIPPI / J. P. COLEMAN GOVERNOR / 1957

Baldwyn

3.5.16 Subject: Baldwyn, City Cemetery Obelisk
Location: Off Cemetery Road, southeast Baldwyn, 38821   N 34 29 50 50 /
W 88 37 41 72
Installed or dedicated: circa 1870s
Medium: Marble
Monument is an obelisk surmounting a three-tiered base.

Inscription
TO THE CONFEDERATE DEAD

Baldwyn, City Cemetery Obelisk

Practically nothing is known about this monument. The time period when it was erected can be inferred, and the graves of Confederate veterans are certainly present. In addition, the proximity of the Brice's Cross Roads battlefield, the railroad, and the rail line extending to Corinth and Shiloh may mean that casualties from any or all of these battlefields were collected in Baldwyn and that the dead were buried here.

Pontotoc County

3.6.1 Subject: Pontotoc, Courthouse Common Soldier
Location: Courthouse grounds, West Washington and South Liberty
N 34 14 51 33 / W 88 59 53 82
Installed or dedicated: 1919
Media: Bronze, marble
Monument is a figure of a private soldier, Confederate, surmounting a shaft and base.

Inscription
[Front]
CS / *[Relief of dove with a sprig]* / C.S.A.
MRS. STELLA WILSON HERMAN / FIRST PRESIDENT OF / R. A. PINSON CHAPTER UNDER WHOSE GUIDANCE / THIS MONUMENT WAS ERECTED *[Raised relief of battle flag, unfurled]*

OUR HEROES / 1861–1865 / *[roster of names]*

C.S.A. / LOVE'S TRIBUTE / TO THE SOLDIERS WHO / MARCHED 'NEATH THE STARS AND THE BARS / AND WERE FAITHFUL TO / DUTY, THE R. A. PINSON CHAPTER, U.D.C. ERECTS / THIS MONUMENT IN / GRATEFUL REMEMBRANCE /

[roster of names]

C.S.A. *[roster of names]*

The full-length figure of a Confederate common soldier, approximately six feet tall, stands atop a tiered base on a four-sided shaft. Facing south, the figure holds a rifle in front of him, butt on the ground, the barrel in right hand. It is another affectionate tribute—"Love's Tribute"—from a local UDC chapter to its veterans, who by now would, if still living at the time of the dedication, be elderly men. The monument stands in the square in front of the neoclassical courthouse.

The decorative reliefs on the shaft are spare but include a relief of an unfurled Confederate battle flag and a dove flying downward, with an olive branch in its mouth. The dove reference may derive from Genesis 6:8, which describes a dove returning to Noah's ark, with a sprig in its beak after the flood, heralding the end of the deluge. Doves are also symbolic of peace and the Holy Spirit, a new creation, and a symbol of hope after a storm.

Pontotoc, Courthouse Common Soldier

The monument was sponsored by the R. A. Pinson Chapter, UDC and was erected at a cost of $2,500. It was erected in the spring of 1919. The rosters were inscribed in 1931.

- Town Square (Confederate Park) Block is the former site of the Pontotoc County Courthouse. In 1916, the present courthouse was constructed on the block to the south, and this block was cleared to become a public park. In the 1930s the Confederate monument was apparently moved to the center of the square where it stands today.

Marshall County
Holly Springs, Hillcrest Cemetery

3.7.1 Subject: Cemetery Statue, Common Soldiers
Location: Center Street, 38635   N 34 45 49 23 / W 89 26 50 26
Dedicated: April 26, 1876
Media: Marble, limestone
Monument is an obelisk draped by a funereal shawl, with two common soldiers, Confederate, surmounting a base.

Inscription
[Front]
[flag relief]
[figure of soldier with sword surmounting pedestal, head bowed, face obscured]

IN MEMORY OF / MARSHALL COUNTY'S / CONFEDERATE DEAD
1876

[three stacked rifles with knapsack and cartridge box inscribed with CS]
[statue of common soldier with rifle in funereal position, barrel up]

IN MEMORY OF / MARSHALL COUNTY'S / CONFEDERATE SOLDIERS
1876

[three stacked rifles with knapsack and cartridge box inscribed with CS] [field artillery piece, draped]

This is a quintessential funereal monument, marking the end of the war and "simply" mourning the dead. The rifles are stacked, as if the soldiers' work is done. Some centennial-era monuments erected at this time extolled the war as a Second American Revolution and glorified the cause for which the war was fought, but not here: no cause is extolled of commemorated. The monument inscription proclaims a pledge to remember the county's Confederate soldiers, living or dead.

The monument is one of the oldest in Mississippi, and the marble is weathered. The figures are only four feet four inches high. There is a rough, vernacular shape to them: they do not have the craftsmanship of the Italian sculptors of Confederate soldiers; however, their downcast countenance is virtually

Holly Springs, Hillcrest Cemetery Statue, Common Soldiers

messianic: bonded to the shaft in high relief, the figures give the impression of being lifted up and bound to a cross looking out on the landscape of the dead as if it were a kind of Golgotha.

- Established in 1837, Holly Springs has been called the "Little Arlington of the South." Among those buried at Hillcrest Cemetery: Brig. Gen. Samuel Benton, Brig. Gen. Winfield S. Featherston, Brig. Gen. Daniel C. Govan, and Brig. Gen. Christopher H. Mott. Maj. Gen. Edward C. Walthal (1831–1898), also buried here, is regarded as the most famous of Mississippi's Confederate generals to survive the war. Walthal fought at Chickamauga, the Atlanta Campaign, and Franklin and survived to establish a law practice, participate in veterans' activities as a speaker, and serve several terms in the US Senate.

Cemetery Obelisk, Hillcrest Cemetery

3.7.2 Subject: Cemetery Obelisk, Hillcrest Cemetery
Location: Hillcrest Cemetery, southwest corner
N 34 45 43 22 / W 89 26 46 28
Installed or dedicated: April 26, 1890
Media: Limestone
Monument is an obelisk surmounting a three-tiered base.

Inscription

[Second National Flag, unfurled, in high relief]

IN MEMORY OF / OUR / CONFEDERATE / DEAD
EVER HONORED, LOVED / AND CHERISHED.

The words "Unknown Confederate Dead" are inscribed on eighty-eight head-stones, arranged in a phalanx formation, in fifteen rows, five deep, although the arrangement may be symbolic. To the, left facing the monument, separate from the Confederate dead, are tombstones of four graves of soldiers of the 3rd US Infantry.

The Confederate cemetery is situated on a one-acre site in the southeast corner of Hillcrest Cemetery. In a 1911 history, *Historic Southern Monuments*, Rosa B. Tyler wrote that this site was "rendered sacred as the resting place

Hernando, City Cemetery, Obelisk

of some three hundred soldiers wounded in the battles of Shiloh, Iuka, and Corinth brought to this place as not on the line of railroad then in possession of the Federals. Books and papers seem to have been lost in burned houses, so that we now know the name of but one of the sleepers."

DeSoto County

3.8.1 Subject: Hernando, City Cemetery, Obelisk, Confederate
Location: 2846 Magnolia Drive (Old US 51), 38632
N 34 39 06 46 / W 89 59 29 68
Installed or dedicated: May 13, 1875
Media: Marble, limestone
Monument is an obelisk surmounting a base.

Inscription
TO THE / CONFEDERATE DEAD / OF / DE SOTO.
ILLIS VICTORIAM NON IMMORTALI-/ TATEM / FATA NEGAVERUNT.
IN MEMORIAM / MULDOON BULLET & CO. / MEMPHIS, TENN

ERECTED MAY 13, 1875.

This is the oldest monument in northern Mississippi, erected in 1875 by the Muldoon Bullet & Co. of Memphis. Local records indicate that Old Hernando

Memorial Cemetery has an estimated one hundred graves of Confederate soldiers, mostly veterans, and that the cemetery's Confederate section has a mass grave for an estimated sixty dead.

Mourning and hope are the prominent themes of this presiding obelisk, which was erected early in the centennial era of monumentation and characterized the war as an honorable Second American Revolution. The Latin encomium beginning, "Illis" may be translated as "The fates which refused them victory did not deny them immortality." That is, fate denied them victory, but they continue. It may be a variation of the expression, "Fate Denied Them Victory, But Crowned Them With Glorious Immortality."

Lafayette County

3.9.1 Subject: Oxford, Courthouse Common Soldier
Location: Courthouse grounds, south side, facing south, 206 North Lamar Boulevard, 38655   N 34 21 57 54 / W 89 31 07 86
Dedicated: May 10, 1906
Medium: Marble
Monument is a figure of a private soldier, Confederate, surmounting a shaft and base.

Inscriptions
[Front]
[Raised relief: CS, Second National Flag]

IN MEMORY OF / THE PATRIOTISM OF THE / CONFEDERATE SOLDIERS
OF LAFAYETTE COUNTY, / MISSISSIPPI. / THEY GAVE THEIR LIVES / IN A JUST AND
HOLY CAUSE. / ERECTED 1907

A TRIBUTE TO / OUR CONFEDERATE DEAD / BY THEIR SURVIVING COMRADES.

THE / SONS OF VETERANS UNITE IN / THIS JUSTIFICATION OF THEIR
FATHERS [*SIC*] FAITH.

A LOVING TRIBUTE TO / THE MEMORY OF OUR DEAD HEROES.
BY THE / PATRIOTIC DAUGHTERS OF / LAFAYETTE COUNTY, MISSISSIPPI.

Given Oxford's prominence as a university town, this may be the prototypical Mississippi Civil War courthouse monument: The figure of a Confederate common soldier, in marble, stands at parade rest facing south, on the south side of the city square, directly in front of the courthouse. On the south face of the shaft is a low relief of a furled Confederate national flag.

A common myth holds that statues of Confederate soldiers face north. It is not true: many Southern courthouses face east or west, and their attendant monuments do likewise. Even when the option is available, it is not always done. In this case, the monument faces south and appears to be less a confrontation with the ancient foe to the north than it is a confrontation with future generations.

Oxford, Courthouse Common Soldier

The Oxford monument celebrates the "Patriotism of the / Confederate Soldiers of Lafayette County." In this regard, it embodies a distinctive kind of defiance and celebration. The federal government would officially classify the events of 1861–1865 as the "War of the Rebellion." Rebellion is not how the Oxford monument defines the war: the war was a "Just and Holy Cause." Moreover, it merited mortal sacrifice. Twice the dead are mentioned: they are "the Confederate dead," and they are "our Dead heroes." Finally, the virtues of family and faith are firmly upheld: by this monument, the sons and daughters of the wartime generation are joined in affirming the devotion and martyrdom of the fathers in their fidelity to a holy cause.

· The monument is a product of the Columbus Marble Works. The court-house behind the monument was erected in 1872. The earlier court-house was burned down by Federal troops in 1864.

University of Mississippi Campus

3.9.2 Subject: University Common Soldier Statue, Confederate
Location: "The Grove," near the Lyceum, University of Mississippi   N 34 21 54 93 / W 89 32 02 56
Dedicated: May 10, 1906
Medium: Marble
Monument is a figure of a private soldier, Confederate, surmounting a shaft and base.

Inscription
[Front]
[shaft with relief of battle flag]

TO OUR / CONFEDERATE DEAD / 1861–1865
ERECTED BY / ALBERT SIDNEY JOHNSTON / CHAPTER 379 U.D.C.

[relief of crossed swords]

JOHN A. STINSON / COLUMBUS MISS.

Ὦ ξεῖν’,
ἀγγέλλειν Λακεδαιμονίοις
ὅτι τῇδε κείμεθα τοῖς κείνων ῥήμασι πειθόμενοι

TO THE HEROES / OF LAFAYETTE COUNTY / WHOSE VALOR AND DEVOTION MADE GLORIOUS MANY A / BATTLFIELD.

"THEY FELL DEVOTED, BUT UNDYING; / THE VERY GALE THEIR NAMES SEEMED SIGHING, / THE WATERS MURMER'D OF THEIR NAME: / THE WOODS WERE PEOPLED WITH THEIR FAME; / THE SILENT PILLAR, LONE AND GRAY, / CLAIM'D KINDRED WITH THEIR SACRED CLAY; / THEIR SPIRITS WRAPP'D THE DUSKY MOUNTAIN. / THEIR MEMORY SPARKLED O'ER THE FOUNTAIN; / THE MEANEST RILL, THE MIGHTIEST RIVER, / ROLL'D MINGLING WITH THEIR FAME FOREVER!" / BYRON.

University Common Soldier Statue

This UDC monument—"To the Heroes of Lafayette County"—stands at a prominent site on the campus of the University of Mississippi. The figure of a Confederate soldier facing northeast overlooks the campus from a knoll at the intersection of University Avenue and University Circle.

This is a county monument—one of two in Oxford, here and on the courthouse square. Two county monuments in the same town is an unusual arrangement—it is unique in Mississippi—but is said to be the outcome of a dispute between commemoration groups. This campus monument stands in honor of veterans, the "Heroes of Lafayette County," and to "Our Confederate Dead," perhaps those who died in the hospital on this campus and were buried on the university grounds. The Ole Miss campus merits attention, however, as a hospital site and Confederate cemetery. The college, founded in 1848, closed after the war began, since most of the student body left to form the University Grays, which became Company A of the 11th Mississippi Infantry, and served in the Virginia theater of war from 1861 to 1865.

Meanwhile, as historian Ben Wynne notes, the "state organized an official military hospital on the campus in anticipation of action in North Mississippi. Following Shiloh, the hospital overflowed with wounded men, causing authorities to commandeer other university buildings and set tents across the campus." The facility was overwhelmed, as were many Mississippi hospitals. The Magnetic Observatory on campus was converted into a Dead House. Some formalities and respect for the dead were observed, but Wynne writes that "as the number of hospital dead grew, corpses were simply thrown onto a wagon, carted away and, as one slave who was there remembered, 'They just buried them like dead chickens.'"

· In the wake of controversy regarding the Confederate statue on the campus of Ole Miss, a granite stele with a bronze tablet was placed at the base of the monument. It displays the following description:

> *[Emblem, University of Mississippi]*
> AS CONFEDERATE VETERANS WERE DYING IN INCREASING NUMBERS,
> MEMORIAL ASSOCIATIONS ACROSS THE SOUTH BUILT MONUMENTS IN
> THEIR MEMORY. THESE MONUMENTS WERE OFTEN USED TO PROMOTE
> AN IDEOLOGY KNOWN AS THE "LOST CAUSE," WHICH CLAIMED THAT
> THE CONFEDERACY HAD BEEN ESTABLISHED TO DEFEND STATES' RIGHTS
> AND THAT SLAVERY WAS NOT THE PRINCIPAL CAUSE OF THE CIVIL WAR.
> RESIDENTS OF OXFORD AND LAFAYETTE COUNTY DEDICATED THIS STAT-
> UE, APPROVED BY THE UNIVERSITY IN 1906. ALTHOUGH THE MONUMENT
> WAS CREATED TO HONOR THE SACRIFICE OF LOCAL CONFEDERATE
> SOLDIERS, IT MUST ALSO REMIND US THAT THE DEFEAT OF THE
> CONFEDERACY ACTUALLY MEANT FREEDOM FOR MILLIONS OF PEOPLE.
> ON THE EVENING OF SEPTEMBER 30, 1962, THIS STATUE WAS A RALLYING
> POINT FOR OPPONENTS OF INTEGRATION.

THIS HISTORIC STATUE IS A REMINDER OF THE UNIVERSITY'S DIVISIVE
PAST. TODAY, THE UNIVERSITY OF MISSISSIPPI DRAWS FROM THAT PAST A
CONTINUING COMMITMENT TO OPEN ITS HALLOWED HALLS TO ALL WHO
SEEK TRUTH, KNOWLEDGE, AND WISDOM.

· The excerpt beginning "They Fell Devoted" is taken from the poem
"The Siege of Corinth," published in 1816, written by George Gordon
Byron. The poem commemorates the Ottoman massacre of the Vene-
tian garrison at Corinth, Greece, during the Ottoman-Venetian War,
1714–1718.

· The Greek inscription is translated as "Go, stranger, and to Sparta tell,
that here, obeying her commands, we fell." Of this passage, historian
Garry Wills writes that "Thucydides put a version of that speech in
his history of the Peloponnesian War, and it became the most famous
oration of its kind, a model endlessly copied, praised, and cited—especially in the early nineteenth century, during America's Greek Revival."
Latin inscriptions appear on many Civil War monuments; however,
this is the only Greek inscription this writer has found in Tennessee,
Virginia, or Mississippi.

· The shaft and base are twenty-four feet high, of Georgia marble, from
the Tate quarries of northeast Georgia. The figure of the soldier is sev-
en feet tall, in Carrara marble, from Italy, by an unknown sculptor.

Oxford, University of Mississippi, University Cemetery Obelisk

---

3.9.3 Subject: University Cemetery Obelisk
Location: South of the Tad Smith Coliseum   N 34 21 39 38 / W 89 32 20 20
Dedicated: May 3, 1939
Media: Bronze, Granite
Monument is an obelisk with a bronze plaque.

Inscription

MISSISSIPPI DIVISION UDC / DEO VINDICE
HERE REST MORE THAN SEVEN HUNDRED SOLDIERS WHO DIED / ON THE CAMPUS
OF THE UNIVERSITY OF MISSISSIPPI WHEN THE / BUILDINGS WERE USED AS A WAR
HOSPITAL, 1862–1865; MOST OF / THE [SIC] CONFEDERATE WOUNDED AT SHILOH; A
FEW FEDERALS OF / GRANT'S ARMY; A FEW CONFEDERATES OF FORREST'S CAVALRY;
EVEN THEIR NAMES, SAVE THESE, KNOWN BUT TO GOD:

[66 names][67 names]

Interred here are soldiers from Alabama, Arkansas, Louisiana, Missouri,
Tennessee, Texas, and Kentucky. Several sports facilities and attendant parking lots surround this site today, but the cemetery is on higher ground, a swale
of sorts. It is likely that drainage was a factor in establishing the site on higher
ground, but it sanctifies the site as well.

Approximately one-half mile to the north is the Lyceum, the University's first building, which served as a military hospital during the war. An estimated two thousand patients were treated; of these, approximately seven hundred died. Many of them were interred here

Local lore holds that this is a mass gravesite. This is not the case. Records were kept, and the dead were laid in orderly rows. At least eleven of those interred were Federal soldiers; however, those remains were removed and re-interred in the Corinth National Cemetery. Individual wooden grave markers in the cemetery were destroyed circa 1900, however. Hospital records were lost either when Federal troops occupied and burned Oxford in 1864, or simply out of neglect. Many of the names of the dead are commemorated on the monument; the identities of the majority remain unknown. When the Center for Archaeological Research at the University of Mississippi conducted several remote-sensing surveys of this site in 2001 and 2004, a total of 432 "anomalies" were detected and verified.

The present monument evidently replaced a granite memorial stone bearing this inscription: "Our Heroes / 1861–1865." Allan Lemon's thesis research on this site reports that the dedication ceremonies on May 3, 1939, began with a procession of the university's ROTC units and band advancing the colors. The last flag in the procession was a "faded, battered battle flag which had seen service with General P. G. T. Beauregard and General Joseph E. Johnston." Two men, dressed in Confederate gray, served as honor guard. They were believed to be the last surviving Confederate veterans of Lafayette County.

The UDC chapter president, Mrs. Calvin Brown, offered these words of devotion:

> Daughters of the Confederacy, this day we are gathered together in the sight of God to strengthen the bonds that unite us together in the common cause, to renew the vows of loyalty to our sacred principles, to do homage to the memory of our gallant deeds unto the third and fourth generations. . . . Our state, Mississippi, the Heart of the South will be the last, the very last to compromise her southern principles for material gain or political preferment . . . after us will come our sons and daughters and the very South itself will depend upon them, the South as we know it and hope to keep it . . . there are things not material, we must instill into the hearts of this generation, or else much that is fine and beautiful of the old South will be forgotten.

- The phrase in the inscription "known but to God," for the unknown dead, has a particular pathos. The phrase does not appear on any Southern monument: it may reflect the use of the phrase on the Tomb of the Unknown Soldier at Arlington National Cemetery (1932), which may in turn draw from British military custom and, in turn, from Deuteronomy 34:5–6, the death and burial of Moses, which was accomplished under God's providence, not that of humanity.

- The Albert Sidney Johnston Chapter of the UDC is responsible for the grounds and continues to hold commemorative services on an annual basis. The cemetery was originally enclosed by an iron fence. The fence was replaced by a brick wall in 1936, with material taken from the remains of Gordon Hall, which burned down in 1934.

Yalobusha County

3.10.1 Subject: Water Valley, Oak Hill Cemetery Obelisk, Confederate
Location: Oak Hill Cemetery, off Blackmur Road, MS 315   N 34 08 56 72 / W 89 37 36 40
Installed or dedicated: circa 1870s
Medium: Marble
Monument is an obelisk surmounting a base.

Inscription
SACRED / TO THE DEAD / OF COMPANY "F," / 15TH REGIMENT, / MISSISSIPPI VOLUNTEERS

BATTLEFIELDS: / FISHING CREEK, / SHILOH, RESACA, / KENESAW MOUNTAIN, / PEACH TREE CREEK, / ATLANTA, / FRANKLIN, / PETERSBURG, VA.

KILLED IN BATTLE [20 names]

DIED IN SERVICE [8 names]

KILLED IN BATTLE [11 names].

This weathered marble obelisk stands on high ground above MS 315, overlooking the town from this hillside cemetery. The grim, weathered obelisk is decorated with four musket reliefs, barrel down, in funereal style, on each side.

- Also in this cemetery: twenty-nine tombstones inscribed "Unknown U.S. Soldier" at N 34 08 51 39 / W 37 39 34 54.

Water Valley, Oak Hill Cemetery Obelisk

3.11.1 Subject: Charleston, Courthouse Common Soldier, Confederate
Location: 1 Court Square, intersection with MS 32, 38921   N 34 00 24 31 /
W 90 03 26 48
Installed or dedicated: n.a.
Medium: Marble
Monument is a figure of a private soldier, Confederate, surmounting a shaft
and base.

Inscription

[Bas relief of Battle flag, unfurled]

ERECTED / UNDER THE / AUSPICES / OF THE / W. SCOTT ESKRIDGE
CHAPTER NO. 1174 / U.D.C. / CSA / TO THE SONS OF / TALLAHATCHIE, WHO / GAVE
THEIR HOPES, / THEIR LIVES, THEIR / ALL FOR THE GRAND / OLD SOUTHERN CAUSE

OUR HEROES / 1861–1865

Little information is available about this monument: there are no dates inscribed, no manufacturer is indicated, and the UDC chapter is not extant,
having disbanded sometime after 1918. However, it stands twenty-six feet high
and offers an affectionate tribute to the Sons of Tallahatchie—"Our Heroes"—
with a particularly sentimental flourish to those "Who Gave . . . Their All for
the Grand Old Southern Cause." "The Cause" is unspecified, but there is something of a "Support our Troops" tone to the inscription. The "why" of the war
is consigned to history, but what the "Sons of Tallahatchie" sacrificed—"Their
Lives, Their / All"—is commemorated on this Confederate monument in
Tallahatchie County.

Charleston, Courthouse Common Soldier, Confederate

3.11.2 Subject: Sumner, Courthouse Common Soldier, Confederate

Location: Court Street, 38957   N 33 58 5 30 / W 90 22 10 64

Dedicated: June 3, 1913

Media: Marble, concrete

Monument is a figure of a private soldier, Confederate, surmounting a shaft and base.

Inscription

[Front]

[Battle flag, unfurled, relief]

1861–1865 / ERECTED / BY THE / WM. H. FITZGERALD / CHAPTER NO. 696 / UNITED DAUGHTERS OF THE CONFEDERACY / JUNE 3, 1913 / OUR HEROES 1861–1865

1861–1865 / "FOR TRUTH DIES / NOT AND BY HER / LIGHT THEY RAISE / THE FLAG WHOSE / STARRY FOLDS HAVE / NEVER TRAILED; / AND BY THE LOW / TENTS OF THE DEATHLESS DEAD

THEY LEFT THE / CAUSE THAT NEVER / YET HAS FAILED." / BY VIRGINIA F. BOYLE TO THE TALLAHATCHIE / RIFLES AND ALL WHO SERVED FROM THIS COUNTY / 1861–1865

1861–1865

This monument has a prominent place in the town of Sumner (population 407, in the most recent census), on the west side of the Yazoo River. Sumner is one of the two county seats of Tallahatchie County; each has a Confederate monument. This figure, standing at parade rest, faces north. No date is inscribed, and no manufacturer is indicated, although it has the look of monuments erected by the Columbus Marble Works, with soldiers sculpted in Italy.

"Virginia F. Boyle" is Virginia Fraser Boyle (1863–1838), dubbed the "Poet Laureate of the Confederacy" by Jefferson Davis, a title that was made official in 1910 by the United Confederate Veterans. Historian Perre Magness writes that she was a poet and novelist as well as an activist with the Red Cross during World War I. In addition, she was known for poetic odes to the Confederate dead, and several notable patriotic poems relating to World War I.

· The intertwining of the war with the civil rights movement is evident: Sumner County Courthouse was the site of the trial and acquittal of Roy Bryant and J. W. Milam in 1955, for the murder of Emmett Till.

Sumner, Courthouse Common Soldier

3.12.1 Subject: Okolona, Courthouse Common Soldier, Confederate
Location: Main Street, 38860   N 34 00 15 20 / W 88 44 48 36
Dedicated: April 26, 1905
Media: Marble
Monument is a figure of a private soldier, Confederate, surmounting a shaft and base.

Inscriptions
[Front]

ERECTED / BY / OKOLONA / CHAPTER / U.D.C. / NO. 117, / 1905.
LOVE'S TRIBUTE / TO A THOUSAND / SOUTHERN / SOLDIERS WHO / SLEEP IN OUR / CONFEDERATE / CEMETERY, WHO DIED IN THE WAR / 1861–65.
[sword, sheathed, in relief]

OUR / CONFEDERATE VETERANS. / 1861–65.
LIST OF THE LIVING / *[Roster]*

LIST OF THE DEAD / *[Roster]*
TO ONE / THOUSAND / CONFEDERATE / SOLDIERS / WHO SLEEP HERE.
OUR / CONFEDERATE DEAD.

NAMES OF SOLDIERS / KILLED OR DIED / DURING THE WAR / NOT BURIED / IN THE CEMETERY.

The Okolona monument stands on Main Street on a plot of ground—today a traffic circle—given by the town. It stands thirty-two feet high, in Georgia marble, displaying a funereal inscription, referencing the dead of the Confederate cemetery on South Church Street, as well as the living and those "killed or died" who are not buried there. The surmounting statue is of Carrara marble, carved in Italy by an unknown sculptor. The monument, along with the columns decorating the First Baptist Church across the street, offer a striking neoclassical juxtaposition in this small Southern town.

The *Historic Southern Monuments* entry for Okolona observes that the "statue is a Confederate scout in an attitude of inimitable grace, standing with left hand shading his eyes as if to shut out the too obtrusive glare and apparently peering to see if danger lurks near. It is beautiful as a work of art in its simplicity, its symmetry of form and magnificent pose."

Okolona, Courthouse Common Soldier

Okolona Confederate Cemetery, stele

3.12.2 Subject: Okolona Confederate Cemetery, stele
Location: MS 245 (South Church Street)   N 33 59 55 48 / W 88 45 17 42
Installed or dedicated: n.a.
Media: Granite, concrete
Monument is a granite stele surmounting a concrete base.

Inscription

1861–1865

[Unfurled CS Battle Flag]

CHICKASAW COUNTY'S TRIBUTE / TO HER SONS WHO WORE THE GRAY /
AND WERE FAITHFUL TO THE CAUSE. / ERECTED UNDER THE AUSPICES OF /
OKOLANA CHAPTER U.D.C. NO. 117.

Wounded from the battles of Shiloh, Corinth, Okolona, Baldwyn, and Brice's
Cross Roads were sent to Okolona via the Mobile & Ohio Railroad, and city
churches, the Female Seminary, Okolona College, and private homes were converted into hospital facilities. In addition, the buildings and grounds of what

was Rose Gates College were taken over by the Confederate government for a hospital.

Many of the dead are interred here: today the Confederate Cemetery maintains the graves of over eight hundred dead, many of them unknown, on sloping ground facing west, toward the four lanes of MS 245 (South Church Street). The topography and setting give it a prominence and poignancy, almost a lack of privacy or intrusiveness: the tombstones stand row on row, facing west on open, sloping ground toward the highway, giving the past a particular, distinctive presence in the twenty-first century.

The Okolona cemetery does not have the notoriety of national military cemeteries or Confederate cemeteries such as the Franklin battlefield in Tennessee. "Northeast Mississippi's largest Confederate Cemetery" claims the following roll of Confederate dead: Alabama 115; Arkansas 49; Florida 1; Georgia 5; Kentucky 12; Louisiana 57; Mississippi 74; Missouri 7; Tennessee 34; Texas 49; unknown 381.

Monroe County

3.13.1 Subject: Aberdeen, Common Soldier, former Courthouse
Location: Old Aberdeen Cemetery, Whitfield Street, Aberdeen   N 33 48 46 52 / W 88 32 23 02
Installed or dedicated: n.a.
Medium: Marble
Monument is a figure of a private soldier, Confederate, surmounting a shaft and base.

Inscriptions
[Front]

C.S.A. / OUR HEROES / 1861-TO-1865.
THIS MONUMENT IS ERECTED BY THE / LADIES OF THE MEMORIAL ASSOCIA- / TION AND THE UNITED DAUGHTERS OF / THE CONFEDERACY OF ABERDEEN, MISS- / ISSIPPI, IN GRATEFUL REMEMBRANCE OF / THOSE WHO RISKED THEIR LIVES, / THEIR FORTUNES, AND THEIR / SACRED HONOR IN DEFENSE OF OUR BELOVED / SOUTHLAND. 1861-TO-1865.
"SOLDIERS, REST, YOUR WARFARE O'ER, / DREAM OF BATTLED FIELDS NO MORE!"

[Relief of Unfurled CS stars and bars]

THE WARRIOR'S BANNER TAKES ITS FLIGHT / TO GREET THE WARRIOR'S SOUL.

[Relief of Seal of the Confederacy]

BATTLES

[Relief of Crossed Rifles]

MANASSAS, FISHING CREEK, FORT DONELSON, SHILOH, SEVEN PINES, GAINES'S MILL, SAVAGE'S STATION, MALVERN HILL, SEVEN DAYS AROUND RICHMOND, PERRYVILLE, MURFREESBORO, 2ND MANASSAS, SOUTH MOUNTAIN, SHARPSBURG,

CHANCELLORSVILLE, CORINTH, GETTYSBURG, CHICKAMAUGA, LOOKOUT
MOUNTAIN, MISSIONARY RIDGE, SPOTSYLVANIA COURTHOUSE, FREDERICKSBURG,
MARYE'S HEIGHTS, ATLANTA CAMPAIGN, RESACA, NEW HOPE CHURCH, KENNESAW
MOUNTAIN, PEACHTREE, CREEK, JONESBORO, WILDERNESS, HARRISBURG, BRICE'S
CROSS ROADS, VICKSBURG, CARTERSVILLE, BAKER'S CREEK, BIG BLACK, OKOLONA,
EGYPT, HIGH POINT, HOLLY SPRINGS, THOROUGHFARE GAP, BOONESVILLE,
PETERSBURG CAMPAIGN, FIVE FORKS, FRANKLIN, NASHVILLE, BLAKELY,
BENTONVILLE, APPOMATTOX.

"OUR CONFEDERATE DEAD / 1861–1865. / IN MEMORY / OF THE / CONFEDERATE
SOLDIERS / OF MONROE COUNTY, MISS., AND / OTHERS WHO REST IN OUR
CEMETERIES. / "WE CARE NOT WHENCE THEY CAME, / DEAR IN THEIR LIFELESS
CLAY; / WHETHER UNKNOWN OR KNOWN TO FAME, / THEIR CAUSE AND COUNTRY
STILL THE SAME, / THEY DIED, AND WORE THE GRAY. /
"THEY TOOK UP ARMS TO RESIST INVASION AND CONQUEST; / A MORE RIGHTEOUS
CAUSE NEVER APPEALED TO THE SPIRIT / OF HEROISM, CHIVALRY, AND PATRIOTISM
IN MAN."
NEEDLESS THIS SHAFT TO THOSE WHO KNEW / THE GALLANT MEN WHOSE
VALOR IT PROCLAIMS, / BUT PATRIOTISM MAY ITS BEACONS FIRE ANEW / WITH
INSPIRATIONS FROM THEIR HALLOWED NAMES. / BUT OH! THE NAMELESS DEAD
WHO SIDE BY SIDE / STROVE WITH OUR LOVED ONES IN THE HAPLESS FIGHT! / THIS
SHAFT WE CONSECRATE TO ALL WHO DIED, / THE NAMELESS AND THE FAMED, IN
CONSCIOUSNESS OF RIGHT.

TRIED AND TRUE. / COMPANIES FROM / MONROE COUNTY:

[Roster of units from the 5th, 11th, 14th, 24th, 27th, 41st, 43rd Mississippi Infantry]

Elaborate dedication festivities attended the dedication of the Aberdeen monument that originally stood at the courthouse, although only a small number of veterans were in attendance and these, of course, were older men. Historic Southern Monuments records that "the roll-call of the companies was an interesting and pathetic feature." The monument has been moved at least twice; it was relocated to this cemetery because of a reconfiguration and widening of MS 45.

The monument is thirty feet high, of "American and Italian marble," according to *Confederate Veteran*. The shaft is surmounted by a life-size figure of a Confederate soldier, said to be "on picket duty in uniform . . . a familiar spectacle to veteran eyes." The figure shades his eyes as he looks north.

· The inscription beginning "The Warrior's Banner" may be excerpted
   from the poem "Ashes of Glory," by A. J. Requier, composed circa 1894.

With its inscribed roster of veterans as well as the list of battles fought during the war, this is a singularly strident, even bellicose monument, especially for Mississippi. This was a war fought "to Resist Invasion and Conquest," it declares. It was a "Righteous Cause," but with a tragic outcome—a "Hapless Fight." The monument is a tribute to many, including the "Nameless Dead Who Side By Side / Strove With Our Loved Ones."

Aberdeen Cemetery, Common Soldier

Amory, Common Soldier, Confederate

3.13.2 Subject: Amory, Common Soldier, Confederate
Location: 1st and Main Streets, Frisco Park   N 33 59 06 25 / W 88 29 21 10
Erected: 1926; Dedicated: June 3, 1931
Medium: Marble
Monument is a figure of a private soldier, Confederate, surmounting a shaft and base.

Inscription
[Front]
[Unfurled CS Battle Flag]

AMORY'S TRIBUTE / TO THE HEROES OF / 1861–1865
MEMBERS OF / STONEWALL CAMP NO. 427 / AMORY, MISSISSIPPI

[Roster of veterans: 53 names]

TO THE WOMEN OF THE / CONFEDERACY WHOSE PIOUS MINISTRATIONS TO OUR / WOUNDED SOLDIERS SOOTHED THE LAST HOURS OF THOSE / WHO DIED FAR FROM THE / OBJECTS OF THEIR TENDEREST / LOVE—WHOSE DOMESTIC LABORS / CONTRIBUTED MUCH TO / SUPPLY THE WANTS OF OUR DEFENDERS IN THE FIELD

[*SIC*] / WHOSE ZEALOUS FAITH IN OUR CAUSE SHONE A GUIDING / STAR UNDIMMED BY THE / DARKEST CLOUDS OF WAR; / WHOSE FORTITUDE SUSTAINED THEM UNDER ALL THE / PRIVATIONS TO WHICH THEY WERE SUBJECTED, WHOSE ANNUAL / TRIBUTE EXPRESSES THEIR / ENDURING GRIEF, LOVE, AND / REVERENCE FOR OUR SACRED DEAD, AND WHOSE PATRIOTISM / WILL TEACH THEIR CHILFREN TO EMULATE THE DEEDS OF / OUR REVOLUTIONARY SIRES. / JEFFERSON DAVIS. CAPTAINS FROM MONROE COUNTY / FROM 1861 TO 1865

[Roster of veterans: 53 names]

Amory was planned, laid out, and established as a railroad town in 1887. Postbellum Southern towns usually do not erect war memorials: this is an exception, and it has always had a prominent place in Amory. As the halfway point between Birmingham and Memphis, Amory served as a maintenance shop for the Kansas City, Memphis & Birmingham Railroad, and progressive towns like this are usually more forward-looking. Evidently, the veterans of the Stonewall Camp thought otherwise; this is an assertive, if elegant tribute to the past. The monument is well maintained and is pristine in appearance: local sources indicate that it is regularly cleaned at the initiative of the city government.

Records at the City of Amory Regional Museum indicate that the monument was erected in 1926 but was not dedicated until 1931. Initially, it stood in the middle of Main Street, but it was moved to Frisco Park on March 23, 1939. The Amory Chapter of the UDC was the sponsor. The Columbus Marble Works served as designers and builders. The cost was $2,500.

The tribute to the "Women of the Confederacy" is taken from the dedication in Jefferson Davis's 1881 narrative, *The Rise and Fall of the Confederate Government*.

Grenada, Common Soldier, Confederate

Grenada County

3.14.1 Subject: Grenada, Courthouse Common Soldier
Location: Washington Street   N 33 47 05 99 / W 89 48 07 98
Dedicated: June 3, 1910
Medium: Marble
Monument is a figure of a private soldier, Confederate, surmounting a shaft and base.

Inscriptions
[Front]
[CS Battle Flag]

TO THE NOBLE MEN / WHO MARCHED NEATH / THE FLAG OF THE STARS AND BARS, / AND WERE FAITHFUL TO THE END

GLORIOUS / IN LIFE / IN DEATH SUBLIME. / UNVEILED JUNE 3, 1910

[Crossed Swords relief]

TO THE NOBLE WOMEN / OF THE SOUTH, WHO / WITH EYES UNDIMMED
BY FEAR AND HEARTS / OF SPARTAN COURAGE, / GAVE THEIR LOVED ONES
TO OUR COUNTRY TO / CONQUER OR TO DIE / FOR TRUTH AND RIGHT
AND WHO ENSHRINED / THEIR DEEDS IN / DEATHLESS LOVE
TO KEEP VIGIL O'ER / SACRED GRAVES

JEFFERSON DAVIS / JUNE 3, 1808 / DEC. 6, 1889
THE ONLY PRESIDENT / OF THE SOUTHERN CONFEDERACY
SOLDIER, STATESMAN / PATRIOT

[CS National Flag]
GRENADA COUNTY'S / TRIBUTE TO HER / CONFEDERATE
SOLDIERS AND SAILORS. / 1861–1865

Faith that endures under trial is a theme of the Grenada monument, a three-tiered marble edifice facing east, erected by the Columbus Marble Works. Thus the "Noble Men / Who Marched Neath / The Flag of the Stars And Bars . . . Were Faithful to the End." They were "Glorious / In Life /," but in "Death Sublime." Extravagant tribute is also given to the "Women/of the South." Davis, the only individual mentioned, is given a eulogistic tribute.

Grenada served as a rail center and supply depot during the war. General John C. Pemberton, commanding Confederate forces, established the "Yalobusha River Line," against Union incursions along the railroad that ran from Greenwood to Columbus. Eight forts were erected around Grenada and more than twenty-two thousand Confederate troops were stationed in and around the city during the winter of 1862. At least two of these forts are extant and accessible to the public at the present-day Grenada Lake Dam. The defenses effectively checked Union General Ulysses S. Grant's advance on Vicksburg by way of the Mississippi Central Railroad during the Vicksburg-North Mississippi Campaign of October–December 1862.

Cleveland, Courthouse Common Soldier, Confederate

Bolivar County

3.15.1 Subject: Cleveland, Courthouse Common Soldier, Confederate
Location: Courthouse lawn, 200 S. Court Street, 38732   N 33 44 39 66 / W 90 43 26 72
Dedicated: May 14, 1908
Media: Georgia marble, Italian marble
Monument is a figure of a private soldier, Confederate, surmounting a shaft and base.

Inscription
[Front]
[Relief of CS Battle Flag, unfurled on pole]

BOLIVAR TROOP / CHAPTER / U.D.C. / C.S.A.
TO THE MEMORY / OF OUR / CONFEDERATE DEAD. / 1861–1865
DEAD UPON THE FIELD OF GLORY. / HERO FIT FOR SONG AND STORY.

C.S.A.

C.S.A.

Most early twentieth-century Civil War monuments across the South took a celebratory, sentimental tone to their subject. Not so in Mississippi. The Cleveland monument, erected in 1908, is like other Mississippi funereal monuments erected at a time when more celebratory monuments were the norm.

The Cleveland monument faces east, at the southeast corner of the courthouse grounds. Much nationalistic fervor is expressed for the nation that, as the monument itself intimates, barely existed, absorbed much blood and treasure during its existence, and collapsed only four years after its inception. The tragic dimension of this story merits no mention, however. Instead, a kind of absolution is evident. Tribute is given to "Our Confederate Dead" who fought for a nation that "Rose So Free From Crime," and "Fell . . . Free From Stain." The UDC mourns the dead by dint of this monument, but they also intimate a life/death/life drama: the nation, though fallen, is pristine. The Bolivar County Board of Supervisors appropriated $2,500 for the project. The UDC Bolivar Troop Chapter 1067 raised $500.

· The whole of the monument stands forty feet high and is a product of the Columbus Marble Works. The figure stands five feet, six inches tall; the sculptor is unknown, but a local history of Cleveland notes that the statue, carved in Carrara, Italy was lost in transit: "When the figure was craned from a boat in the New York harbor, the cradle broke and the figure plummeted to the bottom of the bay. But it was recovered in time for dedication ceremonies that took place on May 14, 1908."

3.16.1 Subject: Greenville, Courthouse Common Soldier, Confederate
Location: Washington Street, 38703   N 33 24 27 11 / W 91 03 11 62
Dedicated: June 2, 1909
Medium: Marble
Monument is a soldier surmounting a shaft and base.

Inscription

[Front]
ERECTED BY PRIVATE / TAYLOR RUCKS CHAPTER / UNITED DAUGHTERS OF
THE CONFEDERACY / TO COMMEMORATE THE / VALOR AND PATRIOTISM
OF THE CONFEDERATE / SOLDIERS OF / WASHINGTON COUNTY.
1861–1865.

[Crossed swords]

1909 / COLUMBUS MARBLE WKS / COLUMBUS MISS.

IT IS DUE THE TRUTH / OF HISTORY THAT THE / FUNDAMENTAL PRINCIPLES
FOR WHICH OUR FATHERS / CONTENDED SHOULD BE / OFTEN REITERATED IN
ORDER THAT THE PURPOSE / WHICH INSPIRED THEM MAY / BE CORRECTLY
ESTIMATED / AND THE PURITY OF THEIR / MOTIVES BE ABUNDANTLY VINDICATED /
CHARLES B. GALLOWAY

THE SUBLIMEST WORD / IN THE ENGLISH / LANGUAGE IS DUTY. / ROBERT E. LEE
NO BRAVE BATTLE / FOR TRUTH AND / RIGHT WAS EVER / FOUGHT IN VAIN. /
RANDOLPH H. MCKIM.

[CS Battle Flag]

FOR THOSE WHO / ENCOUNTERED THE / PERILS OF WAR IN / DEFENSE OF
STATES RIGHTS / AND CONSTITUTIONAL / GOVERNMENT. / JEFFERSON DAVIS.

Solemn declarations characterize the Greenville monument, with its lofty
shaft and common soldier, which stands on the spacious grounds of the county
seat near the Richardsonian Romanesque style courthouse erected in 1891. The
quotation beginning "It is Due the Truth of History" is attributed to Charles B.
Galloway, from an address titled, "Jefferson Davis, a Judicial Estimate," deliv-
ered at the University of Mississippi, June 3, 1908. Galloway (1849–1909) was
a Mississippian, educated at the University of Mississippi, a popular speaker,
preacher, and a bishop of the Methodist Episcopal Church.

The quotation beginning "No Brave Battle for Truth and Right" is credited
to Rev. Randolph Harrison McKim, Confederate veteran (2nd Virginia Cavalry)
and long-time pastor of Epiphany Church in Washington, DC. The passage
is taken from a speech he gave to a United Confederate Veterans reunion at
Nashville, on June 14, 1904.

Archives of the Washington and Lee University contest the attribution of
the quotation to Robert E. Lee, although they do not deny the truth of the
claim or the consonance with Lee's ethos. However, after Lee's death a sheet

Greenville, Courthouse Common Soldier

of paper was found among his effects on which he had written these words: "There is a true glory, and a true honor; the glory of duty done, the honor of integrity of principle."

· The sculpture stands approximately five feet, six inches high. The monument was erected by the Columbus Marble Works at a cost of $4,000.

3.17.1 Subject: Greenwood, Courthouse Common Soldier, Confederate
Location: 310 West Market Street, 38930   N 33 31 13 35 / W 90 11 02 26
Dedicated: October 9, 1913
Medium: Georgia marble
Monument is a figure of a private soldier, Confederate, surmounting a shaft, facing southeast.

Inscription

[Front]
[Figure of Woman tending a wounded soldier]

CSA / 1861–1865
LEFLORE COUNTY'S TRIBUTE / TO HER SONS AND DAUGHTERS / OF THE SOUTHERN CONFEDERACY / ERECTED UNDER THE AUSPICES / OF THE VARINA JEFFERSON DAVIS / CHAPTER UNITED DAUGHTERS / OF THE CONFEDERACY, / OCTOBER 9, 1913

[Figure of Soldier advancing, drawing a sword]

A TESTIMONIAL OF / OUR AFFECTION AND / REVERENCE FOR THE CONFEDERATE SOLDIER / THE MEMORY OF WHOSE BRAVE DEEDS AND HEROIC / LIFE, AND THE PRINCIPLES / FOR WHICH HE SACRIFICED / SO MUCH WE BEQUEATH TO / OUR CHILDREN THROUGH / ALL FUTURE GENERATIONS.

[Figure of Woman praying]

"FATHER, THY WILL BE DONE."
TO THE CONFEDERATE WOMAN / NONE HAS TOLD THE STORY OF HER, / WHOSE HEART AND LIFE WERE A / SACRIFICE. OFFERED AS VALIANTLY AND UNSELFISHLY UPON THE ALTAR OF / HER SOUTHLAND, AS WAS ANY WARRIOR'S LIFE UPON THE BATTLEFIELD. SO TO / HER IN PART WE HAVE PLACED THIS / MONUMENT, THAT ALL MAY KNOW SHE LOVED HER COUNTRY, AND ENFOLD HER / MEMORY IN ETERNAL GLORY, / CHERISHING IT FOREVER.

[Figure of Artillerist bearing rammer staff]

1861–1865
STEAMER STAR OF THE WEST / IN 1861 THE / FIRST GUN OF THE WAR BETWEEN / THE STATES WAS / FIRED AT THIS / VESSEL IN THE CHARLESTON HARBOR REPLICA OF THE PILOT WHEEL OF / THE STEAMER STAR OF THE WEST

[Relief of Pilot Wheel]

THE STAR OF THE / WEST WAS CAPTURED / BY A SQUAD OF / CONFEDERATE / CAVALRY AT SABINE / PASS, AND SCUTTLED / IN 1863 IN / TALLAHATCHIE RIVER AT FORT PEMBERTON, / THREE MILES FROM / GREENWOOD.

This is an opulent monument on the courthouse grounds in a town that was relatively prosperous before and after the war by dint of local agriculture and its railroad and river connections.

The whole of the monument is approximately thirty-five feet in height. Four steps lead up to a pedestal, with a shaft surrounded by statuary tableaux on

Greenwood, Courthouse Common Soldier

pedestals extending from four sides of the shaft. It is a dynamic edifice. The pedestal figures—two women and four men—and the inscription offer a tribute to the wartime generation of men and women, as well as the defense of Greenwood against Union forces in 1862. There is no reference to the outcome of the war.

The role of the women as depicted here merits consideration. Women's suffrage would not be won for another half century, and domestic ideals of a woman's place were certainly esteemed, but the public role of women is also honored in monuments like these. The three men are given homage for their sacrifice and service: an artilleryman holds the rammer staff as a weapon; a soldier is drawing his sword; the surmounting statue, a Confederate artillery officer is evidently looking into the distance to observe the fall of shot of his unit. However, the women of the South are commended for their sacrifices in the same breath as the men. Specifically, the wartime generation of women are those "Whose Heart and Life Were a / Sacrifice Offered as Valiantly and Unselfishly Upon the Altar of / Her Southland, as Was Any Warrior's Life Upon The Battlefield." The depiction of a woman kneeling to care for a wounded soldier on the front pedestal suggests a priestly, ministerial role. The standing figure of a woman, clasping her hands in intercessory, even messianic prayer, intimates that the sacrifice she is called upon to make—"Father, Thy Will Be Done"—is consciously, conspicuously undertaken in the knowledge that it is the will of God (Matt. 6:10). The words are also used by Jesus in the Garden of Gethsemane on the night of his arrest and in anticipation of his trial and crucifixion ("Father, if thou be willing, remove this cup from me: nevertheless not my will, but thine, be done" [Luke 22:42]).

Although it may well be said that women were expected to fulfill domestic roles, and that this ideal was upheld, cherished, and perpetuated before, during, and after the war, there is more to this history. Monuments like these represent two dimensions of the role of women in the war: they mediated between life and death in tending the wounded, and they mediated between heaven and earth by intercessory prayer. In both roles, the women take on a kind of priestly and ministerial function: they were detached from the physical combat of war, but they were immersed in the emotional, physical, and spiritual trials of the war. The women acted; they interceded; they mediated in an intimate, vicariously priestly role. Indeed, the travail was of such a magnitude that the woman as priest became the sacrifice and accepted this destiny—"Thy Will Be Done."

3.17.2 Subject: Fort Pemberton, stele, Confederate
Location: Frontage Road, Fort Pemberton Park, east of intersection of 49E and US 82   N 33 31 51 42 / W 90 14 01 90
Dedicated: January 1, 1958
Medium: Granite
Monument is an inscribed granite stele.

Inscription
[Crossed CS battle flags]

FORT PEMBERTON

IN THE 1863 CAMPAIGN AGAINST VICKSBURG, GENERAL GRANT TRIED SEVERAL APPROACHES, ONE BEING TO SEND TROOPS ON TRANSPORTS DOWN THE TALLAHATCHIE AND YAZOO RIVERS. HE CUT THE MISSISSIPPI RIVER LEVEE IN FEBRUARY[,] WHICH FLOODED THE SEVERAL BAYOUS BETWEEN THE MISSISSIPPI AND TALLAHATCHIE RIVERS, MAKING A NAVIGABLE CONNECTION. TWENTY-TWO TRANSPORTS (WITH 5000 TROOPS), TWO IRONCLADS, TWO RAMS AND SIX LIGHT

Fort Pemberton, Stele

DRAFT GUNBOATS MADE UP THE FIRST EXPEDITION, WHICH WAS LATER REIN-
FORCED WITH ANOTHER BRIGADE AND ADDITIONAL VESSELS. IT TOOK SEVERAL
WEEKS TO MAKE THE TWO HUNDRED MILE TRIP AS THE BAYOUS WERE NARROW
AND TORTUOUS.

APPRISED OF THE FEDERAL PLANS THE CONFEDERATE GENERAL JOHN C.
PEMBERTON ORDERED A FORT TO BE CONSTRUCTED TO BLOCK THE ENEMY FORC-
ES. THE ENGINEERS SELECTED A LOCATION WHERE THE TALLAHATCHIE MAKES
AN ABRUPT TURN EASTERLY, THE RIVER FLOWING TO THIS POINT IN A STRAIGHT
STRETCH. THERE BEING ROOM FOR ONLY TWO GUNBOATS ABREAST, THUS THE
CONFEDERATES WOULD BE SHOOTING DOWN A STRAIGHT ALLEY. THE FORT WAS
HASTILY BUILT OF COTTON BALES COVERED WITH EARTH, AND NAMED FORT
PEMBERTON. IT HAD BUT A FEW LIGHT GUNS, BUT ONE, AN EIGHT INCH RIFLE, WAS
VERY ACCURATE. THE FORT WAS MANNED BY 1500 MEN UNDER COMMAND OF BRIG.
GEN. W. W. LORING. CUTTING THE LEVEES HAD FLOODED THE AREA AND THE ONLY
APPROACH TO THE FORT WAS BY WATER. TO FURTHER IMPEDE THE ENEMY THE
STEAMSHIP "STAR OF THE WEST" WAS SUNK IN THE CHANNEL.

THE FEDERAL FLOTILLA ARRIVED AT FORT PEMBERTON ON MARCH 11TH, AND THE
TWO IRONCLADS ATTACKED AT 1000 YARDS, BUT BOTH WERE DAMAGED AFTER
SEVERAL ATTEMPTS TO REDUCE THE FORT. THE FEDERAL FLEET RETIRED TO THE
MISSISSIPPI. GRANT HAD FAILED TO REACH VICKSBURG BY THE TALLAHATACHIE-
YAZOO ROUTE.

PART OF THE FORT IS INCLUDED IN THE PARK AND SOME OF THE ORIGINAL BREAST-
WORKS MAY BE EASILY RECOGNIZED.

ERECTED BY LEFLORE COUNTY BOARD OF SUPERVISORS / [7 names]

This centennial-era stele commemorates the battle of Fort Pemberton fought on March 11, 1863, when the Confederates denied Union access via the Yazoo River to Vicksburg. No little satisfaction is expressed in the narrative about forcing the Union forces—who were superior in numbers and resources—to retreat. The fort was located on the embankment stretching approximately three hundred yards from the Tallahatchie River to the Yazoo River, and its outline is still discernible.

· The *Star of the West*, a civilian merchant ship, received what have been regarded as the first shots of the Civil War at Fort Sumter on January 9, 1861. Seized by Confederate forces in 1862, it was sunk as a block ship in a channel of the Tallahatchie. The wreckage of the ship remains: it can still be seen in the river when the waters are low. It is now the property of the US General Services Administration.

Carroll County

3.18.1 Subject: Carrollton, Courthouse Common Soldier, Confederate
Location: Courthouse grounds, corner of Lexington and Washington
N 33 30 29 09 / W 89 55 09 54
Dedicated: December 1, 1905
Media: Italian marble, marble base
Monument is soldier surmounting a shaft and base.

Inscription
[Front]
ERECTED BY / CARROLL COUNTY / UNDER THE / AUSPICES OF
P. F. LIDDELL CAMP, / NO 56 AND H. D. MONEY, CHAPTER U.D.C. / 1905

TO THE MEMORY / OF CARROLL'S / CONFEDERATE / SOLDIERS
WHO FOUGHT IN / DEFENSE OF OUR / CONSTITUTIONAL / RIGHTS.

FROM BETHEL / TO APPOMATTOX
JNO. A. STINSON / COLUMBUS MISS.
U.D.C. P. F. RIDDELL CAMP / NO 56

TRUTH CRUSHED / TO EARTH WILL / RISE AGAIN.

In this celebration-era monument, which stands twenty-five feet high, Carroll County's Confederate soldiers are acclaimed as those who fought for justice, "In / Defense of Our / Constitutional / Rights," and who fought well, "From Bethel / to Appomattox." No hint of dishonor or defeat is intimated. Indeed, there is the prospect of a resurrection of the cause, as it were: "Truth Crushed To Earth Will Rise Again." The assertion is excerpted from the poem, "The Battle-Field," by William Cullen Bryant (1794–1878), American poet, journalist, and editor of the *New York Evening Post*. Martin Luther King Jr. used the same quotation in his 1957 speech "Give Us the Ballot."

Carrollton, Courthouse Common Soldier

3.18.2 Subject: Vaiden, Courthouse Common Soldier
Location: Stonewall and Mulberry, 39176   N 33 19 54 83 / W 89 44 32 70
Dedicated: June 3, 1912
Medium: Marble
Monument is a figure of a private soldier, Confederate, surmounting a shaft and base.

Inscriptions
[Front]

SACRED TO THE MEMORY / OF THE / CONFEDERATE SOLDIER, / WHO FOUGHT FOR PRIN- / CIPLES THAT CAN NEVER / DIE, AS LONG AS A / SENSE OF RIGHT AND / PATRIOTISM DWELL IN THE HUMAN BREAST / CONFEDERATE HEROES

"WHEN THE LAST TRUMPET / IS SOUNDED, MAY EACH ONE / ANSWER THE ROLL CALL / OF THE HEAVENLY ARMY." / THE WAR ON THE PART OF / THE SOUTH WAS FOR THE / DEFENSE OF OUR INHERENT, / UNALIENABLE RIGHT. / JEFFERSON DAVIS.

Vaiden, Courthouse Common Soldier

ERECTED BY THE / UNITED DAUGHTERS / OF THE CONFEDERACY, / JUNE 3, 1912
"MANY OF WHOM GAVE ALL, / AND ALL OF WHOM GAVE MUCH."

CSA / 1861 / "LEST WE FORGET." / 1865.

This monument once had a prominent place on the courthouse grounds in front of the picturesque neoclassical courthouse erected in 1905. That courthouse was demolished in 1992, notwithstanding efforts by the state to fund its restoration as a national landmark. The monument was moved when the new courthouse was erected in 1992, and it stands today in a park—in a somewhat unkempt state—on a side street across from the town's city hall.

- "When The Last Trumpet Is Sounded" is a reference to the resurrection of the dead at 1 Corinthians 15:52 ("In a moment, in the twinkling of an eye, at the last trump: for the trumpet shall sound, and the dead shall be raised incorruptible, and we shall be changed" [KJV].)
- The excerpt beginning "The War on the Part of the South" is taken from Jefferson Davis's *The Rise and Fall of the Confederate Government.*

Winona, Courthouse Common Soldier

Montgomery County

3.19.1 Subject: Winona, Courthouse Common Soldier, Confederate
Location: 115 N. Quitman Street, 38967   N 22 28 58 56 / W 89 43 44 56
Dedicated: December 17, 1909
Medium: Marble
Monument is soldier surmounting a shaft and base.

Inscriptions
[Front]
1861–1865

[Relief of Stars and Bars, unfurled]

TO THE / CONFEDERACY / PRESIDENT / JEFFERSON DAVIS, / AND
THE SOLDIERS / WHO FOUGHT / FOR STATES RIGHTS / C.S.A. / 1909

[blank]

THIS MONUMENT IS / THE GIFT OF COMRADE / JAMES C. PURNELL,
TO STATHAM-FARRELL / CAMP OF UNITED / CONFEDERATE VETERANS.

MONUMENTAL COMMITTEE *[List of 4 names]* / C.S.A.

TO THE WOMEN OF / THE CONFEDERACY, / WHO WERE AS FAIR / AS OUR SKIES
AND / SUNNY AS OUR CLIME[.] / THEIR HEROISM, / SACRIFICES, PATRIOTISM, /
AND DEVOTION TO THE / SOUTH, IS [SIC] WITHOUT / PARALLEL IN HISTORY, /
AND FOR THIS WE LOVED / THEM AND WILL FOREVER / HONOR AND CHERISH /
THEIR MEMORY.

Standing approximately seventeen feet high, this courthouse monument was originally erected on the grounds of the former courthouse site in 1909; it was moved when the old courthouse was demolished in 1975. The Winona-Montgomery Regional Library stands on the grounds now, and the monument is adjacent to the library entrance.

The monument no longer has the prominent place it once had, but it proclaims a clear affirmation of states rights, Jefferson Davis, Confederate soldiers and—especially—the women of the Confederacy. Note the unusually overt expression of love for the women—"We Loved/Them"—by the Confederate veterans. At the same time, the monument should be noted for the lack of a domestic calling for the women, who were loved for their spirit and for their "Their Heroism, / Sacrifices, Patriotism, / and Devotion to the / South."

3.19.2 Subject: Duck Hill, Cemetery Obelisk
Location: Corner of Church and Binford   N 33 37 59 97 / W 89 42 35 48
Installed or dedicated: n.a.
Media: Marble, concrete
Monument is a marble obelisk surmounting a shaft and concrete base.

Inscription
[Front]
[CS battle flag, relief]

C.S.A. / IN MEMORY OF / COL. W. S. STATHAM / COL. M. FARRELL, / COL. J. R. BINFORD AND ALL MEMBERS OF / THE 15TH MISS. REGT. INFTRY / C.S.A.
THROUGH THEIR COURAGE / THEY WON IMMORTAL VICTORY / AND DEATHLESS FAME / FOR TO DIE NOBLY IS THE / PROUDEST GLORY OF VIRTUE / "TO THE NOBLE MEN WHO / FOUGHT NEATH THE FLAG / OF THE STARS AND BARS / AND WHO WERE FAITHFUL / UNTO THE END."

C.S.A.

C.S.A.

C.S.A.

The obelisk in this small town faces the tracks of the present-day Grenada Railway, formerly a line of the Illinois Central Railroad. "Company E" of the 15th Mississippi Infantry, known as the "McClung Rifles," organized at Duck Hill. The men of Company E are given lavish praise: they "won immortal victory" by dint of their noble deaths. The praise merits further explanation: "To Die Nobly is the Proudest Glory of Virtue."

- Two flat cars bearing Confederate soldiers were demolished in a train collision near here on October 19, 1862. The dead were buried in a common grave beside the tracks, the "Duck Hill Train Wreck Cemetery," located south of the monument. Thirty-four men were killed. The

Duck Hill, Cemetery Obelisk

Rev. Daniel T. Lake, Methodist minister, reported that "as we came around a considerable curve into straight road in full view of Duck Hill Station, there was a fearful crash, resulting in the destruction of two engines, several cars, and the death of thirty-two men. About forty others were wounded, bruised and mangled . . . some mortally, some seriously and others only slightly. . . . We buried the dead, mostly Arkansas and Texas volunteers, in one long pit grave, wide enough to lay the men crosswise . . . with only their blankets for coffins."

Today there are twenty-nine gravestones; two epitaphs are inscribed unknown. A reenactment group, Stanford's Mississippi Battery, researched the soldiers' names and units and secured headstones for their graves by dint of the Veterans Administration. The precise location of the graves was not determined, but the preponderance of evidence indicated this site.

- The 15th Mississippi Infantry organized at Choctaw in May 1861, with men from Holmes, Choctaw, Quitman, Montgomery, Yalobusha, and Grenada counties. The regiment was engaged at Mill Springs, Fishing

Creek, Shiloh, Corinth, Baton Rouge, the Vicksburg Campaign, the Atlanta Campaign, Hood's Tennessee Campaign, and the Carolinas Campaign. The 15th had 34 officers and 820 men on January 7, 1862, but only a "remnant" surrendered in April 1865.

Oktibbeha County

3.20.1 Subject: Courthouse Stele, Confederate
Location: Corner of Main and D. L. Conner Drive   N 33 27 50 22 / W 88 48 57 82
Installed or dedicated: 2005
Medium: Granite
Monument is a granite shaft.

Inscription
[Front]

IN MEMORY OF THOSE / FROM OKTIBBEHA COUNTY
WHO SERVED DURING THE / WAR BETWEEN THE STATES. / 1861–1865
THEY WERE A BAND OF BROTHERS / AND NATIVE TO THE SOIL.
MAY THEY NEVER BE FORGOTTEN
PUTNAM DARDEN CHAPTER OF UNITED DAUGHTERS OF THE CONFEDERACY / 2005

Two adjacent granite shafts stand on the grounds of the Oktibbeha County. None was present for many years. Two appeared within forty-eight months. Both are provocative in their own way.

3.20.2 Subject: Courthouse Stele, Union
Location: Corner of Main and D. L. Conner Drive
Installed or dedicated: 2006
Medium: Granite
Monument is a granite shaft.

Inscription
IN MEMORY OF THOSE WHO SERVED / DURING THE WAR BETWEEN THE STATES /
1861–1865
THEY WERE BROTHERS THAT STOOD FOR / THE FREEDOM OF OTHERS
COALITION FOR THE / UNION SOLDIERS OF AMERICA / 2006
OKTIBBEHA COUNTY JUSTICE COALITION

The Oktibbeha County Justice Coalition sponsored this Union monument, which was erected in April 2005, as a response to the monument constructed by the UDC and cited above. Jessie Oden, a coalition member, said the memorial was erected to honor Union soldiers in response to the "racism" implicitly attached to the UDC monument. The claim was denied by members of the UDC, who declared that "their monument honors all soldiers of the Civil War."

The Confederate monument (3.20.1) includes the phrase "Band of Brothers," an excerpt from the lyrics of a Confederate anthem "Bonnie Blue Flag," whose

Oktibbeha County, Courthouse Stele, Union

lyrics evidently draw upon the St. Crispin's Day speech in William Shakespeare's *The Life of King Henry the Fifth* (Act 4, scene 3). The phrase "Band of Brothers" is also coincident with the title of a contemporary film series drama of American soldiers set during World War II.

3.21.1 Subject: West Point, Courthouse Common Soldier, Confederate
Location: 205 Court Street   N 33 36 20 03 / W 88 38 51 18
Installed or dedicated: August 8, 1907
Medium: Marble
Monument is two figures of Confederate soldiers flanking the base of an obelisk.

Inscriptions
[Front]
[CS National Flag relief] [Crossed swords relief]

1861 GLORIA VICTIS 1865.
JOHN M. STONE CHAPTER, UNITED / DAUGHTERS OF THE CONFEDERACY, / PAYS TRIBUTE TO THE CONFEDER- / ATE SOLDIERS OF CLAY COUNTY. / C.S.A. / ERECTED 1907.

NO NATION ROSE / SO WHITE AND FAIR / OR FELL SO PURE OF CRIME.
CLAY COUNTY HOLDS IN PROUD / AND GRATEFUL REMEMBRANCE
HER BRAVE AND LOYAL SONS, / WHO PREFERRED DEATH
TO A BETRAYAL / OF HER / DEAREST PRINCIPLES. / MIGHT OVERCAME, / LET NOT OUR SONS / FORGET / THAT THESE UNSULLIED HEROES FOUGHT / FOR RIGHT.

The marble Clay County monument on Court Street stands forty-three feet high. An estimated seven thousand people attended the unveiling ceremonies on August 8, 1907, which was called West Point's "greatest day" in *Historic Southern Monuments*, published in 1911.

The monument was erected as a tribute to the county's "Brave and Loyal Sons, / Who Preferred Death to a Betrayal / of Her / Dearest Principles." The to-the-death stance is as strong a claim as is found in Mississippi monumentation. "Gloria Victis" translated to English reads "Glory to the Defeated" and is likely a reference to the 1874 sculpture titled "Gloria Victis," a tribute to French soldiers of the Franco-Prussian War of 1871, by Antonin Mercie. The inscription "so white and fair . . . so pure of crimes" is attributed to English poet Philip Stanhope Worsley, from a poem dedicated to Robert E. Lee and given to him by the poet in 1866, inscribed in a copy of Worsley's translation of the Iliad. Michael R. Steele notes that Worsley aligns the fallen South with Homeric mythology, with Lee as the tragic Trojan hero Hector and the Confederacy with fallen Troy—"so white and fair . . . so pure of crimes."

West Point, Courthouse Common Soldier

West Point, Battle of Ellis Bridge, Granite Shaft

3.21.2 Subject: West Point, Battle of Ellis Bridge
Location: West of West Point on MS 50, north side   N 33 36 27 01 / W 88 43 45 04
Installed or dedicated: February 1994
Medium: Granite
Monument is a granite shaft.

Inscriptions
[Front]

THE BATTLE OF / ELLIS BRIDGE

[CS Battle Flag]

IN MEMORY OF / THOSE WHO FOUGHT TO / LIBERATE WEST POINT / FEB. 21, 1864 / THEIR ACTIONS RESULTED / IN VICTORY AGAINST / A VASTLY SUPERIOR / FEDERAL ARMY. THEIR / BRAVERY WILL ALWAYS / BE REMEMBERED.

THE BATTLE OF / ELLIS BRIDGE

[CS Battle Flag]

The battle of Ellis Bridge was not a major engagement, but this stele, standing eight feet high, on high ground above MS 50, is one of the few battlefield monuments in the state apart from Vicksburg and Brice's Station. The action here is related to the Meridian Campaign, when some seven thousand Federal cavalry under the command of Brig. Gen. William S. Smith moved from the Memphis area southeastward to join with Maj. Gen. William T. Sherman's command at Meridian on February 11, 1864. Some twenty thousand troops commanded by Sherman had moved east from Vicksburg across the state, February 3–March 5, 1864, in what is regarded as a prelude to his march across Georgia later that same year.

Forrest maneuvered against Smith's approaching Federals to prevent the two forces from uniting. Forrest's campaign was successful. Efforts to trap the Federal force were unsuccessful, but the vigor of the defense here, at West Point, and at Okolona led Smith to withdraw—to Sherman's great ire—and disrupted the Meridian Campaign.

· The bridge crossing at Chuquatonchee Creek—known as Sakatonchee Creek during the war—is at the same site as wartime Ellis Bridge, but the site of the skirmish is not known.

Lowndes County, Columbus, Courthouse Common Soldiers

Lowndes County

3.22.1 Subject: Columbus, Courthouse Common Soldiers, three, Confederate
Location: 5th Street South (US 45 North) and 2nd Avenue North
N 33 29 46 93 / W 88 25 41 30
Dedicated: August 9, 1912
Medium: Marble
Monument is a domed temple with figures of three soldiers, two at the base and one surmounting the dome.

Inscriptions

C.S.A. / OUR HEROES
THIS MONUMENT IS ERECTED / IN HONOR OF THE SOLDIERS / OF LOWNDES
COUNTY, / WHO NOBLY DARED LIFE AND / FORTUNE IN DEFENSE OF THE
1861 SOUTHERN CONFEDERACY. 1865

A TRIBUTE OF LOVE TO OUR / HONORED DEAD, WHOSE MEMORY
WE ENSHRINE IN OUR HEARTS, / WHOSE PRINCIPLES OF RIGHT,
AS A SACRED HERITAGE / WE BEQUEATH TO OUR CHILDREN
THROUGH ALL GENERATIONS. / STEPHEN D. LEE CHAPTER, NO. 34 U.D.C. / 1912

The Columbus courthouse grounds monument consists of a central structure in the form of a domed temple, the whole standing twenty-eight feet high, in white marble, with sculptures of three Confederate soldiers. One figure surmounts the top of the dome, holding a flag, facing southwest. Two figures stand on each side of the temple; each bears a rifle at his side.

The monument has a prominent place on the southwest side of the courthouse grounds. It cost $4,500, with fundraising led by the Stephen D. Lee Chapter, No. 34 of the UDC. The Columbus Marble Works made the monument, which may been the firm's largest in Mississippi. The sculptures were imported from Italy; the sculptor(s) is unknown. John A. Stinson, listed as sculptor, was the founder and owner of the Columbus Marble Works, which erected many courthouse and cemetery monuments in Mississippi. The firm remains in business under the same name at this writing.

The domed temple form intimates the idea of the monument as a hallowed space. The inscription is clear: what the wartime generation did is consecrated; what they stood for is revered: "A Sacred Heritage / We Bequeath To Our Children."

Few county monument designs anywhere outside Mississippi venture to define the space they occupy in this fashion, but this is another Mississippi monument that does so. In particular, Columbus Marble Works monuments such as this example and at Laurel and Ellisville (see chap. 5) offer striking temple forms.

- The tribute beginning "The Soldiers / Of Lowndes County, / Who Nobly Dared Life and / Fortune" may be a reference to the poet Virgil's observation that "Fortune sides with him who dares." It may also be a Second Revolution reference to the signers of the Declaration of Independence. The final sentence of the Declaration is a promise to "mutually pledge to each other our Lives, our Fortunes, and our Sacred Honor." It is, at any rate, by its own proclamation, "A Tribute of Love to Our / Honored Dead."

Friendship Cemetery, Obelisk

3.22.2 Subject: Friendship Cemetery, Obelisk, Confederate
Location: Corner of 4th Street South and 15th Avenue South N 33 28 50 99
/ W 88 25 47 28
Installed: 1873
Media: Marble, brick and mortar base
Monument is an obelisk surmounting a base.

Inscriptions

IN MEMORY OF / OUR / HONORED DEAD. / C.S.A.

ERECTED BY THE LADIES / OF THE COLUMBUS / MONUMENTAL ASSOCIATION. / 1873

This is one of the very early funereal monuments in Mississippi. It stands
between two large, expansive plots of marked graves. It was erected to stand
over a second plot of gravesites of Confederate soldiers. Space in the first plot
on the south side of the cemetery was filled; this plot represents an addition
to accommodate the overflow of soldiers for whom graves were necessary. A
total of 2,194 Confederate soldiers are believed to be interred in Friendship
Cemetery, including three generals: Brig. Gen. William E. Baldwin; Lt. Gen.
Stephen D. Lee; and Brig. Gen. Jacob H. Sharp. The remains of 32 Union soldiers were removed and reinterred at Corinth National Cemetery.

Historic Southern Monuments notes that the "ladies of the Monumental Association labored for years to obtain the means to pay for a monument, and in 1873 when the unveiling took place they felt that they had not labored in vain." The president of the local UDC, "Mrs. Mary B. Harrison," wrote, "We feel that we are doing no less than our duty in this, and a memorial such as we have had erected here will serve to point to succeeding generations now that the living actors in the scenes of the great war are so rapidly thinning[,] what deeds these men did, how generous their sacrifice, how noble the cause for which they battled."

· Founded in 1849, the cemetery is said to be the site of the first Decoration Day. Records indicate that on April 25, 1866, four women of Columbus gathered together to decorate the graves of the Confederate and—it is noted—the Union dead as well.

3.22.3 Subject: Friendship Cemetery, Common Soldier, Confederate
Location: Corner of Magnolia and Hackberry   N 33 28 47 01 / W 88 25 47 90
Dedicated: April 26, 1874
Media: Marble, concrete
Monument is a common soldier surmounting a base.

Inscription

REST

This second monument in Friendship Cemetery may be the earliest statue of a common soldier in the state. The figure—a rough, vernacular rendering—faces north. The musket is missing. However, the one-word inscription, "Rest," reads as a kind of counsel and consolation from the living to the Confederate dead.

This was the original cemetery site for the Confederate dead in Friendship Cemetery. It proved to be too small for the purpose. The casualties of war were high; there were more Confederate dead than expected: it filled quickly. The purchase of a larger tract followed, and this too filled.

Records were kept, however; and the graves were dug in long, even rows. They were originally marked by wooden headboards, each inscribed with a name, regiment, and company. However, the headboards deteriorated or were stolen, and the identities were lost. Today, marble headstones from the Veterans Administration mark most of the graves. The names of approximately 350 soldiers are identified; the remainder are inscribed, "Unknown Confederate Soldier."

Friendship Cemetery, Common Soldier

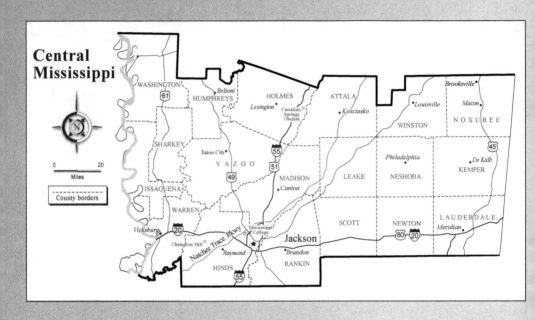

4

CENTRAL
MISSISSIPPI

THE STATE OF MISSISSIPPI'S monument at Vicksburg National Military Park (NMP) was completed in 1912. The state's monument on the Shiloh battlefield, however, was not erected and dedicated until 2015, some 153 years after the battle took place on April 6–7, 1862, and over a century after most of the Shiloh battlefield monuments had been erected. It seems belated, but it should be noted that monuments to the dead from Shiloh are scattered across northern and central Mississippi, even as far south as Meridian, Brooksville, Clinton, Jackson, Canton, and Vicksburg in central Mississippi. Excellent battlefield studies of Shiloh justly focus on the time period leading up to, during, and just after the battle, with due attention to the effects of Shiloh on the course of the war. The participants had a different, more personal perspective on the battle of Shiloh, of course. For the wounded—some eight thousand men—the battle for life and death began at Shiloh and, if they survived, often continued for days, weeks, months, even years afterward.

The political and military events, characters, drama, and consequences of the war dominate our understanding of the time, justly so perhaps, but this facet of the war draws less attention—apart from the monuments that testify to the dead. The full story of the medical history of the war has not been told, and will likely remain so. There are 80,000 graves of Confederate soldiers in Mississippi. Approximately 27,000 of the 78,000 Mississippians who went to war did not return, and many of those who did return were physically or emotionally crippled for life. Historian Ben Wynne writes that one quarter of the white male population of the state who were fifteen years of age or older in 1860 were no longer alive only five years later.

The literature of the Museum of Civil War Medicine in Frederick, Maryland, takes a somewhat optimistic view of medical care during the war. It describes important areas of continuity between the past and present methods of care, for example. Their introductory material observes that medical "technology and scientific knowledge have changed dramatically since the Civil War, but the basic principles of military health care remain the same. Location of medical personnel near the action, rapid evacuation of the wounded, and providing adequate supplies of medicines and equipment continue to be crucial in the goal of saving soldiers' lives." Southern medical facilities were more rudimentary because of the limited rail facilities, a shortage of labor, and limited availability of medicine (in part because of the Union naval blockade of Southern ports). However, a significant factor was the state of medical science at the time. Although much progress was made during the course of the war, the failure to understand what today are regarded as basic principles of hygiene and sterilization led to the death of thousands of soldiers on both sides. The statistics on the impact of disease during the war vary widely, but the consensus is clear: it was devastating to Northern and Southern armies. Quite apart from the battlefield hazard of being shot and killed outright, the war was, as historian James O. Breeden describes it, "a biological holocaust." Historian James McPherson avers that the war coincided with the last chapter what was still a medieval era of medical practice, only a few years before discoveries by Louis Pasteur, Joseph Lister, Robert Koch, and later, Alexander Fleming and Madame Curie, transformed the practice of medicine.

Nevertheless, the medical profession learned and applied many lessons. As time passed, and as the war continued and casualty lists lengthened, some Confederate medical personnel came to recognize that an unclean environment prompted the spread of disease. Dr. Joseph Jones, Confederate surgeon major throughout the war, noted the intuitive deductions doctors made. Jones, as historian Bryan Miller observes, wrote that surgeons recognized that unclean instruments, bowls, sponges, and dressings were contagious. "When wounds were cleansed with sponges or rags," he noted, "which had been used on erypelas [gangrene] patients, it was frequently observed that the disease appeared, and such propagation appeared to be clearly preferable to the transference of contagious matter."

As primitive and unprepared as the medical profession was for war in 1861, historian Alfred J. Bollet, in his *Civil War Medicine: Challenges and Triumphs*, notes that advances in battlefield medical care saved many lives before the war was over. Bollet describes the manifold limitations of medical practices during the conflict, but he also cites the recollections of a Virginia assistant surgeon, William H. Taylor of the 19th Virginia Infantry, whose postwar recollections include the statement that, "as to methods, I say, as a general statement, that we aimed to conform to the science of the time, though the restrictions to which our ever-increasing necessities subjected us often forbade the practice of it. We did not the best we would, but the best we could."

Statues of common soldiers are almost always physically whole, of course: only a few bear evident scars of the war. Historian Bruce Catton has a line that describes a postwar disabled veteran who, on his best days, is able to rise unaided from his bed and look out a window. The image is anecdotal but telling. It bears on the fact that there are no words or images to encompass the travail that was endured by the wartime wounded, sick, and dying in Mississippi during the war and its aftermath. A rhetoric of silence prevails on the landscape, apart from the legacy born by the monumentation. The way the war is remembered in the monumentation in Mississippi is distinctive in this regard. There is an emphasis on the dead and those who remember them that is not evident elsewhere. Virginia's monumentation is instructive as a contrast. Consider the two state capitols, Richmond, Virginia, by comparison to Jackson, Mississippi, for example. Granted, Richmond was the Confederacy's capital, not just the state capital: the scale of commemoration is different. The military leadership of the Confederate Army of Northern Virginia—Gen. Robert E. Lee, Maj. Gen. Thomas J. "Stonewall" Jackson, Maj. Gen. J. E. B. Stuart—is remembered with striking equestrian statues along Richmond's Monument Avenue: no such parallel to this promenade exists in Jackson. Richmond's war dead are duly commemorated, but only within the confines of the public or private cemeteries, such as Richmond's Hollywood Cemetery, the Hebrew Cemetery, and Oakwood Cemetery.

In Jackson, Mississippi, however, it is not the military leadership who are the focus of the most prominent monuments. Instead, the focus is on the war dead and the women of the Confederacy. Belle Kinney's sculpture, "Confederate Women of Mississippi" is in front of the Mississippi state capitol. The lofty state monument to Mississippi's soldiers and sailors, a common soldier, stands on the grounds of the former state capitol and is specifically inscribed as a tribute to the "Confederate dead of Mississippi."

Humphreys County

4.1.1 Subject: Belzoni, Courthouse Common Soldier, Confederate
Location: 102 Castleman, 39038   N 33 10 33 57 / W 90 29 19 04
Installed or dedicated: 1923
Medium: Marble
Monument is a courthouse common soldier and a woman, Civil War era, Confederate; figure of a common soldier, World War I.

Inscription
[Front]
[Below the common soldier]
TO THE MEN WHO / WORE THE GREY / AND WERE FAITHFUL / TO THE END. / 1861–1865

[Under the female figure]
TO THE BELOVED / WOMEN OF THE / CONFEDERACY / AND THE WORLD WAR.

[Below the World War soldier]
HUMPHREYS / COUNTY / TRIBUTE TO / HER SONS OF / THE WORLD WAR / 1917–1918

This is one of several hybrid Civil War/World War I monuments in Mississippi. It was erected in the spring of 1923, only five years after the world war ended, and nearly sixty years after the Civil War's end. The monument displays three figures from two separate generations—two from the Civil War, one from

Belzoni, Courthouse Common Soldier, Confederate

World War I. Each figure surmounts a pedestal; an eagle surmounts the taller center pedestal.

Fidelity and duty are apparent themes of this monument. The figure of the woman in the Confederate monument at Yazoo City—the adjacent county seat—is young. This figure, in contrast, is somewhat older. Hers is a more maternal image: she wears a long dress and apron and holds some knitting in front of her at waist level. The Confederate common soldier is older also, older than the American Doughboy, perhaps intimating a fidelity of service and duty in successive generations, no matter the outcome: "Faithful to the End" is the last word for the wartime generation, a paraphrase of Revelation 2:10.

The monument was purchased on November 6, 1922, from the Columbus Marble Works at a cost of $6,000, by arrangement with the Belzoni chapter of the United Daughters of the Confederacy (UDC) No. 1384. It stands approximately twenty-one feet high.

Smithsonian records indicate that the figure of the World War I soldier is the second made for the memorial. The first statue, deemed unsatisfactory by the UDC, was removed and sold to Mississippi State College. It was replaced with the present figure, which was installed in time for the dedication. (The original figure may be the "University boy" statue, as it is known, located on the east side of Lee Hall at the circle and Lee Boulevard on the Mississippi State campus.)

Holmes County

4.2.1 Subject: Lexington, Courthouse Common Soldier, Confederate
Location: Wall and Spring Streets, 39095   N 33 06 46 40 / W 90 03 10 88
Dedicated: December 2, 1908
Medium: Marble
Monument is a common soldier surmounting a shaft and base.

Inscriptions
[Front]
[CS National flag, unfurled, relief]

ERECTED BY THE / DAUGHTERS OF THE / B. G. HUMPHREYS / CHAPTER NO 463 / U.D.C.

[Crossed swords, relief]

C.S.A.

TO THE HOLMES COUNTY / SOLDIERS OF 1861–1865, / AND MEMBERS OF HOLMES / COUNTY CAMP NO 398 U.C.V. / IN MEMORY OF THEIR / PATRIOTISM AND HEROISM / AND TO COMMEND THEIR / EXAMPLE TO FUTURE / GENERATIONS / 1908

[Relief of anchor with severed rope]

C.S.A. / HONOR TO HEROES, / IS GLORY TO GOD

[Relief of CS Battle flag]

C.S.A. / THE MEN WERE RIGHT / WHO WORE THE GRAY / AND RIGHT CAN / NEVER DIE

C.S.A. / THEIR DEEDS PROUD DEEDS, / SHALL REMAIN FOR US. / THEIR NAMES, DEAR NAMES. [SIC] / WITHOUT STAIN FOR US. / THE GLORIES THEY WON, / SHALL NOT WAIN FOR US, / IN LEGEND AND LAY, / OUR HEROES IN GRAY, / SHALL FOR EVER LIVE, / OVER AGAIN FOR US.

The figure of the common soldier at Lexington is five feet, six inches tall—with brimmed hat and rolled blanket over his shoulder—facing south, surmounting a twenty-five-foot shaft. The inscription proclaims—simply and without further explanation—that "The Men Were Right / Who Wore The Gray / And Right Can / Never Die."

Confederate Veteran reports that the monument was erected at a cost of $3,500. A roster listing the names of Livingston County is inscribed at the base of the monument. Holmes County Camp, United Confederate Veterans (UCV), initiated the project with a resolution on July 1, 1901, but the Bly Humphreys Chapter of the UDC took a leadership role and carried it through to completion with assistance from the UCV camp and the county board of supervisors.

The maker is not cited, but the design and materials are very similar to those known to be the work of the Columbus Marble Works: the common

Lexington, Courthouse Common Soldier, Confederate

soldier standing at parade rest is typical of the firm's statues, which were imported from Italy. The excerpt beginning "In Legend and Lay" is taken from the poem "Our Dead," originally published in 1867 by Fr. Abram J. Ryan. Father Ryan (1838–86), a Roman Catholic priest, came to be known as the "Poet Priest of the Lost Cause."

4.2.2 Subject: Durant, Jefferson Davis Highway Marker
Location: Roadside, near US 51 and MS 12   N 33 04 33 28 / W 89 51 15 00
Dedicated: June 3, 1931
Media: Bronze, fieldstone
Monument is an obelisk surmounting a base.

Inscription

JEFFERSON DAVIS / ERECTED BY / DURANT DAUGHTERS

NO. 973 U.D.C. / 1931

This modest roadside obelisk marks one of several highway networks that were developed in the early years of the twentieth century. This road is one of three named after Jefferson Davis; it was acclaimed as "one of the very greatest works ever attempted by a woman's organization."

Contemporary reports aver that the "idea for the highway was conceived in May 1913, during a conversation between Mrs. Alexander White and a cousin and Confederate veteran, T. W. White." According to Mrs. White, the conversation was as follows: "The Lincoln Highway [today US 30] is ocean to ocean, you can match that with—and I exclaimed 'Jefferson Davis Highway, ocean to ocean.' The conversation led to the following recommendation: 'That the United Daughters of the Confederacy secure for an ocean to ocean highway from Washington to San Diego, through the southern states, the name of Jefferson Davis National Highway; the same to be beautified and historic places on it suitably and permanently marked.'"

The UDC joined a trend that linked together an increasingly sophisticated automobile roadway network. Various groups designated highways to promote commerce, tourism, legacies, and ideals, according to historian Richard F. Weingroff. Other examples of highways that promoted tourism include the Dixie Highway, which ran from Michigan to Florida. Officially speaking, none of these names has endured: numbered systems began to succeed them in the 1920s. However, local roads and such wayside UDC monuments as these remain as vestiges of a legacy that the UDC strove to maintain.

Durant, Jefferson Davis Highway Marker

Castalian Springs, Cemetery Obelisk

4.2.3 Subject: Castalian Springs, Obelisk
Location: Cemetery grounds off West Hill Road, west of Castalian Springs
N 33 04 00 71 / W 89 54 28 76
Installed or dedicated: n.a.
Medium: Marble
Monument is an obelisk surmounting a base.

Inscriptions
[Front]
TO THE MEMORY / OF THE / CONFEDERATE SOLDIERS / OF KY. TENN. / & MO.

ERECTED BY / HOLMES CO. / CAMP NO 398

C.S.A. / SOLDIERS
SENT TO / CASTALIAN SPRINGS / HOSPITAL FROM / SHILOH APR. 1862

LOVES LAST [*SIC*] / TRIBUTE

This modest obelisk stands in an abandoned cemetery on a hilltop approximately one mile west of Castalian Springs. Today Castalian Springs serves as a Christian retreat center, but the area was originally developed as a hotel and health spa. After the Battle of Shiloh, the two-story building and site became a hospital. Wounded soldiers were disembarked from the rail line in Durant and conveyed to the site. Surviving records indicate that ninety soldiers died there from April 1862 to November 1863 and that the dead were buried at Wesley Chapel Cemetery (the chapel is not extant).

Permanent markers were never installed; many of the names and all of the locations of the dead were eventually lost. In the 1990s, headstones were secured for each of the soldiers. The locations of the dead remain unknown, however, and the placement of the tombstones is symbolic.

- The cemetery location is obscure and easily missed in the absence of GPS guidance: From the intersection of US 51 and Mulberry Street, in Durant (Mulberry Street becomes Castalian Springs Street), travel 3.5 miles to crossroads, passing the Castalian Springs site at 3.0 miles. Turn left; proceed 0.4 miles to unmarked gravel road to the left. Turn left again and proceed 0.15 miles to the hilltop cemetery. From the intersection of I-55 and MS 12, travel west 0.9 miles to West Hill Rd., south on West Hill 2.8 miles to an unmarked gravel road, turn left, and proceed 0.15 miles to the cemetery.

Kosciusko, Courthouse Common Soldier, Confederate

Attala County

4.3.1 Subject: Kosciusko, Courthouse Common Soldier, Confederate
Location: 230 W. Washington Street, 39090   N 33 03 30 21 / W 89 35 24 68
Dedicated: June 3, 1899
Medium: Marble
Monument is a common soldier surmounting a shaft and base.

Inscriptions

The Classical Revival architecture of the Attala County Courthouse in Kosciusko erected 1897, offers a backdrop for this seven-foot high statue surmounting a sixteen-foot shaft and base.

The reference to "Lest We Forget" is taken from Rudyard Kipling's 1897 poem "Recessional." The reference to "Spartan Courage" is evidently taken from the epitaph to the Spartans, attributed to Simonides of Ceos, commemorating the Spartan dead from the Battle of Thermopylae (480 BC). Translated, it reads "Go and tell the Spartans, stranger passing by, That here, obedient to their laws, dead we lie." Put more simply, for the Kosciusko UDC, they are the "Boys in Gray . . . Our Heroes."

This is another extravagant Mississippi tribute and testimony to the wartime generation of women. They were/are a breed apart—"Noble Women"—who were willing to give their "loved ones" to the cause of "truth and right" and who now, possessed of "Deathless love," keep vigil over their graves.

- The Attala County seat has been variously known as Red Bud Springs, Greenville, and Paris. The name Kosciusko was adopted in 1836, to honor Andrew T. B. Kościuszko (1746–1817), the Polish émigré who fought as a colonel in the Continental Army during the American Revolution.

Louisville, Courthouse Common Soldier, Confederate

Winston County

4.4.1 Subject: Louisville, Courthouse Common Soldier, Confederate
Location: Columbus and Main Streets, center of street   N 33 07 25 15 / W 89 03 12 82
Dedicated: July 4, 1921
Medium: Marble
Monument is a common soldier surmounting a shaft and base.

Inscriptions
[Front]
[Relief of CS Battle Flag]

A TRIBUTE TO WINSTON / COUNTY'S SONS WHO / FOUGHT IN THE CONFEDERATE WAR / 1861–1865

[12 inscribed stars]

IN MEMORY OF THE BRAVE / SONS OF WINSTON COUNTY, / WHO, SO BRAVELY WERE / WILLING TO MAKE THE / SUPREME SACRIFICE FOR / THE GREAT PRINCIPLES / FOR WHICH THE U.S. / ENTERED THE GREAT / WORLD WAR IN 1917. / MAY THE MEMORY OF / THEIR CHIVALRY AND / PATRIOTISM HANDED DOWN / FROM FATHER TO SON, BE / PERPETUATED FOR / GENERATIONS YET UNBORN

A TRIBUTE TO THE / SPANISH-AMERICAN / HEROES 1898

WINSTON COUNTY'S TRIBUTE / TO HER NOBLE / WOMEN OF THE CONFEDERACY / WHO FED AND CLOTHED / FAMILIES AND ARMIES / FOR FOUR YEARS / 1861–1865

This is less a Civil War monument than it is a collective tribute to the Confederate common soldier, the women of the Confederacy, soldiers of World War I, and the only tribute to Spanish American War veterans—"heroes"—that this writer has found on a Civil War monument. It was originally called a simple "Soldiers Monument." Historian Jennie Newsom reports that the initiative for this monument was undertaken on March 8, 1921, at the request of a "committee of citizens." The Board of Supervisors of Winston County voted to pay $1,750 or half the cost. The committee raised the balance, $1,750, by public subscription.

- The figure is an import, of Carrara marble, and bears a resemblance to a World War I–era figure.

4.5.1 Subject: Macon, Courthouse Common Soldier, Confederate
Location: Corner of Jefferson and Martin Luther King Streets   N 33 06 21
77 / W 88 33 39 20
Dedicated: June 12, 1901
Medium: Marble
Monument is a common soldier surmounting a shaft and base.

Inscriptions
[Front]
[Relief of CS battle flag]
[Relief of stacked muskets]
TO OUR / CONFEDERATE / DEAD

[Roster: 81 names]

[Roster: 77 names]

[Roster: 52 names]

ERECTED BY THE / WALTER BARKER / CHAPTER NO 242. / UNITED DAUGHTERS / OF
THE CONFEDERACY. / 1901.

The Walter Barker Chapter of the UDC disbanded in 1918, a century ago, but
the women of this organization left this monument as an enduring, tangible
public legacy.

The tribute on this monument, which appears to be the work of the
Columbus Marble Works, is preeminent. The roster of the dead displays 230
names, although no unit associations are attached. Rowland, however, lists
24 units from Noxubee County, including elements of the 5th, 11th, 19th,
and 41st Mississippi Infantry, with such colorful company/unit names as the
"Noxubee Blues," the "Mississippi Rip Raps," and the "Mississippi Rebels," aka
the "Noxubee Minute Men."

- The monument stands approximately twenty-six feet high. This is a
  small courthouse town, but in the latter days of the war, when Jackson
  could no longer be secured from Union incursions, Macon was also the
  last wartime capitol of Mississippi.

Macon, Courthouse Common Soldier, Confederate

4.5.2 Subject: Brooksville, Common Soldier, Confederate

Location: S. Post Office and Main Street, 39739   N 33 14 04 78 /
W 88 35 00 86

Dedicated: September 14, 1911

Media: Granite, marble

Monument is a soldier surmounting a shaft and base.

Inscriptions

[Left]

C.S.A. / IN MEMORY OF THE / CONFEDERATE SOLDIERS / WHO DIED IN THE
HOSPITAL / AT BROOKSVILLE, / MISSISSIPPI AFTER THE / BATTLE OF SHILOH /
APRIL 6, 1862 / AND WERE BURIED NEAR / THIS SPOT. "THE MANNER / OF THEIR
DEATH WAS THE / CROWNING GLORY OF THEIR / LIVES." / 1861–1865

C.S.A. *[Relief of CS Battle flag]*

LOVE'S TRIBUTE TO / THE NOBLE MEN WHO / MARCHED NEATH THE / FLAG OF THE
STARS / AND BARS AND WERE / FAITHFUL TO THE END"

OUR HEROES

C.S.A. / "GOD OF OUR FATHERS, / HELP US TO PRESERVE / FOR OUR CHILDREN THE
/ PRICELESS TREASURE / OF THE TRUE STORY OF / THE CONFEDERATE / SOLDIER" /
1861–1865

"ERECTED AUGUST 1911, / BY THE LADIES OF THE / MAIDS AND MATRONS / CLUB,"
AND THE "NOXUBEE / RIFLE CHAPTER" OF THE / UNITED DAUGHTERS OF / THE
CONFEDERACY OF / BROOKSVILLE, MISSISSIPPI / 1861–1865

The women's organizations who gave this monument to the community are no
longer extant, but they left a substantial legacy. Brooksville, with a population
of 1,175 in 2013, is one of the smallest towns in the South with a monument
on this scale. The marble statue and shaft surmounting a granite base may be
the work of the Columbus Marble Works. The statue is likely the work of an
Italian artisan.

Brooksville was established in the 1830s as a farming community. The town
benefitted commercially from the arrival of the Mobile & Ohio Railroad in
1857, and might have looked to prosperity in the near future. With the Battle
of Shiloh, however, Brooksville became a hospital site for the care of the Shiloh
wounded, one of many hospitals established across northern and central
Mississippi. According to local lore and observations, the principal hospital
building remained extant until the 1980s. Unmarked graves of the dead are
believed to be near and beneath this statue, which stands adjacent to the railroad on a very quiet Main Street.

- The Noxubee Rifles mentioned with the UDC chapter formed Company
  F of the 11th Mississippi Infantry.

Brooksville, Common Soldier, Confederate

Yazoo City, Common Soldier, Confederate

Yazoo County

4.6.1 Subject: Yazoo City, Common Soldier, Confederate
Location: Corner of Main and Washington Streets   N 32 51 01 92 /
W 90 24 41 98
Dedicated: July 8, 1909
Media: Bronze, granite
Monument is a common soldier and female civilian surmounting a base.

Inscriptions

[Front]
1861–1865 / AS AT THERMOPYLAE, / GLORY WAS TO THE VANQUISHED / THIS
MONUMENT IS ERECTED TO / PERPETUATE THE MEMORY OF THE / NOBLE COURAGE,
CONSTANCY AND / SELF SACRIFICING DEVOTION OF THE / WOMEN OF THE
CONFEDERACY; AND / THE PATRIOTISM AND HEROIC VALOR / OF THE CONFEDERATE
SOLDIERS, / AND ALL WHO FOUGHT ON LAND OR / SEA FOR THE COUNTRY AND THE
CAUSE / THEY LOVED SO WELL. / BY / JEFFERSON DAVIS CHAPTER, / U.D.C., NO 216;
YAZOO CAMP, U.C.V., NO. 176, / AND THE SONS OF CONFEDERATE / VETERANS AND
THE PEOPLE OF YAZOO / COUNTY / DEDICATED JULY 8, 1909. / TRIST WOOD / DEL.
[at base]

[Seal of U.C.V.]

[Seal of U.D.C.]

SEMPER FIDELIS

[Seal of U.C.V.]

The monument in the Triangle Grounds of Yazoo City is opulent—granite and bronze—and stands twenty-four feet high. It is a rich, complex presentation. Trist Wood (1886–1952), of New Orleans, is credited with the design. Although Wood was not a sculptor, he forged a career as an artist, editor, genealogist, and illustrator and was also the son of a colonel in the Confederate Army, R. C. Wood. The Albert Weiblen Marble & Granite Company is credited with the making of the monument. For decades the New Orleans–based firm, founded by the German-born architect and sculptor Albert Weiblen, was prominent in the construction of monuments and burial structures. In 1969 the firm merged with what is today Stewart Enterprises.

Nothing of the correspondence or any documentation on the design conception for this monument is extant. However, the visual dynamics are particularly arresting and are, in fact, unique. The figure of the man is young, as is the figure of the woman. He is in uniform, ready to move, as if he is about to depart and take the field immediately. However, the drama in the stance is between the two of them. The two face one another: she bears the flag and is placing it in his left hand. With his right hand, the soldier bears a rifle with fixed bayonet. The bayonet nearly touches the female's shoulder in a kind of anointing. There is no embrace, of course: there is, it appears, instead an unspoken assent being communicated to bear the burden thrust upon them by the defining conflict of their generation—a chaste union, yet forever apart—unconsummatable. The exhortation or testimony, "Semper Fidelis," is unique in Civil War monuments, North and South, and may relate to the unspoken, mutual assent the two are undertaking to answer the call to the circumstances of the time in which the soldier and the woman have been placed—wartime, brought about by forces beyond their control or influence. The scene is, at the very least, ironic: this is not a marriage scene, of course, with a vow of devotion of one person to another. It appears instead to represent the mutual consent of this couple to revolution, a war of independence, to the "Cause / They Loved So Well."

Surviving documents housed in the Louis Round Wilson Library of the University of North Carolina—the correspondence of Trist Wood—offer no insight into the designer's intentions, but a great deal of insight into the care that was devoted to the design: the placement of the Enfield Rifle, the fact that the cartridge box on the soldier's belt should be behind him, not in front or side; how attractive the woman should be; and other matters: "The woman's face should be made prettier. The soldier's ankles are too fragile . . . as they are, and should be slightly strengthened. Above all things, the woman's statue (height) must be increased. . . . Her arm is in proportion to her head, but her body must be lengthened and skirt enlarged. Her arm is somewhat stiff—there should a few creases or curves in sleeve to break the straight lines, and her left hand is not as good as the other hands modeled by the sculptor—which are most effectively executed."

Notwithstanding all these annotations, the final word came from the UDC sponsors in a letter to Trist: "We are very much pleased with the design. . . . It certainly is pretty and reflects much credit upon the designer."

Madison County

4.7.1 Subject: Canton, City Cemetery, Column
Location: E. Semmes Street, 39046   N 32 36 26 55 / W 90 01 37 44
Dedicated: April 26, 1881
Medium: Marble
Monument is a column surmounting a concrete base on a mound of earth.

Inscriptions
[Front]
IN MEMORIAM / THE / CONFEDERATE DEAD / ERECTED BY THE / LADIES MEMORIAL ASSOCIATION / OF CANTON, MISS. APRIL 26, 1881. / MRS. CHARLES HANDY, PRESIDENT.

THE SOUTHLAND / MOURNS HER DEAD.

PRO PATRIA

[Inscribed crossed swords, laurel wreath]

THE CAUSE MAY PERISH, / BUT THE MEMORY OF NOBLE / DEEDS SURVIVES

The hospital facility at Canton was established in 1862 as a branch or subhospital of the Jackson Hospital System, according to Patrick M. Harrison, of the Sons of Confederate Veterans (SCV) Canton. Two railroads met here: the Mississippi Central Railroad and the New Orleans, Jackson & Great Northern Railroad. The trains brought casualties from the Battle of Shiloh and perhaps from engagements at Tuscumbia Creek, Booneville, Rienzi, and the second Battle of Corinth. Operations were interrupted by the Vicksburg Campaign, but the hospital may have been in limited use thereafter.

The dead were not buried in mass graves, Morgan notes. Wooden, numbered markers were placed on individual graves, but these either deteriorated and disappeared or were vandalized and stolen. Information that 350 soldiers were buried there led Mrs. Charles Handy, referenced in the inscription on the monument, to place that number of unknown soldier tombstones on the south and west edge of the new cemetery. Research beginning in the 1980s by SCV members has established many identities. Today there are 256 headstones, placed in alphabetical order since the location where each soldier is buried is unknown; the identities of at least 93 soldiers are still unknown.

The climactic tribute in the inscription is funereal, a grim reflection of the struggle that Southerners—and women's groups in particular—had to

Canton, City Cemetery, Column

undertake in caring for men whom they did not know dying in their midst. The Latin "Pro Patria" is the cited cause—"For Country."

· Local units that served in the Confederate Army include "The Madison Light Artillery," as well as "The Confederates," "The Camden Rifles," and "The Beauregard Rifles." These units were assigned to the 18th Regiment Mississippi Infantry CSA, which served in General Robert E. Lee's Army of Northern Virginia.

Canton, Harvey Scouts Obelisk

4.7.2 Subject: Canton, Harvey Scouts Obelisk
Location: City cemetery, east end   N 32 26 31 29 / W 90 01 37 56
Installed or dedicated: 1894
Media: Bronze, granite
Monument is an obelisk surmounting a base.

Inscription
Front
CSA

[Crossed CS battle flags]

ERECTED BY THE SURVIVORS / HARVEY'S SCOUTS / TO PERPETUATE THE MEMORY OF THEIR / CAPTAIN AND COMRADES IN ARMS / 1894 / *[Wreath relief]* / HARVEY'S SCOUTS

KILLED IN BATTLE / *[10 names]*

[Wreath relief]

CAPT. ADDISON HARVEY / BORN JUNE 1837. / KILLED APRIL 9, 1865 / JUST AS THE COUNTRY'S FLAG WAS / FURLED FOREVER, DEATH SAVED / HIM THE PAIN OF DEFEAT.

LONG SINCE HAS BEAT THE LAST TATTOO; / DISBANDED ARE THE GRAY AND BLUE / AND PEACE REIGNS NOW WHERE / TROOPERS DREW / THEIR SABERS TO DARE AND DO— / LED FORWARD BY AD HARVEY

Dunbar Rowland's *Military History of Mississippi, 1803–1898* reports that this independent company was raised in Madison County, with Harvey as its captain. In its various organizational guises and roles, the unit was engaged in

Canton Obelisk: "Faithful Servant and Friend"

reconnaissance on the Mississippi River; Sherman's raid to and from Meridian; the Atlanta Campaign and its aftermath; Hood's Middle Tennessee Campaign; and service with Forrest's command during Wilson's Raid to Macon in 1865. Captain Harvey was murdered on April 20 at Columbus, Georgia—"basely assassinated by a citizen of that place, in Dunbar's account. The unit disbanded with the surrender by Lt. Gen. Richard Taylor of the CS Department of Alabama, Mississippi and East Louisiana on May 4, 1865."

4.7.3 Subject: Canton Obelisk: "Faithful Servant and Friend"
Location: City cemetery, 300 Academy Street   N 32 36 27 24 / W 90 01 49 10
Dedicated: April 26, 1881
Medium: Granite
Monument is an obelisk surmounting a plinth and base.

Inscription
[Front]
ERECTED BY W. H. HOWCOTT TO THE MEMORY OF THE / THE GOOD AND LOYAL SERVANTS WHO FOLLOWED THE / FORTUNES OF HARVEY'S SCOUTS DURING THE CIVIL WAR.

A TRIBUTE TO MY FAITHFUL SERVANT AND FRIEND / WHILLIS HOWCOTT, A COLORED BOY OF RARE LOYALTY / AND FAITHFULNESS WHOSE MEMORY I CHERISH WITH / DEEP GRATITUDE W. H. HOWCOTT

[blank]

LOYAL, FAITHFUL, TRUE, / WERE EACH AND ALL OF THEM

This elegant, polished granite obelisk, standing twenty-one feet high, is a tribute from a Confederate soldier to his "servant and friend," Whillis Howcott. The full story behind this monument is incomplete. Some sources indicate that William Hill Howcott (1847–1927) enlisted with Harvey's Scouts at the age of fifteen. His "manservant," Whillis Howcott, accompanied him. Whillis Howcott did not survive the war, but William Howcott left this personal, public commemoration to his memory. Whillis Howcott's deeds or status are not mentioned. Neither is there any reference to the exploits of Harvey's Scouts. The personal friendship is the theme.

References to "servants" or to slavery are effectively nonexistent in Southern monumentation. Apart from state or federal monuments erected at Vicksburg (Mississippi's African American monument) and Corinth (the Contraband Camp) in the twenty-first century, there are no references to slavery in Southern monumentation, whether Union or Confederate. The role of African Americans in the war was controversial and remains so to this day. For the Union, the question of whether they would fight would be answered in the affirmative at places like the battle of Milliken's Bend, for example. Their place of service in the Confederate Army—what their role was as supporting elements of the army and whether they should be "allowed" to fight in combat—was divisive.

This monument, arguably, belongs in a unique category. The inscription concludes with an extravagant tribute to "All of Them": "Loyal, Faithful, True, / Were Each and All Of Them."

Neshoba County

4.8.1 Subject: Philadelphia, Courthouse Common Soldier, Confederate
Location: Corner of Byrd and Beacon Streets   N 32 46 18 24 / W 89 06 37 76
Installed or dedicated: July 1912
Medium: Marble
Monument is a common soldier surmounting a column and base.

Inscriptions
[Front]
1861–1865
LOVE'S TRIBUTE TO THE / NOBLE MEN WHO MARCHED / 'NEATH THE FLAG OF THE / STARS AND BARS, AND WERE / FAITHFUL TO THE END. / C.S.A. / OUR HEROES. / ERECTED BY THE / DAUGHTERS OF THE / CONFEDERACY. / [14 names] / REV. J. C. LONG CONTRACTOR

[31 names]

[31 names]

[34 names]

Philadelphia, Courthouse Common Soldier, Confederate

Philadelphia, on the banks of the Pearl River, became the county seat of Neshoba County on August 15, 1837. It received this courthouse monument in 1912, at the peak of the monument movement in the South. The monument stands in a prominent place on the courthouse grounds. The figure of the soldier, facing north, surmounts a Corinthian column and base inscribed with 110 names, likely veterans.

The sculpture originally surmounted a multitiered base. The monument was felled by tornado winds in 1990. The Neshoba County Monument Restoration Committee raised $13,500 to restore the monument, which was repaired, restored. and returned to the courthouse lawn in 2006.

A courthouse tablet cites Dunbar Rowland's *Military History of Mississippi, 1803–1898,* which lists nineteen companies of infantry or cavalry from Neshoba County, including the Bogue Chitto Rangers, Co B, 40th Infantry; the Dixie Rangers, Co. G. 40th Infantry; Neshoba Rifles, Co. D., 11th Mississippi; and the Steam Mill Rangers; Co. E, 40th Mississippi.

- The war's effects were pervasive, but Philadelphia was not a firsthand victim of the war's violence. Federal cavalry commanded by Colonel Benjamin Grierson traveled through Neshoba County in the spring of 1863, the only significant action of the war near Philadelphia.

Kemper County

4.9.1 Subject: De Kalb, Courthouse Common Soldier, Confederate
Location: Corner of Hopper Avenue and Veterans Street   N 32 46 03 17 / W 88 39 06 08
Installed or dedicated: n.a.
Medium: Marble
Monument is a common soldier surmounting a shaft and base.

Inscriptions
[Front]
ERECTED / UNDER THE / AUSPICES OF THE / THOMAS H. WOODS / CAMP NO. 1180 / U.C.V. / [2 names] / KEMPER COUNTY'S / TRIBUTE TO / HER SONS WHO / FOUGHT IN / THE WAR OF / 1861–1865 / ERECTED IN HONOR OF / OUR FALLEN HEROES. / [Relief of sheathed sword]

[30 names]

THE MEN WERE / RIGHT WHO WORE / THE GREY AND / RIGHT CAN / NEVER DIE.

[14 names]

[25 names]

The monument, likely the work of the Columbus Marble Works, appears to have a defiant message: the weathered, youthful figure of a Confederate soldier

De Kalb, Courthouse Common Soldier, Confederate

faces north, and a relief of a Confederate battle flag is displayed, unfurled and waving.

The message of this monument is mixed, however. It is not celebratory. The cause for which the "Men in Grey" fought is unmentioned, as is the Confederacy. They were heroes—the names of seventy-one men, the "Fallen Heroes," are inscribed—but their battles are over: the relief of a sword is sheathed.

- The aphoristic claim beginning "The Men Were / Right" is taken from Fr. Abram Ryan's "Sentinel Songs" (ca. 1880).

Lauderdale County

4.11.1 Subject: Meridian Courthouse Common Soldier, Confederate
Location: 6th Street and Constitution Avenue   N 3221 54 58 / W 88 41 56 74
Dedicated: April 26, 1912
Media: Carrara marble for the statue; Georgia marble for the shaft and base
Monument is a common soldier surmounting a shaft and base.

Inscription

IT IS WREATHED / ABOUT WITH GLORY, / AND WILL LIVE IN / SONG AND STORY, FOR ITS FAME ON / BRIGHTEST PAGES, / PENNED BY POETS / AND BY SAGES, SHALL GO SOUNDING / DOWN THE AGES. / CSA / 1861 / 1865

[Relief of crossed swords]

THIS, THE LAUDERDALE COUNTY / CONFEDERATE MONUMENT / IS DEDICATED TO THE MEN, WOMEN / AND CHILDREN OF 61–65, WHOSE / SUBLIME DEVOTION TO DUTY AROUSED / THE ADMIRATION OF THE WORLD; WHO / WERE AMBITIOUS BUT TO SERVE / THEIR COUNTRY, AND WERE EVER READY / TO BE SACRIFICED FOR IT. MAY THEIR / LIVES BE AN INSPIRATION FOR EMU- / LATION TO GENERATIONS YET UNBORN.

The lofty monument stands in a prominent place, facing west, on the northwest corner of the courthouse grounds. It was erected under the auspices of the UDC's Winnie Davis Chapter No. 24, and the W. D. Cameron Camp No. 221, SCV; the county appropriated $5,000 for the monument.

The centerpiece of this monument is the Confederate soldier. This is a forward-looking monument, a prototypical example of celebration-era monuments, which endeavor not simply to mourn the passing of the CSA, nor to mourn the dead, but instead to glorify the sacrifice—the "Sublime Devotion to Duty"—of the "Men, Women / And Children of 61–65," as an example to future generations.

Meridian was the point furthest east reached by troops commanded by Maj. Gen. William T. Sherman, during what came to be known as the Meridian Campaign. The unorthodox march across the state of Mississippi—from Vicksburg to Meridian and back, with two army corps and associated cavalry, without a clear line of supply—has been called a prelude to Sherman's

Meridian, Courthouse Common Soldier, Confederate

notorious March to the Sea that took place in 1864. Much damage was done, especially to Meridian, to such an extent that it remains a sore point with local citizens. In his official report, Sherman wrote that "for five days, 10,000 men worked hard with a will in that work of destruction with axes, crowbars, sledges, clawbars, and fire, and I have no hesitation in pronouncing the work well done. Meridian . . . no longer exists."

- The courthouse was erected in 1903 in a neoclassical style that is consonant with the monument; the courthouse was remodeled to its present art deco form in 1939.
- The poetic excerpt beginning "It Is Wreathed" is taken from "The Conquered Banner," by Fr. Abram Ryan.

Meridian, Cemetery Obelisk

4.11.2 Subject: Meridian, Cemetery Obelisk
Location: Rose Hill Cemetery, 40th Avenue and 8th Street   N 32 21 47 96 /
W 88 43 08 84
Dedicated: May 10, 1890
Medium: Marble
Monument is an obelisk.

Inscription
[Relief of crossed flags: CS national and battle flag]
OUR / CONFEDERATE / DEAD

The "Way Hospital," one of several wartime medical facilities in the Meridian vicinity, served wounded or ill soldiers brought to the town by dint of the Mobile & Ohio Railroad and the Southern Railroad. It stood in downtown Meridian on the site of the present-day fire station, according to researcher Bryan D. McRaven. At least one hundred soldiers who were brought to the hospital did not survive, and their bodies were interred nearby. After the war, their remains were reinterred in Rose Hill Cemetery. Today the dead rest in a mass grave beneath this weathered obelisk, this in addition to graves of veterans elsewhere on the grounds. The obelisk stands on high ground in the cemetery west of downtown Meridian.

A crowd of eighteen thousand was in attendance at the dedication. It is a grim funereal monument, with no roster or sentiment, "just" a simple, direct, permanent remembrance of the Confederate Dead. In recent decades, additional monuments have been raised, and a roster posted nearby lists the names of Confederate soldiers from Alabama, Arkansas, North Carolina, South Carolina, Florida, Kentucky, Louisiana, Mississippi, and Tennessee.

- Dates of dedication vary on this monument: Widener cites June 3, 1891; other sources cite May 10, 1890.

4.11.3 Subject: Charles Savez
Location: Rose Hill Cemetery, 40th Avenue and 8th Street   N 32 21 47 96 / W 88 43 08 84
Installed or dedicated: 1998
Medium: Marble
Monument is a stele surmounting a base.

Inscription

[Seal of CS Navy, inscribed]
CHARLES W. "SAVEZ" READ / NAVAL HERO OF THE CONFEDERACY / LIEUTENANT READ, A NATIVE MISSISSIPPIAN, IS / BURIED HERE. HE WAS AN 1860 GRADUATE OF / ANNAPOLIS. WITH A CREW OF 17, HE CAPTURED / 22 UNION SHIPS IN 21 DAYS AND STRUCK TERROR / ACROSS THE EASTERN SEABOARD. THIS ADVENTURE / HAS BEEN CALLED THE MOST BRILLIANT, DARE- / DEVIL NAVAL ACTION OF THE WAR.

Born in Satartia, Mississippi, Charles W. Read (1840–90), a US Naval Academy graduate, had a multifarious career in the Confederate States Navy. Historian Tony Brown writes that Read saw service in coastal defense, on Mississippi River gunboats, in the fleet engagement at New Orleans, as a battery commander on the CSS *Arkansas*, on a blockade-runner and, as the inscription notes, as a commerce raider off the New England coast. His remains rest beneath a tombstone north of this site.

Texas Stele, one of four in Mississippi

DEDICATED TO THE MEMORY OF THE MEN
FROM TEXAS WHO ARE KNOWN TO BE
BURIED HERE, AND TO ALL BRAVE TEXANS
WHO PASSED THIS WAY

NOTHING IS ENDED
UNTIL IT IS FORGOTTEN

SGT. JOHN L. KILLOUGH
CO. L 2ND TX INFANTRY
DIED 11 JUN 1862

PVT. HENRY STOCKHADT (STOECKHARDT)
CO. H 2ND TX INFANTRY
DIED 21 JUL 1862

PVT. JOHN TAYLOR
CO. H 9TH TX CAVALRY (SIM'S)
DIED 21 JUN 1862

PVT. JOHN H. SCURLOCK
CO. I 6TH TX CAVALRY (WHARTON, STONE'S)
DIED 5 JUN 1862

PVT. R. R. FLOURNOY (ROBERT R.)
CO. A 10TH TX CAVALRY (LOCKE'S)
KILLED BY CARS. 1863

FOR SOME, SERVICE TO THEIR COUNTRY
IS THE GREATEST SACRIFICE
TO OTHERS, IT'S THE HIGHEST HONOR
"WE REMEMBER"

Marion CSA Cemetery Arch

4.11.4 Subject: Texas Stele
Location: Rose Hill Cemetery, 40th Avenue and 8th Street   N 32 21 47 96 / W 88 43 08 84
Installed or dedicated: 2010
Medium: Granite
Monument is a shaft surmounting a base.

Inscriptions

DEDICATED TO THE MEMORY OF THE MEN / FROM TEXAS WHO ARE KNOWN TO BE / BURIED HERE AND TO ALL BRAVE TEXANS / WHO PASSED THIS WAY / NOTHING IS ENDED / UNTIL IT IS FORGOTTEN / *[6 names]* / FOR SOME[,] SERVICE TO THEIR COUNTRY / IS THE GREATEST SACRIFICE. / TO OTHERS[,] IT'S THE HIGHEST HONOR / "WE REMEMBER" / ERECTED BY THE TEXAS DIVISION / UNITED DAUGHTERS OF THE CONFEDERACY / ERECTED APRIL 27, 2010

This is another attestation of affectionate remembrance in Mississippi of Texans who served in the Confederate Army. Texas monuments also stand at Raymond, Vicksburg, and Corinth.

4.11.5 Subject: Marion CSA Cemetery Arch
Location: 6843 Confederate Drive, Marion, 39342   N 32 25 52 82 / W 88 39 22 60
Installed or dedicated: 1994
Media: Aluminum, brick and mortar, granite, marble
Monument is an arch suspended between two brick facades, with adjacent tablets.

Inscriptions

MARION C.S.A. CEMETERY / ERECTED APRIL 1994

ERECTED BY GEN. NATHAN BEDFORD FORREST CHAPTER NUMBER 1649 / SONS OF CONFEDERATE VETERANS / TIME WILL NOT DIM THE / HONOR NOR THE MEMORY / OF THE CONFEDERATE / SOLDIERS WHO GAVE THEIR LIVES / FOR A RIGHT AND JUST CAUSE. THE STORY OF THEIR / VALOR AND SACRIFICE CAN NEVER BE TOLD. / DEATH SPARED THESE 170 / CONFEDERATE SOLDIERS THE PAIN AND AGONY OF / DEFEAT / LOUISIANA / TEXAS / VIRGINIA / ARKANSAS / NORTH CAROLINA TENNESSEE / MISSOURI / KENTUCKY / CSA 1861–1865 / HONOR / THE MOTHERS AND FATHERS WHO / GAVE THEIR SONS IN BATTLE FOR / THE NOBLE CAUSE OF THE SOUTH / SHALL ALWAYS BE REMEMBERED / AND HONORED

The Marion Confederate Cemetery is a tribute to CSA soldiers whose graves are in the vicinity of these grounds. Headstones, technically cenotaphs, for 170 soldiers are arranged in seventeen rows of ten. Each headstone bears the emblem of the Sons of Confederate Veterans, and each is inscribed "Unknown Confederate Soldier." However, no bodies are buried here: the monument grounds commemorate the presence of several mass graves in the area, and the cemetery was placed as near as possible to one of those sites.

- Tablet overlooking the grounds reads:

  2008 / MARION C.S.A. CEMETERY / A PARTIAL LISTING OF THOSE CONFEDERATE DEAD BURIED ON THESE GROUNDS / MAY THEIR SACRIFICES ALWAYS BE HONORED

  [47 names in three columns]

  The names of forty-seven of the soldiers here are based on records at the National Archives. The SCV General Nathan Bedford Forrest Camp 1649, maintains the grounds.

- Another tablet on the grounds lists twenty-two "benefactors," including various SCV chapters and individual donors, Lauderdale County, the Jefferson Davis Society, and the Forrest Cavalry Corps.

- A granite tablet overlooking the field of cenotaphs reads:

  THE CODE OF OUR CONFEDERATE FATHERS
  DON'T CHEAT—IF IT IS NOT RIGHT[—]DON'T DO IT
  DON'T LIE—IF IT IS NOT THE TRUTH[—]DON'T TELL IT
  DON'T STEAL—IF IT IS NOT YOURS[—]DON'T TAKE IT
  ABOVE ALL—HONOR / A.D. 2008

  This is a vernacular catechism of sorts, sponsored by the SCV, commending the presumed ethics of the wartime generation—"Our Confederate Fathers"—to the generations to follow.

4.11.6 Subject: Lauderdale Springs Confederate Cemetery
Location: 9442 Kewanee Road, Lauderdale   N 32 30 35 44 / W 88 29 29 16
Installed or dedicated: n.a.
Medium: Granite
Monument is a stele.

Inscription

LAUDERDALE SPRINGS / CONFEDERATE-UNION CEMETERY / HOSPITAL SITE AND BURIAL SPOT OF / 1020 CSA AND 80 UNION MEN WOUNDED / AT SHILOH, CORINTH, IUKA, JACKSON, / BAKERS CREEK, VICKSBURG, AND IN / FORREST'S NORTH MISS. BATTLES.

PRESENTED BY MEMBERS OF WINNIE DAVIS / CHAPTER #24 UDC, OWNERS

A railroad spur from the Mobile & Ohio brought visitors to this site, called Lauderdale Springs, a fashionable antebellum resort with a main hotel, cottages, a dance pavilion, and bathhouses. Patrons "took the waters" of several local springs, including Black Medicine Springs, White Sulphur Springs, and Colebiate Springs, according to researcher Bill White.

When the war came, the resort was converted to a Confederate hospital, and the railroad brought infirm or wounded soldiers. After the war, the property

Lauderdale Springs Confederate Cemetery

was purchased by the Mississippi Baptist Convention, and until 1878 the site served as a "Home for Confederate Orphans." The Winnie Davis Chapter of the UDC, organized in 1896, purchased this 1.8-acre site for a cemetery in 1897; the Lauderdale County Board of Supervisors purchased an additional 5.46 acres adjoining the cemetery to provide access to the main road. Plans were developed for the cemetery, but World War I diverted the UDC to wartime activities, and the chapter disbanded after the war's end. Thereafter local groups maintained the grounds, and the county Board of Supervisors continued to provide oversight. The Winnie Davis Chapter was reactivated in 1957, and in 1987 the chapter established a Perpetual Care Fund for the site.

Today the dead are memorialized with this stele as well as 1,100 headstones supplied by the federal government—1,020 Confederate and 80 Union. Local historians believe that the remains of Union soldiers were removed and reinterred in national cemeteries. In fact, there are no remains under any of the headstones: technically these are cenotaphs since the dead are buried in mass graves in the vicinity. A kiosk at the site, sponsored by the UDC, identifies the names of approximately 800 soldiers.

4.12.1 Subject: Brandon, Courthouse Common Soldier, Confederate
Location: Courthouse grounds, 201 North College Street; US 72 and North
Street   N 32 16 22 69 / W 89 59 12 92
Dedicated: November 29, 1909
Medium: Marble
Monument is a common soldier surmounting a shaft and base.

Inscriptions

[Front]
"LORD GOD OF HOSTS / BE WITH US YET, / LEST WE FORGET, / LEST WE FORGET."
/ ERECTED BY THE BRANDON CHAPTER / UNITED DAUGHTERS / OF THE
CONFEDERACY. 1861-DEO VINDICE-1865.

LOVE'S TRIBUTE / TO THE NOBLE MEN / WHO MARCHED
NEATH THE FOLDS / OF THE "STARS AND BARS" / WHO WERE "FAITHFUL
TO THE END." / UNDER THE SOD AND DEW / WAITING FOR THE JUDGEMENT DAY

"TO THOSE WHO WORE THE GREY / IN LEGEND AND LAY OUR HEROES
IN GREY, SHALL FOREVER / LIVE OVER AGAIN FOR US"
"THE EPITAPH OF THE SOLDIER / WHO FALLS WITH HIS
COUNTRY, IS WRITTEN IN / THE HEARTS OF THOSE
WHO LOVE THE RIGHT / AND HONOR THE BRAVE."
THE CORNERSTONE LAID BY / THE GRAND LODGE OF F. & A.M. / OF MISSISSIPPI E. J.
MARIN / ACTING GRANDMASTER / NOV. 1, 1907

STATES RIGHTS AND HOME RULE / TRUTH CRUSHED TO EARTH
WILL RISE AGAIN. / MEN DIE, PRINCIPLES LIVE FOREVER
"AND THOUGH CONQUERED / WE ADORE IT;
WEEP FOR THOSE / WHO FELL BEFORE IT / PARDON THOSE WHO
TRAILED AND TORE IT.

The archetypal figure of a common soldier standing at parade rest surmounts
this monument standing thirty-seven feet high on prominent ground facing
west, toward Vicksburg and the western horizon. It has a conspicuous place
at the intersection of Government and North Streets, in front of the Rankin
County courthouse on US 72.

The monument was sponsored by the Brandon Chapter of the UDC, which
organized in 1903 with seven charter members. The chapter, following the
fund-raising models of the time, solicited subscriptions, sponsored fund-raising events, and importuned the Board of Supervisors for a contribution. The
public responded, the Board obliged, the cornerstone was laid with Masonic
ceremonies on November 1, 1907, and the statue was unveiled four weeks later.
Highlights of the dedication included speeches by the mayor of Brandon and by
UDC officers; much applause was directed to schoolchildren who sang "Dixie"
and "The Bonnie Blue Flag."

Brandon, Courthouse Common Soldier, Confederate

The monument faces the direction from which troops under the overall command of Maj. Gen. William T. Sherman entered Brandon on July 19, 1863, during the course of the campaign against Jackson. The monument is said to mark the spot where this force—two brigades of Union troops commanded by Maj. Gen. Frederick Steele—stacked arms. Steele's brigades skirmished with Confederate cavalry outside of Brandon, entered the town, burned elements of the business district, then moved back north on July 22.

Several notable quotations are inscribed.

- The excerpt beginning "To those Who Wore the Grey" (side three, facing east) is taken from the poem "C.S.A.," by Fr. Abram Ryan. The passage beginning "And Though Conquered / We Adore It" (side four, facing north) is excerpted from Fr. Ryan's poem "The Conquered Banner."

- "Waiting for the Judgement Day"—side two, facing south—is almost certainly an allusion to Revelation 20:11–15, the final judgment of humanity by a sovereign God. The phrase "Faithful Unto Death" is taken from Revelation 2:10.

- "Lest We Forget"—side one, facing west—is taken from Rudyard Kipling's poem "Recessional," published in 1897. "Lest We Forget" is consistently invoked on monumentation as a reminder that the dead should not be forgotten, but the poem, first given at the celebration of the sixtieth anniversary of the reign of Queen Victoria, was written as a cautionary note about the corruption and fall of great empires.

- The assertion "Truth Crushed To Earth Will Rise Again" is excerpted from the poem "The Battle-Field" by William Cullen Bryant, the nineteenth-century poet, journalist, and editor of the *New York Evening Post*. Martin Luther King Jr. used the same quotation in his 1957 speech "Give Us the Ballot."

- Dates vary on this monument: the Smithsonian archive specifies September 29, 1907; Widener gives 1908; other sources cite November 1, 1909.

Capitol building, Women of the Confederacy

Hinds County

Jackson

4.13.1 Subject: Capitol building, the Confederate Women of Mississippi
Location: Capitol building, south side, facing Mississippi Street   N 32 18 11
59 / W 90 10 55 88
Installed or dedicated: 1917
Media: Bronze, granite
Monument is three seated figures, two female, one male, the whole sur-
mounting an inscribed base.

Inscriptions
[Front]
[CS Battle Flag]

OUR MOTHERS
TO THE WOMEN OF THE CONFEDERACY / WHOSE PIOUS MINISTRATIONS TO OUR
WOUNDED / SOLDIERS SOOTHED THE LAST HOURS OF THOSE WHO / DIED FAR
FROM THE OBJECTS OF THEIR TENDEREST / LOVE, WHOSE DOMESTIC LABORS
CONTRIBUTED MUCH / TO SUPPLY THE WANTS OF OUR DEFENDERS IN THE / FIELD,
WHOSE ZEALOUS FAITH IN OUR CAUSE SHONE / A GUIDING STAR UNDIMMED BY THE
DARKEST CLOUDS / OF WAR, WHOSE FORTITUDE SUSTAINED THEM UNDER / ALL
THE PRIVATIONS TO WHICH THEY WERE SUBJECT- / ED, WHOSE FLORAL TRIBUTE

ANNUALLY EXPRESSES / THEIR ENDURING LOVE AND REVERENCE FOR OUR SAC- / RED DEAD; AND WHOSE PATRIOTISM WILL TEACH / THEIR CHILDREN TO EMULATE THE DEEDS OF OUR / REVOLUTIONARY SIRES." JEFFERSON DAVIS / UNITED CONFEDERATE VETERANS / HONOR THE MEMORY OF / THE CONFEDERATE WOMEN / OF MISSISSIPPI / UCV

OUR DAUGHTERS
DEVOTED DAUGHTERS OF HEROIC / WOMEN AND NOBLE MEN, THEY / KEEP THE MOUNDS OF LOVED ONES / SWEET WITH FLOWERS AND PERPET- / UATED IN MARBLE AND BRONZE THE / GRANITE CHARACTERS OF A SOLDIERY / THAT WON THE ADMIRATION OF THE / WORLD AND A WOMANHOOD WHOSE / MINISTRATIONS WERE AS TENDER AS / AN ANGEL'S BENEDICTION.

[CS Battle Flag]

OUR SISTERS
THEIR SMILES INSPIRED HOPE; / THEIR TENDER HANDS SOOTHED / THE PANGS OF PAIN; THEIR PRAYERS / ENCOURAGED FAITH IN GOD; AND / WHEN THE DRAGON OF WAR CLOSED / ITS FANGS OF POISON AND DEATH, / THEY LIKE GUARDIAN ANGELS, ENTWINED / THEIR HANDS IN THEIR BROTHERS ARMS, / ENCOURAGED THEM TO OVERCOME THE / LOSSES OF WAR AND TO CONQUER / THE EVILS IN ITS WAKE, / ADOPTING AS THEIR MOTTO: / "LEST WE FORGET."

[Relief of open Bible]

OUR WIVES
THEY LOVED THEIR LAND BECAUSE IT WAS THEIR / OWN, AND SCORNED TO SEEK ANOTHER REASON / WHY, CALAMITY WAS THEIR TOUCHSTONE; AND IN / THE ORDEAL OF FIRE THEIR FRAGILITY WAS TEM- / PERED TO THE STRENGTH OF STEEL. / ANGELS OF COMFORT, THEIR COURAGE AND TEN- / DERNESS SOOTHED ALL WOUNDS OF / BODY AND OF SPIRIT MORE THAN MEDICINES. / THEY GIRDED THEIR GENTLE HEARTS WITH FORT- / ITUDE, AND SUFFERING ALL THINGS, HOPING ALL THINGS FED THE FAILING FIRES OF PATRIOTISM / TO THE END. / THE MEMORY AND EXAMPLE OF THEIR DEVO- / TION SHALL ENDURE.

Local literature describes this memorial to the "Confederate Women of Mississippi" as the oldest public bronze sculpture in Jackson and the only one memorializing women. Public notes describe a central female, "Fame," to her left a dying soldier, and to her right a woman on whose head Fame is placing a laurel wreath, the symbolic gesture of victory, and a recognition of the service rendered. The male figure, who is evidently mortally wounded, has no identifiable uniform, and he bears no weapon.

The sculpture is the work of Belle Kinney; it was cast by the Tiffany Studio and is dated 1917. It is the preeminent monument to the wartime generation of women and their daughters. As a designated Mississippi Landmark, it offers a powerful multimedia, visual, and verbal expression. The setting, an open plaza in front of the 1903 Beaux-Arts style state capitol, gives it a notable prominence among Civil War monuments in Mississippi. A duplicate of Kinney's sculpture (without the lavish inscription) stands adjacent to the War Memorial Building near the state capitol in Nashville, Tennessee. The Nashville sculpture is apparently a copy, but it lacks the inscription on the Jackson example. This monument might have been one of a series of identical monuments for other states: note the ministerial grace of the central figure in the face of suffering, and the consolation in the midst of a cause that will not be won.

Parallels to the New Testament are evident. The women, in "Suffering All Things, Hoping All Things," act in concordance with the "Love Chapter," 1 Corinthians 13, in which the Apostle Paul describes the ways in which love "beareth all things, believeth all things, hopeth all things, endureth all things" (1 Cor. 13:7).

4.13.2 Subject: Archives Building, Common Soldier, Confederate
Location: 199 South State Street, 39205   N 32 17 54 74 / W 90 10 48 46
Dedicated: June 3, 1891
Media: Granite, limestone, glass, iron, marble
Monument is a common soldier surmounting a shaft and base.

Inscriptions
[Front]
TO THE / CONFEDERATE DEAD / OF / MISSISSIPPI
CSA

Although this is called the state monument to Mississippi soldiers and sailors, it is especially devoted to the "Confederate dead of Mississippi." Surmounting the shaft is the figure of a Confederate common soldier. The figure was modeled after CSA Major George M. Govan. The face, however, is that of Mississippi governor John M. Stone, colonel of the 2nd Mississippi Infantry during the war.

The monument stands in Confederate Park south of and adjoining the old capitol grounds, the former state capitol. *Historic Southern Monuments* observes that the monument was erected through the efforts of the "patriotic women of the State, part of the money being raised by private subscription and part by a legislative appropriation." The cornerstone was laid May 25, 1888, with Varina Winnie Davis, daughter of Jefferson Davis, in attendance among the invited guests. The completed monument was unveiled June 3, 1891, with ceremonies attended by some twenty thousand people; the dedication address was given by former CS Maj. Gen. Edward G. Walthall. Jefferson Hayes Davis, grandson of Jefferson Davis, performed the climactic lifting of the veil.

There was reluctance and opposition in the state legislature to appropriate the $10,000 for this project. An "impassioned appeal" by Representative John F. Harris, a former slave, had effects, and the legislation passed. By additional legislation in 1902, the grounds were designated Confederate Monumental Park.

Archives Building, Common Soldier, Confederate

A life-size statue of Jefferson Davis, in Italian marble, occupies a glassed-in vault at the base. The figure stands at ground level facing west. State legislation appropriated funds for the statue after Davis's death. Today, it is encased in latticework and is inaccessible for understandable reasons of security, but at eye level there is a jarring kind of intimacy with the figure of Davis.

- The Greek Revival capitol was completed in 1840. The state legislature voted for the Ordinance of Secession here in 1861. This state legislature abandoned the site when the new capitol opened in 1903; it housed offices from 1917 to 1959 but became a museum site in 1961.

- The art deco War Memorial Building (1939–40) on these grounds commemorates the service of Mississippi soldiers across history. Architectural notes observe that the reliefs of the faces of the soldiers are the same so as to represent the "kinship of Mississippians . . . in defense of their country." The building's cast aluminum doors and panels depict various scenes in Mississippi's military history, including the Vicksburg Campaign, with a relief of ironclads running the bluffs. A marble relief of Jefferson Davis is also displayed.

- The interior vault—now closed off with the Davis installation—is inscribed as follows:

  [North side:]
  OFFICES OF / THE / CONFEDERATE MONUMENT ASSOCIATION / OF MISSISSIPPI. / A.D. 1890

  [5 names]

  THE NOBLE WOMEN OF MISSISSIPPI, MOVED BY / GRATEFUL HEARTS AND LOVING ZEAL ORGANIZED JUNE / 15, 1886, THE CONFEDERATE MONUMENT ASSOCIATION, THEIR EFFORTS AIDED BY AN APPROPRIA-TION / OF THE STATE OF MISSISSIPPI, WERE CROWNED WITH SUCCESS IN THE ERECTION OF THIS MONUMENT TO THE CONFEDERATE DEAD OF MISSISSIPPI IN THE YEAR OF 1891.

  Northeast:

  "ALL LOST! BUT BY THE GRAVES / WHERE MARTYRED HEROES REST HE WINS THE MOST WHO HONOR SAVES— / SUCCESS IS NOT THE TEST."

  Southeast:

  "IT RECKS NOT WHERE THEIR BODIES LIE / BY BLOODY HILLSIDE, PLAIN OR RIVER

  THEIR NAMES ARE BRIGHT ON FAME'S PROUD SKY: / THEIR DEEDS OF VALOR LIVE FOREVER."

  ORGANIZED IN JACKSON MISS. / APRIL 26TH, 1865 / BY SUE LANDON VAUGHN

- A centennial-era granite tablet on the grounds declares Mississippi's remembrance of "Her Heroic Sons and Daughters" in the "War Between the States."

  MISSISSIPPI REMEMBERS / TO COMMEMORATE THE CENTENNIAL / ANNIVERSARY OF THE WAR BETWEEN / THE STATES. MISSISSIPPI GRATEFULLY / REMEMBERS AND PAYS TRIBUTE TRIBUTE [*SIC*] TO HER / HEROIC SONS AND DAUGHTERS WHO / SERVED THE CONFEDERACY WITH SUCH / VALOR AND DEVOTION. / MISSISSIPPI COMMISSION ON THE / WAR BETWEEN THE STATES / 1961–1965 / COMMISSIONERS / [*Roster*]

Greenwood Cemetery Stele

4.13.3 Subject: Greenwood Cemetery Stele
Location: Old Cemetery, Section 1, north of North West Street   N 32 18 29 14 / W 90 10 58 14
Installed or dedicated: April 26, 1931
Medium: Marble
Monument is a stele surmounting a base and steps.

Inscriptions
[Front]
[CS battle flag, unfurled, in high relief]

YOUR GLORY NE'ER SHALL BE FORGOT / WHILE FAME HER RECORD KEEPS
FOR HONOR POINTS THE HALLOWED SPOT / WHERE VALOR PROUDLY SLEEPS
OUR CONFEDERATE DEAD / 1861–1865

PRESENTED TO / W. D. HOLDER CHAPTER / UNITED DAUGHTERS OF THE
CONFEDERACY / BY / MRS. VIOLA ENSMINGER LAKE / IN MEMORY OF / HER FATHER
/ GEORGE CHARLES ENSMINGER / CONFEDERATE SOLDIER / APR. 26, 1931

Front steps:
W. D. HOLDER CHAPTER U.D.C. / 1966 / [19 names]

Claiming the dead as their own even in 1931—sixty-six years after war's end—
this UDC monument stands over Greenwood Cemetery's "Confederate Burial
Ground," which inters the graves of an estimated 1,200 Confederate soldiers:
300 in private lots and the remainder, estimated between 450 and 900, in
these environs.

Historian Timothy B. Smith notes that since the city was situated on major river and rail lines, Jackson saw many wounded and sick soldiers sent from the armies in northern Mississippi in the first two years of the war. Soldiers killed in action during the siege and fall of Jackson in 1863, or who died of disease in area hospitals were interred here. Many were buried in shallow graves where they fell on the battlefield with eventual interment here. Wooden headboards identified many soldiers, but some were reportedly buried in mass graves.

· Six Confederate generals are interred in Greenwood Cemetery: Brig. Gen. Daniel W. Adams, Brig. Gen. William W. Adams; Brig. Gen. William Barksdale; Brig. Gen. Samuel W. Ferguson; Brig. Gen. Richard Griffith; Brig. Gen. James A. Smith. Barksdale and Daniel W. Adams are in unmarked graves. Brig. Gen. James A. Smith is buried near the Veterans Section, among approximately one hundred marked graves. Most of the markers bear the inscription "Unknown Soldier."

· The excerpt beginning "Your glory" is taken from Theodore O'Hara's "Bivouac of the Dead."

· Greenwood Cemetery is a twenty-two-acre expanse founded in 1823 by an act of the Mississippi State Legislature.

4.13.4 Subject: Stele, "Confederate" Trenches
Location: Battlefield Park, east side, off Terry Street and US 80   N 32 17 18 00 / W 90 10 67 38
Installed or dedicated: June 1937
Media: Fieldstone, marble
Monument is a fieldstone stele surmounting a base.

Inscription
CONFEDERATE TRENCHES / WAR BETWEEN THE STATES / 1861–1865
ERECTED BY / W. D. HOLDER CHAPTER / U.D.C. / JUNE 1937

This battlefield stele identifies the ground nearby as Confederate trenches. However, they are believed to be trenches erected by soldiers of the Union 13th Corps during the Siege of Jackson, July 10–16, 1863. If so, the two postwar, breechloading Spanish-American War–era field artillery pieces are—in addition to being inappropriate to the time period—also pointing in the wrong direction.

In fact, extensive fortifications were erected around Jackson in anticipation of action, which took place on May 14 and July 9–17, 1863, when Union forces laid siege to and subsequently occupied the city. These trenches are among the few remaining vestiges of those events. Today's Battlefield Park, once known as Winter's Woods, was acquired by the city in 1927.

4.13.5 Subject: Raymond, Hinds County Courthouse Common Soldier
Location: Courthouse grounds, 127 West Main St., 39154, corner of Oak and Main Street, US 80 and North Street, 39154   N 32 16 22 69 / W 89 59 12 92
Dedicated: April 29, 1908
Media: Bronze; pink and gray granite
Monument is a common soldier surmounting a shaft and base.

Inscription
[Front]
[Bas relief: field artillery piece] [Bas relief: CS Battle Flag, with laurel wreath]

CONFEDERATE / WE OF THE SOUTH REMEMBER, / WE OF THE SOUTH REVERE.

[bronze relief depicting a woman aiding a wounded soldier]

[Bas relief: anchor for the navy]

[Bas relief: crossed swords]

ERECTED BY THE PEOPLE OF / HINDS COUNTY, IN GRATEFUL / MEMORY OF THEIR MEN WHO IN / 1861–65 GAVE OR OFFERED TO / GIVE THEIR LIVES FOR THE / MAINTENANCE OF CONSTITUTIONAL / GOVERNMENT; AND TO THE HEROIC / WOMEN WHOSE DEVOTION TO / OUR CAUSE IN ITS DARKEST HOUR / SUSTAINED THE STRONG AND / STRENGTH- / ENED THE WEAK.

[Relief: crossed muskets for the infantry with slouch hat]

Historic Southern Monuments identifies this as a "beautiful work of art, for the erection of which the Board of Supervisors of the county appropriated the sum of four thousand dollars." It also notes that "all the accouterments" on this common soldier "are perfect, and the details of the uniform accurate, even to the shoestrings and the socks pulled over the lower part of the trousers as our soldiers used to wear them."

It is an elegant monument. Four blocks of Texas pink granite form the base. The shaft is Texas gray granite, twenty-five feet in height, surmounted by a seven-foot bronze statue of a Confederate soldier bearing a musket, standing at parade rest, contrapposto. The monument faces west, in the direction of the Raymond battlefield and, more obliquely, toward Vicksburg.

This is another Mississippi monument that takes particular notice of the tragedy of the war and the fortitude required to endure it. Note the tribute to the priestly, intercessory mercy of the woman in the relief who is caring for a wounded soldier.

Some two thousand people attended the unveiling on April 28, 1908. The Raymond *Clarion-Ledger* called the event a "red letter day and one of the greatest days in the history of Raymond," observing that "as the Jackson Band played a rousing rendition of Dixie, seven little girls pulled the cord to unveil the monument. The crowd was overcome with emotion as they viewed the

Raymond, Hinds County Courthouse Common Soldier

twenty-seven-foot statue placed in memory of the Confederate soldiers of Hinds County."

The monument was sponsored by the Nathan Bedford Forrest Chapter of the UDC. The American Bronze Company of Chicago cast the statue. There is uncertainty about who designed the edifice. The Smithsonian Inventory credits Frank Teich for the base stonework and Frederick Hibbard for the bronze plaque. Teich, a sculptor and businessman of Llano, Texas, supplied the granite for the monument; it is unknown whether Hibbard or Teich designed the statue of the common soldier.

· The Greek Revival–style courthouse was erected 1857–59 by the Weldon brothers, George and Tom, Scotch-Irish immigrants who trained one hundred slaves in construction techniques, among them John Jackson, a slave who worked as a draftsman and architect for the Weldon brothers. The building was used as a field hospital for Union and Confederate wounded after the battle of Raymond when Federal troops occupied the town.

Raymond, Battlefield, Texas Granite Stele

4.13.6 Subject: Raymond, Battlefield, Texas Granite Stele
Location: Raymond battlefield, MS 18, southwest of Raymond   N 32 14 29
27 / W 90 26 33 98
Dedicated: May 4, 2002
Media: Bronze, granite
Monument is a granite shaft decorated with a bronze star surmounting a
base.

Inscriptions
[Front]
TEXAS / REMEMBERS THE VALOR AND DEVOTION OF / ITS SONS WHO PARTICIPATED
IN THE BATTLE OF RAYMOND AND IN OTHER / ENGAGEMENTS OF THE VICKSBURG
CAMPAIGN. / UPON THIS FIELD ON MAY 12, 1863, SOLDIERS / OF THE 7TH TEXAS
INFANTRY, LED BY REGIMENTAL / COMMANDER COLONEL HIRAM B. GRANBURY,
AND OTHER / REGIMENTS OF BRIGADIER GENERAL JOHN GREGG'S / BRIGADE
FOUGHT WITH GRIM DETERMINATION AGAINST / TWO DIVISIONS OF FEDERAL
FORCES UNDER / COMMAND OF MAJOR GENERAL JAMES B. MCPHERSON. / THE
UNION ADVANCE WAS PART OF A LARGER / CAMPAIGN DESIGNED TO CAPTURE THE
STRATEGIC PORT / CITY OF VICKSBURG ON THE MISSISSIPPI RIVER. / LEADING THE
CONFEDERATE ASSAULT AGAINST THE / FEDERALS, GRANBURY'S TEXANS STEPPED
FORWARD / AT NOON AND SURGED ACROSS FOURTEEN MILE CREEK, / WHERE THEY
MET THE ENEMY IN FORCE. / THEY VALIANTLY STRUGGLED WITH REGIMENTS /

FROM OHIO AND ILLINOIS, WHILE ALL ALONG THE / BATTLE LINE THE SOUTHERN SOLDIERS OF GREGG'S / BRIGADE FACED THREE TIMES THEIR NUMBER. / DESPITE THEIR COURAGEOUS EFFORT, THE / CONFEDERATE TROOPS WERE CHECKED AND / FORCED FROM THE FIELD AROUND 4:30 P.M. / THE ENGAGEMENT AT RAYMOND WAS A PRECURSOR / TO THE INTENSE FIGHTING TO FOLLOW / DURING THE SIEGE OF VICKSBURG.

IN THE BATTLE OF RAYMOND, THE TEXANS LOST / 22 MEN KILLED, 73 WOUNDED, AND 63 MISSING / IN ACTION.

A MEMORIAL TO TEXANS WHO SERVED THE CONFEDERACY.

TEXAS UNITS ENGAGED IN THE VICKSBURG / CAMPAIGN

[Roster of 27 infantry or dismounted cavalry units, four batteries of artillery]

TEXAS REMEMBERS AND HONORS HER SONS / THEY SLEEP THE SLEEP OF THE BRAVE

ERECTED THROUGH THE DEDICATION OF / THE TEXAS HISTORICAL COMMISSION

[Adjacent footstone: List of six sponsoring organizations and "Other Friends Who Cherish Undaunted Courage."]

The Battle of Raymond is one of five battles that Union forces led by Maj. Gen. Ulysses S. Grant won during the climactic offensive of the Vicksburg Campaign between May 1 and May 17, 1863. The action at Raymond took place on May 12, 1863. A Confederate force led by Brig. Gen. John Gregg, some three thousand men, disputed the ground along the banks of Fourteen Mile Creek against some twelve thousand Union troops—the 17th Corps, commanded by Maj. Gen. James McPherson. The Confederates fought well but were outnumbered and driven from the field.

Texas monuments in Mississippi are characterized by vivid narratives inscribed on elegant but simple granite stele. This one, sponsored by the Texas Historical Commission, was placed on the recently acquired Raymond Civil War Battlefield, which in turn was sponsored by a local group, Friends of Raymond, in association with the Civil War Trust.

· The Raymond Confederate Cemetery inters the graves of at least 140 soldiers. In recent years, 109 names have been identified based upon research of the Compiled Service Records in the National Archives.

4.13.7 Subject: Champion Hill, Battlefield Stele
Location: Off MS 467, near the Coker House   N 32 18 24 03 / W 90 33 57 22
Installed or dedicated: May 18, 1909
Media: Bronze, granite
Monument is a bronze tablet affixed to a granite boulder.

Inscription

LLOYD TILGHMAN / BRIGADIER GENERAL C.S.A. / COMMANDING FIRST BRIGADE / LORING'S DIVISION / KILLED HERE THE AFTERNOON OF MAY 16, 1863, NEAR / THE CLOSE OF THE BATTLE OF CHAMPION HILL

The Battle of Gettysburg is justly prominent, and the Siege of Vicksburg is duly noted in monumentation and history, but the Battle of Champion Hill, fought on May 16, 1863, was the largest and bloodiest action of the Vicksburg Campaign. It was arguably the decisive battle of the Vicksburg Campaign and thus has also been called the decisive battle of the American Civil War. Here a force of thirty-two thousand Union soldiers commanded by US Maj. Gen. Ulysses S. Grant engaged a force of twenty-three thousand Confederates commanded by CS Lt. Gen. John Pemberton in a struggle for a roadside crossroads between Vicksburg and Jackson. This defeat led Pemberton to withdraw his army from the open field and into the fortifications at Vicksburg, leading to the siege and surrender of his command, the loss of Vicksburg, and the opening of the Mississippi River to Union traffic, control, and further incursions into the Confederacy.

The field is dominated by Champion Hill, where this monument stands. It was from here that Confederate artillery opened fire on the Union army to begin the battle. The first Federal assault on the hill drove the Southerners back, but they were swept away by a counterattack. Grant in turn ordered reinforcements toward the hill. Ultimately the Confederates were driven back again, compelling a general retreat. Confederate Brig. Gen. Lloyd Tilghman was killed at this site while directing the rearguard near the close of the action.

As noted in chapter 1, this is one of three monuments to Tilghman sponsored by his sons, Sidell and Frederick Tilghman. Henry H. Kitson designed this, the Champion Hill monument, which was dedicated on May 18, 1909.

Champion Hill, Battlefield Stele

Mississippi College, Stele

Clinton

4.13.8 Subject: Mississippi College, Stele
Location: The campus quad, looking out on corner of West College and
Jefferson   N 32 90 12 89 / W 90 19 50 10
Dedicated: November 18, 1926
Medium: Granite
Monument is an inscribed granite boulder.

Inscription

LOVE IS IMMORTAL. / THIS BOULDER IS ERECTED BY THE MISSISSIPPI / COLLEGE RIFLES CHAPTER U.D.C. / IN GRATEFUL MEMORY OF THE 104 MEN WHO WENT / OUT FROM THIS COLLEGE AS COMPANY E. 18TH / MISSISSIPPI REGIMENT APRIL 23, 1861. / [7 names] / COMPANY E. WENT INTO ACTION AT THE 1ST BATTLE / OF MANASSAS. ON MANY A HARD FOUGHT BATTLE / FIELD THEIR BLOOD WAS SHED, MANASSAS, LEESBURG, / RICHMOND, MALVERN HILL, SEVEN PINES, CHICKAMAUGA, / SHARPSBURG, THE WILDERNESS, FREDERICKSBURG, / CHANCELLORSVILLE, TERRIBLE GETTYSBURG AND OTHERS. / IN APRIL 1862, W. H. LEWIS OF CLINTON WAS ELECTED CAPT. / OF THE MISSISSIPPI COLLEGE RIFLES. / ON THE 9TH OF APRIL 1865, WITH THE ARMY OF NORTHERN VA. WHICH SURRENDERED AT APPOMATTOX COURT HOUSE, / WAS THE REMNANT OF THE MISSISSIPPI COLLEGE RIFLES. / OF THE 104 WHO ENLISTED, ONLY 8 RETURNED / VALIANT MEN WHOM THE WORLD SPEAKS OF AS / SOLDIERS OF A LOST CAUSE, YET WHOSE NAMES HAVE / GONE DOWN IN HISTORY / WEARING A DEATHLESS FAME.

The Mississippi College Rifles formed in April 1861. Its service as Company E of the 18th Mississippi Infantry is described above. The company initially consisted of 65 men, including 32 students, 3 faculty members, and 1 trustee. It is a secular monument, but this Mississippi College has been affiliated with the Mississippi Baptist Convention since 1852. Note the subtextual biblical allusions to these soldiers as "valiant men" who suffered for their faith in a "Lost Cause" but were vindicated by the remembrance of them in "Deathless Fame" (Heb. 11:37–38).

- Mississippi College, the oldest college in the state, was founded in 1826. The college's Provine Chapel, completed in 1860, was used as a hospital by Union forces during the Vicksburg Campaign. The college managed to remain open during the war, albeit with an average enrollment of about thirty students. The Mississippi "College Rifles" and the Mississippi "College Invincibles" became drill units after the war. The College Rifles and the Invincibles disbanded in the twentieth century as increasingly popular athletic programs fulfilled the functions the military units had once served. ROTC units would be established on campus with the onset of President Wilson signing the National Defense Act of 1916.

4.13.9 Subject: Clinton Cemetery, UDC Stele

Location: Clinton Cemetery, 500 E. College Street   N 32 20 07 74 / W 90 19 14 12

Installed or dedicated: 1928

Medium: granite

Monument is a granite stele.

Inscription

1861–1865 / IN MEMORY OF OUR / CONFEDERATE DEAD
ERECTED BY MISSISSIPPI COLLEGE / RIFLES CHAPTER
UNITED DAUGHTERS CONFEDERACY

This rough-edged granite stele offers a simple declaration by the local UDC chapter. Surrounding it, however, are six bronze tablets set in concrete bases commemorating the service of veterans of the Civil War, World War I, World War II, Korea, Vietnam, and the Persian Gulf. The whole of the site is presided over by a US flag, with landscaping forming a kind of temple or garden of remembrance for the dead.

- Established circa 1800, the Clinton Cemetery is one of the oldest cemeteries in central Mississippi. Buried here are families of early settlers, ten presidents of Mississippi College, and sixty-three Confederate soldiers.

Clinton Cemetery, UDC Stele

Southern Mississippi

5

SOUTHERN
MISSISSIPPI

C HAPTER 5 is devoted to southern Mississippi, including eighteen courthouse sites, the Natchez National Cemetery, and Confederate cemeteries at Natchez, Enterprise, Meridian, Lauderdale, Archusa Springs, and Crystal Springs. Beauvoir in Biloxi is the last home of Jefferson Davis, the site of a Confederate cemetery and, since 1980, the "Tomb of the Unknown Confederate Soldier."

The effects of the war are pervasive across Mississippi, but no major battles were fought in this area, and many of the hospital sites and cemeteries are farther north. Because of Beauvoir, more attention is paid to Jefferson Davis in this chapter than elsewhere. Although Davis was born in Kentucky, he grew up on his father's plantation near Woodville, in southeast Mississippi. Davis established a plantation in Warren County, served as a senator from Mississippi, returned to Mississippi to farm, and lived at Beauvoir in his postbellum years.

As the only president of the Confederacy, Davis remains one of the most famous persons associated with Mississippi, and he, along with fellow Kentuckian Abraham Lincoln, is one of the most famous and controversial Americans of the mid-nineteenth century. At Beauvoir, two bronze statues of Jefferson Davis stand at Davis's last home along with the Jefferson Davis Presidential Library, which opened in 1998 (see Beauvoir, below). (The library was effectively destroyed during Hurricane Katrina but has since been rebuilt.) Originally a facility of 13,500 square feet, the library was established with state funding and contributions by the Sons of Confederate Veterans (SCV). Historian Ben Wynne finds irony in this, observing that the "only President of a nation that barely established itself and did so at the expense of the United States" also has a presidential library.

Paradox, however, seems to define Davis's legacy. He was a reluctant participant in the course of events that led to secession, but he was unrepentant about the Confederate cause after the war, and he always regarded himself as a patriot. He was charged with treason upon his capture in 1865 and spent two years in prison, but his case never went to trial, and he was eventually released on bail. For all the vituperation associated with Jefferson Davis, there are voices that seem to hold the man apart from the cause he fought for. Contemporary historian Edward C. Smith cautions against the hazard of reading the prejudices of the present into the past: "The damage that is done when you start being selective about history is that you are amputating yourself from a significant part of your history. . . . A historian is at his worst when he reads the prejudices of the present into the past." Taking the man as a character, historian Lynda L. Crist, editor of the Jefferson Davis papers, concludes that Davis was, in simple terms, "devoted to honesty and duty and integrity" and was "a loyal American and an American President." Historian William C. Davis marks him as an example of a man "who never gave up, [who represented] in some ways, the essence of the American spirit. . . . He showed an example of someone who risked all and sacrificed all for honor as he perceived it, for the right as he perceived it, for constitution and democratic government as he and his class perceived it, whether right or not is another case. You don't necessarily have to appreciate the cause in order to pay some homage to the dedication he pursued."

In 1888, just a year before his death, Davis called upon the "young men of Mississippi" to "lay aside all rancor, all bitter sectional feeling, and to make your places in the ranks of those who will bring about a consummation devoutly to be wished—a reunited country."

Jefferson Davis continues to be revered by many Southerners in the same way as the Mississippi common soldier is revered: as a flawed figure who is theirs, with an affection bordering on the familial. In this regard, it matters less what cause they fought for or whether their efforts were successful.

The reverse side of the Richmond, Virginia, monument to Jefferson Davis on Monument Avenue may best articulate the way many Southerners came to eulogize Davis.

ERECTED BY THE PEOPLE OF THE SOUTH IN HONOUR OF THEIR LOVE FOR THE MAN, THEIR REVERENCE FOR HIS VIRTUES, THEIR GRATITUDE FOR HIS SERVICES

· Other monuments to Davis stand at his birthplace at Fairview, Kentucky; Davis's gravesite at Hollywood Cemetery, Richmond, Virginia; and on Monument Avenue in Richmond, Virginia. Statues of Davis in Memphis and New Orleans were removed in 2017.

5.1.1 Subject: City Park Common Soldier

Location: City Park, Main and Rankin Streets, 39120   N 31 33 29 76 / W 91 24 03 66

Dedicated: April 26, 1890

Medium: Marble

Monument is a common soldier surmounting a shaft and base.

Inscriptions

[Front]

CSA

[Relief of crossed swords]

THE WARRIOR'S BANNER TAKES ITS FLIGHT / TO GREET THE WARRIOR'S SOUL / IN MEMORY OF / THE / CONFEDERATE DEAD / FROM NATCHEZ AND ADAMS / COUNTY MISSISSIPPI.

DEAR IN THEIR LIFELESS CLAY, / WHETHER UNKNOWN OR / KNOWN TO FAME, / THEIR CAUSE AND COUNTRY / STILL THE SAME, / THEY DIED AND WORE THE / GRAY"

AND EACH LIFE THAT MEN / DEEM LOST, / WHEN ITS HOLDER COUNTS / THE COST, / AND FREELY LAYS IT DOWN, / SHALL WEAR A DEATHLESS / CROWN."

ERECTED BY THE / CONFEDERATE MEMORIAL / ASSOCIATION / OF / NATCHEZ AND ADAMS COUNTRY MISS. / 1890.

"FROM EACH 'LOST CAUSE' / OF EARTH / SOMETHING PRECIOUS / SPRINGS TO BIRTH, / THOUGH LOST IT BE TO MEN / IT LIVES WITH GOD AGAIN."

This monument stands in Memorial Park, formally a church cemetery, and adjacent to St. Mary Basilica in downtown Natchez. It is an especially picturesque monument, funereal in appearance and inscription, but one that is also suggestive of the changing South. The monument reflects the changes Natchez has faced since the city's founding in the eighteenth century—the oldest city on the Mississippi River. For example, St. Mary Basilica on the adjacent block was built during the years 1841–51. Its Gothic Revival design reflects the French and Spanish Catholic influence on the city from the sixteenth and seventeenth centuries, but as a cathedral in the newly established Diocese of Natchez, it was intended to serve the Italian and Irish immigrants coming to the city in the nineteenth century. The monument's placement in Memorial Park in 1890 reflects concerns and interests that would be associated with the City Beautiful Movement, the nationwide, turn-of-the-twentieth-century trend in urban planning to revive and enhance the aesthetics, culture, and livability of urban space.

Natchez, City Park Common Soldier

The monument was sponsored by the Confederate Memorial Association of Natchez. At the time of its dedication, the Natchez *Democrat* declared:

> It must be remembered that [the monument] is a tribute of a people wasted and impoverished by war, whose country was overrun by invading armies and who after the storm of war was over, witnessed desolation on all sides—not only in the their fields, but socially and politically—let it be remembered that out of and through this desolation, the people who are erecting this monument have never lost their gratitude, reverence, and devotion to the memory of their heroes who died a quarter of a century gone by but are not about to accomplish the crowning touch in enduring marble their undying sentiment.

- The excerpt beginning "The Warrior's Banner" is taken from the poem "Ashes of Glory," by A. J. Requier (ca. 1880). The excerpt beginning "Dear In Their Lifeless Clay" is taken from "March of the Deathless Dead" by Fr. Abram J. Ryan. The renewal associated with "From Each 'Lost Cause' / Of Earth" may be associated with Ephesians 2:5 ("Even when we were dead in sins, hath quickened us together with Christ, [by grace ye are saved;]").

- The origin of "And Each Life That Men Deem Lost" is undetermined, but it is so lavish a tribute to the messianic sacrifice of men that it bears comparison to the New Testament book of John 10:18, and the words of Jesus: "No man taketh [my life] from me, but I lay it down of myself. I have power to lay it down, and I have power to take it again."

5.1.2 Subject: Natchez, City Cemetery stele
Location: 2 Cemetery Road   N 31 34 34 89 / W 91 23 36 36
Installed or dedicated: n.a.
Medium: Granite
Monument is an inscribed stele.

Inscription
[CS Battle Flag]

1861–1865 / IN MEMORY OF THE / SOLDIERS OF THE SOUTHERN / CONFEDERACY / TIME WILL NE'ER DIM THEIR GLORY

Natchez is a deceptively appealing city: it once had the second largest slave market in the South, but its antebellum charm and opulence shaped its present status as an attraction for tourism in the twenty-first century. The city surrendered to naval forces commanded by Flag Officer David G. Farragut in July 1863 after the fall of New Orleans in May 1862; it remained occupied for the

Natchez, City Cemetery Stele

duration of the war. As a result, the city escaped the damage and devastation that other Southern cities endured.

There is no battlefield cemetery, nor was it a refuge for the wounded from other battlefields after May 1862, when Union forces occupied the town. An early twentieth-century narrative, attributed to "Frzd. J. V. Le Cand," of the Natchez United Confederate Veterans (UCV) and the Natchez Memorial Association, observes that "there is a burial lot which was set aside for Confederate soldiers in the Natchez Cemetery, and which contains the remains of about fifty soldiers. The lot is enclosed, and fairly well kept by the Memorial Association of Natchez. Those who were buried in this lot, were strangers. The dead of the commands which left Natchez and which were sent home, or died here, were buried in private lots. The Veterans' Association acquired an additional lot, where veterans are buried."

5.1.3 Subject: Natchez National Cemetery
Location: 41 Cemetery Rd, Natchez, 39120   N 31 34 84 44 / W 91 23 70 54

There is no central monument here, but the Federal government purchased eleven acres for a national cemetery in 1866, on a bluff overlooking the Mississippi and near the City Cemetery. The grounds were enclosed by a brick wall in 1873. Original interments on these grounds included transfers from sites within a fifty-mile radius of Natchez. By 1871, the cemetery interred the remains of 3,086 Union soldiers, only 253 of whom were identified.

Fayette, Courthouse Common Soldier, Confederate

Jefferson County

5.2.1 Subject: Fayette, Courthouse Common Soldier, Confederate
Location: Fayette Town Square, 39069   N 31 42 41 65 / W 91 03 40 20
Dedicated: November 19, 1904
Media: Granite, marble
Monument is a common soldier surmounting a shaft and base.

Inscription
[Front]
[C.S. National flag]

ERECTED 1904 / JEFFERSON COUNTY'S / TRIBUTE TO HER / CONFEDERATE
SOLDIERS / CONFEDERATE SOLDIERS

[inscribed crossed cannon barrels]

CSA

[inscribed crossed cannon barrels]

CSA
THE NAMES OF THE MAJORITY / OF THESE CONFEDERATE / SOLDIERS HAVE BEEN /
OFFICIALLY PLACED IN THE MISS[.] STATE ARCHIVES IN THE YEAR 1904

[inscribed crossed cannon barrels]

CSA

The Fayette county courthouse common soldier is depicted as an older man in
full uniform, including a tunic, standing at parade rest, in marble, surmounting an opulent granite shaft and base. The figure faces west toward the courthouse. It is an unassuming, unpretentious veterans' monument. There are no
expressions of mourning, defiance, or affection. This is a tribute to services

tendered by the county's Confederate soldiers, taking note that the veterans' names have been archived and will be remembered. *Confederate Veteran* simply called it "a beautiful Confederate monument, erected in 1905, at a cost of about $2,500, inclusive of the iron fence surrounding it."

Claiborne County

5.3.1 Subject: Port Gibson, Courthouse Common Soldier
Location: 410 Market Street, 39150   N 31 57 43 56 / W 90 59 01 58
Dedicated: October 24, 1907
Media: Marble
Monument is soldier surmounting a shaft and base.

Inscriptions
[Front]
[relief of C. S. battle flag] [relief of crossed muskets]

ERECTED BY / THE UNITED DAUGHTERS / OF THE CONFEDERACY / OF CLAIBORNE COUNTY'S / TRIBUTE TO / HER SONS / WHO SERVED / IN THE WAR OF / 1861–1865

[relief portrait bust of Maj. Gen. Van Dorn]

C.S.A. / MAJOR GENERAL EARL VAN DORN / 1820–1863

C.S.A.
PORT GIBSON RIFLES / COMPANY C. 10TH REGT. MISS. VOLS. / CLAIBORNE GUARDS / COMPANY K. 12TH REGT. MISS. VOLS / FAIRVIEW RIFLES / COMPANY G. 16TH REGT. MISS. VOLS / CLAIBORNE VOLUNTEERS / COMPANY F. 48TH REGT. MISS. VOLS / CLAIBORNE LIGHT INFANTRY / COMPANY D. 24TH BATTALION CAVALRY / VAN DORN GUARDS / COMPANY B. 38TH REGT. INFANTRY / COMPANY C. 4TH REGT. CAVALRY / COMPANY D. REGT. CAVALRY / ABBAY'S BATTERY / COMPANY K. 1ST / REGT LIGHT ARTILLERY. / SONS OF CLAIBORNE COUNTY / WHO SAW SERVICE IN OTHER COMMANDS / MILITIA COMPANY

[relief portrait bust of Brig. Gen. Humphreys]

C.S.A. / BRIG. GEN. BENJAMIN GRUBB HUMPHREYS. / 1808–1882

Port Gibson, Courthouse Common Soldier

This is a veterans' monument in the courthouse square, an affectionate familial tribute to the "Sons / of Claiborne County 'Who Served in the War of / 1861–1865.'" The roster of units is extensive; the tributes to generals who are from Port Gibson are prominent. There is no mention of the outcome of the war, however, and no mention of the battle of Port Gibson fought here on May 1, 1863, as part of the Vicksburg Campaign. Like the Fayette monument in the adjacent Jefferson County, the veterans' service is enough to merit a tribute, irrespective and—in some measure despite—the outcome of the conflict in which they served.

- The figure stands about six feet high; the whole of the monument is twenty-one feet high. The Columbus Marble Works served as fabricator; the sculptor of the statue is unknown. This is likely an Italian import sculpted by an anonymous craftsman.

- The action at Port Gibson on May 1, 1863, has a large importance in the Vicksburg Campaign as well as American military history. When two army corps commanded by Maj. Gen. Ulysses S. Grant crossed the Mississippi River at Bruinsburg, they undertook a successful amphibious landing and advance on a scale that would not be surpassed until World War II. Grant's forces then marched north toward Vicksburg, but Confederate forces commanded by Brig. Gen. John S. Bowen offered a vigorous resistance at Port Gibson. They were outnumbered, however: the Union force under Grant numbered some twenty-three thousand men, the Confederates about eight thousand. The Southerners were driven back.

- Among the dead at Raymond's Wintergreen Cemetery are 140 Confederate soldiers, believed to be mainly from the 3rd Tennessee and 7th Texas Infantry, who were killed during the battle of Port Gibson. Interred by local townspeople, the Confederate dead were laid to rest in rows—"Soldiers' Row." The dead were eventually marked with footstones inscribed "C.S.A." placed by the United Daughters of the Confederacy. These footstones are still in place, but individual gravestones from the Department of Veteran Affairs were installed in 1986, based on research undertaken by Roger Hanson.

- Benjamin G. Humphreys raised a company of infantry and was commissioned a captain in the Confederate Army in 1861. He eventually rose to the rank of brigadier general in the Army of Northern Virginia, survived the war, and served as governor of Mississippi, 1865–68.

- A West Point graduate, Earl Van Dorn (1820–63) had a mixed record as a general at the battles of Pea Ridge and Corinth. As commander of

Pemberton's cavalry, however, he led his troops against the supply depots at Holly Springs in December 1862, effectively disrupting Grant's operations against Vicksburg. It was a high point of his service. He was killed within six months, and his end was ignominious. He was shot and killed May 7, 1863, after a dispute in which Van Dorn was accused of committing adultery with another man's wife.

Copiah County

5.4.1 Subject: Hazlehurst, Courthouse Common Soldier, Confederate
Location: Courthouse grounds, corner of Caldwell Drive and Gallatin Street, 39083   N 31 51 35 91 / W 90 23 47 54
Dedicated: April 26, 1917
Media: Granite, marble
Monument is a common soldier surmounting a shaft and base.

Inscriptions

INFANTRY CAVALRY ARTILLERY NAVY
IN HONOR OF THOSE / WHO FOUGHT AND DIED; / OF THOSE WHO FOUGHT AND LIVED; / THIS MEMORIAL IS ERECTED BY / COPIAH COUNTY / AND THE / CHARLES EDWARD HOOKER CHAPTER / NO. 1179 / UNITED DAUGHTERS / OF THE CONFEDERACY / APRIL A.D. 1917
"LOVE MAKES MEMORY ETERNAL"

(On each side of the round pedestal, below soldier:)

(Incised on circular wall:)

CSA 1861 TO THE MEMORY OF OUR CONFEDERATE SOLDIERS 1865 CSA

Hazlehurst, Courthouse Common Soldier, Confederate

This monument, standing fourteen feet high, stands directly in front of the Copiah County courthouse, which was erected in 1902. This is a wartime monument: it was dedicated April 26, 1917; on April 4, 1917, the US Senate voted to declare war on Germany. It is the most prominent testimonial on the courthouse grounds, but it shares space with several other veterans' monuments, including substantial memorials to servicemen and women of World War I, World War II, Korea, Vietnam, and Iraq, with space left over for future conflicts. The monument faces north. The surmounting figure has a mature appearance: he is evidently an able figure, armed and ready—a citizen-soldier, neither bellicose nor willingly hostile, but alert to a call to service if and when that call comes.

This is the only monument in Mississippi with a fountain (which is no longer operating) but, like many such monuments (e.g., Laurel, Ellisville, Hattiesburg), the fountain intimates a narrative of life, loss, cleansing, rebirth, and renewal—"Love Makes Memory Eternal."

- Charles Edward Hooker (1825–1914), for whom this chapter of the United Daughters of the Confederacy (UDC) was evidently named, was a state representative before the war, a Confederate officer during the war, and a US congressman after the war.

5.4.2 Subject: Crystal Springs, City Cemetery, Obelisk, Confederate
Location: Jackson Road, 39059   N 31 58 42 35 / W 90 21 31 80
Dedicated: June 3, 1876
Media: Marble, concrete
Monument is a marble obelisk surmounting a concrete base.

Inscriptions
[Front]

OUR CONFEDERATE DEAD 1861–1865

ERECTED BY THE / LADIES OF / CRYSTAL SPRINGS / MISS. / 1876.

Crystal Springs, City Cemetery Obelisk

Brookhaven, Rose Hill Cemetery Obelisk

This is a very early postwar, centennial-era monument with a terse inscription, surmounting a mound that evidently marks the site of unknown and undocumented graves. The wooden canopy and benches, painted white, are an apparent twentieth-century addition. They may be taken to have a sacred symbolism—intimating a kind of sacred space—as well as practical purpose in sheltering the marble shaft from the elements.

Lincoln County

5.5.1 Subject: Brookhaven, Rose Hill Cemetery Obelisk, Confederate
Location: 443 E Monticello Street, 39601   N 31 34 40 80 / W 90 26 01 66
Installed or dedicated: 1896
Medium: Marble
Monument is an obelisk surmounting a shaft and three-tiered base.

Inscription
[relief of CS Battle Flag]

LEST WE FORGET / IN MEMORY OF / THE CONFEDERATE DEAD / BY THEIR
COMRADES IN / ARMS AND THE SONS / AND DAUGHTERS OF THE / SOUTHERN
CONFEDERACY / IN MEMORY OF JULIOUS BOWSKY / BY GEO. BOWSKY HIS BROTHER

Erected in 1896 in memory of Julious Bowsky, 3rd Battalion, Co. E, 45th Mississippi Infantry, by his brother George, this twenty-foot-tall monument was deeded to the Sylvester Gwin Camp UCV in 1924, and now serves as a memorial for the Confederate soldiers who died and were once buried at Whitworth College. That college was founded in 1858 and disestablished in 1984. During the war, the college facilities served as a Confederate hospital. This obelisk serves as a memorial for Confederate soldiers who died and were buried at the wartime hospital at Whitworth College but whose remains were reinterred after the war. Twenty-two headstones are arranged around the monument, each inscribed "Unknown Soldier Confederate States Army."

·   The brothers Elias and George Bowsky were among a number of Jews who established community ties in Mississippi in the nineteenth century.

Amite County

5.6.1 Subject: Liberty, Town Square Obelisk, Confederate
Location: 131 Church Street, adjacent to Liberty Presbyterian Church   N 31 09 31 01 / W 90 48 32 80
Installed or dedicated: 1866–71
Medium: Marble
Monument is an obelisk with a funereal urn and drape atop, the whole surmounting a plinth, base, and shaft.

Inscription
[Front]

CO E 22 MISS REG'T / *[40 names]* / CO A 10 MISS REG'T / *[6 names]* / SACRED / TO THE MEMORY OF / THE SOLDIERS FROM / AMITE COUNTY / WHO LOST THEIR LIVES IN THE CONFEDERATE ARMY / ERECTED BY / THE CITIZENS OF AMITE COUNTY IN / 1871.

CO K 7 MISS REG'T *[33 names]* / CO K 4 MISS REG'T *[4 names]* / CO C 7 MISS REG'T *[38 names]*

CO K 44 MISS REG'T / *[40 names]* / CO A 3 LA REG'T / *[1 name]* / CO I 33 MISS REG'T / *[45 names]*

CO K 33 MISS REG'T / *[43 names]* / CO E 2 LA MISS REG'T / *[4 names]* CO B 3 MISS REG'T / *[22 names]*

Located on North Church Street in Liberty, adjacent to Liberty Presbyterian Church, this monument is the names of 279 soldiers. The cornerstone was laid in 1866; the site was donated by the Liberty Lodge of Masons. It was designed and built by A. J. Lewis of Brookhaven at the direction of the Amite County Monument and Historical Association. The association organized in 1866 and over the next five years raised $3,300. The memorial was completed in March 1871 and dedicated on April 26 of that year. The obelisk, surmounted by a funereal Grecian urn, is approximately twenty-one feet high and surmounts a base

Liberty, Town Square Obelisk, Confederate

of Kentucky granite and a shaft of Italian marble. It was the first Confederate monument erected in Mississippi and was one of the first raised in the country.

Jones County

5.7.1 Subject: Laurel, Courthouse Common Soldier, Confederate
Location: 415 North Fifth Avenue, 39441   N 31 41 39 32 / W 89 07 51 92
Installed: March 1912; Dedicated: April 12, 1912
Medium: Marble
Monument is a common soldier surmounting a colonnade.

Inscriptions
[Front]
1861 / 1865 / CSA / CONFEDERATE SOLDIERS
ERECTED BY THE STEPHEN DILL LEE CHAP. U.D.C. LAUREL, MISS. MARCH 1912

IN MEMORY OF OUR FALLEN HEROES.

1861 / 1865 / CSA / CONFEDERATE SOLDIERS
HONOR DECKS THE TURF / THAT WRAPS THEIR CLAY / ENOUGH OF MERIT HAS EACH / HONORED NAME / TO SHINE UNTARNISHED ON / THE ROLLS OF FAME.

Mourning is a theme of the Laurel courthouse monument, which faces west and stands at the northwest corner of the courthouse. It is one of two courthouses and two courthouse monuments in Jones County. The memorial is a colonnade supported by eight columns. Within the colonnade are two stone benches—exedra—forming a kind of temple space. The monument is sentimental: the canopy is decorated with reliefs of two pairs of crossed swords, as well as a wreath and ribbon with the letters "CSA" intertwined.

The whole of the temple form intimates profound grieving, however: it is, after all, erected "In Memory of Our Fallen Heroes." Four funereal urns are displayed on each side of the steps. Surmounting the colonnade is a pedestal supporting the figure of a Confederate soldier, but in the center of the colonnade is the figure of a kneeling woman whose downcast face looks upon the Confederate flag in her lap.

- The McNeil Marble Works provided the monument, which was erected at a cost of $3,300. The county board approved $2,250; the UDC chapter and local firms were other contributors.
- The statue was damaged in the late 1950s or early 1960s by a storm. A replacement wooden rifle was installed in the 1980s to take the place of the damaged original.

Laurel, Courthouse Common Soldier, Confederate

5.7.2 Subject: Ellisville, Courthouse Common Soldier, Confederate
Location: 101 Court Street North, 39440   N 31 36 14 56 / W 89 11 44 46
Dedicated: June 3, 1912
Media: Marble
Monument is a common soldier surmounting a four-column colonnade.

Inscriptions
[Front]
CSA / CONFEDERATE SOLDIERS

1861–1865 / LEST WE FORGET

ERECTED BY / JEFFERSON DAVIS CHAPTER U.D.C. 1912

1861–1865
"THE PRINCIPLES FOR WHICH THEY FOUGHT / LIVE ETERNALLY."

This is another example of eastern Mississippi monuments that mourn rather than "simply" celebrate or sentimentalize the Confederate soldier. True, the monument makes the strident claim that "The principles for which they fought / live eternally." Notwithstanding the inscription, the circular planter at the center of the monument is more symbolic of hope, healing, and renewal than defiance or justification.

This is also a more modest version of the monument that stands in the other county seat of Jones County at Laurel. This is a four-column colonnade, the whole standing approximately sixteen feet high, with one sculpture of a surmounting soldier—facing north—but without the sculpture of a female in mourning beneath, within the colonnade, that Laurel displays.

The county's Board of Supervisors authorized $2,250 for the monument on March 7, 1911. The surmounting figure, facing north, has a younger appearance than his counterpart at Laurel.

· Jones County, with its two county seats, took care to erect two county seat Confederate monuments. However, resistance to CS authorities in Jones County became militant and violent as the war continued, to the point where, as historian James R. Kelly Jr., observes, the "Natchez Courier reported in its July 12, 1864, edition that Jones County had seceded from the Confederacy." Although there was no official secession document, Kelly observes, "for a time in the spring of 1864, the Confederate government in Jones County was effectively overthrown," and the legend of the "Free State of Jones" began.

Ellisville, Courthouse Common Soldier, Confederate

Heidelberg, Common Soldier, Confederate

Jasper County

5.8.1 Subject: Heidelberg, Common Soldier, Confederate
Location: MS 528: Mary Weems Parker Memorial Library, 1016 Pine Avenue,
39439   N 31 53 49 24 / W 89 59 42 48
Installed or dedicated: 1911
Medium: Marble
Monument is a common soldier surmounting a shaft and base.

Inscriptions
[Front]
[Relief of CS Second National Flag]

CSA / JASPER COUNTY'S TRIBUTE / TO HER SONS /
WHO FELL IN THE WAR / 1861–1865

TO THE WOMEN OF / JASPER COUNTY, / THE RECORD OF / WHOSE SUBLIME / SELF-
SACRIFICE / AND DEVOTION TO / DUTY IN THE SERVICE OF THEIR / COUNTRY IS THE
/ PROUD HERITAGE / OF A LOYAL / POSTERITY.

TO THE NOBLE / MEN WHO / MARCHED NEATH / THE FLAG OF / THE STARS AND /
BARS AND WERE / FAITHFUL TO / THE END

CSA / ERECTED BY BOARD / OF SUPERVISORS / OF JASPER COUNTY / THROUGH
THE EFFORTS / OF THE JASPER COUNTY / CHAPTER NO. 1221 U.D.C. / MISSISSIPPI
DIVISION / HEIDELBERG MISS. / "LEST WE FORGET" / 1911

The surmounting figure of the Jasper County Confederate monument in Heidelberg holds a cross before him at chest level, uniquely so in Civil War monumentation, North or South. The monument stands forty feet high, facing south, in front of the county library west of the downtown.

The figure of a woman holding a wreath at her side and a common soldier on the right side are like the monument at Hattiesburg, suggestive of the impact of the war and the need to bereave, remember, and praise the dead on the part of the woman, as well as the willingness of the next generation to meet its challenges. The cross, however, is notable as a soldier standing against evil, interposing the cross against evil as a veritable soldier of Christ (2 Tim. 2:3; cf. Eph. 6:13).

Crosses on Confederate monuments are infrequent, but there are a few, most notably perhaps the monument at the Confederate cemetery, Lexington, Kentucky, erected in 1874. As a rule, crosses were associated with a Catholicism that was often looked on with suspicion in some elements of American culture in the nineteenth century. Historian Ryan K. Smith writes that in the "eyes of many American Protestants, and in the words of one Presbyterian magazine, the cross was 'not a symbol of redemption through the blessed Saviour, but a perverted, abused symbol of a great system of superstition and imposture.'" This was destined to change, however: by the time of World War II, crosses would be standard issue features on headstones of the dead interred in national cemeteries.

Clarke County

5.9.1 Subject: Quitman, Common Soldier, Courthouse, Confederate
Location: Courthouse grounds, South Archusa Avenue   N 32 02 24 79 / W 88 43 39 20
Installed or dedicated: October 24, 1911
Medium: Marble
Monument is a common soldier surmounting a shaft and base.

Inscriptions
[Front]
[CS National flag in high relief]

TO THE CONFEDERATE / SOLDIERS
THOUGH YOUR RANKS / NOW FAST ARE MELTING / AND THE STARS AND / BARS ARE FURLED, / YET THE SOUTH / WILL LIVE FOREVER / IN THE GLORY / OF YOUR WORLD

[Relief of crossed swords]

1861–1865 / CLARKE COUNTY'S / TRIBUTE TO / THE NOBLE MEN / WHO MARCHED / NEATH THE FLAG / OF THE STARS / AND BARS AND / WERE FAITHFUL / TO THE END.

[blank]

C.S.A.

Quitman, Common Soldier, Courthouse, Confederate

The Quitman monument offers a sentimental tribute to the wartime generation, with much praise for their devotion to the Confederacy. There is no sponsorship, and no extant records of a period SCV, UCV, or UDC in Quitman could be located, but this monument inscription bears noting for its affectionate, nostalgic, and perhaps overly optimistic climax: "Yet the South / Will Live Forever / In the Glory Of Your World."

- "Faithful to the End" is an apparent reference to the New Testament book of Revelation 2:10. "Faithful unto death," in the Authorized Version, is excerpted from the letter to the "faithful church" at Smyrna, which intimates that that community's trials have a divine purpose and that redemption is in prospect. The phrase is also inscribed on the monuments at Grenada (see chap. 3, Grenada County); Duck Hill (see chap. 3, Montgomery County); Brandon (see chap. 4, Rankin County); Poplarville (see chap. 5, Pearl River County); and Philadelphia (see chap. 3, Neshoba County).

- Dates vary on this monument: Widener cites 1914; the Smithsonian file cites October 24, 1911.

The Texas Hospital and Confederate Cemetery, Archusa Springs

5.9.2 Subject: The Texas Hospital and Confederate Cemetery, Archusa Springs
Location: South end of Quitman, off High Street (MS 145/18)   N 32 01 19 75 / W 88 43 42 52
Installed or dedicated: 1937
Media: Brick, marble
Monument is an inscribed stele.

Inscriptions

"TRY TO PROVE TO THE WORLD THAT ALTHOUGH WE WERE NOT SUCCESSFUL IN OUR EFFORTS / FOR INDEPENDENCE, WE WERE WORTHY OF SUCCESS." / ROBERT E. LEE

TO ALL THOSE WHO PAID THE SUPREME PRICE IN / THEIR PURSUIT OF AN IDEA THAT CHANGED A WAY / OF LIFE FOR US ALL—WE HUMBLY DEDICATE THIS / MEMORIAL AND THAT ALL BE JUDGED BY THE / ALMIGHTY AND NOT BY MAN."

ADD RILEY V.F.W. POST 4982 / MAY 25, 1987

The Confederate Memorial Cemetery may be found at the end of a dirt road off MS 145, south of Quitman.

The Texas Hospital at Archusa Springs opened in July 1862 as an initiative by citizens of Galveston and Houston, Texas. Although it opened for the sake of Confederate soldiers from Texas, the facility also treated soldiers from Tennessee, Mississippi, Arkansas, Alabama, and Louisiana, as well as the general public. Federal forces commanded by Maj. Gen. William T. Sherman burned the facilities on February 17, 1864, and the hospital did not reopen.

The site was abandoned until the 1930s, when the hospital's cemetery was reportedly rediscovered "by a Black farmer, plowing in order to put in a corn crop." Federal Writers of the WPA researched the site; identifications were made, and headstones were eventually put into place for the graves of the estimated three hundred soldiers interred here. Over the course of the following decades, the grounds were cared for by a unit of the Mississippi National Guard, several Boy Scout troops, and various citizens and local firms. Today the Add Riley VFW Post 4982, oversees the perpetual care of the grounds. Records indicate that the cemetery was formally dedicated on Memorial Day, May 25, 1987.

· Sources are lacking to confirm that the quotation attributed to Robert E. Lee is by Lee, but the commitment to duty is consonant with Lee's persona and legacy.

5.9.3 Subject: Stele, Roster of Confederate Dead
Location: South end of Quitman, off High Street (MS 145/18)
Installed or dedicated: n.a.
Medium: Granite
Monument is two intersecting stelae.

Inscription

CSA / LISTED DEATHS JUNE 1862 TO FEB. 18, 1864

[65 names with unit association and date of death]

Although the source of this roster is uncited, monuments with lists of previously unidentified names who are buried in Confederate cemeteries have been added in recent decades, as local researchers have accessed such sources as the National Archives in Washington, DC.

The Arch at Archusa Springs

5.9.4 Subject: The Arch at Archusa Springs
Location: South end of Quitman, off High Street (MS 145/18)
Installed or dedicated: circa 1920s
Medium: Concrete

Inscription

CONFEDERATE CEMETERY

The arch to the cemetery stands in the northwest corner of the grounds, on the edge of the surrounding woods. No road runs through it. The arch gives the site the look of a splendid ruin. It was designed by George Weir, a veteran of World War I, was damaged by Hurricane Isabel in the 1970s, and has never been repaired.

Enterprise, City Cemetery Stele

5.9.5 Subject: Enterprise, City Cemetery Stele
Location: Cemetery Road, east of Old Mill Creek on North Street   N 32 10
44 92 / W 88 49 29 12
Dedicated: April 21, 2012
Medium: Granite
Monument is a stele.

Inscriptions

ENTERPRISE CONFEDERATE CEMETERY / 1861–1864

[95 names in three columns, each inscribed with units and dates of death]

PARTIAL LISTING OF CONFEDERATE SOLDIERS BURIED ON THESE GROUNDS /
INFORMATION FOUND IN RECORD GROUP 109 NATIONAL ARCHIVES WASHINGTON D.C.

[95 names in three columns, each inscribed with units and dates of death]

The Enterprise Confederate Cemetery is east of the railroad tracks of what was
the Mobile & Ohio Railroad. More than four hundred soldiers are buried here,
according to the Enterprise Woman's Club, which has overseen the tending of
the grounds since 1930, this in a town with a population of 526 in 2010.

The Enterprise Woman's Club's monument, erected in 2012, commemorates
the sesquicentennial of the Battle of Shiloh in April 1862 and lists the names of

219 of the dead, many of them casualties brought to Enterprise after the battle. Flagpoles for the grounds were erected in 2013. Granite memorial benches—exedra, as it were, for the sacred space—were erected circa 2012 from Missouri and Mississippi.

- Enterprise was active during the war as a supply depot and a recruiting base for troops. In addition, a prisoner exchange program brought paroled Confederate soldiers to Enterprise after the surrender of the Vicksburg garrison on July 4, 1863.

Wayne County

5.10.1 Subject: Waynesboro, Courthouse Common Soldier, Confederate
Location: Chickasawhay Avenue   N 31 40 28 13 / W 88 38 49 92
Dedicated: August 2, 1911
Media: Marble
Monument is a common soldier surmounting a shaft and base.

Inscriptions
[Front]
1861–1865 / WAYNE COUNTY'S / LOVING TRIBUTE / TO THE / NOBLE MEN / WHO MARCHED / NEATH THE FLAG / OF THE / STARS AND BARS / C.S.A.

LEST WE FORGET

C.S.A. / ERECTED / BY THE LUNDY / GUNN CHAPTER / UNITED DAUGHTERS / OF THE / CONFEDERACY / AUGUST 2, 1911

FURL THAT BANNER / TRUE 'TIS GORY / YET 'TIS WREATHED / AROUND WITH GLORY, / AND 'TWILL LIVE IN / SONG AND STORY / THOUGH ITS FOLDS / ARE IN THE DUST.

The Lundy Gunn Chapter of the UDC was still active as late as 1918. They left this weathered, vernacular work of art standing just west of the railroad and east of the Wayne County courthouse, facing south toward Chickasawhay Avenue, in front of the present-day justice building. The inscription—a "Loving Tribute"—faces the railroad, presumably giving notice to passing travelers of the legacy the war left. Placing a monument beside a railroad line is unusual but not singular. Others stand at Brooksville and Duck Hill in Mississippi as well as such diverse locations as Pulaski, Virginia, and the Fredericksburg and Stones River battlefields.

Surmounting the shaft is the statue of a common soldier, standing at parade rest: a thin, even spindly-looking figure—consonant no doubt with the generally hardy but food-deprived health of true wartime soldiers. The figure is placed off-center on the shaft in a way that may make one wonder if the figure's base was cut down because it was too large for the shaft or if it was damaged in some way.

Waynesboro, Courthouse Common Soldier, Confederate

- Records indicate that the monument was originally placed in front of the Waynesboro High School but was moved when that school building was torn down.
- The inscription beginning "Furl That Banner" is taken from the poem "The Conquered Banner," by Fr. Abram J. Ryan.

5.13.1 Subject: Hattiesburg, Courthouse Common Soldier, Confederate
Location: 630 Main Street, Main and Eaton Streets, 39401   N 31 19 39 35 /
W 89 17 30 08
Dedicated: April 26, 1910
Medium: Marble monument is a common soldier surmounting a shaft and
base.

Inscriptions
[Front]
[CS National flag in high relief] [crossed rifles, three swords]

CSA / 1861–1865 / TO THE MEN AND WOMEN OF / THE CONFEDERACY / 1861–1865

CSA

CSA / WHEN THEIR COUNTRY CALLED / THEY HELD BACK NOTHING. / THEY
CHEERFULLY GAVE THEIR / PROPERTY AND THEIR LIVES. / THROUGH THE
DEVOTION AND / UNTIRING EFFORTS OF THE / HATTIESBURG CHAPTER NO. 422 / OF
THE UNITED DAUGHTERS / OF THE CONFEDERACY, THIS / MONUMENT IS ERECTED
TO / THE HONOR AND MEMORY OF THOSE WHO WORE THE GRAY
ERECTED 1910

CSA

Mississippi's monumentation reflects a profound paradox and ambivalence
that is perhaps best illustrated by the monument at the 1905 Hattiesburg
courthouse.

The monument stands approximately thirty-five feet high on a base approximately ten feet by ten feet.

There are three figures on the monument: a common soldier in Confederate
uniform surmounting the shaft who is evidently a veteran, who faces north,
and who appears to be manifestly ready to take on Northern aggressors if/
when they come again. At the base is a second figure—a young female, holding
a wreath, barefoot, dressed in classical garb, a *peplos*—evidently mourning
the death of Southerners and the defeat of the South. Adjoining the base is a
third figure, a male youth in Confederate uniform with a readiness to serve
but arguably one who, as Robert Leckie puts it, senses the "impossibility of any
man's ever ascertaining the justness of his cause, bidding him, if he believes his
leaders to be honest, to obey them and shoulder arms." Mourning, vigilance,
and youth form a collective trinity, it seems, reflecting successive generations
confronting the conflicts and challenges of each generation.

· The figures at the base, each about five feet high, are the work of Frank
  Hartman, a local artisan. The courthouse, which is still in use, was
  erected in 1905.

Hattiesburg, Courthouse Common Soldier, Confederate

5.12.1 Subject: Poplarville, Courthouse Common Soldier, Confederate
Location: Courthouse grounds, Main Street, 39436   N 30 50 37 08 /
W 89 32 09 62
Dedicated: June 3, 1926
Media: Marble

Monument includes four sculptures: an eagle surmounting a central shaft
with common soldier, flanked by Confederate common soldier and a woman,
each surmounting a pedestal, adjoining exedra.

Inscriptions
[Front]
[Common Soldier, Confederate:]

TO THE / MEN WHO / WORE THE / GRAY AND / WERE / FAITHFUL / TO THE END /
1861–1865

[Central World War Common Soldier]

PEARL RIVER / COUNTY'S / TRIBUTE TO / HER SONS OF / THE WORLD WAR / 1917–
1918 / ERECTED UNDER THE AUSPICES OF / J. M. SHIVERS CHAPTER /

[Figure of a woman, Civil War-era]

TO THE / BELOVED / WOMEN / OF THE / CONFEDERACY / AND THE / WORLD / WAR

[List of 14 service men]

[Names of Pearl River County citizens: committee, sponsors, and participants]

This is a commemoration to military veterans of the Civil War and World War I
as well as the women of the time. Three figures stand on pedestals: one in the
center is a uniformed World War I soldier—"The / World/War"—standing at
attention; the figure of a uniformed Confederate common soldier appears in
a similar stance on the left pedestal, and a female figure stands on the right
pedestal. Behind and above them is a central pedestal surmounted by an eagle
with partly open wings.

Note the careworn, ordinary appearance of the woman, in midcalf-length
dress and apron, this in contrast to the neoclassical figures of other monuments, in mourning, such as those standing at Laurel, Hattiesburg, and
Heidelberg. A "Mrs. Whitten of Pearl River County" was photographed in work-
aday period garb, and the image—in something of an American Regionalist
style—was used as the model for the female figure.

There is a timelessness to the portraiture: the Confederate soldier looks
younger than the World War I figure, and the figures as a whole represent
down-to-earth people, drawn from ordinary life, consumed by the defining
conflict of their time but able to endure and even transcend their times.

Poplarville, Courthouse Common Soldier, Confederate

· This is the central monument on the Pearl River County grounds: monuments in front of it commemorate Pearl River County citizens who served in World War II, the Korean War, the Vietnam War, Grenada, Panama, and the Persian Gulf War.

· The county appropriated $10,000 for the monument and the landscaping of the grounds. The statues were executed in Italy and cost $500 each. It was erected under the auspices of the Col. J. M. Shivers Chapter of the UDC and the Orville Carver Post No. 100, American Legion.

Lucedale, Courthouse Obelisk

George County

5.13.1 Subject: Lucedale, Courthouse Obelisk
Location: George County Courthouse grounds, 368 Cox Street, Lucedale, 39452   N 30 55 23 01 / W 88 35 25 22
Installed or dedicated: May 2016
Medium: Granite
Monument is obelisk surmounting shaft and base.

Inscriptions
Front
[Seal of CSA] [crossed swords]

IN HONOR OF / THE MEN OF THE / GEORGE COUNTY AREA / WHO SERVED IN THE / ARMY OF THE / CONFEDERATE / STATES OF / AMERICA / THESE ARE THE MEN WHO WORE / THE GRAY / 1861–1865

[30 names]

[30 names]

[30 names]

[29 names]

This veterans' monument is the most recent Confederate courthouse monument at this writing. It revives a neoclassical temple form of the obelisk in a kind of plaza, or stereobate, with flags surrounding it. The monument faces southwest on a concrete base painted dark gray, with an adjoining walkway painted red. It has the appearance of a more modest version of the neoclassical sacred spaces/temples at Ellisville, Laurel, and Columbus, as well as several state monuments at Vicksburg. At the same time, it has the modernist simplicity and lack of adornment of the 2001 and 2009 Kentucky monuments at Vicksburg or the 1982 Vietnam Memorial at Washington, DC. In addition, it displays documented rosters of soldiers from George County in the same fashion of those contemporary monuments.

Harrison County

5.14.1 Subject: Gulfport, Courthouse Common Soldier, Confederate
Location: Courthouse grounds: 1801 23rd Avenue, corner of 19th Street
N 30 22 23 04 / W 89 05 25 80
Installed or dedicated: October 1911
Media: Bronze, granite
Monument is a common soldier surmounting a column and base.

Inscriptions
[Front]
[unfurled CS Battle flag]

1861–1865 / "IN MEMORY OF / OUR CONFEDERATE DEAD," / LEST WE FORGET

"ERECTED BY THE DAUGHTERS / OF THE CONFEDERACY AND / BOARD OF SUPERVISORS," / OF HARRISON COUNTY / MISSISSIPPI."

[BLANK]

UNVEILED, OCTOBER 1911

Dedicated in October 1911, the peak of the Civil War monument movement, this opulent sculpture, standing twenty-five feet high, depicts a figure of a mature-looking common soldier in bronze, standing at parade rest, surmounting a granite shaft and base. The monument faces east; the bust of the sculpted figure faces northeast. The monument is adjacent to the courthouse, however, not in front of it. In fact, the monument is located around the corner from the courthouse doors. It stands—incongruously—beside the vehicle entry to the utterly pragmatic, brutalist-style, two-story parking garage for the courthouse.

The Gulfport monument was erected at a cost of $3,500. The UDC chapters at Gulfport, Biloxi, and Pass Christian raised $2,500; the Harrison County Board of Supervisors authorized $1,000.

· Gulfport is a postwar city incorporated in 1898. Today it is second only to Jackson in size. Postwar cities do not always erect Civil War monuments. The materials and style are stylistically unusual by Mississippi courthouse monument standards, which, in many cases were erected by the Columbus Marble Works.

Gulfport, Courthouse Common Soldier, Confederate

Jefferson Davis statue, Beauvoir

Beauvoir

5.14.2 Subject: Jefferson Davis statue
Location: Jefferson Davis Home and Presidential Library, 2244 Beach
Boulevard   N 30 39 20 49 / W 88 96 96 13
Installed or dedicated: 1998
Medium: Bronze
Monument is a statue surmounting a base.

Beauvoir was the retirement estate of Jefferson Davis from 1877 until his death in 1889. Beauvoir was also the site of the Mississippi Confederate Soldiers Home from 1903 to 1957. Davis died on December 6, 1889, and his remains were interred in Hollywood Cemetery, Richmond. The disposition of Beauvoir was uncertain, but the grounds were established as a state home for Confederate veterans and their wives in 1903 and remained open until 1957.

This uninscribed statue of Jefferson Davis, sculpted by Mississippian William Beckwith, once stood in the rotunda of the Presidential Library. The building, dedicated May 30, 1998, was destroyed by Hurricane Katrina in 2005; it was rebuilt and rededicated June 3, 2013.

· In fact, seven buildings on-site were destroyed, and the remaining two, including Beauvoir, were seriously damaged; much restoration was accomplished, but the process was still ongoing at this writing.

Jefferson Davis statue, with Joseph Davis and Jim Limber

5.14.3 Subject: Jefferson Davis statue, with Joseph Davis and Jim Limber
Location: Beauvoir Memorial Cemetery, Jefferson Davis Home and
Presidential Library, 2244 Beach Boulevard
Installed: 2009
Medium: Bronze
Monument is three figures surmounting a base.

The Sons of Confederate Veterans (SCV) of Virginia intended to erect this un-inscribed statue in Richmond, next to the Lincoln statue at the Tredegar Iron Works. The monument, the work of Gary Casteel, depicts Jefferson Davis with his biological son, Joseph Evan Davis, who died in 1864 from a fall. Also posed with Davis is his African American "adopted" son, Jim Limber.

The statue was the subject of controversy when it was cast. Historian John Coski reports that the "SCV offered the statue to the American Civil War Center at Tredegar Iron Works to balance the statue of US president Abraham Lincoln and his son Tad placed at Tredegar in 2005. In August 2008, the Center's board voted to accept the statue, but the board would not guarantee where or wheth-er the statue would be displayed or explain how it might be interpreted."

In response, the SCV rescinded its offer in November 2008 and found a place for it at Beauvoir.

- For the record, Coski also reports that "nineteenth-century Virginia law did not provide for formal adoption of children. Jim's status in the Davis household seems to have been informally that of a ward or what modern Americans would call a 'foster child.'"

UDC Arch

Beauvoir Memorial Cemetery

5.14.4 Subject: UDC Arch

Location: Entry point, east side of Beauvoir Memorial Cemetery, Jefferson Davis Home and Presidential Library, 2244 Beach Boulevard   N 30 23 41 95 / W 88 58 17 22

Installed or dedicated: ca. 2007

Media: Bronze, marble

Monument is an inscribed arch.

Inscriptions

[Front]

ERECTED BY THE MISSISSIPPI DIVISION UNITED DAUGHTERS OF THE CONFEDERACY / 1917 / TO COMMEMORATE JEFFERSON DAVIS AND OUR CONFEDERATE VETERANS BURIED AT BEAUVOIR / 1861 / 1865

[Bronze Relief of Jefferson Davis]

JEFFERSON DAVIS PRESIDENT OF THE SOUTHERN CONFEDERACY

This relatively modest UDC arch replaces a larger version that once stood facing US 90. The original arch was destroyed when it was struck by an unmoored ocean barge during Hurricane Katrina in 2005. Insurance coverage facilitated the rebuilding of the arch, but restoration constraints compelled its erection here, as well as its downsizing.

The Beauvoir Memorial Cemetery was founded when the Jefferson Davis Beauvoir Soldiers' Home was opened on December 2, 1903. Today, 771 graves of Confederate veterans and their wives are located here. The graves are numbered; the superintendent of Beauvoir maintains records of the name and grave number of decedents. Records are, however, incomplete, although research is ongoing in this matter. A "Register of Marked Graves" was completed in 1941, but it includes notations about unmarked graves and notes such as "aluminum marker without name" or "no marker." Other records were lost as a result of Hurricanes Camille in 1969 and Katrina in 2005.

· Among those buried in the cemetery is Samuel Emory Davis, the father of Jefferson Davis.

5.14.5 Subject: Stele, the Confederate Dead
Location: Entry point, east side of Beauvoir Memorial Cemetery, Jefferson Davis Home and Presidential Library, 2244 Beach Boulevard
Installed or dedicated: ca. 1920s
Medium: Granite
Monument is a stele surmounting a base.

Inscription

CONFEDERATE DEAD

"NO NATION ROSE SO WHITE AND FAIR / NONE FELL SO PURE OF CRIME."

ERECTED BY / MRS. C. W. BYRNUM

This undated, privately erected monument was the only one on the cemetery grounds until the UDC arch was erected in the twenty-first century. The expression "No Nation Rose So White" is common, especially in Georgia monuments, as an expression of the Lost Cause; its origins are unclear.

5.14.6 Subject: Unknown Confederate Soldier, Sarcophagus
Location: Beauvoir Memorial Cemetery, Jefferson Davis Home and Presidential Library, 2244 Beach Boulevard
Installed: May 20, 1980; Dedicated: June 6, 1981
Medium: Marble
Monument is a sarcophagus surmounting a base.

Unknown Confederate Soldier, Sarcophagus

Inscriptions

[Front]
THE UNKNOWN SOLDIER / OF THE / CONFEDERATE STATES OF AMERICA

KNOWN BUT TO GOD

THE UNKNOWN SOLDIER / OF THE / CONFEDERATE STATES OF AMERICA

AH! FEARLESS ON MANY A DAY FOR US, / THEY STOOD IN FRONT OF THE FRAY FOR US, / AND HELD THE FOEMAN AT BAY FOR US; / AND TEARS SHOULD FALL / FORE'ER O'ER ALL / WHO FELL WHILE WEARING THE GRAY FOR US.

FATHER ABRAM J. RYAN / POET-PRIEST OF THE CONFEDERACY.

The remains of this soldier—by all accounts a Confederate soldier—were discovered near Vicksburg in December 1979 and were reinterred in a cypress casket, with military honors, on April 19, 1980. The idea of a national unknown soldier for the former Confederacy is consonant with the tomb of the unknown soldier at Arlington National Cemetery. The sarcophagus has the status, as the Arlington soldier does, of a kind of monument to the unknowns who are buried elsewhere.

· The excerpt beginning "Ah! Fearless on Many a Day" is taken from the poem "C.S.A.," by Fr. Abram J. Ryan.

The 1903 Arch

5.14.6 Subject: The 1903 Arch
Location: Former entry gate, Beauvoir Memorial Cemetery, Jefferson Davis
Home and Presidential Library, 2244 Beach Boulevard   N 30 23 41 54 / W 88
58 21 62
Installed or dedicated: ca. 1903
Media: Granite, limestone
Monument is an inscribed stele.

This modest arch facing west fronting on Beauvoir Street has aluminum spear-
top fencing running across it now, and is no longer in use as an entryway.
However, it was constructed when the home and cemetery grounds were established, it has survived a century's worth of Gulf Coast storms, and it retains
such decorative flourishes as four granite columns and a heart inscribed in
the keystone.

Jefferson Davis Highway, Stelae. The second highway stele can be seen on the upper left of this image, further west on US 90.

5.14.7 Subject: Jefferson Davis Highway, Stele
Location: US 90, in front of Beauvoir Memorial Cemetery, Jefferson Davis Home and Presidential Library, 2244 Beach Boulevard   N 30 23 30 49 / W 88 58 13 46
Installed or dedicated: ca. 1920s
Medium: Marble
Monument is an inscribed stele.

Inscription

[Mississippi coat of arms: "Virtute et Armis"]

JEFFERSON DAVIS / MEMORIAL HIGHWAY / PRESIDENT / OF THE CONFEDERACY

Beauvoir was never isolated. Railroad tracks were laid out just north of the estate after the war, and these facilitated travel to and from this Gulf Coast location. Today this stele stands in front of a major highway, US 90, which in turn is adjacent to a man-made beach. In 1928 what was then billed as the world's longest seawall, spanning twenty-five miles of the coastline, was dedicated, facilitating the construction of the highway. Midcentury saw the making of a sand beach by dint of the use of hydraulic dredges.

5.15.8 Subject: Jefferson Davis Highway, Granite Stele
Location: 2244 Beach Boulevard, US 90, in front of Beauvoir Memorial
Cemetery, Jefferson Davis Home and Presidential Library   N 30 23 30 54 /
W 88 58 11 94
Installed or dedicated: ca. 1920s
Medium: Granite
Monument is an inscribed stele

Inscription

JEFFERSON DAVIS / HIGHWAY / BEAUVOIR / LAST HOME OF JEFFERSON DAVIS

The plan to designate a transcontinental highway to honor the President of
the Confederate States of America was conceived in 1913 and was sponsored
by the UDC. In addition to the transcontinental route, historian Richard F.
Weingroff notes that the UDC designated two auxiliary routes: a route through
Irwinsville, Georgia, traced Davis's route at the end of the Civil War before his
capture, and this one, which begins at Davis's birthplace at Fairview, Kentucky,
and terminates here, where he lived in later years.

Selected Sources

Print Resources

Aaron, Daniel. *The Unwritten War: American Writers and the Civil War*. New York: Alfred A. Knopf, 1973.

Adams, Michael C. C. *Living Hell: The Dark Side of the Civil War*. Baltimore: Johns Hopkins University Press, 2014.

Ayers, Edward L. *In the Presence of Mine Enemies: The Civil War in the Heart of America, 1859–1864*. New York: W. W. Norton, 2004.

Ballard, Michael B. *Civil War Mississippi: A Guide*. Jackson: University Press of Mississippi, 2000.

Bearss, Edwin C. "Monuments and Memorials: Battlefields." In *Encyclopedia of the Confederacy*, edited by Richard N. Current, 1071–74. New York: Simon & Schuster, 1993.

Blair, William. *Cities of the Dead: Contesting the Memory of the Civil War in the South, 1865–1914*. Chapel Hill: University of North Carolina Press, 2004.

Blight, David. *Beyond the Battlefield: Race, Memory and the American Civil War*. Amherst: University of Massachusetts Press, 2002.

Bollet, Alfred J. *Civil War Medicine: Challenges and Triumphs*. Tucson, AZ: Galen, 2002.

Brown, Thomas J. *The Public Art of Civil War Commemoration*. Boston: Bedford/St. Martin's, 2004.

Campbell, Edward D. C., Jr., and Kym S. Rice, eds. *A Woman's War: Southern Women, Civil War, and the Confederate Legacy*. Richmond: Museum of the Confederacy and University of Virginia Press, 1996.

Cmiel, Kenneth. *Democratic Eloquence: The Fight Over Popular Speech in Nineteenth-Century America*. New York: William Morrow, 1990.

Cooper, William J., Jr., *Jefferson Davis, American*. New York: Alfred A. Knopf, 2000.

Cox, Karen L. *Dixie's Daughters: The United Daughters of the Confederacy and the Preservation of Confederate Culture*. Gainesville: University Press of Florida, 2003.

Cozzens, Peter. *The Darkest Days of the War: The Battles of Iuka and Corinth*. Chapel Hill: University of North Carolina Press, 2006.

Cushman, Stephan. *Bloody Promenade: Reflections on a Civil War Battle*. Charlottesville: University Press of Virginia, 1999.

Davis, Stephen. "Empty Eyes, Marble Hand: The Confederate Monument and the South." *Journal of Popular Culture* 16 (Winter 1982): 2–21.

Davis, William C. *The Cause Lost: Myths and Realities of the Confederacy*. Lawrence: University Press of Kansas, 1996.

———. *Jefferson Davis, the Man and His Hour*. New York: HarperCollins, 1991.

Dew, Charles B. *Apostles of Disunion: Southern Secession Commissioners and the Causes of the Civil War*. Charlottesville: University of Virginia Press, 2001.

Downs, Gregory P. *After Appomattox: Military Occupation and the Ends of War*. Cambridge, MA: Harvard University Press, 2015.

Dumas, David B. *The Original Vicksburg National Military Park and Vicinity*. Bloomington, IN: AuthorHouse, 2017.

Fahs, Alice, and Joan Waugh, eds. *The Memory of the Civil War in American Culture*. Chapel Hill: University of North Carolina Press, 2004.

Faust, Drew Gilpin. *Mothers of Invention: Women of the Slaveholding South in the American Civil War*. New York: Vintage, 1996.

———. *This Republic of Suffering: Death and the American Civil War*. New York: Alfred A. Knopf, 2008.

Foner, Eric. *Reconstruction, 1863–1877*. New York: Harper, 1988.

Foote, Shelby. *The Civil War: A Narrative*. 3 vols. New York: Random House, 1958–74.

Foster, Gaines M. *Ghosts of the Confederacy: Defeat, the Lost Cause, and the Emergence of the New South, 1865–1913*. New York: Oxford University Press, 1987.

Fullenkamp, Leonard, Stephen Bowman, and Jay Luvaas. *Guide to the Vicksburg Campaign*. Lawrence: University Press of Kansas, 1998.

Gallagher, Gary W., and Joan Waugh. *The American War: A History of the Civil War Era*. State College, PA: Flip Learning, 2016.

Giambrone, Jeff. *An Illustrated Guide to Vicksburg Campaign and National Military Park*. Jackson, MS: Communication Arts, 2011.

Guelzo, Allen C. *Fateful Lightning: A New History of the Civil War and Reconstruction*. New York: Oxford University Press, 2012.

Hess, Earl J. *The Civil War in the West: Victory and Defeat from the Appalachians to the Mississippi*. Chapel Hill: University of North Carolina Press, 2012.

———. *Civil War Logistics: A Study of Military Transportation*. Baton Rouge: Louisiana University Press, 2016.

Hicken, Victor. *Illinois in the Civil War*. Urbana: University of Illinois Press, 1991.

Hills, Parker. *Art of Commemoration: Vicksburg National Military Park*. Vicksburg: National Park Service—Lower Mississippi Delta Initiative, 2011.

Hines, Thomas S. *William Faulkner and the Tangible Past: The Architecture of Yoknapatawpha*. Berkeley: University of California Press, 1996.

Isbell, Timothy. *Vicksburg: Sentinels of Stone*. Jackson: University of Mississippi Press, 2006.

Janney, Carolyn E. *Burying the Dead But Not the Past: Ladies' Memorial Associations and the Lost Cause*. Chapel Hill: University of North Carolina Press, 2008.

Kammen, Michael. *Mystic Chords of Memory: The Transformation of Tradition in American Culture*. New York: Vintage, 1991.

Leckie, Robert. *Helmet for My Pillow: From Parris Island to the Pacific*. New York: Bantum Books Trade Paperbacks, 2010.

McKay, John. *Brave Men in Desperate Times: The Lives of Civil War Soldiers*. Guilford, CT: Twodot, 2007.

McMurry, Richard M. *Two Great Rebel Armies: An Essay in Confederate Military History*. Chapel Hill: University of North Carolina Press, 1989.

McPherson, James M. *Battle Cry of Freedom: The Civil War Era*. New York: Oxford University Press, 1988.

McWhiney, Grady, and Perry D. Jamieson. *Attack and Die: Civil War Military Tactics and the Southern Heritage*. Tuscaloosa: University of Alabama Press, 1982.

Meringolo, Denise. *Museums, Monuments and National Parks: Toward a New Genealogy of Public History*. Amherst: University of Massachusetts Press, 2012.

Mills, Cynthia, and Pamela H. Simpson, eds. *Monuments to the Lost Cause: Women, Art, and the Landscapes of Southern History*. Knoxville: University of Tennessee Press, 2003.

"Monumentation Survey of the Vicksburg National Military Park." Works Project Administration, 1942.

Neff, John R. *Honoring the Civil War Dead: Commemoration and the Problem of Reconciliation*. Lawrence: University Press of Kansas, 2005.

Panhorst, Michael W. *Memorial Art and Architecture of Vicksburg National Military Park*. Kent, OH: Kent State University Press, 2014.

Parson, Thomas E. *Work for Giants: The Campaign and Battle of Tupelo/Harrisburg, Mississippi, June-July 1864*. Kent, OH: Kent State University Press, 2014.

Rotundo, Barbara. "Monumental Bronze: A Representative American Company." In *Cemeteries and Gravemarkers: Voices of American Culture*, edited by Richard E. Meyer, 263–92. Logan: Utah State University Press, 1992.

Savage, Kirk. *Standing Soldiers, Kneeling Slaves: Race, War, and Monument in Nineteenth Century America*. Princeton, NJ: Princeton University Press, 1997.

Schantz, Mark S. *Awaiting the Heavenly Country: The Civil War and America's Culture of Death*. Ithaca, NY: Cornell University Press, 2008.

Sedore, Timothy. *An Illustrated Guide to Virginia's Confederate Monuments*. Carbondale: Southern Illinois University Press, 2011.

Sifakis, Stewart. *Compendium of the Confederate Armies: Mississippi*. Westminster, MD: Heritage, 2007.

Smith, Timothy B. *Champion Hill: Decisive Battle for Vicksburg*. New York: Savas Beatie, 2004.

———. *Corinth 1862: Siege, Battle, Occupation*. Lawrence: University Press of Kansas, 2012.

———. *The Golden Age of Battlefield Preservation: The Decade of the 1890s and the Establishment of America's First Five Military Parks*. Knoxville: University of Tennessee Press, 2008.

———. *Shiloh: Conquer or Perish*. Lawrence: University Press of Kansas, 2016.

Stout, Harry S. *Upon the Altar of the Nation: A Moral History of the Civil War.* New York: Penguin, 2007.

Waldrep, Christopher. *Vicksburg's Long Shadow: The Civil War Legacy of Race and Remembrance.* Lanham, MD: Rowman & Littlefield, 2005.

Warner, Ezra J. *Generals in Blue: Lives of the Union Commanders.* Baton Rouge: Louisiana State University Press, 1964.

———. *Generals in Grey: Lives of the Confederate Commanders.* Baton Rouge: Louisiana State University Press, 1959.

Wills, Brian S. *The Confederacy's Greatest Cavalryman: Nathan Bedford Forrest.* Lawrence: University Press of Kansas, 1992.

Wills, Garry. *Lincoln at Gettysburg: The Words that Remade America.* New York: Touchstone, 1992.

———. *While God Is Marching On: The Religious World of Civil War Soldiers.* Lawrence: University Press of Kansas, 2001.

Wilson, Charles Reagan. *Baptized in Blood: The Religion of the Lost Cause, 1865–1920.* Athens: University of Georgia Press, 1980.

———. *Judgment and Grace in Dixie: Southern Faiths from Faulkner to Elvis.* Athens: University of Georgia Press, 1988.

Woodworth, Steven E. *Nothing But Victory: The Army of the Tennessee, 1861–1865.* New York: Albert A. Knopf, 2005.

Wynne, Ben. *Mississippi's Civil War: A Narrative History.* Macon, GA: Mercer University Press, 2006.

Memorial Volumes

Confederated Southern Memorial Association. *History of the Confederated Memorial Associations of the South.* New Orleans, LA: Graham, 1904.

Emerson, Mrs. Bettie A. C. *Historic Southern Monuments. Representative Memorials of the Heroic Dead of the Southern Confederacy.* New York: Neale, 1911.

Periodicals—selected, various

Confederate Veteran.
Southern Historical Society Papers.

Other Media

Jefferson Davis: An American President. DVD. Directed by Brian Gary. Kultur Video, 2008.

Websites—selected

Dyer, Frederick H. "Regimental Index: Union Regimental Information." *A Compendium of the War of the Rebellion* (Dyer's Compendium) (Part 3). http://www.civilwararchive.com/regim.htm.

Map. Vicksburg. Google Map. https://www.google.com/maps/@32.3436914,-90.8510716,41m/data=!3m1!1e3?hl=en.

Map. "Vicksburg National Military Park, Miss." Washington, US Geological Survey, 1935. https://www.loc.gov/item/99447430/.

Smithsonian Institution Research Information System. "Civil War Sculpture, Mississippi." http://siris-collections.si.edu.

Interviews

Various personnel: Corinth Civil War Interpretive Center, Vicksburg National Military Park; Vicksburg Visitors Center; John Davis Williams Library of the University of Mississippi; Brice's Cross Roads National Battlefield; Old Capitol Museum, Jackson; Mississippi Department of Archives and History; the Amory Museum, Amory; Holly Springs Public Library.

Index

campaigns summarized, 8–10

Campbell, Robert (Maj.), 170

Canton, MS, *ix*, 7, 23, *298*, 300, 320–324, *321, 322, 323*

Carolinas Campaign, 41, 286

Carr, Eugene A. (Brig. Gen.), 192

Carroll County, *ix*, *202*, 280–282, *281, 282*

Carrollton, MS, 280–281, *281*

Castalian Springs, MS, *ix*, *xvi*, 25, *298*, 308–309, *308*

Casteel, Gary, 95, 394

Catholicism, 217, 305, 360, 377

Catton, Bruce, 60, 301

Celebration Era, 4, 280, 328

Chambers, Alexander (Col.), 135

Champion Hill, Battle of, *ix*, 9, 38, 59, 73, 88, 99, 102, 106, 157, *168*, 176, *180*, 182, 183, 188, *298*, 350–351, *351*

Charles City, VA, 6

Charleston, MS, *ix*, *202*, 204, 258–259, *259*

Charleston Harbor, SC, 276

Charlottesville, City Council of, xi, 5

Chattanooga, TN, 6, 53, 75, 99

Chickasaw Bayou, 9

Chickasaw County, *ix*, *202*, 262–265, *263, 264*

Churches, 264, 266, 274, 370, 379

Cianfarani, Aristide B., 46, 108, 137

Citizen-soldiers, 11, 50–51, 60, 64, 90, 368. *See also* common soldiers, monuments/tributes

City Beautiful Movement, 360

Civilian Conservation Corps (CCC), 31–32, *127*, 135, 175

"Civil War," as name for the war, 27n1, 99

Claiborne County, *ix*, *356*, 365–367, *365*

Clarke County, *ix*, *298*, 377–384, *378*, *380, 382, 383*

Clay, Henry, 88

Clay County, 289–291, *289, 290*

Clay Street, Vicksburg, *viii*, *28*, 35, 37, 119, 171, 200, *201*

Cleveland, MS, *ix*, *202*, 272–273, *272*

Clinton, MS, 24, 300, 352–355, *352, 355*

Clio, muse of history, 8, 13, 74, 75, 86, 87, *169*

Cockerill, Joseph (Col.), 137

Coe, M. Herring, 84, 174

Coleman, J. P., 237–241

Colleges and universities: Female Seminary, 264; Mississippi College, 352–355, *352, 355*; Mississippi State University, 5, 84, 286–287, 303–304; Okolona College, 264; Rose Gates College, 264–265; United States Military Academy, xvi, 22, 59, 72, 77, 78, 84, *158*, *191*, 366; University of Mississippi, *ix*, xvi, 5, *18*, *202*, 248, 250, 252–256, *251, 254*, 274; University of North Carolina, 319; University of Wisconsin-Madison, 81; Washington and Lee University, 274

Colonnade, 372, *373*, 374, *375*

Columbus, MS, *ix*, 7, 10, 84, 199, *202*, 204, 250, 271, 292–297, *292, 294, 297*, 391

Columbus Marble Works, 229, 250, 260, 269, 271, 273, 274, 275, 280, 293, 303, 304, 314, 316, 326, 366, 391

common soldiers, monuments/tributes: overview, *1–2*, 4, 6–8, 10–12, *13*, 15, *18*, *19*, *20*, 33, 118, 300–301, 359; Adams County, 360–362, *361*; Alcorn County, 205–207, *206*, 217–218, *217*; Attala County, 310–311, *311*; Bolivar County, 272–273, *272*; Carroll County, 280–282, *281*; Chickasaw County, 262–263, *263*, 264–265, *264*; Claiborne County, 365–367, *365*; Clarke County, 377–379, *378*; Clay County, 288–289, *289*; Copiah County, 367–368, *367*; Forrest County, 386–387, *387*; Grenada County, 270–271, *270*; Harrison County, 391–392, *392*; Hinds County, 346–347, *347*; Holmes County, 304–305, *305*; Humphreys County, 302–304, *303*; Jasper County, 376–377, *376*; Jefferson County, 364–365, *364*; Jones County, 372–375, *373, 374, 375*; Kemper County, 326–328, *327*; Lafayette County, *18*, 248–253, *249, 251*; Lauderdale County, 328–329, *329*; Lee County, 227–229, *228*; Leflore County, 276–278, *277*;

Hurricane Katrina, 358, 393, 396

TIMOTHY SEDORE is Professor of English at
the City University of New York, Bronx Community
College. He regularly teaches undergraduate courses
in composition, literature, and religious rhetoric.
He is also an ordained Baptist minister.

Rev. Dr. Sedore is the author of a trilogy on
Civil War monumentation in the American South.
His book *Mississippi Civil War Monuments: The
Illustrated Field Guide* joins *Tennessee Civil War
Monuments: The Illustrated Field Guide* (Indiana
University Press, 2020) and *An Illustrated Guide
to Virginia's Confederate Monuments* as a survey
and analysis of the legacy of the war on the
American landscape.